Persons Emerging

SUNY series in Chinese Philosophy and Culture
Roger T. Ames, EDITOR

PERSONS EMERGING

Three Neo-Confucian Perspectives on Transcending Self-Boundaries

GALIA PATT-SHAMIR

Cover art: Ma Yuan, *Scholar by a Waterfall*, Southern Song dynasty (1127–1279), late 12th–early 13th century.

Published by State University of New York Press, Albany

© 2021 STATE UNIVERSITY OF NEW YORK PRESS

All rights reserved

Printed in the United States of America

No part of this book may be used or reproduced in any manner whatsoever without written permission. No part of this book may be stored in a retrieval system or transmitted in any form or by any means including electronic, electrostatic, magnetic tape, mechanical, photocopying, recording, or otherwise without the prior permission in writing of the publisher.

For information, contact
State University of New York Press, Albany, NY
www.sunypress.edu

Library of Congress Cataloging-in-Publication Data

Names: Patt-Shamir, Galia, author.
Title: Persons emerging : three neo-Confucian perspectives on transcending self-boundaries / Galia Patt-Shamir.
Description: Albany, NY : State University of New York Press, [2021] | Series: Suny series in Chinese philosophy and culture | Includes bibliographical references and index.
Identifiers: LCCN 2020057308 | ISBN 9781438485614 (hardcover) | ISBN 9781438485621 (ebook) | ISBN 9781438485607 (paperback)
Subjects: LCSH: Neo-Confucianism.
Classification: LCC B127.N4 P38 2021 | DDC 181/.112–dc23
LC record available at https://lccn.loc.gov/2020057308

10 9 8 7 6 5 4 3 2 1

JENNY: Do you ever dream, Forrest, of who you wanna be?

FORREST: Who I'm gonna be? Aren't I gonna be me?

JENNY: You'll always be you. Just another kind of you. You know?

FORREST: I want to reach people on a personal level.
I want to be able to say things, just one to one.

—Eric Roth, *Forrest Gump*, movie script

For Boaz

CONTENTS

Acknowledgments ix

Introduction A Riddle: The Person as the Way? 1

ONE. I Think, Therefore You Are: Emerging Out of Self-Boundaries in Early Confucianism 17

TWO. Emerging to a Self through Transcending the Infinitude-Finitude Dichotomy: Zhou Dunyi's Anthropocosmic Riddle and Its Response 47

THREE. Emerging through Transcending the In-Out Duality: Shao Yong's Epistemological Shift 103

FOUR. Emerging Out of Life and Death: Zhang Zai's Pragmatic Point of View 163

Appendix A Brief Methodological Remark: Chan Buddhism and Living Riddles 205

Notes 217

Bibliography 247

Index 261

ACKNOWLEDGMENTS

Persons Emerging was reaching its final stage in spring 2020, when the COVID-19 pandemic was turning into a member (albeit undesirable) of the global community. My annual neo-Confucianism seminar in Tel Aviv University was, in some senses, a reflection of the strange time we are living in. Against the dark background of chaotic events, and when the class—students and teachers alike—was reduced to online entities locked up in pixel squares, the idea of emerging out of boundaries and thriving had special magnitude. Neo-Confucian ideas of personhood were revealed as a source of optimism and hope for us all.

For this hope and its time-specific sense, I am indebted to my students in Philosophy as a Practice: The neo-Confucian Case of Spring 2020. I am grateful to all my students—my partners in pursuit of the Way over the years, who ask and challenge, dare and open up new horizons. Some of my former and present graduate students—Sharon Small, Roy Porat, Galia Dor, Inbal Shamir, Niva Sharon, Keinan Mariasin, and Karine Vieman—will find here echoes to their own poignant voices. For the love for the world of ideas, spur for research and faith in the human ability, I am forever indebted to my teachers, Tu Weiming, Benjamin Schwartz, Hillary Putnam, Ben-Ami Scharfstein, Yoav Ariel, and Shlomo Biderman. Heartfelt thanks to Roger Ames, who has been an inspiration to ideas on becoming persons in writing and in presence; one of his remarks at a conference in Beijing was adopted by me as the title of this book. I am fortunate to have exchanges on ideas that appear here with brilliant scholars who have been broadening my mind and influencing my work: Robin Wang, Yong Huang, Michael Puett, Zhang Ping, Nechama Verbin, Noa Naaman Zauderer, Daniel Raveh, and Roy Tzohar.

Earlier versions of chapter 2 on the synchronicity of *The Diagram of Supreme Polarity Explained*, and of chapter 4 on Zhang Zai's sense of immortality in *The Western Inscription* were originally published in *Dao: A Journal of Comparative Philosophy*. I am grateful to the Israeli Science Foundation for the generous support of research toward this book, to Brian Bowles for language editing, to Cynthia Col for indexing, and for its realization I am grateful to James Peltz, Jenn Bennett-Genthner, Laura Glenn, and the people of SUNY Press. Last is my thankfulness to Boaz, Alma, and Karmi for merging their ways with mine.

INTRODUCTION

A Riddle

The Person as the Way?

....

"Who are YOU?" said the Caterpillar.

This was not an encouraging opening for a conversation. Alice replied, rather shyly, "I—I hardly know, sir, just at present— at least I know who I WAS when I got up this morning, but I think I must have been changed several times since then."

"What do you mean by that?" said the Caterpillar sternly. "Explain yourself!"

"I can't explain MYSELF, I'm afraid, sir," said Alice, "because I'm not myself, you see."

"I don't see," said the Caterpillar.

"I'm afraid I can't put it more clearly," Alice replied very politely, "for I can't understand it myself to begin with; and being so many different sizes in a day is very confusing."

"It isn't," said the Caterpillar.

> "Well, perhaps you haven't found it so yet," said Alice; "but when you have to turn into a chrysalis—you will some day, you know—and then after that into a butterfly, I should think you'll feel it a little queer, won't you?"
>
> "Not a bit," said the Caterpillar.
>
> "Well, perhaps your feelings may be different," said Alice; "all I know is, it would feel very queer to ME."
>
> "You!" said the Caterpillar contemptuously. "Who are YOU?"
>
> —LEWIS CARROLL, *Alice's Adventures in Wonderland*

A PROBLEM OF RELATEDNESS

Once, so the sages say, the Way (*dao* 道) prevailed on earth and the world was in peace and harmony. Then, it had been abandoned and lost and times of turmoil, fighting, corruption and disunity darkened the face of the earth. Maybe it was forgotten (the cynics might say repressed) and as this was before the advent of history, people's true sentiments were confined to oblivion. Then better times arrived and yet, the memory of this loss may have lingered on for generations and accordingly people perhaps never quite attained the sense of well-being they had had before. The ages have handed down many varying and incongruous accounts concerning the Way and the ways to attain it, but as a devoted disciple testified, the more he came closer the farther away it had gotten. Ever since, it is our task to find it again and bring back the serenity that we had had. The toll for this loss is, however, that we the seekers of Way carry the responsibility not only to travel it but to broaden it too, with only minor clues for how we, mortal and limited, can enlarge the mighty Way. We incessantly return to it, whether to idolize it or to criticize it, whether to escape it or to yearn for it, whether to describe it or take it to pieces—or perhaps simply to question it.

In this book I want to do something similar to the latter. Not so much to question it but to be questioned by it. The two protagonists in this book are, thus, the Way and its traveler, the person. They are the core of early Chinese thought and in fact, they are what human life is about. We have learned so as early as Confucian *Analects*' teaching that the Way can be broadened by the person who travels it, rather than that it broadens the person (*Lunyu* 論語 15:28). Indeed, these protagonists are much more than two: the first is as numerous "as the stars in the sky and as the sand on the seashore" (Gen. 22:17); the second is endless, ongoing and abstract, and its manifestations are abundant. Then again, some suggest that these two are, in some sense, one.

The person—the one about whom voluminous studies were produced in philosophy, literature, psychology, history or cultural studies—is always hard, if not impossible to define. She and her ilk are the seekers of where to go, who to be inspired and guided by, and how to live a better life and burgeon. They belong with a certain form of life having its community and traditions. In general, they are considered (by their peers) as having unique qualities and capacities, including reason—at least a type of reason and reasoning other animals are not known to have. Morality is attributed to them only; animals can be helpful to each other in various ways, but cannot morally deliberate on their next or previous actions. Self-consciousness and being part of a culturally established form of social relations include a responsibility that is solely theirs. Indeed, the defining features of personhood and consequently of what makes a person may differ among cultures and contexts and yet, one thing is quite certain: people's task is to realize their potentiality as human beings. The task of the Confucian follower is to broaden the Way; perhaps better to say, the human task from the Confucian perspective is to broaden the Way.

As for the Way, it is not less sneaky. The Way is what we aspire to and yet, it is also how we advance toward; while not one of us, it is commonly among us, it is in our commonality (*yong* 庸) as coined by Tu Weiming (1989), or in activities that are ordinary and common, as we are embedded in the world. It is near us, and yet, it sometimes appears besides us, above us, in front of us, and at times, as Yan Yuan attested, one may even "look at it before him, and suddenly it appears behind" (*Analects* 9:11). It cannot be hermetically delineated or defined; as Yan Yuan suggested, the closer to it we get, the more distanced it appears. It is something that is always greater, more virtuous, farther-reaching, all-embracing, and more complete than anything we experience and anything we conceive. It is something similar to the "that then which nothing greater can be conceived" in Saint Anselm of Canterbury's reference to God. It is the height of moral knowledge and practice; it is the sociopolitical ideal order, the boundless perfection a person can wish for, and the lofty ideal of incessant self-cultivation. There again, this Highness turns into a common and concrete human way. It is us, humans, who can broaden the Way.

The apparently innocent stand exposes a fundamental philosophical problem regarding the relatedness between ultimate and nominal, infinite and finite, or boundless and limited. How, one may ask, can the person—limited in space and time, by body and mentality—enlarge the boundless Way? How can those who travel the Way as ultimate perfection create it in their striving for perfection? What does the Way imply about the person, the alleged agent of the way? Given that the Way is ever-growing and unlimited, does the person who broadens it share similar characteristics? If so, how?

Confucius denotes the unattainable as the given: Not only the Way can be broadened, it is human beings, limited and flawed as they are, who can broaden it. Any monotheistic framework would see this philosophical attitude as scandalous; in fact, in monotheistic terms, the saying that human beings can broaden the Way, rather than that the Way broadens humans can be rendered as analogous to saying that rather than God created human beings, it is human beings who create divinity in each and every step in their walk—somewhat anarchistic, indeed. From the Confucian perspective, however, we can only attain perfection when we cocreate it, and we create it in our own self-cultivation; what alternative do we have? Moreover, cultivating our own selves is, in fact, cultivating others (*Analects* 6:30). In other words, the task is attained in human deeds, in moral deeds. So, in order to broaden the Way, that is to reach others, we broaden ourselves, and we can only broaden ourselves by taking care of others. Moreover, this broadening necessitates overcoming boundaries and obstacles, including ones that we usually consider nonpassable, like one's own predispositions, rooted conceptions and biases that create these boundaries. Then again, what means do we have to overcome these boundaries and obstacles and transcend them?

One may suspect that a Confucian antinomy is revealed regarding the two Confucian notions of the Way and the person. Recalling the German philosopher Immanuel Kant, we may think that the Way as perfection is beyond concrete experience, yet when our thinking transcends the limits of possible experience, it becomes entrenched in antinomies that are equally rational but contradictory. In this line, the relatedness of person and Way could be seen such an antinomy: Thesis: The Way as perfection is bigger than any creature, including humans (hence it cannot be broadened by any other creature). Antithesis: The person broadens the Way. Indeed, an anomaly concerning human-ultimate relation appears: First, the idea of Way annuls radical transcendence (either as the religious idea of God or the philosophers' Truth) and thus, apparently, looses firm standard for perfection. Second, in the very broadening of Way, a discrete subject disappears too, as broadening shifts the experience of a defined unique individual to incessant relatedness, self-broadening and self-transcendence.

But can we truly determine the limits of possible experience? Can one know in advance what is possible and what is not? Antinomies isolate themselves: they are like discontinuous points scattered in the field of logic. The discussion that was part of Kant's plan to set limits to science and philosophical inquiry is replied to in our days through interdisciplinary thinking, acknowledging the fact that human rationality must be negotiated and expanded, and strict boundaries are both impossible and unhelpful in search for human understanding.[1] Perhaps, contrary to the accepted principle of logic, according to which a contradiction may lead to every possible conclusion, the antinomy of the Way does not isolate itself. It may be disastrous to a formal system but it agrees with the riddle of life.

According to the present study, if broadening the Way can be considered the Confucian task, it was not until the days of the Song dynasty (960–1279) that more systematic approaches were offered for *how* the Way is to be broadened, giving the antinomy a living sense. As suggested by the philosophies that are exemplified here, the focus then turns to finding the boundaries that we can remove, or obstacles we can overcome, and the means to do so. The latter is tightly connected with inquiring for a foundation for human spirituality, and the alternative sense of transcendence that may be suggested in the system that lacks a notion of absoluteness.

PERSON AND WAY: THE CONFUCIAN CONVICTION

The Confucian idea of the person as always related to others is traced here back to the Mencian spirit according to which "humanity is the person" (*renyezhe renye* 仁也者人也; *Mencius* 孟子 7B:16). A person (*ren* 人) is a related person—or a person in two—(*er* 二), or human (*ren* 仁). It is a person in relationships, or person to person, implying a lack of idea of person as an isolated individual. This attitude stands in sharp opposition to the philosophical (typically Western) idea of subject, meaning a unique being with a distinctive experience and a singular consciousness who considers himself a discrete entity that relates to additional entities, usually referred to as others or as objects of one's knowledge. The Confucian presupposition, in contrast, does not arise from an underlying principle that the world consists of objects, which the subject allegedly considers to be separate entities, with the resultant duality of experience, and the problem of relating subjects to objects.² Pondering the idea of subject as distinct, or an individual, one might find oneself puzzled with the difficulty of isolating both subjective experiences and subjective consciousness from one's surroundings. The Confucian-related person is free from this bafflement.

In analytical terms, this characterization is quite an achievement: the relation between the person as human being (*ren* 人) and the virtue of being human (*ren* 仁) is similar to the inherent natural relation between the predicate raining and the noun rain: When one says, it rains, others know that it is the rain that is raining, and there is no need to ask what is raining? or who is raining? or what does the rain do? Subject and predicate are introduced as one: the rain rains and anything that rains is the rain. (We may say that someone rains favors on another, but then clearly we use rain as a metaphor, wishing to indicate that the favors were given in a natural flow reminiscent of rain.) We tend to think that the more complex our subject is, the harder it is to self-define; and we consider the human extremely complex. In this Confucian line, however, the distinctive characteristic of the human being amounts to being morally related to others; a human "humans," in the way rain rains. When Mencius defines *person* on its own terms, he introduces Confucian humanistic terms as not only the words or the language through which we deal with ideas and values, but also—conditions. A necessary and sufficient condition for being a person is one's being related to others; caring and living in dialogue.

Accordingly, in every given situation, we live, we know, we feel and we act within a human net of relationships, and any specific relationship commits to a certain attitude and a distinctive set of values. This is quite simple and self-explanatory: I am my parents' daughter, my children's mother, a partner, a neighbor, a teacher, a student, a colleague, a customer, and so on. Being a caring mother is definitely different from being a caring daughter, a caring teacher, customer, or neighbor; each role demands different skills and responsibilities. In this way, the ethics that is based on virtues accords with one's concrete roles in differing situations.³ In this way, in all roles, one is bound to answer the practical question, how can I realize myself in this particular context? Or how should I act so that it brings me closer to the Way? The practice whereby we realize ourselves in all relations is being human as caring for others and as morally committed to act accordingly. The self-knowledge that one gains is knowledge of oneself as morally related, or as reaching others through transcending one's boundaries. *Doctrine of the Mean* (*Zhongyong* 中庸) describes this characterization.

> Only the perfectly sincere person can actualize his own essence. Actualizing his own essence, he can fully actualize the essence of others. Fully actualizing the essence of others, he can fully actualize the essence of all things. Being able to fully actualize the essence of all things, he can assist Heaven and Earth in their transformation and sustenance. Able to assist in Heaven and Earth's transformation and sustenance, he forms a trinity with Heaven and Earth. (ch. 22)[4]

The understanding of a single person as inherently related to others, even embodying others is given sense when we understand that everyone is a subject, as actualizer of others, an agent, an and a co-creator with heaven and earth in actualizing him- or herself. In this way boundaries that are sometimes considered strict may dissolve between oneself and another, even between oneself and heaven and earth. This is the essence of self-transcendence.

Mou Zongsan's 牟宗三 idea of immanent transcendence (*neizai chaoyue* 內在超越) is valuable in this context.[5] Accordingly, rather than having a transcendent ultimate being that carries the responsibility for every immanent phenomenon in the human world, in Confucianism, through moral transformation, every person can transcend him- or herself to ultimately become larger, as a sage. In Mou's immanent transcendence, heavenly principle and human nature are never distinct or substantially separate from each other. However, despite the spiritual (perhaps religious) overtones in this perspective, it is vital to note at this point that the sense of transcendence this book refers to has little to do with religiosity in its strict sense.[6] Transcendence is used here in the sense of the human ability to rise above or go beyond accepted limits, to triumph over restrictive aspects of one's existence, to overcome serious difficulties and thus find oneself above material existence, yet never beyond existence. Importantly, the essence of this overcoming is human, located within a moral framework, rather than the divine sphere. Indeed, the ability to transcend one's boundaries does carry a spiritual alternative with regard to ideas such as infinitude or immortality, and yet the ideas are based on human effort and morality, rather than divine omnipotence. Then again, questions come up: Can one, in this system, be at all limited in space and in time? Can we make clear conceptual distinctions between that which is within life and that which is external to it? What sense does death—the ultimate boundary of life—have in this view? Is there at all a sense to the end of life? Is it the end of the world? Or does the Confucian system necessarily imply that as eternally related, something must live forever? But then again, we have no clue for an idea of immortality in early Confucianism.

I undertake this study seeking to understand the later frameworks and methodologies that enable this transcendence of boundaries of the person who broadens the Way. Early Confucian philosophers offer a moral tip for understanding the cultivated traveler of the Way. Accordingly, by way of a never-ending commitment, one transcends one's so-called corporeal or spatial boundaries through person-to-person relatedness; one's temporal boundaries through conveying past traditions into present practices; and one's symbolic boundaries through ritualistic practice. The elevation of oneself over personal boundaries allows one to live morally in others' lives.

However, the mystery remains unsolved in terms of methodology and left open to its later renovators in the Song dynasty. Not disclosing the idea in early times and holding onto the idea of broadening oneself through moral interaction also explains the fact that Song dynasty philosophical texts, which lean on early Confucian morality, also apply ideas from Daoist mysticism and naturalness, correspond with Buddhist ideas of emptiness, and perhaps even use methodological cues from other schools.[7] Focusing on Zhou Dunyi 周敦頤 (1017–1073), Shao Yong 邵雍 (1011–1077), and Zhang Zai 張載 (1020-1077), I suggest that the renewed philosophical attitudes can be better understood as echoing the early Confucian mystery in various ways, not as a bewilderment or a flaw, rather as a *riddle* of a special kind, that can be responded to only in the practice that reflects the philosophical system.

A BRIEF ON LIVING RIDDLES AND RIDDLE AS METHODOLOGY[8]

When something is difficult to solve or to achieve, we refer to it as a problem. In a philosophical context it may be an unsettled question raised for inquiry, deliberation, discussion, and hopefully, some kind of solution. At times, problems of this kind are revealed a source of perplexity, unease, frustration, and sometimes even agony. In this sense, broadening the Way could be seen such a problem; indeed, broadening the Way is not easy to achieve; it is always demanding more inquiry and consideration, it is never fully settled, and can turn into a source of perplexity for its learners. Broadening the Way, however, is not aspiring for a theoretical solution; rather, it calls for a response in action. Only upon traveling, the idea of Way and what broadening amounts to, can be understood. Hence, rather than being a source for frustration or agony, it is a source of action, in particular moral action.

An early hint for understanding as living riddle in the Chinese tradition, can be found in the early philosophy of the *Book of Change* (*Yijing* 易經) and its appreciation of life as transforming and unforeseen, suggesting a concrete practice of "foretelling" that cannot simply be understood in reference to telling future events only. It is a forecasting not as casting an event into a fixed mold; rather, it is causing to move or sending forth, like casting a fishing lure. What one tells in advance is one's position regarding the issue in question. We cast our movements beforehand, but not their outcomes not knowing what it will bring back. This understanding corresponds with Jung's explanation of the sixty-four hexagrams as the tool by which sixty-four different paradigmatic conditions can be interpreted but never determined. The fact that the conditions are paradigmatic necessitates consideration of nuances and subtleties. Realization that there are various possible responses for any question relies on one's reflection and projection, yet never on one firm solution.⁹ The book's foretelling can thus be understood better as deciphering a mystery or understanding through riddles. In this way, it offers a first methodological clue on *how* we can address life as a riddle.

Seeing life and death as a riddle, deciphered step by step, by means of subtle clues given by sixty-four symbolic shapes and enigmatic words, which can never be disclosed, is assisted by the *Xici Zhuan* 繫辭傳 (or the *Great Appendix*, 大傳 *Dazhuan*), the philosophical appendix regarding the relationships of the hexagrams as embodying clues for understanding. The most important characteristics of the first two hexagrams—those of Qian 乾 and Kun 坤, according to the Appendix, address the question of boundaries: "Qian knows the great beginnings; Kun brings them to completion" (*Xici* I). First, Qian is the knowledge of great beginnings (*qianzhi dashi* 乾知大始), never of ends that are typically unknown. Kun refers to completion (*cheng* 成), signifying process again, rather than a full-stop or an ending (*kunzuo chengwu* 坤作成物). Hence, beginnings are to be known for endings to be reached appropriately. The basic presupposition of the system as the human capability to "trace things to their beginning, and turn back to their end—thus knowing death and birth" (原始反終, 故知死生 *yuanshi fanzhong guzhi sisheng*) is cited in the times of the Song dynasty as part of the cosmic process that humans embody. The use of images in the *Book of Change* as means of focusing organic changes enables practitioners to reflect on moral implications of paradigmatic states as representations of personal occurrences. Seeing life as ongoing transformation understood by various combinations and variations of two basic powers brings practitioners to a new perspective on understanding regarding transformation, relatedness, and the lack of concrete boundaries—including those between life and death.

The point that life is seen in riddles is quite explicit in texts of the Lao-Zhuang 老莊 tradition, then with the assimilation of Buddhism in China, reaching its peak in the Chan practice of *gong-an* 公案.[10] Confucian philosophizing in riddles is less explicit and yet, in major texts we encounter points in which the text appears to contradict itself. Examples, as shown hereafter to refer to the most significant terms in the system; just think of Confucius's different and at times apparently contradictory replies to what humanity is about (e.g., *Analects* 4:3 vs. 4:4).

Rather than settling apparent contradictions and interpreting away significant passages, we may treat them as riddles of a special kind that cannot be responded by theoretical means. Implying what Ludwig Wittgenstein called "the riddle of life and death in space and time," it is a living riddle, or a riddle that must be responded to in practice.[11] According to the present suggestion, the Way embodies a living riddle that is responded to in the Confucian form of life.

In the present book, the riddle is not only an idea, but moreover, it is a methodology for reading philosophical texts that belong to forms of life that are not one's own. With regard to the Chinese case, sinological methodologies are necessary in any research that aims at learning anything about Chinese culture from Chinese texts yet, their strength in clarifying, classifying, and forming good taxonomic schemes of terms and contexts is liable to leading one to overlook the philosophical point in a text. My choice to apply the conceptual methodology of riddles takes its cue from Wittgenstein's own attempts at understanding other cultures and others' beliefs.[12] In this context, Wittgenstein refers to two senses of understanding: first, the sense in which understanding a sentence is one's ability to construct another sentence that says the same thing in different words; second, the sense in which understanding a sentence involves seeing why it cannot be replaced by any other words (referred to hereafter as "the uniqueness sense").[13] Wittgenstein stresses that the two senses together form our concept of understanding. Replacing words by other words is a practice with which we, researchers and teachers in the Humanities, are quite familiar; it is what we usually call explanation and at times interpretation. Yet, we also want to show the uniqueness of a system, in its own terms, even when not habitually used by us. In these cases, we may find the comparative riddle methodology useful.

According to this suggestion, encountering a textual paradox or ambiguity may signify a key idea that cannot be hermetically defined, and *has to be* textually expressed through contradiction. Usually it denotes a real-life conflict, for which the response can be provided only in life and practice. Finding textual riddles as signs for living riddles is therefore joy rather than agony. With the Wittgensteinean philosophical spirit, I wish to offer a systematic approach, according to which in understanding a form of life as living riddle, one acquires *a point* (PI §564) rather than rules and techniques, regarding its beliefs and practices. If one can show that a certain text embodies a living riddle, and that riddle language is necessary for the issue at hand, one may acquire some understanding of that text in Wittgenstein's second sense, as the uniqueness sense of understanding a form of life.[14]

The philosophies of Zhou Dunyi, Shao Yong, and Zhang Zai, which originated around the same time during the Northern Song, indicate the renewal of Confucianism as a humanistic philosophy that takes the cultivation of the person not as a hermetically defined goal, but as the proper response to the Way as introducing a riddle of a unique type; that of a perfection that can be perfected by human beings, imperfect as they are. As this study suggests, each of the three philosophers offers a unique perspective on what the early Confucian vision of the person who broadens the Way amounts to, and on the way in which it can be attained. Each perspective contributes to forming a more complete concept of a Confucian sense of transcendence that is never separate from the Confucian person; rather, it is inherent in the self-creation of the person who has to incessantly transcend self-boundaries as part of the natural engagement in self-realization as a realization of others, or of something bigger than oneself. The renewed neo-Confucian idea also influences the understandings of core thinkers in contemporary Confucian humanism, as indicated in the first chapter of this book.

THREE NEO-CONFUCIAN RIDDLES AND THEIR RESPONSES

What, then, does this book suggest? After a background chapter on Way and person in early Confucianism, the rest of this book addresses the attitudes of Zhou Dunyi, Shao Yong, and Zhang Zai as three different responses to the Confucian riddle of how the finite can broaden the infinite Way, or of broadening oneself as perfecting the ultimate. As there is no radical transcendence—each of the three neo-Confucians embarks on the Way, searching for his own response. The understanding that broadening the Way presupposes broadening oneself, and broadening oneself is attained by an ongoing process of removing self-boundaries that delimit and delineate who one is brings each of the philosophers to transcend boundaries and suggest their own unique philosophical understandings. Although all three philosophies are multidimensional, in the present context Zhou Dunyi's perspective on broadening the Way is focused on here as a *metaphysical* perspective; Shao Yong's is explored as adding an *epistemological* perspective; and Zhang Zai's is viewed as offering a *pragmatic* sense to the broadening of the person as broadening the Way. All perspectives, though absorbed with foreign ideas, stem from Confucian morality, and reaffirm the early Confucian idea of broadening the Way through human virtues and moral relations.

First, we encounter Zhou Dunyi's metaphysical understanding. Seeing reality as a process of becoming that necessitates ongoing creative movement and transformation, *one* transcends the boundary between infinitude and finitude as that between the Non-Polar and Supreme Polarity (*Wuji er Taiji* 無極而太極) and the myriad things (*wanwu* 萬物)—of which the person is only one manifestation. We first address the short treatise *Diagram of Supreme Polarity Explained* (*Taijitu Shuo* 太極圖說, abbreviated hereafter as TJTS). The early Daoist diagram is explained by Zhou as an impressive Confucian statement on the continuity between the ultimate and the world under heaven. In the present context, the daring opening "Nonpolar and Supreme Polarity" of the treatise presents its reader with the riddle: what is Nonpolar and Supreme Polarity? and, more importantly, how Nonpolar and Supreme Polarity at once?

In his explanation, reminiscent of a Laozian attitude, Zhou offers a dialectic of Duality/Nonduality, in which he refers to the world through analogous references, represented in the diagram by five symbols in the spirit of the *Book of Change*—both graphically and textually. Accordingly, Nonpolar and Supreme Polarity as the archetypal One that is at once its own negation, sets the framework (and also the nonframework) of discussion. Manifested then through the interpenetration of tranquility (*jing* 靜) and activity (*dong* 動) of yin-yang, the transformations of the five phases (*wuxing* 五行), and the dynamics of Qian and Kun 坤, the harmonious progression in seasons and natural changes are created. The myriad things, including humans, embody the process as a whole. In this way, the cultivated person as sage is depicted as the human manifestation of Nonpolar and Supreme Polarity.

Zhou's work leans heavily on the philosophy of *Change* and the understanding that life is transformation from a moral-metaphysical perspective. Dealing with the aspect of *wu* as nonbeing, Zhou accommodates terms that were foreign to the Confucian spirit. However, if the terms are indeed foreign, the *use* Zhou makes of them is genuinely Confucian, in a way that creates a renewed and more open version of the doctrine. Zhou's new use of the unified concept Nonpolar and Supreme Polarity (WJTJ) in the Confucian context is taken here to be *a living riddle* that can only be responded to in one's life and practice; in his case in elevating oneself over the strict boundary between One and many, or in attaining infinitude in finitude.

Projecting TJTS on ideas from *The Penetrating Book* (*Tongshu* 通書, abbreviated as TS) demonstrates how the person can embody the riddle. In short, the boundary between One and many disappears through sincerity (*cheng* 誠), presented in terms of an earthly manifestation of Nonpolar and Supreme Polarity. TS opens in three chapters on sincerity, each referring, according to the present understanding, to a different dimension of the idea, first as analogous to Supreme Polarity; then, to the myriad things; last, to Nonpolar and Supreme Polarity. The suggested response is described through the interpenetrating of activity and tranquility in human tasks—manifesting the succession of yin-yang, five phases, and Qian-Kun dynamics in the human heart, and the attempt at being a sage (*shengren* 聖人). The striving for sagehood is thus presented as Zhou's response to the riddle of WJTJ in "to be and not to be a sage," both at once.

The next response to the riddle of the Way takes an epistemological perspective in the philosophy of Shao Yong, who broadens the Way by observing its travelers. Shifting the focus to his inquiry of observation (*guan* 觀), self-realization and the ability to expand one's boundaries revolves around an ability to observe the world and one's position in it. As observer, Shao transcends the distinction between in (*nei* 內) and out (*wai* 外). Shao's understanding of life through observing a game of Weiqi 圍棋 (more familiar by its Japanese name of Go) in his "Great Poem on Observing Weiqi" (*Guanqi dayin* 觀棋大吟) serves as cue, leading to Shao's broader philosophical ideas. The three-hundred and sixty lines of Shao's poem refer through correlative thinking to life and game at once.[15] The choice of game as a model enables understanding of the person both from within as a player, and from without as an observer, thus forgoing the boundary between in and out, entering others' lives through game. Shao's text has clear Daoistic overtones, including as part of his observation a process of forgetting both (*liangwang* 兩忘), with a Confucian twist, reaffirming the necessity of a framework that enables this forgetting.

First, the chapter refers to the cultural significance of using games as a model, then to playing the game of Weiqi. Next, Shao's idea of observation, which opens the poem, is introduced with the aid of his philosophy of observation of things (*guanwu* 觀物), as introduced in the *Book of Supreme World Ordering Principles* (*Huangji jingshi* 皇極經世, hereafter abbreviated as HJJS), and the central topic of his major philosophical treatise *Inner Chapters on Observing of Things* (*Guanwu Neipian* 觀物內篇). Then, Shao's ideas are exemplified in the poem, first by describing how he observed the game and drawing from this observation analogies to life. Moving from in to out, the observer transcends his own subjective boundaries to understand the players and the game as a microcosm of life. Then, observing history, Shao moves this time from out to in. Seeing the game in history brings him to transcend history as such and reveal the game in one's life. The poem implies a theoretical perspective on an unceasing interchange between in and out, between observing and playing, between game and life. Transcending dichotomies, one is led to seeing the single world order.

Last, Zhang Zai's pragmatic personal transcending of the most essential boundary in human life—that between birth (*sheng* 生) and death (*si* 死)—is presented through Zhang's use of the family as a model for universal interactions. Within the various relationships with living and dead family members, one creates oneself beyond the boundaries of birth and death. This perspective brings Zhang Zai back to the significance of moral practice of all human beings as reverent sons and daughters (*xiao* 孝). As suggested, he makes relentless attempts to overcome death—both as his own fear of death and as overcoming pain and loss upon the death of others. As his philosophy of qi 氣 suggests, he even seeks to overcome any loss in the world. While the tendency to see the harmony of the natural world as a model for human harmony in the spirit of the *Book of Change* is an almost all-Chinese philosophical tendency, the analogy of cosmic harmony to family relations suggests a clear Confucian flavor.

Accordingly, in his writings Zhang Zai takes the perspective of an involved seeker of the Way. As a seeker, heaven and earth are introduced as embodying an ontogenetic nature as the origin and development of the human being, in a way that inherently denotes and delimits one's identity as son or daughter. The denotation as sons and daughters—necessitating the family as a frame of reference—by definition cannot be fixated or limited. This family connectedness attributes the cosmic powers with a human flavor, in terms and sounds that are familiar to the Confucian ear. Zhang's call for engagement in the universal order through moral practice is a pragmatic call to move on from daily practice to universal morality, or from existence to essence, and reverses Zhou's and Shao's emanation from ultimate perfection to the myriad things, thus introducing his unique sense of human broadening of the Way.

To follow this understanding, we will take up from a concise text, this time that of the *Western Inscription* (*Ximing* 西銘, hereafter abbreviated as WI) with references to the broader Works of Zhang Zai (*Zhangzaiji* 張載集, hereafter abbreviated as ZZJ). We first addresses WI as reference to the remarkable view of Qian and Kun as parents; the relatedness within the different branches of the universe as one body; the commitment to the universe as family reverence; and the conclusion that serving one's parents with reverence during life enables one to die in peace. In order to suggest that through family reverence one may overcome the boundary between life and death, we then move on to Zhang's philosophy of qi as that which builds and fills any living creature; its functioning as void (with both Daoist and Buddhist overtones); its moral perspective; and its suggesting a continuity that transcends the strict boundary between life and death. Last, I suggest that looked at jointly, the two former perspectives—on universal relatedness and on qi—necessitate a unique moral sense of immortality or a Confucian idea of transcending one's boundaries as timelessness or morally living in the present.

Granted, the scope of this inquiry prohibits me from addressing each philosophical attitude from all or even most of its perspectives—historical, personal, religious, and others. Hence, I do not discuss or only briefly mention central issues that do not reflect directly on the present theme, such as Zhou's political ideas, Shao's elaborate philosophy of numbers, or Zhang's deliberations on spiritual forces.[16]

The weaving of perspectives together into one fabric reflects my own attempt at understanding, as an attempt at transcending my academic and personal boundaries, and enter the philosophies of three great thinkers, trying to understand others through their own eyes, rather than explaining away ideas that might appear counterintuitive in our day inconceptual schemes. It then calls to transcend yet another boundary: that between then and now. The practical sense of the latter is, however, left for a future discussion, and more importantly—the practice thereof.

ONE

I Think, Therefore You Are

Emerging Out of Self-Boundaries in Early Confucianism

No man is an island,
Entire of itself,
Every man is a piece of the continent,
A part of the main.
If a clod be washed away by the sea,
Europe is the less.
As well as if a promontory were.
As well as if a manor of thy friend's
Or of thine own were:
Any man's death diminishes me,
Because I am involved in mankind,
And therefore never send to know for whom the bell tolls;
It tolls for thee.

—JOHN DONNE, "No Man Is an Island"

INTRODUCTION: PERSON AND BEYOND

The Confucian presupposition of the human ability to broaden the Way rests on a firm belief that we are more than our psychophysical dispositions. Who one is embraces how one actualizes predispositions, and actualization is associated with who one relates with and how it serves one's realization, as well as why a certain set of practices is the best realization, and what concrete practices one should undertake. In Confucian philosophy of the Way, the Way always can be made even broader, as the person—him- or herself—broadens it, and making the ultimate—as Way—what it is. Accordingly, a person becomes the specific Way she or he travels and creates.

The point of departure to the present journey is thus, that since old times, the Confucian world was engaged with an essential interest in expanding self-boundaries, or changing that which we consider the given limits of the person. This expansion is to be revealed later on in history as an occasion for a spirituality that does not rest on ideas of transcendence as God; highest aspiration as Truth; morality as Law and immortality as eternal life (in any of its common versions). Broadening the Way by human beings signifies the broadening of the person who is not a creator of the Way in the cosmic sense, and yet who is a creator of the ever-expanding net of human relationships; hence, of human morality. As we see hereafter, this point of departure is to be easily found in the Confucian classics, and in particular in the later on grouped Four Books (*sishu* 四書), including the *Analects* (*Lunyu* 論語); *Great Learning* (*Daxue* 大學, hereafter GL); *Doctrine of the Mean* (*Zhongyong* 中庸) and *Mencius* 孟子.

Looking for concrete clues with regard to the person, or the traveler of the Way, we find ourselves puzzled; the philosophy of Way—in particular, of a moral Way—introduces its agent with neither a clear definition, nor with clear boundaries in space and time. This lack of concreteness is inherent to the notion of the person as incessantly becoming and changing. Looking for Confucian understandings of the person, we realize that the idea of person entails a basic identity between moral relatedness as the virtue of humanity, and the indispensable opportunity for self-empowering and flourishing. Prior to calling for a reexamination of the nature of this relatedness in the neo-Confucian case, we will focus in this chapter on its Confucian roots, with regard to three connected questions: First, what boundaries can we transcend? And second, how far can we expand ourselves? Then, what does this expansion imply in practice?

This chapter addresses early Confucian sources with regard to the person and one's apparent boundaries—or rather the lack of definitive boundaries—as reflected in an idea of a *self-transcending personality*. This point of departure addresses neo-Confucianism as a search for a response to *Analects*' presupposing that it is the person who can broaden the Way, rather than the Way can broaden the person (*Analects* 15:28), by taking it as a demand to transcend one's apparent boundaries for the sake of moral flourishing. This chapter briefly returns to some major ideas regarding Confucian life as process and relatedness, offering grounds for future Confucian developments of ways to transcend accepted self-boundaries. First, "spatial" boundaries dissolve by relating to others and living in dialogue; next, temporal boundaries fade away by means of living joyfully in the present; then, symbolic boundaries disappear through ritual practice—altogether bringing to overcoming the boundary between life and death through the never-ending ritualized moral commitment to others, alive and dead.

TRANSCENDING SPATIAL BOUNDARIES

A Dialogical Person

The Confucian person is characterized by means of a dialogical nature. In fact, dialogue is presented as the essence of being human and the foundation for human understanding, as the Master says.

> Even when I walk in a group of three people, I am assured to find a teacher among the other two. The good in them—I will follow; the non-good in them—I will correct in myself. (*Analects* 7:22)

One may assume that the short saying refers directly to a question a disciple posed to the Master. It could have been, How is morality attained? What practices do you, Master, exercise for learning? Or perhaps, Who is a teacher? or simply, Can others contribute to one's understanding? The reply is quite straightforward: every person can contribute to others' progress by the very virtue of being a person; everyone can be a teacher to her partners. Among any two partners, there is something positive to follow, and if one sees negative, or nongood (*bushan* 不善) aspects in others, this provides an opportunity for self-reflection and learning about the nongood within oneself.[1] Through others we can better judge ourselves, as the other mirrors one's morality. Serving as human mirror for the other and seeing the other as one's mirror is the main method for paving the Way and for better orienting oneself through moral deeds. Neither scientific progress, nor complex psychological theories are required in order to understand the rule: if anything bothers me in the other, I should first search for it within myself; if something truly irritates me, I should examine myself more thoroughly, and correct it within myself.

Since the *Analects* presents no organized system of premises, inference, and conclusion, reflexivity and dialogue turn into its main methodology for human flourishing. As we see in the plenty of segmented conversations between Confucius and his disciples: a disciple wonders, consults, or places a difficulty, and the Master responds; the Master challenges and a disciple suggests and challenges back. Through ongoing dialogue, the Master and his disciples pave the Way and together create its perfection. Thus, the dialogical form of *Analects* is not coincidental; it fits well with the gist of Confucius's tips to his disciples. Rather than acting as philosopher whose main interest is thinking better—or who knows something that is hidden, or sometimes even forbidden to others, or who represents some higher authority for knowing the Way—Confucius is a teacher and a partner for the Way, and as teacher Confucius travels with his disciples, copaving the Way on their steps. Hence, despite the fact that he was (and still is) considered in China the greatest teacher of all times, Confucius presents himself as a learner. Within any company of two, he is certain to find a teacher. Perhaps this type of reasoning is what made him so great.

This idea comes clear by Confucius disciple, Zigong.[2]

> A human person wishing to be established himself also establishes others; wishing to realize himself, he realizes others. The ability to make those who are nearby your own model can be called the art of humanity. (*Analects* 6:30)[3]

The main point about humanity, the core Confucian virtue, as Mencius later on clearly suggests (*renyezhe renye* 仁也者人也; *Mencius* 7B:16), is that it defines a person as "person in two." A living person, a flourishing person is someone whose self expands to others, whose self-realization necessitates that one's self eventually includes others in terms of others' needs, feelings, or knowledge. This understanding helps explaining the relationship between Confucius and his disciples, who never receive fixed hermetical and predetermined responses. Rather, the Master responds to every disciple in his own way. When, Zilu and Ziyou each asks whether a true learner should immediately carry into practice what he heard, the Master responds to each of them differently, perhaps even in contradictory ways.[4] When asked why he gave different responses, the Master says, "Qiu (Ziyou) is restrained; therefore, I urged him forward. You (Zilu) is vigorous; therefore, I restrained him" (11:22). Confucius sees "practicing the doctrine" as having different senses according to the different practitioners and the ways they are related to others.

In a similar spirit, when asked about humanity, which one would expect him to be clear about, Confucius suggests different understandings, probably as addressed to different disciples, or in different contexts: humanity is presented an expansion of family reverence (1:2); it is inherent to rites and music (3:32); the human hearted is never isolated (4:25); without human heartedness one cannot subsist in misfortunes or in fortune (4:2); only the human-hearted person can love or hate others (4:3); and when the will is set on the virtue there is no hatred (4:4).[5] When Fan Xu poses the same question, Confucius further suggests that it is to love allhumans, then when asked to clarify, he surprisingly suggests an altogether different direction of thought as employing the upright and putting aside the crooked, so that the crooked can be made to be upright (12:22); then again, in yet another occasion he tells Fan Xu that to be human is to have good manners at home, be reverently attentive in public, and strictly sincere with others (13:19).[6] While the differences are important, the general spirit of the sayings embodies a feeling that the virtue of humanity receives different nuances, as related to different disciples. Yet, in all cases, cultivated people are those who open themselves to others, whether it is through love, music, ritual, or something else. In Confucian ethics, caring for others is seeing one's role not in relation to virtue as absolute, but as related to a concrete person. Cultivating a personality or learning to be human means learning to be sensitive to the growing network of possible social connections.

The point of dialogue in the present context is that through the ongoing exchange with others, people expand themselves in a way such that their cultivated selves are "made of" the others from whom they have learned, or have others within. The process of expanding oneself is best exemplified in the *Great Learning* as an expanding learning. The book opens with a clear statement that the way of the GL exists in, is present in, lies in, or simply is at (*zai* 在) the three moral intents of illustrating illustrious virtue (*ming mingde* 明明德), congregating the people (*qingmin* 親民), and resting in the highest good (*zaizhiyu zhishan* 在止於至善). Yet, as the text immediately shows, this "at" is never a specific locus, it is always a movement toward others. This movement is described as succession of systematic structural progress of eight phases (*batiaomu* 八條目) functioning as a guide to the practitioner in achieving a particular kind of knowledge of his own self, society, state, and the world at large. The guidelines that the text offers can be structured as a three-dimensional system, according to which its two opening ideas—of the investigation of things (*gewu* 格物) and of the extension of knowledge (*zhizhI* 知至)—form a dynamic framework for the process, from which three deepening phases of better relating with oneself, and three broadening phases of better relating with others follow.

Accordingly, functioning as the infrastructure to the process of self-expansion, investigating things, as "vertical" growth, and extension of knowledge, as "horizontal" growth, are in fact pursued at every phase throughout the learning process, as one adds new spheres of information; therefore, learning is never fully acquired. Once the framework is set and before being able to expand oneself and relate to others, three deepening phases represent the process of investigation: First, "When knowledge is extended, the will becomes sincere," with reference to the exegesis saying, "Making the will sincere means not to lead oneself astray . . ." (ch. 6).[7] In order to sincerely understand one's own motivations, one should question oneself as a first step to self-transforming. Then, the next phase reads: "When the will is sincere, the heart-mind is stabilized" (ch. 7). Sincerity yields a grasping of the importance of having a stabilized heart-mind and the extent to which one's heart-mind is unstable. In this way, through one's own search, a person realizes the difference between authentic feelings and erroneous emotions that stir the mind and bring about extreme behaviors. Emotive stability may bring about true change, in the last of the deepening phases: "When the heart-mind is stabilized, the self is cultivated," as opposed to: "When the heart-mind is not present—we look and do not see" (ch. 7). The mind is sometimes nonpresent: at times we overlook things, or look at without seeing. Only with self-awareness can one transform and relate to others.

Deepening brings about broadening too, described in the text by three broadening phases, representing the process of the expansion of knowledge, as a practice. First, "When the self is cultivated, the family is regulated." The family that provides the person with her first relations with others also provides her with the ground for moral flourishing. Taking responsibility allows one to truly experience caring for others, broadening further as: "When the family is regulated, the country is well ordered" (ch. 9). Treating others with kindness, as the exegesis adds, implies acting "as if watching an infant" with care and tenderness. Even if one does not hit the target, one still gets closer to it (ibid.). To complete the process, one reflects on the significance she can give to the last broadening step as "When the country is well governed, there will be peace in the world."

The first broadening step, as regulating the family has a special status in the Confucian framework and carries a major weight in the understanding of the person as embodying others through living dialogically, simply by virtue of being others' son or daughter.

Analects tell us about the unprecedented importance of the family:

> The accomplished person follows the roots; once the roots are established, the Way grows. Reverence to parents and elder siblings, isn't this the root of humanity? (*Analects* 1:2)

Family reverence is the root for humanity, and humanity is first practiced at home among family members. *Analects* sets the ground for Confucian moral personality as springing from the root of family reverence (*xiao* 孝). The latter cannot be taken to reflect a simplistic understanding of morality in a traditionalistic manner, as Confucian moral realism is revealed in the passage such that no one is devoid of the capacity to practice morality to its utmost. The root of any human *qua* human is what an accomplished person devotes himself to, and it appears as the necessary and sufficient condition for a person to be moral or person to person.[8] Morality subsists through family relatedness—as both biological and moral relatedness.

The *Book of Family Reverence* opens with this point, as Confucius asks his disciple Zengzi about the perfect virtue of the sage kings that enabled them to harmonize with all under heaven.[9] Zengzi believes that as an individual, who is not a sage king, he is unable to know the virtue Confucius is looking for. However, the response is as follows:

> It is family reverence, said the Master, that is the root of excellence, and whence education itself is born. Sit down again, and I will explain it to you.[10]

In contrast with one's possible expectations, according to the passage, the sage kings are distinguished neither through rightness, nor wisdom, nor courage; rather, family reverence is the root of all virtues of the sage kings (the same point reappears later on in chapter 14). The answer that Zengzi gets for his question "How can a simple person like me be able to know the virtue of sage kings?" implies that since everyone is someone's son or daughter, everyone is morally capable. The family unit serves as the root of the Way and the primary foundation for morality. Family kinship and values lie at the core of the sociopolitical fabric; the traveler of the Way makes the first steps at home, by means of family relationships and rites. The concern with kinship derives not from a vision of precedence of family members over others; rather, family is a microcosm for moral human relationships. Mencius keeps up this spirit, adding his own humanistic flavor to the idea in connecting duty as family reverence and as self-cultivation.

> What is the most important duty? One's duty towards one's parents. What is the most important thing to watch over? One's own character. (4A:19)

In the same line, he also teaches that family reverence is intuitive, such that every human born is endowed with it.

> What a man is able to do without having to learn it is what he can truly do; what he knows without having to reflect on it is what he truly knows. There are no young children who do not know loving their parents, and none of them, when they grow up, will not know how to respect their elder brothers. Loving one's parents is benevolence; respecting one's elders is rightness. What is left to be done is simply to extend these [principles] to the whole Empire. (7A:15)

Seen as the natural source of all moral virtues, in the proposed moral model it appears that there is no sense in moral virtuosity that does not accord with family reverence. Being moral and not filial is not even a possibility. Personal considerations should not interfere with family relations; and moreover, under certain conditions, legal, social, political, and even some ethical considerations appear negligible if they conflict with family values. Such is the story in *Analects* about the governor who proudly told Confucius that in his place if a father stole a sheep, the son gives evidence against him. Confucius replies that in his place sons and fathers conceal (*yin* 隱), or cover for each other (13:18).[11] The point of the story can be understood under the important presupposition that being a caring family member is the root of morality, and thus of the Way. Turning in the father who stole the sheep is not just being irreverent; more importantly, it is not being moral, despite the fact that it is behaving according to law. Acting according to the law and turning in the father is also abandoning him, and moreover, abandoning his likelihood to cultivate his wrecked morality, while concealing his act enables taking care of him, especially taking care of his moral perfection. Children and parents likewise show reverence to the Way through moral learning, which amounts to being good sons, daughters, siblings, and parents. In a similar vein, we read in *Mencius* about an official asking what would Shun, the sage king, do if his father had murdered a man.

Mencius replies: "The only thing to do was to apprehend him"; but then, an explanation is added.

> Shun looked upon casting aside the empire as no more than discarding a worn shoe. He would have secretly carried the old man on his back and fled to the edge of the Sea and lived there happily, never giving a thought to the Empire. (7A:35)

While Confucius clearly rejects blind obedience (*Book of Family Reverence* 15), observance in serving parents is vital; in case of a disagreement, one ought to argue with them about their wrongs in the gentlest way (*Analects* 4:18). Every aspect of Confucian ethics as mentioned thus far—relatedness, self-realization as realizing others, learning from others and finding teachers in one's close vicinity, is based and first learned at home, within one's family. The Way as a transformative process becomes more meaningful than ever. The idea of realizing oneself through realizing others in learning and in practice, as GL states, helps personal growth to advance the global aspiration for world peace by contributing small shares, even if not completely attaining it. The text uses the metaphor of root (*ben* 本) and branches (*mo* 末), not necessarily in a diachronic sense, but rather in a conditional, biological sense: roots have no life without branches; branches cannot live without roots, and both are vital in the ongoing process of realization. Without roots and branches there is no Way.[12]

Through the process of gradual relating to others we expand our circles of relatedness and expand ourselves. This expansion requires expanding self-perception beyond one's ego and overcoming obstacles that are found within, such as presuppositions, prejudices, emotions, and preferences that can and should be changed.

The relationships one has with others are vital to who one is, to one's self and to one's moral development. Human heartedness is essential to the Confucian person as a moral agent. Treating the other with open-minded spirit is vital for one's health, in the way that water and air are necessary for it. By implication, analogous to the person's dying absent any water or air, so is a person who is not open to others morally dead. The subject is created as a meeting point or a crossroad of relationships that enable moral blossoming.[13] Hence, one is committed to others throughout life, through an ongoing process of self-realization among others, of which the awareness regarding the presence, feelings, and needs of the other is inherent. In this way, touching others' lives is immanent to one's self-definition and the sense overcoming one's so-called spatial boundaries is its realization.

The Self-Expanding Person in Contemporary Eyes

The vitality of the Confucian suggestion of the person as ever-expanding develops later on, in the writings of three Song dynasty Confucians, as discussed in the rest of this book. Importantly, the understanding of this unique characteristic of the person is echoed in focal stands in the present generation of Confucian scholarship, each with its nuanced understandings of the Confucian person. Let us briefly mention some of them.

Tu Weiming remarks on the uniqueness of the form of life that is exemplified by this process of self-transformation.

> A person becomes a personality not by conscientiously obeying conventional rules of conduct but by exemplifying a form of life worth living; indeed by establishing a standard of self-transformation as a source of inspiration for the human community as a whole.[14]

Tu's model of concentric circles represents the person who expands self-boundaries, as a never-ending process of becoming a subject, through a *creative tension* that is inherent in the process of self-cultivation.[15] This ongoing process of invariably expanding oneself is a practice of overcoming psychological challenges: First, overcoming egoism is necessary in overcoming one's limitations through relating with one's family; then nepotism is overcome when a family member relates with the broader community; next, parochialism is overcome through relating with people from other communities; nationalism or ethnocentrism is overcome through relating to people from ethnicities or nations that are not one's own; and last, anthropocentrism is overcome through taking care of nonhuman creatures. However, each of the above restraints—that is, our family, our community, and our nation—also enables us being who we are, as Tu says.

> Self-realization, in the final analysis, is ultimate transformation—that process which enables us to embody the family, community, world, and cosmos in our sensitivity.[16]

According to Tu, the ongoing process of ever-expanding oneself is a practice of overcoming psychological obstacles of egoism, nepotism, parochialism, ethnocentrism, nationalism, and ultimately even anthropocentrism. The faith in one's ability for self-transformation is a source of inspiration for the human community, given that everyone can be perceived and understood only in relation to others. The relationships one establishes with others are vital to who one is, to one's attitudes, beliefs, and deeds. In this way, the person is created as a point of meeting or a crossroad of relationships that enables one's moral growth.[17] Hence, one is committed to others throughout life, through an ongoing process of self-realization, among other things. Being human is, therefore, being involved in others' lives.

Hall and Ames stress that the Confucian world is immanent.[18] The Confucian alternative for absolute transcendence is a dynamic and bidirectional relationship between the individual and the community—which the individual influences and is influenced by, at every moment. They add that Confucianism leans on ontology of events rather than of substances. Hence, the understanding of human events does not require that one address fixed qualia or attributes; rather, it comprises an engagement in explaining a certain behavior of a certain person in a certain context. In this way, the agent and the deed cannot be considered separately from each other. An agent is a projection of her deed exactly as she is the reason for it. Hence, similarly to the Sartrean view (in *Existentialism Is a Humanism*, 1946), essence does not precede existence in one's experience. Moreover, the ontology of events is characterized by change and not by some context-independent fixity. Hall and Ames suggest an alternative for the Western "conceptual polarity," such that polar concepts relate to each other symmetrically with each pole conditioning the existence of the other and existing within a process of change toward the other pole. Just as each pole necessitates the other for explanatory purposes, so does a person necessitates the other for understanding oneself, such that we cannot define the person by means of a definition that has no reference to the other. Hall and Ames define the Confucian subject through a model that applies a spatial image of relationships—the *focus field*. They see the self as a shared consciousness of one's roles and relationships, which does not include a capability for separating the essential self, or, according to my understanding, for allowing a reflective intuition on the subject "from outside," as an object. Rather, it is the consciousness of the person comprising a focus that others distinguish. Moreover, internal self and external self are never divided.[19] The latter, as I see it, also stresses the difference from Western rationality, which is always oriented to the "real" or internal self as distinguished from the external, solely as an expression of it. They explain their idea of field.

> The variety of specific contexts defined by particular family relations, or socio-political orders, constitutes the fields focused by individuals who are in turn shaped by the field of influences they focus.[20]

The sense of human relatedness is thus reflected in understanding the individual as being shaped by the fields of influence that she focuses on and is the focus of. Hence, one should refer to a correlative self who is in constant transformation: oneself is always a becoming other, and an other is always becoming oneself.[21] Being involved in an ongoing process of becoming another, stresses the nondichotomous relationships of self-other and the constant presence of the other in the self. As seen earlier, being always present in others is quintessential in the Confucian attitude toward life and death.

David Wong accepts Hall and Ames's claim that the community is a field that is constituted by the individuals who compose it, yet constantly seeks to understand who is the subject maintaining the relations and the roles. If Hall and Ames might have implied a possible search for a self in the Western sense, Wong suggests an altogether *relational self* as a biological organism.[22] Accordingly, the person is related to other persons as subjects in the developmental sense of the human being, who is born needy and helpless and ready for nurturing by others. In this way, the person becomes who he is by means of assistance or delay of those who surround him.[23] Wong argues that these characterizations indeed explain who the subject is, yet they do not give a sense in which the subject is *constituted* by his own relationships. Hence, he suggests the idea of context-specific traits.[24] He assumes that potentially, many of our traits involve tendencies that are evolved by specific people in specific contexts. For example, he notes the traits of generosity and warmness, which are expressed so differently toward family members and colleagues. If so, the traits we attribute the subject with are not global, in that they are not essential or expressed beyond specific situations. According to Wong, if generosity and warmth are part of the person, then those people toward whom he reacts in warmness and generosity are also part of the person. Hence, the answer to the question, who am I? depends on the situation the subject is part of and on the people who also form part of the specific situation. According to my understanding, who the person is changes according to the specific context and in reference to the others who are part of the situation as well.

Li Chen-yang expands the relational vision of the self using categories from *care-ethics* to explain this caring for others. According to his view, the Confucian moral dilemma is not how to realize human's rights without hurting others; rather, it is how one can conduct a moral life that includes commitment to oneself, to one's family, and to human beings in general. Therefore, Confucian ethics leave no room for a notion of individual rights; ethics is fulfilling one's role in the social fields as son, brother, mourner, ruler, or citizen. He explains,

> If benevolence, love, altruism, kindness, charity, compassion, human-heartedness, and humaneness all translate the concept of Jen, what do all these terms have in common? The word emerging in my mind is "caring." Taken as a virtue of human relations, "caring" is the essence of every one of these terms.[25]

Li claims that if a person does not express care for others, then none of the traits that usually translate *ren* as morality, humanity, or benevolence can be attributed to her. According to his view, "Only with care can a person be a moral person, only in the practice of caring, can a person become a moral person."[26] He claims,

> Both *ren* and care focus on the tender aspect of human relatedness. Second, in contrast to Kantian and rights-based moral theories, both Confucians and feminists advocate the human person as socially connected, not as disinterested, separate individuals. Third, both ethics emphasize situational, personal adjustment, character building, instead of rule-following.[27]

Michael Puett accentuates the idea of relatedness through the prism of ritual, emphasizing the centrality of human self-realization in setting and practicing ancient traditional rites. According to Puett, rites involve a process of a domestication of the inner self-dispositions, the basic emotional qualities that all humans have at birth. Created by humans, the rites embody a set of normative relationships—links and connections to one`s inner tendencies, social, and environmental relations. In his interdisciplinary work he shows how rituals allow us to live in our imperfectly fragmented and incoherent world. Through the conventions of ritual, we learn to live together in a broken world. He suggests that ritual—like play—creates *as if* worlds rooted in the imaginative capacity of the human mind to create a subjunctive universe. Ritual defines the boundaries of these imagined worlds of human creativity. Crossing between imagined worlds is focal not only for the Confucian personality, but to human beings in general, and in particular for developing empathy for one another.[28]

Roger Ames and Henry Rosemont follow this line in coining the idea of Confucian *role ethics*, in which morality is based on a person's fulfillment of a role, such as those known to us from the family context. As morality is derived from a person's relationship with their community, unlike other ethical systems, role ethics is not individualistic. The holistic philosophy presented through roles is grounded in the primacy of relationality and a narrative understanding of person, and is a challenge to liberal individualism that has defined persons as discrete, autonomous, rational, free, and self-interested agents. Confucian role ethics centers around family reverence as elaborated in the Confucian *Book of Family Reverence*. According to Ames and Rosemont, Confucian normativity is defined by living one's family roles to maximum effect. These roles are established as relationships, and are not individualistic. Confucian roles are not rational, and originate through the heart-mind (*xin* 心). In the context of Confucian roles, special significance is given to the idea of rites, or rules of propriety, as reinforcing family relationships, and binding together the community. As rites have to actually be performed, the idea underscores the person's moral commitment as a human being. In this way Confucian role ethics begins from a relationally constituted conception of person, takes family roles and relations as the entry point for developing moral competence, invokes moral imagination and the growth in relations that it can inspire as the substance of human morality, and entails a human-centered, atheistic religiousness that stands in sharp contrast to the Abrahamic religions. [29]

Robin R. Wang focuses on the ongoing necessary process of self creation, when she analyzes the idea of self-cultivation from the perspective of the nutrition of the physical body (*shen* 身). Wang argues that Confucian self-cultivation, from the prism of body-cultivation enables a link between inner/personal and external/social dimensions of the self, also implying a unified cosmic structure. Throughout her work, she displays *yin-yang* as a paradigm of process in Chinese thought, or a lens through which the Chinese people have viewed and continue to view the world for thousands of years. *Lived yin-yang* represents a dynamic system of thought and way of dealing with the world. Accordingly, the term *yin-yang* can refer to any aspect of life, nature, and the world, including cosmology, functions in society, warfare, ethics, ontological substance for the human body, and visual presentations. The ontology of yin-yang goes back to the *Book of Documents* (*Shang Shu* 尚書, 772–476 BCE), where the qi 氣, or the vital energy of yin-yang, is understood as a generative force underlying all existence and serving an essential role in making the ontological link between a unitary source and the diversity of the myriad things (*wanwu* 萬物). Wang notes that with regard to ethics, on the one hand, yin-yang furnished a sense of human connection to broader processes of the universe, which was highlighted later in the term *daode* 道德 (the virtuous Way); on the other hand, it structures human obligations through particular human relationships and hierarchies, which is emphasized in the term *lunli* 論理 (patterned relations).[30]

Tu, Hall and Ames, Wong, Li, Puett, Wang, and Rosemont and Ames all see the process of self-cultivation as creating the self in relation to others and thus transcending the common dichotomies between one and others. Only a person who is related to others can be considered an accomplished person, and a person who accomplishes lives in others too. Cheng Chung-ying adds that in a *harmonious community* of this kind, there is no doubt or fear. He claims,

> Here we see how the individual self is cultivated to make changes in one's behavior toward others with the vision that when everyone does this, the society will be transformed into a state of mutual respect and reciprocal empowerment. It is a social vision in which the harmony of the society is created from the *ren*-motivated individuals and the potential of an individual will be fully realized in a state of this human mutuality. It is a state of harmonization by mutual comprehension in which no misgiving, no fears and no doubts will arise, for the conditions for their manifestation will be eliminated in the process of mutual transformation.[31]

TRANSCENDING TEMPORAL BOUNDARIES: THE PERSON WHO IS MORALLY LIVING IN THE PRESENT

The person's ever-expanding relatedness embodies a unity of heaven and human, as Mencius says,

> All things are already complete in us. There is no greater delight than to be conscious of sincerity on self-examination. If one acts with a vigorous effort at the law of reciprocity, when he seeks for the realization of perfect virtue, nothing can be closer than his approximation to it. (7A:4)

Mencius sees sincerity (*cheng*誠) as the most genuine manifestation of human virtue and the reality of man's heavenly endowed nature.[32] When Mencius turns inside, he finds all things within himself, in their sincere or authentic form, and in fact, in his own sincere authentic form. Among the myriad things, his fellow humans are found within, such that he meets others within himself. This existence within oneself cannot be understood in any solipsistic manner, since the self constantly relates to others, constituting who she is. This intuition is also observed in *The Doctrine of the Mean* (DM).

> The enlightenment that comes from sincerity is our own nature. The sincerity that comes from enlightenment is called education. If you are sincere, you will be enlightened. If you are enlightened, you will be sincere. (DM 21)

If one wonders which precedes the other: sincerity or enlightenment, the response is that their codependence entails a process: our nature as sincere brings forth enlightenment, which necessitates sincerity again. The endless simultaneous process brings past and future into the present as explained in the next lines, by means of transcending oneself to the magnitude of forming a trinity with heaven and earth. By ongoing actualization of morality, the person is revealed a full partner not only of others in daily life, but moreover, the partnership in daily life makes each participant a partner in creation. By creating morality, the person is considered an equal collaborator or a cocreator.[33]

The explanatory power of simultaneity of creation is tightly related to the Confucian moral view as present oriented or nonutilitarian. In one occasion, when Confucius is asked about humanity, he explains that its essence is in acting in humane ways, disregarding the obstructions one must overcome; the benefit can be reaped as secondary, only after completing the act (6:20). The inferiority of profit in Confucianism is reaffirmed in this way, emphasizing that a moral act springs from and is conducted by morality itself; therefore, the moral act itself is what one should desire, rather than its consequences. Confucian humanity cannot be conceived in teleological or consequentialist terminologies in which extraneous effects are valued, rather than morality itself; all the more so regarding utilitarian terminology. If profit is to be considered, it may only have secondary significance; it could be added into one's deliberations as an afterthought, after the moral act was performed, and not as a parameter to consider before engaging in the act. According to Confucius, to attain wisdom, one should live in the vicinity of the good (4:1) rather than orient oneself to some unknown future good.

This reasoning is apparent in the famous example for the rejection of profit in the Mencian conversation with King Hui of Liang, when Mencius, the lover of humanity, dismisses even a mention of the word *profit* (*li* 利) and contrasts profit with rightness and humanity as mutually exclusive (*Mencius* IA:2). Interestingly, in the next recorded conversation in their series of meetings, Mencius emphasizes the significance of aesthetic pleasure enjoyed by the wise (IB:1). While the King is worried that if he becomes a virtuous person, he risks his ability to enjoy simple beauty, since a virtuous person should be always engaged with morality, Mencius explains that only a virtuous person can enjoy beauty. This is true precisely because he does not seek the profit that can be reaped of a beautiful pond; as a moral person, while standing by it simply enjoys the moment. The significance of pleasure-oriented deed is crucial to understanding the moral person who, as we have seen above, transcends his designated space and enters others' lives, as a person who also transcends the ordinary boundaries of time, such that he is able to incessantly live in joy in the present. To elaborate on this understanding, let us take a look in the opening of *Analects*.

> Learning and timely getting back to the learning—is it not a pleasure? Having friends visit from afar—is it not a joy? Not taking offence, even when others fail to appreciate you—is it not being an accomplished person?

Readers who are accustomed to grandiose openings for canonic texts might be surprised by an apparently quite tedious opening. Diametrically opposed the grandeur of the opening of *Genesis* with a clear beginning in time (or even, a beginning of time), for which one God is responsible, the *Analects*' opening refers to daily experiences of learning with joy, having friends with pleasure, and responding to offensive behavior without offence. This could be somewhat disappointing; we may even suspect again, egotistic and hedonistic overtones. However, if one wonders whether the Confucian-cultivated person is aiming at egotistic joy and pleasure, the idea is quite the opposite. Learning is learning morality, being a friend is acting morally, and disregarding what others say is the know-how of the cultivated person.[34]

The way to appreciate the full might of the passage lies in the orientation of a moral deed being neither in the past that no longer exists nor in the future that is not yet existent and is unknown—an orientation to morality as acting in the present. Similarly to Kant, and much earlier in history, this idea is embodied in Confucianism, giving a special status to joy and pleasure, calling for appreciating the morality of a person who lives in the present, rather than being oriented toward future benefits. Pleasure is the pleasure in learning the moral doctrine and in rehearsing what is learned. When the passage suggests the joy in one type of moral conduct—in this case hospitality toward visiting friends—it accentuates the type of moral personality Confucianism suggests as belonging to the world we live in and never beyond it. Pleasure and joy characterize a moral experience as oriented to itself, never to future outcomes. This idea becomes clearer when we read about Yan Hui, who was noticeable, in his Master's words, for his love of learning (6:3) added to Confucius's misgiving: "Hui is no help to me at all. He is pleased with everything I say" (11:4).[35] Confucius appreciates Hui, who does not seek to profit from learning; by not being profitable to his Master, Confucius cannot see him as means, rather, he is an end-in-himself.[36] According to Confucius, having joy rather than profit appears the highest moral response. Unlike profit, which is necessarily oriented toward something in the future that is external to the moral deed, pleasure is within the deed itself, and referring to the present. In the case of moral learning, the pleasure is in the deed itself, and is in contrast with profit.

In this spirit, when Confucius describes himself as the sort of man who forgets to eat when he tries to solve a problem, and who is so joyful that he forgets his worries and does not notice the onset of old age (7:19), we understand that his morality, experienced as joy, enables his engagement in life and practice without fear, not even in the face of death. The Confucian Way is thus revealed an ideal and never an attainable goal. Since an ideal cannot be fully attained, striving toward it is joyful, and yet it requires continuity and endless ongoing effort. This is what the Way is about. The Way is ideal in the sense of a standard to always aspire to and to be constantly realized, even if the realization is by definition never complete.[37] From within the framework of the moral ideal, when learning is discussed, it can never be intended for seeking profit, or even be directed toward an achievable aim; it is never future-oriented. In this model, any type of goal-oriented learning, such as learning for exams, would not be considered true learning. (Notably, this includes the imperial exams in China, despite the fact that they include the Confucian classics. In fact, such learning should be seen as an abuse of Confucian texts, for confusing an aim with a means for success, instead of being undertaken for its own sake.) The moral standard is always in the instant in which morality is actualized, as part of an ongoing process.

Importantly, pleasure is an indication of morality, rather than an outcome. It rests precisely in the moral act (as opposed to profit, which accompanies other acts), while the moral person is an agent who performs morality as a joyful task. In this sense, both learning and rehearsing and the hosting of friends (in 1:1) are pleasure and moral practice at once. Confucius brings his reader back to beginnings that are close to each and everyone: learning, joy, having a friend, a pleasure. These beginnings, as the beginnings of morality, are not within time, but rather without time, or timeless. In this way, the ongoing moral self creates eternal moral-time. Contrary to both hedonistic and utilitarian worldviews, joys referring to the action in the present, as opposed to profit referring to future consequences, characterize the Confucian moral world. This view of moral life is idealistic, yet the ideal is practiced daily, and not only by sages. While teleological reasoning can be defined easily and consistently in terms of causes and effects, means and aims—the philosophy of Way necessitates process reasoning. Whereas consequential reasoning may focus on argumentation, process reasoning may only focus on human practice, as moral and present.

In opposition to a "small person" (*xiaoren*小人) who is worried about the profit she can gain (or lose) (4:16o), the morally accomplished person (*junzi* 君子) is distinguished, in this way, as joyful. Coming back to the last part of the opening passage of *Analects*, we then realize the moral ability of the accomplished person to express indifference toward nonappreciation by others. What matters, primarily, is what one knows within. While others, as we have seen, play a major role in the constitution of who one is in terms of one's moral realization, one never depends on others for recognition or fame for her or his own self-assessment. Just as one never aspires to have a joyful deed end, so one never wishes for full attainment of morality; hence, in *Analects*, both sagehood and accomplished personality are unattainable. This nonattainability keeps the open-ended nature of moral life as a never-ending story; everyone learns ceaselessly in order to be a sage. From a concrete perspective, no one is a sage (since there is always more to learn); from the universal perspective, everyone, as a learner of morality, is a sage (since sagehood is the activity of ever-learning morality).[38] In fact, even if one appears to be a sage, that person should keep learning, and Confucian moral learning is the learning *to be a sage*. The framework of the moral standard as ideal, rather than a goal, is established without neglecting the motivation for self-cultivation; yet, as an ideal it is oriented toward the very instant of realization.

The idea of living morally in the present proceeded Mencius, as implying a deep faith in human nature and human moral feeling. Morality is not about making a great effort to conquer a desire to hurt others. Rather, being moral is about having an intuitive repulsion to harming others. Instead of, "I successfully restricted myself in time and hence I am a moral person," being moral corresponds to, "I cannot have pleasure when the other is in pain." As the outcome of our natural feelings of sympathy, *acting* morally is innate in us.[39] The feeling of immediate repulsion to the suffering of others is a moral feeling, and since any human being cannot live with the suffering of others, there is no human being who is not inherently moral. For example, a common person cannot understand the situation of a young child at risk for drowning through parameters such as a presupposition that the child enjoys her reflection in the water, or is about to dive in and come out, or that the sight of falling down is only a figment of the imagination, or a misinterpretation of the observing mind to sense-data. A person's feeling alarm, seeing distress, or hearing a cry for help (rather than a sound) all comprise part of the event as present and experienced as moral. Having a heart-mind that cannot bear to see the suffering of others, the person who sees a child about to fall into a well, feels alarm and distress as part of the event and an inner call to act (2A:2).

Through moral deeds that are introduced here as living incessantly in the present, the Confucian person transcends temporal boundaries. The idea, as shown in this section is quite comprehensible: the moral deed is never oriented to a future aim or outcome. A moral deed carries the past into the present, as one's moral tradition, as oriented to joy and pleasure in the deed. The moral Way, which is always in search, always in the present, and always an ideal, is embodied in the Confucian vision of life as an ongoing moral duty that is also a joy.[40] A cultivated person is thus a person who transformed past as well as future into present, a person who lives morally in the present. In this understanding, longing for profit is not being capable of understanding what life is. Longing for afterlife is understood in this way as treating morality as a means for an end that is external to it, and seeking to profit from this life instead of morally living life as moral, for its own sake, in a continuous joyful present.

TRANSCENDING SYMBOLIC BOUNDARIES: ETERNITY THROUGH RITUAL

A Ritualized Family

Always in the present and always related to others, the moral person is not higher than others, or beyond this very life. As the boundaries of corporality are transcended by entering others' space through moral relations, and the boundaries of time are transcended through living joyfully in the present, the moral person transcends boundaries between symbol and the symbolized as well, through practicing rites (*li* 禮).[41] Amid the practice, the practitioner turns (even if for an instant) into a different, fully cultivated person. In this way, as Michael Puett opines, the imaginary world created through ritual changes to the way we live.[42] Importantly, the first place for learning the rites is one's home. Through the family, parents spread the tradition, holidays or memorial days are practiced and honored, and through rituals one learns about family members that are not physically present. As we will see in the following discussion, learning from family-based rites comprises the practical component of one's ability to transcend one's own boundaries through the symbolic activity of ritual practice. The detailed ritual corpus regarding family reverence as family worship connects the person as a family member within a living tradition. While family reverence is the root of morality, it is then preserved through the ongoing practice of rites.

The significance of rites is seen in their serving one system, in which the full sense of a certain ritual is derived from the system as a whole. This is clearly observed when *Analects* says that returning to the rites even for one day is being human, holding onto the symbolic reasoning that observance of rites is the framework through which the world is seen, heard, and known.

> Do not look unless it is in accordance with rites; do not listen unless it is in accordance with rites; do not speak unless it is in accordance with rites; do not move unless it is in accordance with rites. (12:1)

The passage explicitly states that one should not see, hear, speak, or move "unless it is in accordance with rites." Rites as symbolic forms (using Ernst Cassirer's terminology) or rather the language game in which we take part (using a Wittgensteinean terminology) function as rules that enable the knowledge of the world as well as the proper conduct in it; they constitute a Confucian form of life. Ritual enables the person to see herself from outside as part of a larger context, as rooted in an ongoing tradition. Functioning in this way as a type of epistemological framework, the rites afford the related self with practical foundations. The alternative framework that those who perform the ritual create reformulates the limits of the person, such that when performing a ritual, we directly relate ourselves with the tradition and cross the concrete context of time and space within which the rite is performed. Thus, through rites, the self relates to something that is larger than bodily limits, which is open and abstract.

Rites maintain a relationship of great moral significance with the family and the virtue of family reverence. Indeed, family reverence is equally maintained through rites during one's parents' life and death (1:11), and in particular through the three years of mourning ritual (4:20). When a disciple asks about being filial, the Master replies with "never fail to observe." When asked to explain, Confucius stresses,

> When your parents are alive, observe the rites in serving them; when they die, observe the rites in burying them; and observe the rites in sacrificing to them. (2:5)

The idea that one follows the rites through life and death is not only about the continuity of tradition; the point is the continuity of morality. Performing rites for a person becomes more significant after that person's death, and the dead are served as if they live. In the same spirit, the closing chapter of the *Book of Family Reverence* is devoted to the responsibility of children to their parents and ancestors, through love and respect in life, and through grief and mourning in death.[43] Similarly, *Doctrine of the Mean* 19 praises King Wu and the Duke of Zhou for actualizing family reverence through which they correctly passed down the wills of their forefathers by observing every detail of the ancestral-worshiping rite. The importance of following one system of rites through life and through death embodies in it the crossing of the ultimate limit—that between life and death as distinct states. When *The Book of Rites* (*Liji* 禮紀) describes the rites of bringing spirits, in particular ancestor spirits from above, into our world (9:7), it stresses that in the moral sense, we and our deceased ancestors live one life, in the same world, dealt with according to the same rule.

The significance of keeping the rites involves the ability to transcend one's biological and genealogical limits for the sake of preserving the living moral feeling or the continuity of the moral person. The opening of *Book of Family Reverence* shows that the virtue of the sage kings is no other than family reverence, as the root for appropriate moral service in every human circle:

> Your physical person with its hair and skin is received from your parents. Vigilance in not allowing anything to do injury to your person is where family reverence begins; distinguishing yourself and walking the proper Way (*dao*) in the world; raising your name high for posterity and thereby bringing esteem to your father and mother—it is in these things that family reverence finds its consummation. This family reverence, then, begins in service to your parents, continues in service to your lord, and culminates in distinguishing yourself in the world.

Confucius's words, in the example, refer not only to the continuity of the rites, but moreover to that of our own bodies with those of our ancestors. Confucius explains that every human disposition is a parental endowment. In fact, one's physical body, every hair, and every bit of skin, as well as one's tendencies and moral virtues, are all received from one's parents. Who we are and what we are made of is rooted in them. For this reason, nurturing our bodies is a primary expression of family reverence and of respect for our parents, which establishes one's character and assists in cultivating oneself as reviving one's parents and continuing their Way. Knowing that our relationships with our parents can then be broadened to other members of the moral community, the point cannot be taken as a mere biological line; an adopted child, in this sense, continues his parents just as well, even if not biologically.

The centrality of honoring parents through cultivating oneself as shown in the *Book of Rites* in the case of Zengzi's reference to his body that was respected as part of his parents' bodies (24:26), is expressed in the same spirit in *Analects* 8:3, in the context of Zengzi's dying and asking his disciples to uncover his hands and legs and see that he had protected his body, thus showing the extent to which he revered his parents. The *Book of Rites* likewise tells that the sages built temples and established ancestor worship "not forgetting those to whom they owed their being" (24:20). As consequence, the multitudes submitted to their lessons and listened to them with readiness.

The significance of rites-following in Confucianism is shown in the story on Zai Wo's reservation with regard to the three-year mourning period.[44] Zai Wo sought permission to enact one year of mourning for his father, instead of three, making clear that he feels comfortable dressing, eating, working, and enjoying music, to which Confucius reacts in giving him permission to do so. Yet, an accomplished person would not have reacted in this way; a moral person feels the pain—one that makes garments uncomfortable, food not tasty, and music unpleasant. Hence, when Zai Wo leaves, Confucius teaches his disciples that Zai Wo is lacking humanity. According to the present understanding, his reservation regarding the symbolic mourning ritual is in fact a reservation regarding the entire moral system, and in particular regarding grieving as the moral feeling for one's parents (7:21).

While on the surface the dispute is about a specific ritual, a careful reading exposes that the ritual signifies much more than what is ordinarily taken as its face value; it serves as a channel to address the human difficulty in expressing feelings in the face of death. Through the system of rites, Confucius who does not address death in theory and discourse, is dealing with death profoundly; perhaps there is no other way to do so. His reverence to life and hence to death, and the great awareness of the feelings of mourners, is shown in a short laconic reference to his own practice of never eating to the full in the presence of mourners (7:9).[45] Whereas Confucius does not openly discuss the pain, the fear in the face of death, or one's feeling, he does stress the importance of a meaningful practice of ritual in one's life with regard to others' deaths. Mourning rituals do occupy a significant part in Confucius discussions, expressing that the ritual cannot lack inner intention and feeling; it cannot be conducted mechanically.[46]

Through the rites, we keep up the moral tradition of our deceased ancestors; we relive their morality and expand it, and sometimes we have to correct it. In this way, the rites assist in preserving the continuity among generations and forging continuity between life and death. In some practices, through simple gestures, one symbolically brings the deceased back into human daily context—for example, by placing food and wine to satisfy ancestors in family fests. In this way, past experiences and deceased ancestors are present in everyday practices, as part of moral life. The rites are thus keeping a living thread of morality. Through them, the past enters the present, and the deceased indeed come back to life—not in body, yet neither only symbolically, since through the performance of rites their morality never dies; rather, it is preserved and transferred. Ancestral worship, in this way, not only reminds sons and daughters of the life and traditions of the deceased ancestors, moreover it brings them back as members of the moral community. The above suggestion clarifies the idea that Confucian self-relatedness, sprouting from family relations and preserved in rites is a morality of living eternally in the present, or as explained hereafter, it is a sense of immortality.

Cultivating morality through rites is at once cultivating oneself and honoring parents and past traditions. Therefore, by means of cultivating one's own character, one preserves her parents as if they are alive. Ancestral worshiping brings humans to an appreciation of who we owe our life to, and to an awareness of the gift of life and the value of preserving it as our own moral selves in becoming more humane toward others. *The Book of Rites* ties ancestral worship with a continuity that transcends every accepted limit; in particular, it transcends the distinction between life and death, such that the memory of moral ancestors ties the dead with the living in a way that brings the presence of the dead back to life (24:21) in our own living morally in the present, carrying on our ancestors' lives symbolically. In this way, morality lies both beyond space and beyond concrete existence in time, as well as beyond the dichotomy between symbol and symbolized. On this ground Confucius gives a moving statement that is highly revealing in terms of his view on the person and one's boundaries.

> The Master was very sick. Zilu assigned the disciples to serve as formal ministers. Upon the illness' relief, he said, "For a long time your conduct has been deceitful! Having no formal ministers and pretending to have ministers, whom do I mislead? Do I mislead heaven? Moreover, I'd rather die in your hands, my disciples, than die in the hands of formal ministers. And even if I may not get a lavish burial, do I die on the road?" (9:12)

Confucius's last wish implies an understanding of what being a person amounts to.

The Master's wish to die among his disciples—his closest partners to the Way—rather than in the hands of respected ministers to whom he is not related, is of extreme importance to the Confucian understanding of the person as living morally with others and dying among them. In the quest of showing his sick Master the esteem and admiration he deserves, Zi Lu (You) preferred a lavish ceremony. He sought to respect and honor his Master by acting as if the Master had a formal office that allowed him formal ministers. Confucius, on his deathbed, used the harsh judgment of "deceitful" (zha詐) with regard to Zi Lu's suggestion, applying irony: pretence is useless; one cannot deceive heaven. Moreover, Confucius does not want to deceive himself; his own wish is to die among the ones who know him and care for him, who precede morality to ceremony, and who see life and death as he does. Confucius who lived among his disciples wishes to die among them. I posit that the continuity of rites in life and death may give one a sense of immortality, while in fact this is a sense of morality.

Morally Related and Eternally Alive

When the teacher tells his disciples that "hearing about the Way in the morning—one can die in the evening" (4:8), the ultimate boundary is crossed—between life and death, through the Way. Questioning this relatedness may bring one to wonder: is there an ontological overtone regarding the independency between the moral Way and the ability to prolong life? Or is there an epistemological nondeterministic perspective regarding life as a game in which knowing the rules is impossible? Can one suspect this as a fatalistic statement about a life with no safe haven? Perhaps a warning is implied in saying that following the Way cannot grant some antidote for disaster. In the present understanding, the passage also suggests some moral comfort, implying that after hearing the Way one can rest peacefully, with no fear or worries.

It is quite puzzling that Confucius, who was primarily concerned with the person and one's life, gives only sparse hints regarding death. For most humans in most places, no issue is more mysterious, more disturbing, and more terrifying than the end of life: We have neither a solid clue to what happens when we die, to the possibility of afterlife, to our ability to affect it and whether at all it is connected to this life, nor to an explanation and comfort regarding the deaths of people we love. Interpreters made attempts to extract from Confucian sayings ideas that relate to death, in order to locate Confucius's stance with regard to the issue.[47] One question that interpreters grapple with is the great Master's silence following the tragic early death of his beloved disciple, Yan Hui. Keeping his focus on life rather than on death; when Zilu inquires about death, Confucius replies: "You do not yet know life—how will you understand death?" (11:12).

One who is not seasoned with the laconically told story could suspect that Confucius avoids the issue, since he has nothing significant to say; this simplistic solution is not probable, especially given the "yet" (*wei zhisheng yan zhisi* 未知生焉知死) in the passage: Zilu cannot understand death *yet*, when neither life is disclosed to him nor his person is accomplished. The importance of this phrasing should not be overlooked, given the great admiration Confucius held to Yan Hui's moral cultivation. According to *Analects* 6:7, it is Hui alone who was able to stick to humanity for three whole months (either realistically, or as a metaphor for a long time). Clearly, throughout his short life, his Master praised him for his love of virtue and his consistent embodiment of it. We read that Hui is appreciated as exceptional listener who does not utter a word when the Master teaches, while later his actions show his vast knowledge of the doctrine (2:9, 9:19, 11:4). When Zigong admits that as a fellow student he cannot measure with Yan Hui's knowledge, his prompt ability to understand, and the comprehensiveness of his understanding, the Master admits that just like Zigong, neither can he himself measure up to Hui (5:9). Moreover, Hui is praised not only for his exceptional talent as a student but moreover for his moral character. For example, the teacher mentions his satisfaction with little, as he lives in a narrow alley and subsists on some grain and water, and still has joy in life (6:11).

The above references make Confucius's subtle reactions to the death of his young disciple even more moving. The Master expresses deep sorrow over the fact that Hui passed away too young to fully realize his promise (9:20), comparing him to a sprout that failed to flourish (9:21). Without detailed description of lamentations and extravagant acts of mourning, Confucius grieves the true virtue of his student, the modesty, the wit, and the endless love for moral learning (11:6).

The explanations of Confucius's refusal to discuss death refer back to the laconic sources that leave room for interpretations. Zhu Xi, the great synthesizer of Confucianism in the Song dynasty, wonders about the Master's refusal to speak about death, yet believes that Confucius had some teachings on death and on spirits, for which he did not see in every disciple a ready learner, and thus is recommending that they complete basic learning before moving on.[48] Contemporary interpreters take this up; for example, Edward Slingerland refers to the humanism, which many see in this passage, and to the practical orientation of the doctrine, focusing on moral conduct rather than speculative discourse of the unknown. Slingerland mentions in this context Confucian commentaries such as Huang Kan's remark on emphasizing the here and now, especially in Confucius's sayings.[49] Chen Tianxiang, sees in Confucius a teacher of daily human affairs, who never digresses to the esoteric; P. J. Ivanhoe makes the point that in Confucian ethics, to understand death one must understand life.[50]

If one might still suspect that Confucius, who does not discuss feelings, avoids discussing death, since it is so painful, it is revealed that with neither grandeur of ceremonies nor of words, Confucius *does* express great pain over Yan Hui's death. Indeed, Confucius expresses the tragedy in this loss with few moving words repeated twice, "Heaven bereft me! Heaven bereft me!" (11:9). The text tells that when Yan Hui died, the Master cried for him to the point that the disciples wondered if the grief was not excessive. Confucius replied asking rhetorically: "if not for him, for whom should I express pain?" (11:10). Confucius's treatment of Hui as his own son also motivates his objection to an extravagant funeral that shifts the focus from authentic feelings to a fixed format of burial and mourning ceremonies. The ritual is performed, preserving a sincere expression of feelings; and for Confucius, these feelings express the relation between father and son. In this way, when Yan Hui's father asks for an outer coffin for his son, Confucius refuses, since he wants Hui to be treated like his own son who had no outer coffin (11:8). Similarly, when the disciples suggest a lavish burial, Confucius, who sees this as improper, apparently refers to the fact that his own son was not buried in this fashion. When the disciples insist and act accordingly, Confucius states, "Hui treated me as a father," and objects to the fact that he was "prevented from treating him as a son" (11:11). In Confucius's response, actual family boundaries are crossed: Yan Hui is treated as his son, and in this way keeps living in him. This boundary crossing is a crossing of accepted spatial, temporal, and symbolic boundaries at once.

The understanding that life is morality brings us again to Mencius's stressing that when one is occupied with morality, one neither fears death nor aspires to longevity. This idea is evident in the fish versus bear's paws analogy, taken from Chinese culinary world. In Mencius's circle, fish is not considered a bad dish, but neither is it considered a delicacy; it thus represents a simple noninspiring life without morality, which is not necessarily bad or antimoral, yet it is indifferent, basic, and amoral. In contrast, the delicacy of bear's paw is analogous to moral life, or life with rightness (*yi* 義), which is meaningful and inspirational. According to Mencius, if he cannot have the two together, he gives up the fish and takes the bear's paws. The allegory is explained right away: he likes life, and he also likes morality. If he cannot keep the two together, he will give up life, and choose morality; even though he dislikes death, it is immoral life that he dislikes even more. Mencius concludes: "Though life is what I want, there is something I want more than life" (6A:10).

Therefore, on occasions in which morality is at stake, he does not flee from danger. When Mencius discusses morality, he makes certain that morality is what life is truly about and, therefore, he does not cling to life at all costs (6B:15). Morality gives life its meaning, and without it, death is preferred. On a different occasion, Mencius refers to a prince wishing to become sovereign by the wrong means, through the analogy to a very sick person seeking a wormwood plant, which can be effective only after three years of drying. The analogy is unmistakably compelling: Immoral life is sick life. If not taken care of on time, the sickness is incurable. Hence, if the rulers do not set the wills on morality at all times, the people are "in sorrow and disgrace, and they will be involved in death and ruin" (4A:9), and a ruler should be prepared to die for morality (1B:20). Taking delight in not being benevolent is, according to Mencius, like "hating to be drunk, and yet exaggerating in drinking wine," as one's joy in not being moral is pure self-deception and self-destruction, which are worse than death (3A:3). Confucian life is revealed as meaningful only when the person is morally cultivated such that it transcends all boundaries, including that between life and death. Mencius accentuates his point:

> He who has exhausted all his mental constitution knows his nature. Knowing his nature, he knows Heaven. To preserve one's mental constitution and nourish one's nature is the way to serve Heaven. When neither a

premature death nor long life causes a man any double-mindedness, but he waits in the cultivation of his personal character for whatever issue, this is the way in which he establishes his Heaven-ordained being. (7A:1)

Morality is the power to live unthreatened. Being harmonized with heaven and earth, one is indifferent to longevity or premature death in a similar way to that in which heaven and earth are. Similarly to his Master's "hearing the Way in the morning and possibly die in the evening," according to Mencius,

> There is an appointment for everything. A man should receive submissively what may be correctly ascribed thereto. Therefore, he who has the true idea of what is Heaven's appointment will not stand beneath a precipitous wall. Death sustained in the discharge of one's duties may correctly be ascribed to the appointment of Heaven. Death under handcuffs and fetters cannot correctly be so ascribed. (7A:2)

Since we do not live to experience death, the mystery is vast. Regarding one's own death, anything we say can only be speculative; regarding to the death of a close person, the pain makes the expression in words hard, if not altogether impossible. Yet, the explanation for Confucius's choice to pass over in silence is rooted deeper in his moral philosophy. Death upon fulfilling the Way (*jinqidao* 盡其道) or, as Legge translated it, "in the discharge of one's duties," reflects moral life, as related to others and always present. Moral duty is one's task that cannot be terminated, not even by death; it is not subject to time. In fact, like the person, it is timeless.

Living morally in the present is living as timelessness is necessary since the person is a person in dialogue that is never temporally limited and can be always symbolically performed, and since one's identity is comprised of the meetings with others throughout one's life. In particular, with regard to the ultimate limit of the person—that of death—a person who passed away persists through living in the others she influenced throughout her life. The living person experiences death as the death of the other within himself, as others become part of who we are (not in a solipsistic manner of realizing oneself by means of swallowing the other, but by means of others realizing themselves through us).

The early Confucian perception of person is not well defined but rather remains blurred and unbounded, since one inherently transcends boundaries: in particular, the boundary between one and the other, the boundary between present (as actual) and past or future (as ideal), and the boundary between symbolic ritualistic act and real act, it even exceeds the boundary between life and death. I posit that the continuity of rites in life and death may give one a sense of immortality, while in fact this is a sense of morality. As we will see, the Confucian revival during the Song dynasty takes up the old moral perspective on the person with sophistication that originates in Chinese attitudes that are not solely Confucian or not Confucian at all.

CONCLUDING NOTE

Confucian life is living in dialogue with others as a personal, communal, and cosmic commitment. The person as an ongoing process of dialogue is a Confucian depiction of the person regardless of where and when he or she lives. When living is defined as being related to others, one is realized in dialogue. As Confucius describes it, it is the walking with others and learning from them. Being in dialogue, as Buber suggests, is given to man as a task. Buber addresses his readers, in particular, those who believe in a creator and see the *task* of living on earth in *dialogue* as a gift from God that cannot be realized without the human contribution. In Confucianism, the world is not a given, it is *created* by humans; the ultimate as the Way is created by those who travel it and broaden it with their deeds. In this form of living, the person as inherently related with others and incessantly transforming transcends one's own boundaries and enters the lives of others. By doing so through moral deeds, one lives in others, such that transcending oneself is also transcending known boundaries of finitude and infinitude (as seen in Zhou Dunyi's philosophy), in and out (as in Shao Yong's philosophy), and ultimately, life and death (demonstrated in Zhang Zai's philosophy). By entering into other's lives as if entering a new game and letting others enter our own, we are then staying in each other's lives after we are gone. In this way, in terms of one's moral, metaphysical, and epistemological boundaries, being human is *living* in others eternally. We are thus introduced to the person who transcends boundaries of space and time, as well as accepted symbolic forms, as a Confucian version for understanding homo sapiens as an alternative to the Cartesian suggestion in a way that in the end of the day reflecting within, one discovers the *other*. Paraphrasing the familiar words: I think, therefore *you* are. Therefore, you are an ongoing process. In this way "a person can broaden the Way, but the Way cannot broaden a person" (*Analects* 15:28).

TWO

Emerging to a Self through Transcending the Infinitude-Finitude Dichotomy

Zhou Dunyi's Anthropocosmic Riddle and Its Response

To witness the mystery of our mind, all we have to do is stare at ourselves in the mirror and wonder, What lurks behind our eyes? This raises haunting questions like: Do we have a soul? What happens to us after we die? Who am "I" anyway? And most important, this brings us to the ultimate question: Where do we fit into this great cosmic scheme?

—MICHIO KAKU, *The Future of the Mind*

EXPANDING RELATEDNESS: AN INTRODUCTION

The Task: A Confucian Sense of Metaphysics

The early Confucian insight that relating with others is the central manner of broadening the Way shifts in the Song dynasty to relating with every living creature and cosmic phenomena. These attempts are presented here as a major contribution, not only to neo-Confucianism, but to worldly humanistic philosophy and its concern with human boundaries and one's capabilities to transcend them and overcome inherent limitations. A creative and key voice in forming this uniquely Confucian inclusive cosmological perspective was Zhou Dunyi周敦頤 (1017–1073)—the protagonist of this chapter—commonly considered the pioneering thinker in the Confucian revival in the Song dynasty, who challenged the most fundamental dichotomy up to the vanishing of the very distinction between One and many, or de-dichotomizing infinitude and finitude.

Zhou's basic attitude toward life remains faithful to early Confucian humanism, while making extensive use of the early philosophy of the *Book of Change* (*Yijing* 易經 abbreviated hereafter as *Change*) as both cosmological and methodological anchor to establishing a unique metaphysical perspective on the person as a growing relatedness with every part of the universe, or an anthropocosmic vision (as coined by Tu Weiming, 1994). Using the term metaphysics for Zhou's humanistic philosophy is neither trivial nor is it precise. If ancient and medieval philosophers in the West saw metaphysics, like astronomy or biology, as inherently defined by its subject matter, the subject matter of metaphysics appears in question and dispute. It was the science that studied that which never changes, or the first causes of things, considered later on by Kant, who aimed at finding the one thing that lies behind all things in the universe, the being as such (thing in itself, *Ding an sich*). Looking for one unifying aspect behind everything that is yet giving rise and existence to the many things and events in the world of phenomena, this being was traditionally articulated through the problem of the One and the many, or the infinite and the finite. Finding a science of this kind appeared (and still is) problematic in every conceptual scheme; even more so when considered from the Chinese perspective, and in particular from the Confucian humanistic one.

In the latter, some philosophical problems that are commonly considered metaphysical (or partly metaphysical) are in no way related, in the conceptual scheme, to a first cause or an unchanging thing of the kind of a self-created being like God. Some major examples include the inherent relatedness of the Way to its partakers, rather than that of God and the created world as strictly distinguished from its creator; similarly, a natural characterization of Way is human morality, opposed to the question of the moral status of the transcendent God and the derived problem of evil; likewise, the centrality of change in Chinese philosophy is in sharp opposition to the constitution of identity over time, and the aspiration for an eternity that stands in contradiction to the human experience of change; and even more so, the unity of heart-mind (*xin* 心) as one idea, rather than the infamous mind and body problem that became focal in philosophy since Descartes times in the seventeenth century.

The roots of Chinese metaphysics in the *Book of Change* may shed some light on the uniqueness of this way of thinking. The *Change* offers a noncausal thinking, such that first causes or unchanging things disappear in the fluidity of life and its categories of explanation; in this way, neither there was a tradition of argumentations for the existence of an ultimate cause. Accordingly, with no first cause for the series of observable phenomena, the strict conception of causation falls apart in this philosophical tradition. While World Philosophy, at large, takes the problem of One and the many, as the relation between God and the created world was never solved and remained in the core of the search for a metaphysical foundation, in Confucianism this vital relation was never truly considered a problem. A success in explaining the One-many as the cosmic manifestation of infinite-finite relationship was always aspired to, and was taken as offering explanation to related questions, including the relations between eternal and temporal; constant and discrete; absolute and relative; simple and complex; space and matter, and other implications of the infinite-finite relatedness. Similarly, it was also assumed that if the problem of the One and the many is to be solved, we must understand the nature and structure of the universe, and hence we may know the One thing that is giving rise to, is common to, and connects the many things within the universe. Only then we will understand the natures and structures of the various material things.[1]

In the Chinese context, we encounter an alternative inclusive metaphysics taking into account that the ultimate itself is to be seen as the very process of relating and transforming in space and time, thus transcending infinitude-finitude dichotomy in theory and in practice. According to the present suggestion, Zhou Dunyi undertakes this relation as his task that from then on informs the Confucian revival in the Song dynasty. As explained hereafter, through a renewed use of existing terminology, Zhou sees person as Way, or the finite as infinite as a practical commitment. If offering a metaphysical foundation to early Confucian ethics (similarly to that offered by Kant's philosophy to Aristotle and Plato) is sometimes anticipated from Zhou by his interpreters, as presented here, Zhou's philosophy does offer a foundation, yet this foundation is human life, thought, and practice, as shown through his systematic attempt to transcend the infinitude-finitude boundary. In this way metaphysics loses its Parmenidean significance as the fundamental nature of reality that is separate from events. Perhaps it also loses the justification to be called metaphysics. In this sense, Zhou's metaphysics is what Roger Ames titles ametaphysics, or perhaps it should be titled supra-metaphysics.[2] If so, what it gains, as suggested here, is much more than an impressive title.

Infinitude and Finitude in Zhou's Biography

When Zhou was still a child, his father died prematurely and by the age of fourteen, he had been taken in and raised by his uncle. Throughout his youth, while yearning for his lost father, he expressed remarkable care for life, and his great love for nature and for living creatures was well known among those surrounding him.[3] As anecdotes tell, out of a sense of kinship with every living and growing being, he was unable to cut the grass of his lawn; he admired the lotus flower—the famous Buddhist symbol—as allegorical of the life of the accomplished person, who is rooted like the lotus in mundane muddy affairs of samsara (or phenomena), while realized and flourishing in pure air—analogous to nirvana (or noumena).[4] In this way, his life story sheds light with regard to his philosophical yearning for the transcending boundary between finitude and infinitude, many and One.

As Confucian offspring, Zhou established a reputation as a teacher of Confucian learning. A personal testimony by his disciple Cheng Hao refers to the ways Zhou taught him and his brother Cheng Yi to investigate the places in which Confucius and his favorite disciple Yanzi found their happiness.[5] The idea of happiness in one's life as a sign of Oneness brought Cheng Hao later on to give up the ambition to pursue civil service examinations or to orient his studying toward the examinations, that in fact stand in sharp opposition to the Confucian idea of joy in learning for its own sake. The emphasis on taking happiness in the study rather than benefiting from it for the purpose of passing examinations is central to Confucianism as a whole, and has special importance for understanding Zhou's view of focusing on natural flow rather than on external cause or purpose.

Zhou was promoted several times to different state offices, a significant event in this context was his promotion to an official post as a settler of legal cases; as we learn, his performance was admirable, and he was known for his peace-making attitude.⁶ Zhou was known as always giving special attention to learning and teaching the Confucian doctrine, as well as to active implementations of it, so for him that knowledge was unified with practice and his appreciation for human life was demonstrated not only in his writings, but also in practices such as his active refusal to accept unjustified verdicts, in particular, the most horrifying violation of the natural course in unjustified death. In one famous incident, the regional finance commissioner intended to execute certain prisoners, while of all the officials only Zhou protested against the harsh sentence and in fact succeeded in saving the prisoners' lives.⁷

Zhu Xi 朱熹 (1130–1200), the great synthesizer and commentator of Confucianism, who later established the Confucian line of transmission, mentions that he translated Zhou's *Taijitu shuo* 太極圖說 (*Diagram of Supreme Polarity Explained*, abbreviated hereafter TJTS),⁸ as well as the forty chapters of the *The Penetrating Book* (*Tongshu* 通書, abbreviated as TS) in their initial editions, in which they were passed down through generations of students in the most accurate form possible. In this context, Zhu Xi accentuates Zhou's influence on his students, especially on his most prominent ones, the Cheng brothers, giving justification for his quite consensual position as the beginner in the succession of the Way (*daotong* 道統). Of special interest in this context is Joseph Adler discussion on Zhu Xi's elevation of Zhou Dunyi and the re-creating of the accepted line of transmission from Confucius and Mencius to his own time, by predating Zhou—hitherto a minor figure—to the Cheng brothers by almost a century.⁹ Zhu Xi's choice of Zhou, which has never enjoyed a satisfactory explanation, is given by Adler in the explanation that the idea that inspired Zhu Xi's understanding self-cultivation (*xiushen* 修身) and becoming a sage lies in Zhou's TJTS, in his understanding of the interpenetration of activity and tranquility (*dongjing* 動靜) as the first manifestation of Supreme Polarity, applicable to both the cosmos and the human mind.¹⁰

Zhou's philosophical treatises rely on classical Confucian sources through extensive cross-references; yet they also apply Daoist and Buddhist terminologies, methodologies, and ideas. Presenting a single nonlinear process in which Supreme Polarity is embodied in activity and tranquility, yin and yang, the five phases, and the myriad things, of which the sage's mind is its utmost manifestation, TJTS presents the cultivation of human mind as mirroring the natural Order.

The Book of Change as Initial Model

The ideas of *Change* played essential role in the revival of Confucianism in the Song dynasty, and as mentioned above, its explanatory power, as reflected through the wide acceptance the book received by almost all Chinese thinkers, served a major role in Zhou's philosophy as well.[11] Zhou refers back to the *Change* and extensively applies its terminology; moreover, Zhou's use of the TJT diagram in the core of his philosophy might testify that the *Change* had influenced his philosophical methodology as well. The significance of the *Change* can't be underestimated when recalling Confucius, the Master of moral learning, who testifies that had he been given fifty more years of life, he would have devoted them to studying the *Book of Change*, so that he could be free of faults (*Analects* 7:17).[12]

Before delving into Zhou's philosophy, it is helpful to recall that according to the *Book of Change*, aspects of all existence are understood through the flux between the polar contrasts of yin 陰 and yang 陽, representing female as completing male, dark as completing bright, low as completing high, negative as completing positive, wet as completing dry, and so on. Yin and yang are in this way presented not as two opposing forces and pairs of fixed attributes, they are contextual, meaning that one thing can be yin at one time and yang at another. Hence, although it is understood through pairs of concepts, the system cannot be considered dualistic; rather, it reflects an important play on the ontological oneness of reality, manifested as one ongoing motion between poles.

Of great significance to the present context is the uniqueness of the *Book of Change* lying in its noncausal explanation to the various happenings in the world, in particular regarding the relatedness of human and Way. The noncausal explanation is taking into consideration the coincidental aspects of life and phenomena that are "greater than us," like natural disasters or wonders, as well as in personal smaller aspects of reality, including concrete events, emotions raised in specific contexts, and influences. When Carl Gustav Jung commented on the book, he coined the term *synchronicity* for the understanding according to acausal connecting principle that the book offers. According to Jung's suggestion, the synchronicity in Chinese thought portrays the endless concurrent happening of events in the world, rather than superstitiously assuming that X preceded Y and made it happen. As he explains, it is "a peculiar principle active in the world so that things happen together somehow and behave as if they were the same, and yet for us they are not."[13] In other words, the world is perceived as mutual codependence, in a way that makes any cause-effect explanation inadequate and useless.

This outlook comes through in the broader Chinese context, as Joseph Needham opines, applying to the physical world as well as the social. Things behaved in particular ways not necessarily because of prior actions or impulsions of other things, but because their position in the ever-moving cyclical universe was such that they were endowed with intrinsic natures, which made that behavior inevitable for them. If they did not behave in those particular ways they would lose their relational positions in the whole (which made them what they were), and turn into something other than themselves. They were thus parts in existential dependence on the whole world-organism.[14] The acausal dynamics of the spontaneously self-generating life process of Chinese cosmology are based on the yin-yang system of contrasts, referring to the ongoing movement between poles, which characterizes life. Frederick Mote opines,

> The genuine Chinese cosmogony is that of organic process, meaning that all of the parts of the entire cosmos belong to one organic whole and that they all interact as participants in one spontaneously self-generating life process.[15]

Referring to the opening of Zhou's TJTS, Cheng Chung-ying understands the idea of Nonpolar and Supreme Polarity (*wuji er taiji* 無極而太極) in terms of the *Book of Change*'s vision of that which is (*you* 有) and that which is not (*wu* 無). While *you* is the totality of things and affairs in the world, apparently *wu* is their absence. However, the latter does not amount to a world of nothingness; rather, both are experienced aspects of reality. This relation necessitates a special notion of a changing reality, of creative unity and a transforming, dynamic world. In this view, *wu* can be explained in terms of indeterminate qi (vital power 氣[16]), and *you* in terms of Order (*li* 理[17]). Reality as Nonpolar and Supreme Polarity is not limited to a specific product or even a process; it is a reality in which *wu* and *you* are interdependent. Hence, according to Cheng, the first statement of TJTS, Non-Polar and Supreme Polarity means that

> Creativity cannot but be, yet is not to be exhausted by the process of transformation. The first statement points to the fact that the concrete world of things manifests the infinite source of creativity or that *you* manifest the *wu*, the delimitation of *you*.
>
> The second statement points to the fact that the unlimited reality of creativity manifests, indeed cannot but manifest, a process of change and production of life—or that *wu* manifests *you*, the determination of *wu*.[18]

According to the present suggestion, the rootedness of the idea of Nonpolar and Supreme Polarity in the *Book of Change* reaffirms the significance of a paradox: if we acknowledge life as transformation, we have to acknowledge its contradictory nature. In his use of Nonpolar and Supreme Polarity, when Zhou takes the reader back to the *Book of Change* and the Chinese yin-yang thinking, he introduces the person as an integral part of a cosmic process of relational transformation.[19]

While Zhou uses the book's insight for his anthropocosmic understanding, it is likely that the book also influenced Zhou's philosophical methodology. In this context, one should note that the original use of the *Change* as a work of divination displays an apparent paradox. On the one hand, the main practice the book promotes is divination, or fortune-telling, apparently assuming that the future can be known and told. On the other hand, everything is in constant flux, changes occur, and transformation is unavoidable. Anything we know is learned through our own experience in the present (embodying the past in it); the future is beyond a human's reach, and the ongoing transformation necessitates an inability to foreknow; therefore, the only way to treat one's life is through the present instant. Likewise, seeing the foretelling of the book, not in reference to the telling of future events in advance, we realize that what one tells in advance is one's position with regard to one's situation and context, similarly to casting a dice in a game, knowing beforehand that this is how we play, but never possessing knowledge of the exact outcome. Moreover, the casting is always relational to a situation.

Jung's explanation of the sixty-four hexagrams as the tool by which sixty-four different paradigmatic conditions can be interpreted but never determined elucidates the conditions as paradigmatic, necessitating consideration of nuances and subtleties.[20] The realization that there are various possible responses for any question relies on one's reflection and projection. Hence, the book never pretends to offer one firm solution.[21] The knowledge one aspires to is knowledge of the world as projected in the ever-expanding transforming self. Jung writes,

> The *I Ching* does not offer itself with proofs and results; it does not vaunt itself, nor is it easy to approach. Like a part of nature, it waits until it is discovered. It offers neither facts nor power, but for lovers of self-knowledge, of wisdom—if there be such—it seems to be the right book. To one person its spirit appears as clear as day; to another, shadowy as twilight; to a third, dark as night. He who is not pleased by it does not have to use it, and he who is against it is not obliged to find it true. Let it go forth into the world for the benefit of those who can discern its meaning.[22]

Zhou brings to the front the book's foretelling as representing a call to decipher a mystery. As shown hereafter, in Zhou's philosophy, the person is one manifestation of the mysterious all-encompassing process of becoming through incessant creative movement and transformation, which requires transcending of the fundamental boundary between Infinitude and finitude as One and many, and also related to transcending other boundaries as well, including those between activity (or motion) and tranquility (or stillness) and the boundary between that exists, perceived and experienced as being and that which is not. This philosophical stand necessitates seeing all elements as one unity that enables the requisite space for creation. The removal of boundary between infinitude and finitude yields a vision of one transforming universe, in which the person is inherent; since the dynamics of cosmic creation is the creation of the myriad things, it necessarily includes the person. The universe, the self, beginnings and endings, and birth and death, are all one endless transformation. The synchronic organic whole that is embedded in the *Change* leaves place for open-ended understanding, or as presented here, for understanding in riddles.

Riddle and Response

As Zhou's TJTS shows, investigating universal beginnings and endings (*shizhong* 始終) yields understanding regarding one's self-boundaries known as those of death and birth (*sisheng* 死生). This understanding responds to questions on first cause and its derivatives, on infinitude-finitude relatedness, on One and many, or in large on the metaphysical, through one's life and practice. In this sense, Zhou's attitude is not simply viewed as a metaphysical curiosity; it is rather introduced here as a *living riddle*—explained hereafter as a riddle that can only be responded to in one's life and practice.

The *living riddle* in Zhou's philosophy is presented in the rest of this chapter as a true linguistic revolution in which he responds to the riddle of life with understanding Non-Polar and Supreme Polarity as *a new conceptual construct* (hereafter referred to as WJTJ). Calling for action in the ending of TJTS is a call to investigate beginnings and endings not as first and last causes, or as One that is responsible for the many, but rather as one's life and practice. Following Zhou's own investigation through reading TJTS and TS as one whole philosophy, demonstrates how the person embodies the cosmological.

The following refers first to Zhou's TJTS introducing Nonpolar and Supreme Polarity as living riddle, moving on to the embodiment of the Supreme in the ongoing process of emergence through yin-yang, the five phases and *Qian* and *Kun*, in the spirit of the *Book of Change*, and ultimately its embodiment in the myriad things, including human beings. Next, the embodiment of the Supreme in oneself is introduced in TS as a moral-practical commitment, as humanly transcending the boundaries of One and many. The sage, according to the present reading, is the human embodiment of the riddle of Nonpolar and Supreme Polarity responded in unlimited moral transformation. The relatedness between the anthropocosmic vision of TJTS and Zhou's moral philosophy in TS suggests that the paradoxical attitude in which the One is the many is inherent to the Confucian anthropocosmic vision—in fact, it is inherent to life.

THE DIAGRAM OF SUPREME POLARITY EXPLAINED: INFINITUDE IN FINITUDE AND THE RIDDLE OF ONE AS MANY

The TJTS—including a diagram (see figure 2.1) and a short explanatory text—comprises an impressive Confucian statement on the universe as one dynamic continuity, from the heavenly whole and perfection to the flawed partiality of the world below. Scholars usually celebrate the daring opening statement of the short piece, Nonpolar and Supreme Polarity, as the essence of Zhou's renewed metaphysical perspective.[23] I posit that the metaphysical perspective embodied in the short treatise does not suggest a metaphysical *foundation* to Confucianism in the accepted sense of a Grand Metaphysical explanation for life (leading traditionally to believing in the existence of a supreme eternal and infinite deity). Rather, following the treatise from beginning to end leads the reader to a conclusion that, in fact, the supreme, eternal, and infinite *is* the very ever-becoming of the myriad finite things on earth. This process constitutes both the continuity between here and beyond, and the unity of the One and the many. Taking its cue from TJTS, this chapter delves into the significance of the person as the embodiment of the Ultimate, whose exploration necessitates transcending the decisive boundary between infinitude and finitude, and living as infinitude within finitude.[24] As suggested here, this idea is not only the essence of TJTS but also a core concept in understanding the broader anthropocosmic philosophy of Zhou Dunyi as shown in TS.

Transformation according to TJTS occurs through an ongoing movement toward transcending the boundary between Infinity—as Non-Polar and Supreme Polarity (*Wuji er Taiji* 無極而太)—represented in the upper circle of the diagram, and the finite—as the myriad things, including the sage as its human embodiment—represented by the lower circle. According to the

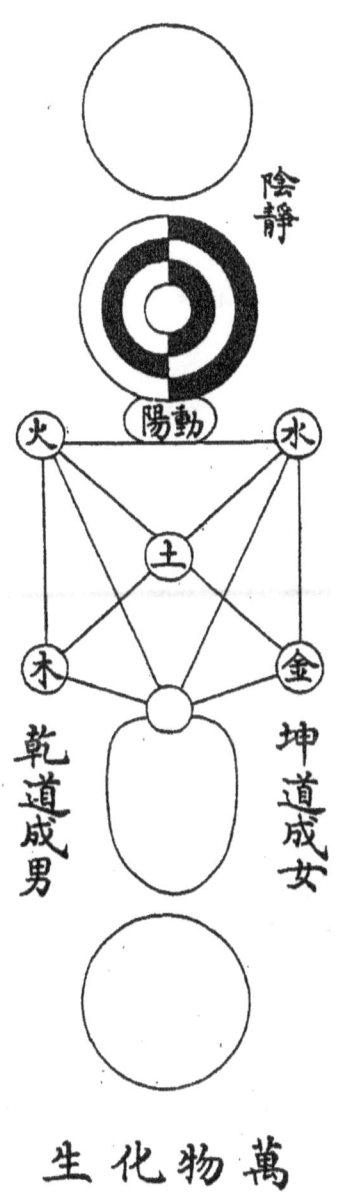

FIGURE 2.1. *Taijitu Shuo* 太極圖說. *Source*: Fair use.

present suggestion, despite its linear graphic form, the diagram has to be read synchronously rather than diachronically, such that each of its figures reflects all others, while the opening with the contradictory expression Non-Polar and Supreme Polarity is exposed in the end as the ultimate expression to the multitude of finite beings.

The treatise's unusual opening with the unified concept Non-Polar and Supreme Polarity comprises an unprecedented expression in Confucianism, in which the idea of ultimate cannot accept a conception of distinct contrariety or of a discrete preeminence; rather, it is a dynamic polarity. To fully appreciate the conceptual breakthrough, let us note again the characterization of Confucian thinking as a thinking of *you* 有 as existence—diverse, active, and seen, as opposed to Daoist *wu* 無 as nonexistence—unified, reactive, and hidden.[25] Along this line, Benjamin Schwartz stressed that the only knowledge admissible in Confucianism is a practical intelligence wholly based on know-how or know what to do, which immediately relates to practice as existence. Confucianism requires that being is acting (*youwei* 有爲), which amounts to various intentional purposive actions. Daoist spontaneous, unified nonaction (*wuwei* 無為) works wonders in nature, yet is not suitable for human beings.[26] If so, what sense can the unification in the opening statement of TJTS make within a renewed context of philosophy in the Song dynasty?

It might be helpful to first refer to the scheme of the diagram in TJTS, that is likely borrowed from the *Diagram of the Nonpolar* (*Wujitu* 無極圖) associated with the Daoist tradition. In particular, as Robin Wang notes, Zhou stated that the Daoist hermit Chen Tuan, who allegedly inscribed it in a cave on Hua Mountain, had the mystery of the transformations of yin-yang.[27] While the diagram relates to the religious tradition in Daoism, its reading order (from top to bottom) and the written text represents the yin-yang tradition in a Confucian conceptual spirit.[28] As for the expression *taiji*, it may be understood as signifying a pole beyond all poles, an extreme of all extremes, or as more (*tai* 太) than the most (*ji* 極). One may even think of it in terms of St. Anselm of Canterbury's "that than which nothing greater can be conceived," however, not in a sense of a divine being, but in the conceptual sense of a unique construct in language, the essential construct of a discussion about something that we cannot conceive not to exist.[29] Since we conceive of something that cannot be conceived not to exist, it must exist *as such*—and it is precisely in this sense (that is, that it cannot be conceived any differently)—that it is the greatest, or the preeminent. There is neither a proof of existence nor a myth of creation;

rather, the significance of the idea lies in the conceptual suggestion itself. *Wuji*, as the negation of *taiji*, can be demonstrated through an allegory to arithmetical infinity, which refers to a quantity without bound or end; which in some senses is pretty much like zero, and in fact represents the other aspect of zero: it is a quantity that does not measure; it can be both positive and negative; it is the perfect balance in the point of no end, or no finitude, in which biggest can always grow bigger and smallest become smaller.[30]

Zhou's method of representing perfection as *wuji* and *taiji* at once overtly relates that for him, the Confucian Way has to be expressed in more than just nuanced terminology; nonetheless, the use of paradoxical terminology adds to one's understanding the idea of ultimate. The Supreme Polarity as the upper bound—which is also the boundless Non-Polar—later on presented by various facets, expressed through the dynamic powers of life, such that each of the myriad living creatures embodies the whole process. The dialectic structure of the text is reminiscent of the Laozian two as one dialectic. According to this dialectic as rooted in the first verse of the *Laozi*, the Way is a unity that when expressed in language, it cannot escape the duality of Way as limited, and conditioned *daokedao* 道可道, which is also One, ineffable, limitless, and eternal *chang dao* 常道. Despite their incommensurability (*fei* 非) in language, in the end the two are revealed as One (*ciliangzhe tong*此兩者同).[31] The *wu* in *Laozi* is not absolute nothingness; rather, it stands beyond distinctions.[32]

Zhu Xi offers an important observation for understanding the paradox, stressing that "*ji* is the highest moral principle (*daoli* 道理),"[33] and then that "WJTJ correctly means that there is no specific form but there is specific moral principle."[34] In contrast to the belief that the neo-Confucian project turns to metaphysics, Zhu Xi reminds his reader that in Zhou's acclaimed metaphysical treatise, the point is Order, and Order is first and foremost, moral. While TJTS presents similar poles as Supreme Polarity and Non-Polar that are together beyond distinctions, unlike in the *Laozi*, in the case of TJTS, the transformation demanded in the walk between the poles is necessarily appreciative of the moral features of the Way. While the reality of things is not denied, reality is presented as nonconcrete. As we will see later on, this way of expression is revealed consequential also to Zhou's moral-practical understanding.

The opening statement—*wuji er taiji*—then, refers to a unity of Supreme Polarity and Nonpolarity, or that which ultimately is, and that which ultimately is not. It is the limit of all limits, such that the utmost limit as such is ultimately limitless. When referred to as *taiji*, it includes within it everything;

it is the perfection of all perfections, similar to traditional monotheistic idea of God; however, unlike monotheistic God (and more similar to a Spinozistic idea of God as Nature or a Kabbalah notion of Einsof[35])—by including everything, in particular including in it the limitless—the boundary fades away, and wipes out the very existence of perfection as a separate entity. To eliminate excessive associations to ideas of perfection, let us from now on refer to it as the linguistic construct WJTJ.

One's ability to develop a meaningful discourse on a reality that cannot be grasped except in contradiction is not a trivial task. I therefore suggest taking the opening to the treatise as a *riddle* that Zhou posits to his readers, bringing it to a new understanding. Taken as riddle, WJTJ suggests a description in a promissory sense only, that is, it can be referred to only in terms of *wu* and *you* at once. As the distinctive feature of a riddle is shown by its own grammar, in the case of WJTJ, great has a grammar entirely different from the one we are used to: it is the grammar of a being whose nonexistence cannot be conceived otherwise; hence, it is necessary for understanding the conceptual structure. In its renewed Confucian grammatical form, great is not to be measured; it is not a definite (nor indefinite) quantity (reminiscent, perhaps, of the way in which infinite is understood in Set Theory).

The response to any riddle of this kind can be attained only in finding a *system* in which the object can exist. In the present case, the object is a nonobject: it is the transcending of the boundaries that constitute an object, and the emerging of one as many. Only when the system is found, the riddle that seemed to be lacking sense is given a new practical sense. By seeing the *Book of Change* as the riddling system in the background of Zhou's text, it is then seen that the text does not reflect an attempt to form a new ontology claiming the existence of WJTJ; rather, WJTJ, as a *response* to the riddle of life, exists. As WJTJ is a conceptual construct, the solution is thus not an object of any kind, but rather a renewed system of thought and discourse. In this way the riddle embodies its response. When one is committed to a Confucian life, one no longer needs to seek the answer to the living riddle or even to think of one's life as the response to the riddle; one simply lives life as a *living riddle*. Thus, the opening line of the text is understood here as a call to practically see oneself as the living riddle: how WJTJ? for which we are given clues in the rest of the text through a clear emphasis on process, concluded at the ending of the treatise with yet another riddle.

Living as Transforming

I LIVED YIN-YANG AND FIVE LIVING PHASES

Moving from the opening statement to the rest of the diagram, after setting the configuration (and also the nonconfiguration) as WJTJ represented in the top circle, Zhou moves on to describing universal dynamics, in the spirit of *The Book of Change*—represented in the second circle—as follows:

> The Supreme Polarity in activity generates yang. Extreme activity is tranquility. Tranquility generates yin. Extreme of tranquility is activity.[36] Activity and tranquility become the root of each other, bringing about the division to yin and yang. This is where the two modes are established.[37]

Representing the yang movement of the Supreme Polarity, which at its utmost is tranquil Zhou introduces what Robin R. Wang calls Lived yin-yang. According to Wang, Lived yin-yang represents a dynamic system of thought and a way of dealing with the world.[38] Yin-yang can refer to any aspect of life, nature, and the world, including cosmology, functions in society, warfare, ethics, ontological substance for the human body, and visual presentations. The ontology of yin-yang goes back to the *Book of Documents* (*Shang Shu* 尚書, 772–476 BCE), where the qi 氣, or the vital energy of yin-yang, is understood as a generative force underlying all existence and serving an essential role in making the ontological link between a unitary source and the diversity of the myriad things (*wanwu* 萬物).[39] Wang notes that with regard to ethics, on the one hand, yin-yang furnished a sense of human connection to broader processes of the universe, which was highlighted later in the term *daode* 道德 (virtuous Way); on the other hand, it structures human obligations through particular human relationships.[40] One basic function of yin-yang is building a system for classifying and relating things and events in both the human and the natural worlds, serving as the pivot and legacy of Chinese thought. Wang categorizes various relationships between yin and yang as multiple manifestations that she claims can be seen through six different relationships between the two poles: (1) contradiction and opposition (*maodun* 矛盾); (2) interdependence (*xiangyi* 相依); (3) mutual inclusion (*huhan* 互含); (4) interaction or resonance (*jiaogan* 交感); (5) complementary or mutual support (*hubu* 互補); and (6) change and transformation (*zhuanhua* 轉化). In all the above categories, according to the yin-yang system, the essential characteristic of living is movement and transformation.

Acknowledging this requires the understanding that absence of such ongoing activity prohibits the occurrence of knowledge, too; a still world is a world with no interactions, let alone interactions between knower and known. While yang is activity, tranquility is the movement of yin, as no pure stillness is to be found in life. Movement and tranquility are in constant continuity, such that they are becoming each other (a propeller moving at a high speed that seems completely still is a simple example). In this way, yin and yang divide, as modes (*yi* 儀) only, yet not as divided essences or separate entities. The yin-yang circle of the diagram, introduces WJTJ as dynamic forces that are known through two interrelated modes of one movement. While every living being moves and transforms, and through this movement we understand phenomena such as growth and decay, only dead things have no inherent movement, they disintegrate, split up, collapse, and break down. Yin-yang's paradoxical explication of the WJTJ paradox brings Zhou to the next level in the diagram, this time describing movement through a fivefold manner that reflects the yin-yang dialectic.

> The alternation of yang and unification of yin generates water, fire, wood, metal, and earth. The five-fold *qi* follows and spreads, the four seasons proceed within them.

Yang is a movement of alternation, while yin is the subtle movement of congealing and assimilating as the merging movement, such that the unifying of yin and yang in itself is a yin movement.[41] The third level of the diagram then, unfolds the natural consequence of the dynamics of alternation and unification as the five phases (*wuxing* 五行) of water, fire, wood, metal, and earth, interestingly referred to in the text as a fivefold qi (*wuqi* 五氣), stressing again the apparent movements as one dynamic power: water flows downward, fire bursts upward in flames, metal coalesces inward, wood sways back and forth, and earth breathes and blows, and all are qi. Within the general dynamism, the five phases create each other, through the interaction in which each receives its clear features and distinctions, as relational to the other phases. Accordingly, for both explanatory-theoretical and practical purposes, no phase is either understood or existent without all others. All five amount to the undivided qi, which *is* yin and yang. Zhou states then that the five follow each other (as yin) and spread (as yang), and this very movement is experienced as the four seasons, representing movement again, this time accentuating time cyclicality.

Life as movement is represented in this way as time. It is the generation of seasons as indivisible and nonlinear; the appearance of distinct seasons as manifestations illustrates humans' experience in the flux of time. Accordingly, rather than seeing movement as existent *in* time, time *is* movement. Using Bergsonian terminology, we may say with regard to life that "time is its fabric itself" or reality itself.[42] In fact, time is reality as never mediated and experienced directly through maturing and aging, through growing and decaying. It cannot be taken as a priori form of all intuitions (as in Kantian transcendental idealism) or as an empty container to be filled with experience (as in the Newtonian reductionist paradigm). Life as time is movement, activity, experience; in other words, nothing is real except movement, and likewise, reality cannot be defined except as movement. Indeed, reality cannot be defined at all, since as Bergson opines that "a perfect definition applies only to a completed reality"[43] and reality is always in process, always changing, never done. The uncompleted harmony of life functions both as the Order of the present and as the source of life, and (like in Bergson's approach) this harmony is to be found at the end and not in the beginning of life, as an incentive and not an aspiration. Stressing the movement of the Way as unity, before moving on to the fourth level in the diagram, TJTS offers a midway summary.

> The five phases are yin and yang; yin and yang are Supreme Polarity; Supreme Polarity is fundamentally NonPolar. When the five phases generate, each one has its own nature.

The above passage denotes the first three levels of the diagram as undivided and synchronous; as such they function as various representations of one reality. They are neither different planes of reality, nor are they separate realms of activity. The process can thus be envisioned along one endless plane, understood from three perspectives: first, of WJTJ; next, of yin-yang; and then, of the five phases. What we refer to as the nature of things, according to which we know other living beings, is understood as the various representations of WJTJ.

QIAN 乾 AND 坤: ARCHETYPES OF REALIZATION

The fourth level in the diagram moves back to a unifying movement, emphasizing the yin Nonpolar aspect of the living world.

> The reality of Nonpolar and the essence of the Two and Five mysteriously unify and congeal. "The Way of *Qian* becomes the male; the Way of *Kun* becomes the female; "the two *qi*s interact and move, transform and generate the myriad things. The myriad things generate and regenerate, changing and transforming endlessly.

Emerging to a Self through Transcending the Infinitude-Finitude Dichotomy

The text that focused, up to this point, on transforming through accentuating the perspective of *you* as the existing transformation, shifts now to accentuating the reality (*zhen* 真) of the Nonpolar as *wu*, the absent component, or the space that gives rise to change, in particular as embodied in *Qian* and *Kun*. The absence of limit is thus presented not as lack of existence, but rather as full potentiality: it is the Nonpolar that endows us with the openness to various realizations, unlimited by a framework or fixed form, which is a necessary power in the creative process. Zhou cites the Appended Remarks from the *Book of Change*, referring to *Qian* and *Kun*—the first two hexagrams of the book.[44]

Indeed, *Qian*—consisting of a series of six yang lines (or two trigrams of three yang lines on top of each other)—denotes the ultimate representation of *yang*. *Kun*—composed of six yin lines (or two yin trigrams on top of each other) suggesting the complementary features of creativity as earthly receptivity, responsiveness, and containment—is the ultimate representation of *yin*. *Qian* and *Kun* represent an instant of perfection, when all dispositions are in order and movement is in perfect balance, not yet realized.

The condition of the *Qian* hexagram represents activity and creativity, referring to their actualization in the human world as success; its image symbolizes heaven's movement with unceasing power. The lines employ an image of a dragon—a most capable legendary creature that has the versatility of living in water, on earth, and in heaven, symbolizing the exemplary person in gradual movement and transformation. Within the six lines of the hexagram, each position signifies a different stage in the single natural process; hence, although all lines are yang lines, each signifies an altogether different perspective of yang movement. Read from the bottom up, the hexagram is an attempt to represent movement rather than fixed positions: the bottom line represents the dragon when hidden; then moving upward as the lines are added, the dragon appears in the field on the second yang line; then, awakens until sunset as the third line; next, it soars above an abyss; flies in heaven; and finally, the top yang line represents the arrogant dragon bringing remorse. The image the hexagram offers is of constant yang movement as developing and soaring, which should always be in balance, as excess brings remorse. According to this reasoning, reaching the peak (symbolically, as the top line) already amounts to moving down, as depicted in the famous yin-yang symbol.

The reader of the hexagram is called on to change perspective of perception, then to move and transform accordingly. According to the Commentary on the Judgments (*Tuan Zhuan* 彖傳[45]), *Qian* indicates the great and originating power of everything under heaven, such that

It allows clouds to scud and rain to fall and things in all their different categories to flow into forms. Manifestly evident from beginning to end, the positions of the six lines form, each at its proper moment. When it is the moment for it, ride one of the six dragons to drive through the sky. The change and transformation of the Dao of *Qian* in each instance keep the nature and destiny of things correct.... So one stands with head above the multitudes, and the myriad states are all at peace.⁴⁶

The passage, which has been celebrated in neo-Confucian times, presents the world as in constant flux, in which the task of the sage is to follow and understand creation. The sense of *Qian* being the originator signifies that all things are created into activity, and this activity flows into concrete forms, which may still transform. The movement (or the person who rides on this movement) mounts upward toward heaven, as exemplified in the mythical image of the dragon, symbolizing ongoing initiation, activity, and outburst. This model of movement and transformation applies to the person as an organic part of the world; the human ability to follow the six hexagram lines as riding the dragons keeps nature and destiny correct. From the cosmic perspective, the power of transformation is consequential in seeing the person as an integral part of the myriad things, affected by transformations and affecting the transformations of her surroundings. The Way of change and transformation (乾道變化 *qiandao bianhua*) is thus presented as the fundamental power by which each thing takes its nature and mandate in forming great harmony (保合大和 *baohe dahe*).

Polar opposite to the *Qian* hexagram is *Kun* (the second hexagram), referring in the judgment to its actualization in the human world as an act of perseverance following, which brings the success of serene resolve. The lines describe an inner movement, followed by the commentary:

> How great is the fundamental nature of *Kun*! The myriad things are provided their births by it, and in so doing it compliantly carries out Heaven's will....
>
> The mare is a metaphor for the Earth, for it travels the earth without limit.... For one who is yielding and compliant, it is fitting to practice constancy here, and the noble man who sets out to do something, if he takes the lead, will be in breach of the Dao, but if he follows and is compliant, he will find his rightful place.⁴⁷

The mare serving as metaphor for movement as earthly contrasts with the active movement of *Qian*: While *Qian* is origination and creating multiplicity,

Emerging to a Self through Transcending the Infinitude-Finitude Dichotomy 65

reaching everything by means of penetration, *Kun* embraces everything by means of containment and composure. Opposed to *Qian*—the creator that initiates, motivates, and spreads out, *Kun*—as co-creator, complies, yields, and corresponds with heaven, carries all in harmony, and embodies everything. This more sublime aspect of transformation applies to every phenomenon and to every person, and more particularly to the exemplary person. If *Qian* spreads in a sort of extroverted and independent nature, *Kun* is characterized by means of stable, docile, introverted nature, stressing codependence and unification, without which initiation and growth can neither be fully realized, nor understood. *Kun* is responsive movement, and like *Qian*'s movement never ceases.

The fourth circle in TJTS representing the instant that precedes concrete realizations depicts the living perspective according to which everything remains a potentiality, and yet it is already there. The coalescing of the one and its various manifestations is wondrous, and in it *Qian* and *Kun* represent heaven and earth; yet, the male and female characteristics appear in everything in the living world. In line with Robin Wang's ideas, within this context, the social function of yin-yang is realized in the differentiation between male and female, revealing various facets of possible balances, in which sexual intercourse is a specific way to promote the circulation of qi, both on a personal level and more broadly within the cosmos, where it helps one to attain the unification of yin and yang in heaven, earth, and the human world. Men and women play the roles of heaven and earth, and together create this cosmic unity and generativity.[48] The person as an organic part of the world can follow the six hexagram lines as riding the dragon or as the firmness of mare, paving the way to understanding the nature of human beings as the entirety of realizations, as depicted by the diagram's fifth and lowest circle, representing the world under heaven. Within it, humans alone obtain the most refined and efficacious qi.

Infinitude in the World of Finitude

EMBODYING WJTJ IN THE MYRIAD THINGS
(AND THE PERSON IN PARTICULAR)

The bottom circle of the diagram, standing for the myriad things, is explicated by the following passage, followed by three other passages:

> The myriad things generate and regenerate, changing and transforming endlessly.

Only humans receive their refinement most efficaciously. When form is manifested, they are born; when spirit is manifested, they have awareness; when their five-fold nature is aroused into movement, good and evil are divided, and the myriad affairs ensue.

In this description, the mystery of the diagram can be disclosed as the mystery of life, expressed in the riddle of birth and death. According to the progression of the diagram, a human being—like every other thing in the world—is qi, which is, no other than WJTJ, revealed through yin and yang and the five phases. As Zhou states, qi is realized in human beings in a more refined way, or through human-refined capabilities of awareness and morality. Representing a process of emanation of qi, it appears that whereby the more multidimensional the being is, the more it transforms and realizes qi in a refined manner. Human beings are introduced in this way as more complex and varied than other creatures, who essentially are made of the same qi. Through qi the text connects humans and heaven as equal embodiments of WJTJ, stressing this as one movement that yields a multitude of transformations. As human beings are all of the same qi, that is, morally refined, the text implies a demand for a human moral commitment to the process of cosmic creation as moral commitment for the knowledge of good and evil. Human beings are presented as creators of morality, while morality reflects WJTJ as boundless. The fivefold nature acts and moves humans in a concrete human dynamic, manifested in virtues, originated in knowledge of good and evil.

According to the text, when form is taken, human beings are born; and when the spirit is realized, they know and make proper distinctions. Good and evil characterize human deeds after taking form and not as part of raw nature. Humanity is rooted in the universe in a fivefold nature (*wuxing*五性) as the human manifestation of the natural five phases, revealed as the five cardinal virtues of humanity, rightness, rites, trust, and knowledge. Through the correlation between universal-natural movement and human virtues in the diagram, Zhou suggests his own dynamic version of correlative thinking.[49] When one acts, it is impossible not to have mistakes, and evil ensues; yet, following the structure of the diagram, an action of this type cannot be seen as intentional evil, it is part of a natural progression and transformation that can always be further transformed. Zhou makes it quite clear that the correspondence between nature and person is perfect, but they are differentiated since nature is creation itself and the human is one aspect only. Accordingly, upon birth, humans receive their human form; as soon as spirit is realized in human beings, they gain knowledge or awareness and in this sense, every person is potentially WJTJ. The Genesis story of the Garden of Eden and the knowledge of good and evil that human beings attain (or perhaps steal) by eating the forbidden fruit can serve as instructive opposition in this context, in particular as including the serpent representing an inherent evil inclination.[50]

> And the serpent said unto the woman, Ye shall not surely die: For God doth know that in the day ye eat thereof, then your eyes shall be opened, and ye shall be as gods, knowing good and evil. (Gen. 3:1–5)

The serpent told woman that God was, as matter of fact, insincere. He had said they would die, but He knew they would be like Gods; and indeed what the serpent said was revealed as the truth when his advice was taken. Moreover, not only the possibility that God lied about the tree is less than satisfactory, there is an even more severe discrepancy relating the issue of being created "in the image of God" (Gen. 1:26–28), when it appears that human beings were created having no moral judgment. Is it possible that God plays the cynic, endowing them (or us) only with a degree of potentiality to resemble him, yet with no real intention of allowing this potentiality to be actualized? What then is left of the sense of the image of God? The disharmony goes on: it appears that God created a human partner, in order to not threaten His own uniqueness, and was challenged by the couple's eating of the fruit despite His command. Not taking another risk, man and woman are not allowed anymore to stay close to the other forbidden tree—the tree of life; they might become completely "one of us," said God to His angels, and drove away the sinning humans from the Garden. The serpent was punished too (Gen. 3:12–22). The Garden, however, perfect and vital, belongs to the divine, guarded now not by men, but by cherubim and a flaming sword. While in both sources, the knowledge of good and evil is what makes us human, the Genesis story presents this knowledge as an outcome of corruption and a fracture in the original harmony; the opposite case is presented in TJTS introducing knowledge of good and evil as a manifestation of the existing original harmony.

In this way in TJTS, the person is depicted as a manifestation of WJTJ. Indeed, sagehood is supremacy; it is the supreme realization of the creative process, Zhou refers to the sage, the exemplar of human perfection.

> The sage settles this with centrality, correctness, humanity and rightness; (the Way of the sage is none other than humanity, rightness, centrality and correctness) and underscores tranquility (without desire, there will therefore be tranquility).[51] The ultimate human is established. Therefore, "the virtue

> of the sage equals that of heaven and earth; his brilliance equals that of the sun and moon; his timeliness equals that of the four seasons; his good fortune and bad fortune equal those of ghosts and spirits."[52]

The Way of the sage as finite and limited person embodies the infinite limitless cosmos by making choices using the active virtues of centrality, correctness, humanity, and rightness, on the one hand; and by embodying Nonpolar through tranquility, on the other. Zhou parallels the cosmic creation such that just as *taiji* is supremacy in the cosmos, so the sage is in human beings; in the way the universe is *wuji* or cosmically unbounded, so is the sage analogously, morally unbounded. A human deed—a moral deed—by implication is the ultimate as boundless (as can be observed in the simple act of giving to those in need: while every concrete act of giving is definite and limited to a certain location and time, as well as to a certain amount or act of giving—the very idea of giving has no limit).

Zhou addresses the *Book of Change* with reference to the original moral aspect of this cosmology. The accomplished person's cultivating these virtues brings auspiciousness, as opposed to the lesser person who opposes them and bringing inauspiciousness, since opposing virtue is opposing nature. Zhou ends the treatise in citing the *Change* again.

> Therefore it is said, "Establishing the Way of heaven, one speaks of yin and yang; establishing the Way of earth one speaks of supple and firm; establishing the human Way one speaks of humanity and rightness."[53] It also says, "Starting with beginnings and returning to ends; one understands death and birth."[54]
> How great is the *Change*! This is its excellence.

What indeed is its excellence in Zhou's philosophy?

FROM BEGINNINGS AND ENDINGS TO DEATH AND BIRTH

Coming back to the *Book of Change*, life is constantly fluxing and transforming, and foretelling is in this way a call for *understanding through living a riddle*. In this way, it offers an attitude on *how* we can address questions regarding life, offering a first methodological cue to understanding. The implied idea is that ordinary language cannot suffice to express something meaningful regarding life, while a riddle can perhaps imply something in this regard.

The idea of the riddle of life and death, deciphered step by step, by means of subtle clues given by sixty-four symbolic shapes and enigmatic words, which can never be fully disclosed, is assisted in Zhou's short treatise by the *Xici Zhuan* (or the *Great Appendix* 大傳 *dazhuan*): "*Qian* knows the great beginnings; *Kun* brings them to completion" (*qianzhi dashi, kunzuo chengwu* 乾知大始, 坤作成物), enfolds in it the riddle of infinitude and finitude as expression to the riddle of life and death. As *Qian* is the knowledge of great beginnings, knowledge belongs with creation and multiplicity; not with unknown ends. Moreover, *Qian* refers to the great beginnings as embodying Order and not as concrete points in time. Opposed to *Qian* knowing beginnings, *Kun* is characterized by completing (*cheng* 成), signifying one's activity of bringing the process to completion as coming back to oneness, rather than to a full stop or an ending. Beginnings are to be known for endings to be reached appropriately.

The Appendix presents the basic presupposition of the system of accordance with heaven and earth as the human capability to "trace things to their beginning, and turn back to their end—thus knowing death and birth" (*yuanshi fanzhong guzhi sisheng* 原始反終, 故知死生). As the first section of the text referred to *Qian* as knowledge of beginnings and *Kun* as actual completion, calling onto one's ability to follow this Way, is a call to live the riddle. Thus, the opening line of the text is understood here as a call to practically see oneself as the living riddle: How WJTJ? for which we are given clues in the rest of the text through a clear emphasis on process, concluded at the ending of the treatise with yet another riddle as expressed in quoting the *Book of Change*: through starting with beginnings and coming back to endings, one knows death and birth, followed with an exclamation about the greatness of the change and/or of the greatness of the *Change* (*dazai yiye, siqi zhiyi* 也易哉大 斯其至矣)—and most likely of both at once—we are called to realize that life as transformation embodies a riddle of an emergent person, as a concrete demonstration of Oneness as a dialectic process of embodying polarities, in which *wu* signifies a lack of boundary between the One and the many.

Zhu comments on the closing of Zhou's treatise in this spirit, as follows:

> *Yang*, firmness, and humanity are the beginning of things; *yin*, yielding, and rightness are the end of things. If we are able to trace back to their beginning and understand how they are generated, then we can revert [*fan*] to their end and understand how they die. This is the ineffable mystery of the orderly process of creation.[55]

Zhu Xi, the great Confucian commentator, unequivocally connects the cosmology of TJTS with the moral way. Yang in the universal Order is identified with humanity as the beginning in the human world. Yin in universal Order is identified with rightness as outcome.⁵⁶ Tracing the beginning as humanity allows us to turn back and understand death. Yet, Zhu Xi suggests that the text calls for a reverse reading too. After reading from top to bottom in order to be able to "trace back to their beginning and understand how they are generated," the diagram should be read again from bottom up, in order to revert to their end and understand how they die. Life is the riddle of ongoing flux, in which beginning and endings are one transforming unity, like yin and yang, the Five Phases and *Qian* and *Kun*.

The understanding Zhou leads his reader to is that in terms of cosmic events, we know birth and death as part of life as blooming and withering, developing and stagnating, thriving and decomposing; from the personal perspective, though, there is only life, in constant transformation, expressed in riddle. The instant of birth as one's coming to be and that of death as ceasing to be are never experienced by oneself, as unity. As Birth and death are experienced by others, the transformation between the oneness of nonbeing and the plurality of being, and then between being and nonbeing as death, is a projection of beginnings and endings, as happening *to the cosmos* and belonging to it, while also affecting others as part of the same life and world. Since birth and death are not experienced by a particular subject as one among many, the idea offered by the book takes life as the ongoing transformations *in* the unified world, while birth like death happen *to* this world. As one's ultimate boundaries of birth and death—the boundaries that make a distinguished subject are never experienced by the subject—the boundaries between infinitude and finitude, or One and many ultimately disappear. The beginning of life is the transformation of one body into two; the end of it is the disintegration of qi that then remains in others who live, as memories, feelings, and thoughts as well as DNA and body marks. From the perspective of infinitude and finitude, a cultivated person lives in the myriad transformations, or as shown earlier with regard to the moral perspective, a cultivated person lives in the present.

Reminding his readers of the analogy of heaven, earth, and human at the end of the text (revealed also as the beginning): finitude and infinitude are revealed as one. Ready to conclude, Zhou endows his readers with a key for deciphering the riddle How WJTJ? WJTJ offers a conceptual construct that acts differently from what we are used to, representing the investigating beginnings and turning to endings as knowing death and birth as response. As TJTS shows, in the limitless cosmos, there are no definite ends and beginnings; therefore, as embodiments of WJTJ, we do not experience death or birth. In this understanding, the mystery is disclosed. The experiencing I—the person—is only a small fraction in a larger unity as the ongoing emergence between birth and death. The secret of WJTJ is that we are our lives.

The riddle of WJTJ, responded in using it as linguistic construct that allocates the riddle of One as many, or infinitude as finitude is presented in Zhou's TJTS as implied in what Wittgenstein called, "the riddle of life and death in space and time, or the riddle *par excellence*" (*Tractatus* 6.4312). Zhou's response to the riddle in pointing to the transforming world suggests that for humans, the transformation is first and foremost moral. Living harmoniously with transformations as taught in the *Change* is embodying WJTJ. A person who embodies WJTJ experiences death and birth, not as the limits of one's life, rather death and birth are experienced as the cosmic transformations of the infinite as finitude. To understand how this is applied with regard to human life and its practical significance, we should move on to Zhou's moral-pragmatic philosophy.

COSMOS AS PERSON: TWO TEXTS—ONE PHILOSOPHY

Zhou's ideas in TJTS were questioned by later neo-Confucians: in particular, the idea of WJTJ and the significance of tranquility within the cosmic dynamism was referred to as his metaphysical thought, and seemed foreign to Confucian notions emphasizing human morality and practice. Indeed, there is no particular reason to categorize the text as Confucian; as characteristic of Northern Song, it is eclectic, mixing elements from Confucianism, Daoism, and Buddhism to create what is usually referred to as moral metaphysics. Unlike TJTS, Zhou's TS, commonly considered his ethical thought, deals with sincerity, self-cultivation, sagehood, and other ideas that are in accord with the Confucian tradition.[57] Zhu Xi tries to overcome what might seem to be a discord between Zhou's two texts and their main notions. In his concluding remarks to TS, Zhu Xi gives an impression of unease about the fact that Zhou's famous disciples, the two Cheng brothers, never mentioned TJTS and its ideas in their own writings. Trying to exhibit a continuity of ideas with Zhou's, Zhu makes a remarkable effort to justify Zhou's ideas from a Confucian perspective.[58] Zhu takes substantial strides at showing that not only TS but also TJTS is essentially Confucian, making particular reference to the relatedness of TS to the *Great Learning* and its subtleties, which even profound people find hard to understand. The important clue that Zhu offers is that GL itself focuses on the continuity between the universe and the person, through the investigation of things bringing to an extension of knowledge, leading then to a moral process of self cultivation, which ultimately yields peace under heaven.

The idea that an investigation of things, and not solely of morality brings about moral knowledge, similarly to those of form, size, color, and so on, presents morality as a necessary category of knowledge, not solely of practice. In this way a chair can be brown, round, tall, and wooden, and also helpful by nature, as it can, for example, be offered to a weary person as aid. The traveler of the Way is understood as one whose self, by definition, is always in an ever-deepening, ever-broadening process of becoming, in which the boundaries between personal, social, political, and cosmic are all surpassed, and distinctions among realms disappear, or transcended. In line with the Confucian eightfold path suggested in GL, there are beginnings and endings, or roots (*ben* 本) and branches (*mo* 末), yet the eightfold path for attaining world peace does not signify discrete steps; rather, one who cultivates the self necessarily investigates things, makes the thoughts sincere, or takes care of the family in an ongoing maintenance of all aspects of the process.

Perhaps as part of his attempt to Confucianize metaphysical ideas that were considered Daoist or Buddhist, Zhu Xi explains that Zhou's learning as a whole is so profound that its moral ideas can be communicated through images, and that it is "nowhere more complete than in the single Diagram of the Supreme Polarity."[59] According to Zhu, the forty chapters of TS explicate Zhou's store of knowledge as a whole. In particular, the chapters dealing with *sincerity, activity, tranquility, Order, nature,* and *mandate* are those from which one can learn more clearly about "the lofty ideas" of the TJTS.[60] Hence, according to Zhu Xi, not only is there a way to decipher Zhou's metaphysical ideas and restate them in ethical terms, but in fact, there is no other way to understand his philosophy as a whole.[61] *Song Biographies* presents Zhou as a believer in the unity of the Supreme Polarity and the Moral Order. Accordingly, since the two are not separate, they do not have to be adjoined by complicated argumentative techniques or heuristic devices, for both belong to one reality and one Order.[62] Zhou's suggestion leads to an ethical significance of metaphysical notions, especially regarding the process of becoming a person through transcending accepted boundaries.

In the spirit of the dialectics of duality/nonduality or two as one in TJTS, I want to show that his two philosophical treatises can also be seen as one, rather than two different discussions on life; moreover, that they jointly form one transformative philosophy that employs metaphysical terms and flavors, and yet is fundamentally moral. If this is so, then the dialectics of WJTJ embodied in life as unifying One and many is applicable also on TS. I suggest that in TS Zhou delves deeper in investigating beginnings and endings, while turning back to traditional Confucian moral issues including sincerity, rites, learning, self cultivation and moral realization. In this way, the human perfection is a perfect accordance with yin-yang transformations, and an embodiment of WJTJ. When Benjamin Schwartz notes that Chinese thought exhibits a deep faith "that the nonhuman universe is the source of all values," he points out that this idea demonstrates a lack of emphasis on intentionality, as is the tendency of the *Book of Change*, where "human intentionality is almost regarded as a snake in the Garden of Eden."[63] This observation suggests how moral virtues are introduced in TJTS as a trait, or as one concrete case in the comprehensive workings of the five phases; that is to say, when the five phases are manifested in the human realm as a natural manifestation of WJTJ, they are known as the five cardinal virtues. According to the present reading, morality is introduced in TS as the more explicit and detailed representation of WJTJ in human conduct. Seeing a continuity of Zhou's two texts reaffirms the essential Confucian continuity of heaven and man.

In this way it is suggested here that TJTS can be read as a brief or a guidebook to TS, such that WJTJ can be read into TS. In this understanding, searching for a metaphysical *foundation* for the doctrine is seen as both unhelpful and unnecessary, not only because it is foreign in spirit, but more importantly, since the foundation it calls for is separate from the life we live. TJTS preserves a structure that avoids the dichotomy between that which resides in our world and that which does not. As mentioned above, it certainly provides a foundation; yet the foundation for who one is, is one's world, one's life, and one's practice rather than metaphysical presuppositions. According to this reading, Zhou's philosophy is an assertion of Confucian moral ideas in new terminology. While foreign influences on terminology and on methodology enable a new cosmological discourse, the question that guides the present inquiry is *why* Zhou adopts specific foreign ideas and what they serve in his moral philosophy. In short, using foreign terms and renewing an old dialectic, not commonly used in Confucian humanism, allows the understanding of the Confucian moral person as emergence or as having a self who transcends cosmic boundaries—the most important being the boundary between infinitude and finitude as that between One and many.

THE MORAL SENSE OF INFINITUDE IN FINITUDE: FROM SINCERITY TO SAGEHOOD

The riddle of Non-Polar and Supreme Polarity responded in understanding WJTJ as the linguistic riddling construct that stands for infinitude embodied and realized in the finite is not easy to grasp, and moreover to apply on the human world. Yet, if as suggested in TJTS, the response to WJTJ is to be found in investigating endings and turning to beginnings, then the task can and has to be pursued only from the human moral perspective—the only perspective Zhou, as human, has. Then again, applying the ideas of TJTS on TS shows that with regard to human relatedness and transformation, the commitment to the broader cosmic transformation is a commitment to moral cultivation, reflected at its best by the sage as single-minded, vacuous, and tranquil, while necessarily moral, practical, and straightforward.

The first three chapters on sincerity in TS, each referring, according to the present understanding, to a different dimension of the idea, reveal its apparent contradictory nature, which can be read as analogous to WJTJ. TS opens first as analogous to Supreme Polarity, then—to the myriad things, last—to WJTJ. Through the first three chapters of TS the multifaceted nature of sincerity is revealed, embodying both metaphysical senses like reality, authenticity, and perfection; and moral senses like realization, accomplishing words, integrity, and resolve, as well as their verb forms, such as to integrate, to make true, to authenticate, or to make sincere. Having an essential role in both cosmic-order and the human world, sincerity brings in moral weight to the relevant dimensions of the universe, and cosmic weight for human morality. From the human perspective, in its fullest, sincerity is embodied in the sage, rather than being some ultimate source. In Zhu Xi's terminology, the transforming aspect of sincerity results in its various appearances in human life, as functions (*yong* 用) that realize the cosmic in oneself. Seen in this way, the first three chapters of TS mirror sincerity as WJTJ, by each taking a different perspective regarding the realization of the riddle in the human sphere. The first chapter introduces sincerity as Supreme Polarity (as One, or infinite); the second chapter discusses sincerity as *you*, or as realizations among the myriad things (or in the finite many); the third chapter corresponds to the *wu* perspective of the Non-Polar, in which dichotomies fall apart (One is many). The latter brings forth the understanding that sagehood as ultimate moral transformation is WJTJ manifesting One as many as infinitude within finitude.

Sincerity as Infinitude: Metaphysics and More

The *Penetrating Book* (TS) opens as follows:

> Sincerity is the foundation of the sage.
>
> "Great is *Qian* the originator, it avails the beginnings of the myriad things,"[64]
>
> It is the origin of sincerity.
>
> "The way of *Qian* is to transform everything according to its appropriate nature and mandate."[65]
>
> Sincerity, in this way, is established in it.
>
> It is extremely pure and perfect.
>
> Therefore it is said:
>
> "The successiveness of yin and yang is what is referred to as the Way.
>
> That which continues it is good.
>
> That which completes it is one's nature."[66]
>
> Its origination is going smoothly, and its comprehensiveness returns to profiting and purity.
>
> Great is the change, the origin of nature and mandate.[67]

The first appearance of sincerity introduces the moral idea in terms of purity, perfection and origination that may remind unseasoned readers of ideas of divinity and absolute transcendence. Introducing sincerity as the foundation of the sage, it first appears as an authentic natural power, rooted in *Qian*. As such, it is "extremely pure and perfect" (*chuncui zhishan zheye* 純粹至善者也), implying that it functions as ultimate with regards to earthly perfection, or as infinite virtuosity that is the foundation to finite goodness. As cited from the *Book of Change*—the moral Way is described as the natural succession of yin and yang, whose prolongation is good. The discourse in the first chapter relates sincerity, *Qian*, the sage, and perfection in a procession that corresponds with classical Confucianism. Zhou adds the citation regarding the completion of sincerity in human nature, reaffirming the Mencian presupposition on human nature as originally good. Sincerity, as introduced in *Mencius* and in the *Doctrine of the Mean* (DM), is indeed the Way of heaven (*chengzhe tianzhi daoye* 誠者天之道也) appearing as some ultimate standard.[68]

Zhu Xi comments on the opening of TS that sincerity is the rectifying Order (*li* 理) that is bestowed by heaven and received by things, then makes one of his most vigorous, and compelling comments in the treatise, that sincerity is what we call Supreme Polarity. The latter, however, raises the question: what grounding does Zhu Xi have for his daring suggestion? Apparently, Zhu follows Zhou who opens with grounding sincerity in the *Qian* hexagram of the *Book of Change*, explicitly mentioning that as the originator *Qian* avails the beginnings of the myriad things and stresses, in particular, that this is the origin of sincerity. Sincerity is thus presented by Zhou in accord with the early tradition, as heavenly, perfect, and almost divine. Taken up by Zhu, as heavenly perfection, sincerity is inherently related to *Taiji* as the originator of everything in the universe, hence is naturally also the foundation of the sage.

Sincerity in this way appears to provide a so-called metaphysical foundation to morality. Depicted as the ongoing process of creation through yin-yang dynamics, sincerity is the process in which the sage manifests the natural orderly alteration of yin-yang as one's own (good) nature, leading to human perfection. In his commentary, Zhu Xi offers a linguistic analysis according to which,

> This is the language of the *Yijing*. Yin and yang are *qi* and are posterior to shape (*xinger xia* 形而下). That by which there is the alternation of yin and yang is the Order which precedes shape (*xing'er shang* 形而上). The Way therefore means Order. That which continues it refers to *qi* that begins to come out but has not yet taken complete form. Good is therefore the name of the Order beginning to act yet before it has been established. This is the yang category and the origin of sincerity. Thus being complete is when things are already completed, and nature is when Order is already established.[69] This is the category of yin and the establishing of sincerity. (TS, 1c)

The cosmological analysis of existing before taking shape and after taking shape can be explained as analogous to the Lockean primary/secondary quality distinction, concerning the nature of reality. Before taking shape the primary quality as Order is embedded in the pure abstract organization of the universe, namely, it includes properties that are independent of any observer and exist in the thing itself, can be determined with certainty, and do not rely on subjective judgments. Existing after shape, Order is mixed together with qi, hence containing superfluous information that strips Order of its genuine nature, and characterizes it by its derivative secondary qualities, as properties that can be described as the effect things have. Knowledge that comes from mixed Order (as secondary qualities) involves also subjective impressions about things that are necessarily in any interaction with being and life processes. According to Zhu, the Way depicted as yin-yang before taking shape, is Order. Continued by qi—it is good as the yang origin of sincerity; its completion as human nature establishes the yin perspective of the Way as sincere. In this way, Zhu Xi reaffirms Zhou's metaphysical understanding of sincerity (emphasizing that Zhou's "that which continues it is good" is qi as human nature is in good, hence in line with the Mencian tradition[70]).

This understanding of sincerity is reiterated later in the text; for example, chapter 11 of TS, titled "Follow and Transform" (*shunhua* 順化) is a call to follow heavenly transformations on earth, opening with the following words:

> Heaven uses yang to produce the myriad things and uses yin to complete the myriad things. To produce is humanity, to complete is rightness.
>
> Therefore when the sage rules, he uses humanity to produce the myriad things, and uses rightness to correct the thousands of people.

Zhou reemphasizes the cosmic perspective of the production process, stating explicitly that in the myriad things yang and yin are reflected in morality such that production is humanity and completion is rightness, endowing morality with glaring cosmological tones. Then, according to Zhou, when the way of Heaven operates, the myriad things follow, the virtue of the sage is cultivated, and all the people transform, in a way that appears natural and effortless. As consequence, knowledge is realized as the true know-how of transformations, and therefore the root of the multitudes in the world is in one person.

In his commentary to the chapter, Zhu Xi refers the reader to TJTS's anchoring human moral transformation in the cosmic process in a way in which the human-practical is endowed with metaphysical qualities. Adding the comment, the world and the sage, their way is one, Zhu Xi asserts that the Way is one in the outer world and in the perfect personality; unifying knowledge is unified as primarily metaphysical. Accordingly, he ends his commentary,

> The root of the world under Heaven is in the profound person. The way of the profound person is in the heart-and-mind. The skills of the heart and mind are in humanity and rightness.

Zhu Xi's clear unifying of the world with the person, as one's heart-and-mind, then as its moral capacity, makes it only natural to read toward the end of TS that Supreme Polarity is attributed to a single human being, the one among myriad who reached perfection:

> As for the virtuous Way being high and deep, enlightening people through education without end, and being truly equal with heaven and earth and the four seasons—who else is like that except for Confucius? (II.39)

Zhou describes Confucius—the concrete finite person and the infinite limitless heaven, earth, and four seasons—as one. In this way, without mentioning the term, he attributes to a single finite person the nature of Supreme Polarity. Zhu Xi, in his comment, identifies the single human exemplar with Supreme Polarity unequivocally.

> One whose Way is as high as heaven is yang. One whose virtue is as profound as earth is yin. One whose teaching is without end like the four seasons is the five phases. Confucius must be Supreme Polarity.

In a theistic context, one might have suspected that Confucius is introduced as God, or at least—a god. This possibility collapses the very core of Confucian learning and the idea regarding self-cultivation as open to every person qua person. Yet, through moral practice Confucius attains a perfect match between the heavenly and the daily, thus transcending the boundary between infinitude as One and divine, and finitude as many, mortal and limited, rather than creating himself as divine and distinct from earthly practice. One's behavior, including thought, actions, and speech reflects one's proximity to Oneness, Supreme Polarity, or perfect sincerity in a way that is open to all. Later on, Zhu Xi takes up when applying cosmological language to the moral realm when he claims in his own treatise that humanity is origination and production and—as substance (*ti* 體)—it is spontaneous, natural, uncalculating, and has nothing in view.[71] In his discussion of the Supreme Polarity, he takes the other direction to complete the identification, applying human-moral language to Supreme Polarity in a specific reference to Zhou Dunyi.

> What Master Zhou calls the Supreme Polarity is a name to express all the virtues and the highest good in Heaven and Earth, man and things.[72]

Zhou indeed sets a foundation for morality, and yet, a careful reading cannot present it as a metaphysical foundation in the traditional sense. In line with the tradition, the justification for moral actions is to be found in notions of perfection that cannot be considered metaphysical or justified from outside the human world. In this way, Grand metaphysical theories are not only hard to justify, but also insufficient. As external to our world, their power to justify moral actions or to reject immoral ones is limited. Zhou's merit is revealed in this way in creating a renewed philosophical language in which metaphysics turns into ametaphysics (or supra-metaphysics) reaffirming Confucian morality and its inherent justification in human life as natural following and transforming. In this way, rather than endowing Confucianism with a metaphysical foundation, through introducing sincerity as Supreme Polarity, Zhou endows it with a new terminology that reaffirms the old doctrine in a way that reinforces it as having a broader explanatory force.

The first sense of sincerity as infinite according to the opening chapter of TS is that sincerity as perfection is ultimately *Taiji*, and it is humanly realized only by the sage. The question then arises: what about the rest of us? If sincerity is Supreme Polarity, can anyone, then, be Supreme Polarity? Put in a more disturbing way: can one be sincere?

Sincerity in the World of Finitude

EARTHLY SINCERITY

If chapter 1 introduced sincerity from the perspective of *Qian* as Supreme Polarity, identifying the cosmic as moral, endowing sincerity a status of a metaphysical foundation, as infinitude, the second chapter of TS shifts the perspective. Referring to sincerity through activity and tranquility as characteristics of the transforming world, Zhou introduces the relationship between sincerity and sagehood as a pragmatic one, ending with a call for intentional action, emphasizing the hard practice toward attaining perfection within the realm of the myriad things.

> Sagehood is no more than sincerity.
>
> Sincerity is the foundation of the five cardinal virtues and the source of all conduct.
>
> When tranquil it is not there, when active it is there. It is supremely correct and clearly pervading.
>
> The five cardinal virtues and all conduct, without sincerity are not there. They are then askew, hidden and blocked.
>
> Therefore when it is sincerity, then there are no affairs.
>
> Extremely easy, yet practicing it is very hard.
>
> With certainty and firmness there is no difficulty in it.

Therefore it is said: "if you for one day conquer yourself and return to the rites, all under Heaven returns to humanity."

"Sagehood is no more than sincerity" (*sheng chengeryiyi* 聖誠而已矣) in the second chapter is slightly but significantly different from "sincerity is the foundation of the sage" (*chengzhe shengren zhiben* 誠者聖人之本) in the first chapter, referring to the sage as a person. The second chapter presents sincerity as a necessary and sufficient condition for sagehood, through identifying sincerity and sagehood as having equal ontological status. When sagehood is identified with sincerity the sage reiterates his known status as human practitioner, who in fact never attains sincerity in its entirety. Since, as the first chapter shows, sagehood (*sheng* 聖) *is* sincerity, sincerity can be the foundation of a sage (*shengren* 聖人) as concrete person. Zhu Xi reminds the reader that "this is precisely Supreme Polarity" (TS 2c). However, as Zhou moves on, the second chapter offers a perspective on sincerity as the primary human task; it is realized as the foundation of the five cardinal virtues and the source of *all* conduct (*baixing zhiyuan ye* 百行之源也), not of sagely ones alone (TS 2). Zhu Xi comments in this case: "they are the image of the myriad things" (TS 2c).

We will return to the second chapter, after looking into this earthly aspect of sincerity as exemplified in chapters 31–32 of TS, in line with the *Book of Change*, by means of referring back to its hexagrams. First, chapter 31, refers to the movement among the hexagrams *Qian* (hexagram 1), Diminution (*sun* 損, hexagram 41), and Increase (*yi* 益, hexagram 42). It opens with a reminder to the relatedness between sincerity and profound personality as *Qian*, similarly to the way it is presented in the first chapter of TS, saying: "The profound person stands firm and does not give up sincerity."[73] To accentuate its status, Zhu Xi comments that *Qian*, as activity is the substance (*ti* 體), before moving on to the functions (*yong* 用) without which the substance has nothing to organize. According to Zhou, the profound person, who is living in the realm of functions, "curbs his temper and desires" and "changes his evil ways and reforms, and afterwards reaches."[74] In other words, the sage lives among the myriad things, and her greatness is the ability to curb herself and to change the evil that exists in the realm of myriad things only, as the hexagrams of Increasing and Diminution teach. Sagehood in this way is revealed in the functions of sincerity. Carrying on this understanding, chapter 32 connects sincerity to four hexagrams that depict familiar earthly experiences of Family (*jiaren* 家人), Separation (*kui* 睽), Return (*fu* 復), and Without Falsity (*wuwang* 無忘), again with reference to sincerity.

When we talk about the existence of a foundation for governing the world, we are referring to the person. When we talk about the existence of a model for governing the world, we refer to the family. The Foundation must be correct. A well-formed foundation is no more than making the heart-mind sincere. The model must be good. A good model is nothing other than making relatives harmonious.

According to the passage, in governing the realm under heaven, the correct foundation is the person, as the (active) making of one's heart-mind sincere. Sincerity, in the human realm, is no more presented as given perfection, rather, it is an attainment, and the suggested model for it is one's family. Family, as quite obvious, is far from perfection and yet one cannot conceive of a more elementary model; each person is born into a family. Referring to world governing, as modeled in the family, and rooted in one's making the heart sincere, Zhou follows an argumentation that is familiar to his reader from GL's relating world-governing, family ordering, and sincerity of heart-mind; accordingly, sincerity of one's thoughts comprises a precondition for the regulation of the family, which is itself a precondition for state and world-ordering. It then follows that to get closer to the Confucian Way, we should not seek for external sources; rather, the foundation lies in everyone's ability be filial. Good family relations, however, is no easier to achieve than world order, as expressed in the simple straightforward statement.

Family is hard and the world is easy.

Family is close and the world is distant. (TS 32)

Importantly, the close is harder than the distant, and yet it cannot be skipped, in order to be able to deal with the distant. Moving on to Separation brings in the difficulties involved in relating to others in one family and the ease by which troubles arise.[75] Zhou notes that the world models the family that models the self as sincerity of heart-mind, as the practice of return. When one's heart-mind is sincere one can turn back, or repent and rectify wrong deeds, as expressed in the Return hexagram.[76] Without Falsity (following Return in the organization of the *Book of Change*) is then a rational derivation of sincerity. Accordingly, first, one detects a foundation and finds a model; then problems can occur and the unity may be broken, yet there is always a way to turn back and reach no-falsity; in this way all dimensions of the process, rather than only its "pure aspects," reflect sincerity. In his comment, Zhu Xi refers to Cheng Yi who follows Zhou, when more distinctly than his teacher he defines no-falsity by means of sincerity. Heaven and earth, which reflect cosmic Order, are Without Falsity or without irregularity; accordingly, humans have sincerity as long as they follow Order.[77] While heaven is naturally without falsity and sincere, human beings that follow it have sincerity as a contingent. Zhou ends chapter 32 in citing the *Book of Change*, saying that by means of the possibility of attaining the state of no-falsity, the sage kings used people to match the seasons and produce the myriad things. While the moral path can thus be outlined according to nature, this can only be done with an ability to transform like seasons do; never in one definitive form, rather in a plurality of manifestations, as summers differ from each other and so do falls, winters, and springs.

Chapters 31–32 offer an explanation to the statement in the second chapter that when it is sincerity, then there are no affairs and the idea that despite being natural and hence extremely easy, practicing it is hard. The rudimentary stand regarding sincerity turns in this way into some fundamental constituent of reality that embodies within it an inherent possibility and even an inclination toward perfection.

TRANQUIL AND ACTIVE SINCERITY

Returning to the second chapter of TS, with sincerity as the source of moral perfection, as well as the source of all conduct, an important addition to the nature of sincerity is brought in through referring to it as "when tranquil it is not there, when active it is there" (*jingwu erdongyou* 靜無而動有). Zhou's referring to sincerity as tranquil and as active can be found instrumental for understanding the mysterious nature of sincerity.

Summing up the conflicting expressions by means of which Zhou refers to sincerity and following Zhu Xi's comment that when sincerity is tranquil it is not there, has to be understood as yin and not inexistent, Joseph Adler renders it as "imperceptible" when tranquil, and "perceptible" when active. Adler stresses the unique nature of sincerity not as sometimes is and at others is not; rather, when sincerity is tranquil it is not there *for us*, its human partakers. Perhaps, it is us that have to be tranquil in order to find our sincerity within. The significance of activity and tranquility for understanding the nature of sagely transformation and that of the reality in which we live is crucial for understanding the indispensable role of riddle for understanding and living the life we live.

Chapter 16 of the text can assist in this understanding when introducing the dynamics of transformations by opening with a clear distinction regarding activity and tranquility as exclusive either/or possibilities in things (*wu* 物), opposed to an inclusive unrestrained relationship in living organisms.

> That which when active is not tranquil, when tranquil is not active, is a thing. If when active—it is yet without activity; when tranquil it is without tranquility, it is spirit. (I.16)

Adler sees the interpenetrating modes of activity and tranquility as key for understanding Zhou's philosophy, as well as for understanding one of the most important innovations in Song dynasty neo-Confucianism's idea of cultivating the self. He suggests that Zhou's innovation of the interpenetrating of activity and tranquility applied to both the cosmos and the human heart-mind (*xin* 心) enables a crucial bond between theory as ideal and perfect, and practice that is never single and never perfect, which offers Zhu Xi a cosmologic theory to support the idea of self-cultivation.[78] Complete tranquility does not allow development and flourishing, while complete activity does not allow meditation and introspection. According to Zhou, complete tranquility alongside complete activity are possible only in things as inert, otherwise activity and tranquility are inherently mixed; while a lifeless thing is always either in activity or in rest as necessarily limiting each other, a living organism is never in pure activity or pure tranquility.

The idea of interpenetration of activity and tranquility that at times might seem odd and paradoxical, makes more sense in reality than in theory. An object is a clear either/or situation: having no internal activation, when completely in rest, it can be moved only by means of an external force, like a human hand, the wind, mechanical ignition, or a collision with another object. When objects move, they are without rest; things are in this sense one-dimensional. However, with regard to the human world, simple experiences demonstrate its inherent multi-dimensionality; for example, one can walk, run, or swim when senses, mind, or emotions are all at rest, although the body is active; on the other hand, when lying down, as if still, something within constantly moves through breathing, blood circulating, or dreaming that can make a dreamer exhausted when waking up. In the moral sense, resting without being given to the stirrings of emotions, or to selfish concerns is the working of spirit. Spirit is distinguished from things not in being empty, but rather in being able to influence and affect without leaning to one side, and never depending on an external mover. As Zhou puts it,

To be active and without activity, to be tranquil and without tranquility, is not the same as not active and not being tranquil. Things are not penetrating Spirit works wonders with the myriad things. Water, which is yin, is rooted in yang. Fire, which is yang, is rooted in yin. The five phases are yin and yang. Yin and yang are the Supreme Polarity. (TS 16)

Zhu Xi comments on the above affirmation of TJTS's words, in a simple outspoken way: "In activity there is tranquility. In tranquility there is activity" (TS 16c).

From the human perspective, it is clear to both thinkers that having a spirit is not being fixed. Spirit moves and changes and ought to move and change by nature. Rooted in the dynamics of yin and yang and in the five phases, spirit is the transforming feature of the living realm. The neo-Confucian notion of tranquility implies in it a criticism on the Buddhist and Daoist's *wu* 無 tradition by which it is influenced. Tranquility does not refer to a vacuum or to inexistence, rather, it is an inclusive state in which spirit embraces all aspects of existence as part of the all-pervading nature of the becoming process. A human being, having a spirit has an inherent activating force; independent of concrete positions. Analogous to water as yin rooted in yang and fire as yang rooted in yin, spirit is activity and rest not as alternating states, but as one process with simultaneous expressions. In this process, unlike things that do not penetrate each other, in the spirit neither exclusive yin nor yang qualities exist, nor do pure water, fire, earth, wood, and metal as distinctive elements. In this context, Zhou gives an explicit reference to Supreme Polarity, as if saying that while TS refers primarily to ethics and the human life, it is not alienated from TJTS. Indeed, he reminds the reader again that the five phases are yin and yang; yin and yang are Supreme Polarity.

Having spirit, one's acting without activity (*donger wudong* 動而無動) signifies that activity always has tranquility in it, and tranquility is in incessant activity. The activity that has no action can therefore be described in terms of yin and yang as always nourishing each other and present within each other. When Zhou ends the chapter with a sense of wonder—"How undifferentiated! How developed! How limitless!"—it appears that he does not refer to a mystery in the sense of what lies beyond one's perception; he simply points to the mystery of the daily wonders of life. While Zhou shows the versatility of reality, Zhu Xi comments in applying his own terminology of substance and function.

> The foundation of the substance is thus one, therefore it is said "undifferentiated." The function spreads out and differentiates, therefore it is said "developed." ' One is in action and one is tranquil. Its activity is like the limitless circular activity. This discusses the topic of substance and function simultaneously. This chapter illuminates the ideas of the *Diagram*; it is worthy to be consulted for reading the *Diagram*. (TS 16c)

The point that Zhu Xi is trying to make by means of his dualistic methodological inclination is that, according to his understanding of Zhou's ideas, substance is never separate from its functions, yet the distinction must be made for explanatory purposes. According to Zhou, just like in TJTS and like his discussion of sincerity in TS, so with reference to activity and tranquility in TS, the dichotomy collapses again. The dialectic of duality/nonduality reappears in the passage with reference to the ambiguous nature of life. In Zhu Xi's terminology, if the substance of nature governs *all* activities, specific leanings cannot disturb the harmonious limitless motion. Understood as substance, one is always both active and tranquil. As substance is meaningless without actualizations or functions, its various functions are ultimately undifferentiated from it; hence, activity can take the limitless course. Zhu Xi's application of the relationship between substance and function is reflected also in the relationship between the one Order and the many affairs (*shi* 事) as manifestations of it. If substance-function relatedness stresses an operative view on life, Order-affairs relatedness stresses the perspective of realization in the world.

Chapter 35 brings in the practicality of this dual citizenship of sincerity, again.

> When perfectly sincere, one acts. Acting, then one changes. Changing, then one transforms. Therefore it was said, "Consider, and afterwards speak, discuss, and afterwards act. Consideration and discussion are used to complete one's transformation."[79]

Sincerity brings to action. The idea of sincerity embodies a promissory meaning such that it cannot suffice to just be theoretically sincere; rather, a sincere person is defined in practice, change, and transformation—all characterizing the phenomenal world. In this way perfect sincerity requires consideration and discussion not only as essential for action and transformation, moreover as *committing* to action and transformation. If one inquires how to change as outcome of perfect sincerity and remain perfectly sincere, Zhu Xi replies in his commentary that "being perfectly sincere is the self-nature of actualized

Order. Considering and discussing is used for making oneself sincere" (TS 35c). In other words, Zhu Xi acknowledges two forms of sincerity: First, natural sincerity that does not demand effort and brings to action. Recalling the first chapter of TS, this sincerity is rooted in *Qian* as the originating active force, or the spur for action. The second form is the sincere *action* as derivative sincerity, demonstrating a living (practical) human aspect that belongs with sincerity in addition to its understanding as Ultimate or perfection. Sincerity in this second sense is not natural or intuitive, it demands effort, and is therefore necessarily nonpure anymore; a sincere act is never pure, precisely because it is active. In the world under heaven, however, these are the sole realizations of sincerity. What may then amount for a realization of sincerity in the world we live in?

ONE DAY AS SAGELY REALIZATION:
RITUALIZED SINCERITY

The second chapter on sincerity ends in a practical suggestion going back to *Analects* 12:1: "if you for one day conquer yourself and return to the rites, all under Heaven returns to humanity." Recalling the interrelatedness of moral virtues in Confucianism as the virtue that refers to realizing one's speech or intentions, sincerity appears to run through other virtues as a guide for their realization in the transforming world. The chapter that opens with sincerity as sagehood giving an impression that perfection is naturally in the world, ends in *a single day*. How can we understand the system in which morality is introduced as heavenly and yet a single day of moral practice suffices to fulfill it? The answer must lie in the significance of practice in Confucianism.

As we have seen, Zhou does not appear to be alarmed by identifying the heavenly perfection with a human attainment as corresponding the early idea of DM: sincerity is the Way of heaven, and yet the Way of man is to "sincere it" (*chengzhizhe renzhi daoye* 誠之者，人之道也),[80] corresponding with the *Analects'* presentation of the person as capable of broadening the Way rather than the Way broadening humans. The human face of sincerity demands ongoing practice.

Along this line, TS chapter 13 on rites and music (*liyue* 禮樂), offers an explanation to Zhou's attitude identifying Order (as infinite) with rites (as finite), opening in saying that "Propriety is used to put things in Order. Music is used to harmonize things" (*liliye yueheye* 禮理也，樂和也). Zhou invites his reader to focus on the moral-pragmatic value of Order, introducing the universal category that enables our knowledge of the world, as implied already in the classical Confucian concept of rites, functioning as a filter through which

Emerging to a Self through Transcending the Infinitude-Finitude Dichotomy 87

we come to know the world. Indeed the passage that Zhou cites from *Analects* in the second chapter precedes with the instruction not to look, listen, speak, or move, unless it is in accordance with the rites, presented in this way as an organizing epistemological system. Highlighting the role of Order as the new extended understanding of rites brings about an extension of the relatedness between humanity and rites to a relatedness between humanity and Order; since moral categories are innate in our perception of the world, Order is related to humanity. According to the chapter, when yin and yang are in Order, the five human relationships are established appropriately, bringing to harmony in the human world as following the cosmic process,] that is, thus introduced as a single process with various realizations such that "the myriad things each attain their Order; this being so, then there is harmony" (TS 13). Rites, as the system that reflects the manifestation of Order, have to be practiced.

In this framework for the phenomenal world, there is special significance for human instructors, with whom we discuss and consider our ideas on practice, prior to its carrying out in action, as appears in the seventh chapter of TS.

Someone had asked: How can the world be good?

I answered: Teachers.

He said: Why do you say that?

I answered: Human nature is nothing other than when firm and supple; good and bad are at their center.

He did not get it.

I said: when firmness is good it is rightness, decisiveness, determination and solid action. When it is bad it is fierceness, narrowness, and coerciveness. When suppleness is good, it is kindness, subservience, and mildness. When it is bad, it is cowardliness, indecisiveness, and obsequiousness. (TS 7)

Zhou opens his lesson replying that teachers are the human mediators of the process of making the world good. Through the use of firm (*gang* 剛) and supple (*rou* 柔) for explaining goodness and badness in the human world, Zhou relates to practice. Zhou, in this case, makes no explicit reference to either sincerity or to Supreme Polarity or yin-yang, leaving the gap to be filled by the reader. Zhu Xi, the most influential reader and commentator clarifies that the discussion belongs with *The Book of Change* and with TJTS, according to which firm and supple are manifestations of yang and yin, and like yin and yang, each can be good and useful when balanced properly or bad and harmful when losing the right balance. The process can improve if human nature is guided toward a well-balanced manifestation of its potentialities, moreover, one can attain the realization of the inherent well-balanced nature if only guided by the right teachers.

In his commentary to these lines, Zhu Xi uses the terminology of *li* and *qi* for interpreting Zhou's puzzling idea that ultimate world Order is in fact attained in human practice through education. According to Zhu's distinction, when firm and supple, good and bad are balanced, it is a sign for properly cultivating qi. This idea has its roots already in *Mencius*'s 2A.2, referring to the difficulty to describe flowing qi, as it is exceedingly great, and strong, and yet fills up all between heaven and earth; it has to be nourished by virtues. Qi can be realized partially and yield unintended results, if the realization of Order is not inherent in it; and it is a human responsibility to apply necessary effort in the process of realization, and respond according to world Order. A reference to *Mencius* 5A:7 at the end of chapter 7, regarding the responsibility of those who embody Order more fully to teach those who do not, yields the conclusion, as follows:

> Therefore, those who understand first teach those who are last to understand. Those still in the dark seek the enlightened ones, and the Way of teachers is established. When the Way of teachers is established, then good people will be numerous. When good people are numerous, then the imperial court is correct and the world under Heaven is well-governed. (TS 7)

The description of the naturalness of morality as Supreme Polarity as appearing on the opening chapter of TS could have resulted in an impression that effort is needless, if one ignores the fact that there are those who are first and last to understand. Cultivating the self always in relation to others demands ongoing maintenance, as introduced in classical Confucianism. Part of the self-fulfillment of teachers is the responsibility to cultivate students, who in turn, as part of their own cultivation, will cultivate the multitudes in the imperial court and ultimately, in the whole world beyond.

Zhu Xi, in his concluding comment to the chapter, stresses human agency even more, saying that any differences in understanding Order or in realizing the potentiality results from the fact that "the depth or shallowness with which people look at it is different" (I.7c). A difference in depth is something that can be worked on as the differences in the realization are due to the fact that in the myriad things qi rules, which can always be realized to a greater degree.

Zhu applies analogies for explaining how Order can be one in different things and still account for diversity in manifestations or in moral natures.[81] While heavenly transformation may be spontaneous, in the human realm transformation is attained in effort as part of the practice.

In this line, in chapter 22, titled "Order, Nature, and Mandate" (*li xing ming* 理性命), without mentioning the terms Order, nature, or mandate in the chapter's body even once, Zhou relates directly to the One-may issue, with the fact that some things are obvious while others are subtle, and education is required to be able to realize the subtle. According to Zhu Xi, Order includes both the obvious as yang and the subtle as yin. Zhou moves on from obvious and subtle to firmness and suppleness as both good and evil, referring to the significance of getting to the mean. Zhu Xi comments that nature is the human disposition as both firm and supple, each with its potentiality to develop into both good and evil. Last, Zhou refers to yin and yang as the two vital powers, and the five phases that transform and create the myriad things.

> The two *qi* and the five phases transform and create the myriad things. The five are distinguishing, the two actualize. The root of the two is therefore, one. In this way ten thousands are one: one actuality and ten thousand differentiations. The myriad and the one each has its correctness: the small and the big have definitions. (TS 22)

Zhou returns here to TJTS's terminology of duality as nonduality, giving more than a clue for those familiar with the philosophy of the *Change*. The two qi of yin and yang as mandate reflect Order: they are the initiation and realization of movement, as the actualization of Order. While two qi create the finite myriad, Order is one and infinite. Stressing that the root of the two is One, the ten thousands are then One as well. Accordingly, the myriad and the single each has its correctness, in other words, there is no one correct form opposed to myriad illusory alternatives. Zhu Xi adds that this refers to mandate as the given nature of yin and yang and five phases. While Zhou does not distinguish three separate aspects (perhaps since he wishes his reader to see how human moral nature reflects the single Order), he allows it as part of his philosophy of infinitude in finitude. Zhu Xi makes the distinctions according to his own dualistic methodological tendency. Trying to resolve the problem of the One and the many that Zhou does not explicitly address but that his words imply, Zhu Xi first makes clear distinctions among Order, nature, and mandate—and then returns to unifying all as Order again. Order is one's Master; and yet, it is one's choice to follow it. Only in this way, can Order be considered inherent in human nature. Order as human nature penetrates everything, and a human being wishing to coexist with heaven and earth should obey Order. As shown in chapter 2, disobeying Order is selfishness as a demolition of order. A lack of morality as the outcome of disobeying Order reflects the inability to transform, or to follow yin-yang and the five phases. As the second chapter shows, the human way to follow Order is in returning to the rites.

Zhou offers a daring look into the tradition and explicitly reaffirms its conflicting ideas, rather than simply represent traditional orthodoxy. In line with Mencius 7A:4, studying the Order of things is investigating oneself, since things are complete in oneself. If Order is there, it is human responsibility to do one's best to not lose it. Since the one Order is manifested at different levels in each particular thing, from the perspective of the Orderly process, humans and things can be discussed with a single terminology. In the human sphere, to be moral one must know what is morally good, and to know good is to follow Order.[82] From the point of view of Order, it is already there and nothing must be done except for looking within, since world Order, political organization, and personal morality are one. From the perspective of a human manifestation, effort is the key to realize Order, not to create it.

Zhou refers to this idea of the balancing between the naturalness of Order and the need for effort in his own words in the opening of chapter 22: "One thing is obvious, another thing is subtle; if you are not educated, it is not transparent." The model of natural Order as the ongoing yin-yang transformations manifested in the human world, it is the source of the myriad things—progressing through yin and yang and the five phases, and reaching the human world, culminating in the sage.

Coming back to sincerity in the first two chapters, they jointly require two apparently opposing understandings of the life we live as related to sincerity. First, sincerity is Supreme Polarity—an infinite cosmic perfection. In this sense of sincerity, we receive a clue that Confucius is *Taiji*, hence, it cannot be separated from human life. This clue can be helpful in understanding the second aspect of sincerity as part of the myriad things. From this perspective, sincerity is human and likely flowed as well. Sincerity endows the heavenly with inherent moral qualities and human beings with qualities of the metaphysical. While the sincerity of heaven is ultimate, the sincerity of human beings includes sagely perfection as ideal; yet it is also the sincerity of others, always partial and attained by effort. It appears then, that sincerity is both the actual description of heaven that embodies the full moral potentiality and the partial actualization of the person, either as accomplished or on the way to accomplishment.

In this way, the ultimate as One is introduced as stipulated by the multitudes, limited and flawed as we are. The dual nature of sincerity embodies an inherent paradox: sincerity is the only virtue that is depicted the Supreme Polarity itself, and yet it is human imperfect behavior at the same time. Sincerity simultaneously discloses the One and the many; it functions as the ideal heavenly virtue, as well as a goal in everyday human deed. Applied to heaven, sincerity is dealt with in terms of an unattainable ideal or a model for humans to aspire to and to wish for, similarly to Yan Yuan's description of the Way in *Analects* 9:11, as getting farther the more we get closer to it. What human beings may achieve is concrete sincere instances as goals. In this way, sincerity bonds heaven and humans; it embodies the paradox of the desired Way of heaven and also the incomplete Way of humans, as one's ability to expand the heavenly.

WJTJ: From Sincerity to Sagehood

SINCERITY IN WU TERMINOLOGY:
INFINITUDE WITHIN FINITUDE

As if responding to the riddle of sincerity as infinitude in the first chapter and as finitude in the second, by means of adding yet another riddle, TS's third chapter, titled "Sincerity, Subtle Activation and Virtue" (*Cheng, ji, de* 誠幾德) opens bluntly with "sincerity is non-action" (*cheng wuwei* 誠無爲 TS 3). It goes on.

> Sincerity is non-action.
>
> Subtle origin is good and evil.
>
> The virtues, when they appear as love are called humanity, when as doing right are called rightness, when as Order are called rites, when as penetration are called wisdom, when as protection are called trust.
>
> Being by one's own nature in it, and at peace in it is called sagehood. Returning to it and holding on to it is called worthiness (*xian* 賢). Manifesting that which is so minute that it cannot be seen, filling up that which is so complete that it cannot be exhausted, is called spirit (*shen* 神).

To complete and reaffirm the linguistic construct of WJTJ in the human world, Zhou now applies the *wu* perspective, employing the Daoist idea of nonintentional action, as annulling the duality as well as the exclusiveness of both former alternatives. It is neither solely Supreme Polarity as the heavenly infinitude, nor is it solely earthly transformations of the finite. Reminiscent of TJTS—Zhou's full idea of sincerity is that its understanding as heavenly and supreme and also as the myriad, necessitates its unification with the *wu* aspect in the dynamics of sincerity as both tranquil and active. This perspective offers substantial explanatory power for the imperfection that is implied in the second chapter. Ultimate polarity (demonstrated in the first chapter) unified with the ongoing process of becoming of the myriad manifestations (in the second chapter) can be complete in the sage, the worthy., and the person of spirit only through *wuwei* negating both One and many or infinitude and finitude as exclusive. With the aid of *wu*, the supreme and the myriad are both reaffirmed at once in the sage's oneness embodying the riddle as ultimate perfection, on the one hand, and ceaselessly transforming with the myriad things, on the other.

In coping with this Daoist-sounding statement, Zhu Xi explains that there is no action in the true Order (*shili* 實理) existing by its own nature, or in spontaneity (*ziran* 自然), adding yet another Daoist term, as if making sure that Zhou's use of *wuwei* is not an outcome of carelessness, or worse, of misunderstanding. Internalizing sincerity through continual practice of rites brings one into acting in a "Confucian *wuwei*," in which things happen as if by themselves. Sincerity is nonaction in a sense that makes use of the new construct WJTJ, rooted in cosmic spontaneous transformation. In this way, when Zhou states that sincerity is nonaction, he can be understood as presenting a new understanding of sincerity as WJTJ while also going back to original Confucian reference to the person as broadening the Way. Thome Fang opines on this point with an interesting twist.

> Axiologically considered, the truthfulness of sincerity abides by itself in a state of non-action, yet it is the fundamentum of human virtues as well as the spring of human actions. It is non active in that it is the spontaneous embodiment of reason in the form of substance having under its sway all potentialities of modes ... Whenever it is motivated to action by the mind, it will be specifically achieved as the moral excellencies.[83]

According to Zhou, as sincerity itself is presented as nonaction, its subtle activation (*ji* 幾) is the source of good and evil, which also enables the choice between them.⁸⁴ The nature of sincerity as in an ever-continuing activity and also as always tranquil is inherent in the human Way: in this way it is both pure (純 as the first chapter states) and is manifest in the impure world as the "source of all conduct" (*baixing zhiyuan* 百行之源, TS 2) being the subtle activation of good and evil (*jishane* 幾善惡). The role of subtle activation cannot be undermined in the essence of sincerity, as neither existing nor nonexisting. It is *always* an emergence through betweenness of *wu* and *you*; it is always in process and transformation, never finite or bounded and never perfect or done. In other words, subtle origin embodies perfect potentiality that gains significance only when coming to being, such that the very coming to being necessarily includes imperfection. The pragmatic significance of this betweenness can be beautifully illustrated by the *Zhuangzi*'s examples of the perfection of the lute virtuoso Zhao Wen heard in the instant *before* a single sound is played; of the harmony of conducting by Maestro Shi Kuang, silently manifested when his staff is raised, an instant before the orchestral music fills the air; and the gesture of the brilliant logician Huizi when leaning on his wooden table ready to express his views yet without saying a word.⁸⁵ In all these examples, perfection lies in the instant between nonbeing and being; embodying infinite possibilities for realization and a concrete finite realization.

The philosophical exposition of sincerity as moral WJTJ involves the adaptation of old ideas in renewed and more open philosophical language and terminology borrowed from other schools and appreciative of classical Confucian ideas. In the neo-Confucian context, showing the significance of sincerity by means of metaphysical terminology of Supreme Polarity and Order serves the old doctrine and justifies it.

Chapter 9, titled "Thinking" (*si* 思), may be helpful for understanding the special role of Zhou's idea of subtle activation with regard to the *wu* aspect of sincerity, presented as a codependence.

> Being without thought is the foundation, penetrating thinking is the function. Subtle origin acts in the latter, sincerity acts in the former. Not to think and yet to be all-penetrating is to be a sage. (TS 9)

Sincerity as not having a thought is regarded the foundation; thinking penetratingly is a function and an outcome of realizing the power of subtle activation. A sage, as we will soon see, as the human embodiment of WJTJ, must be capable of both. Zhou asserts that thought is indispensable, and that one can neither reach the minute nor encompass all without it. With the foundation of having no thought, and a function of penetrating thinking, sincerity is revealed a living moral reflection of WJTJ. Pure thought, in Confucianism, has no significance if not practically realized; this is the essence of the inherent relatedness between knowledge and action. To have this purest type of thought realized is to have it penetrate everything. In other words, it does not suffice that a thought is sincere; it must be initiated by subtle activation in order to penetrate, such that everything happens as if it were spontaneous and with no effort. Only when all three aspects of sincerity are realized as One, many, and neither-One-nor-many; or as infinite, finite, and infinitude within finitude, can one be a sage as reaffirming infinitude in finitude as one. In this way, thinking penetratingly is, in fact, an outcome of having no thought, understood within the system as having no interfering thoughts, or having moral thoughts solely. When the foundation is no-thought (and thinking is hence the function), thinking appears as the ground for the know-how in the core of Confucian ethics.[86] The *wu* form enables Zhou the reaffirming of being WJTJ in the human world, as emerging in the dynamics between finitude and infinitude.

THE SAGE AS RESPONSE TO THE RIDDLE OF WJTJ[87]

Zhou's depiction of the sage in TS 20 is according to this understanding the culmination of living the riddle of WJTJ.

[To the question] Sagehood, can it be studied? Say: Yes!

If asked: is there any essence? Say: there is.

If asked to hear about it, say: Oneness is the essence.

What I mean by Oneness is having no desire. Being desireless, when tranquil one is empty, and when active one is upright. When tranquil and empty, one is enlightened. Enlightened, one is then penetrating. Moving upright, one is then unbiased. Unbiased, then all-pervading.
Being enlightened, penetrating, unbiased, and all-pervading, one is near.

The first part of TS ends with chapter 20 in a way that echoes WJTJ in a human moral version. The idea of One that is many appears this time with reference to the ideal person. First, sagehood can be studied, apparently as a finite task. However, echoing Supreme Polarity, its essence is One (*yi* 一). In the latter case it has a *wu* form as desirelessness; as such it negates both exclusive Oneness and plurality, as well as the dichotomy between them. Sagehood is in fact manifested as two types of desirelessness: first, in action one is upright; then, through tranquility one is empty. In this way, the sage follows

Order with no insurmountable obstacle or impediment. The reconstruction of the dialectic of WJTJ as one, continuous, indivisible, and whole, and yet as realized on earth through activity and tranquility, brings about a renewed perspective on the human attainment. The chapter can be schematized as in figure 2.2, depicting the dual citizenship of the sage.

The structure of the chapter in a Confucian dialogical way is essential for understanding the human application of the dialectic leading to the riddle: a student asks Zhou whether sagehood can actually be attained; the Master answers in the affirmative. When asked about the requirements of the study, the Master suggests Oneness or singleness in *taiji* terminology, defined as having no desire (*wuyou* 無 欲) in *wuji* terminology. Then, he moves on to describing it through the duality of activity and tranquility. As if this does not suffice for showing the riddle, Zhou then concludes that on fulfilling all the conditions, one is *near* (*shu* 庶) to sagehood. In this way, what Zhou finally draws from his own presentation of the sage seems to contradict the premises: while the first intuitive response is in the affirmative, the final conclusion is in fact a negative one: near is not there. It turns out that while sagehood *can* be studied, what is studied and acquired is *not* quite sagehood. In other words, from the concrete perspective, no one is a sage, since transformation toward sagehood reflects the universal ceaseless transformation. From a universal perspective, however, everyone can be a sage, since morality is embodied in the very universal process.[88]

To understand this dialectic one should first address the question how non-desiring leading to tranquility can make sense in the Confucian context, or how this *via negativa* description of the sage fits with the Confucian moral ideal. Indeed, Zhu Xi raised serious doubts about the aptness and compatibility of emptiness and desirelessness as a Confucian description of a focused state of mind.[89] Truly, saying that when tranquil one is empty cannot be understood in this context, in the sense of being without sensations, perceptions, and hence, also without moral values. Wing-tsit Chan suggests that Zhou is influenced by Daoism and Buddhism to the extent that he contradicts not only early Confucianism, but also his own stand.[90] Elsewhere, Chan notes that the spirit of neo-Confucian rationalism is diametrically opposed to that of Buddhism: Whereas Buddhism insists on the unreality of things, neo-Confucianism stressed their reality; Buddhism asserted that existence came out of, and returned to, nonexistence, whereas neo-Confucianism regarded reality as a gradual realization of the Supreme Polarity; Buddhists relied on meditation and spiritual practice to attain enlightenment; neo-Confucians relied

Sagehoood *sheng* 聖

Oneness *Yi* 一

Desirelessness *wuyu* 無欲

Empty in tranquility *jingxu* 靜虛	Upright in activity 動直 *dongzhi*
Enlightened 明 *ming*	Impartial 公 *gong*
Penetrating 通 *tong*	Pervading 溥 *pu*
Enlightenedly penetrating 明通 *mingtong*	Impartially pervading 公溥 *gongpu*

Near 庶 *shu*

FIGURE 2.2. The dialectic of sagehood according to *Tongshu* 通書, chapter 20: "A schematic representation." *Source*: Fair use.

on moral practice and reason for attaining moral perfection.[91] Indeed, while clear examples for desirelessness can be found in texts from both Lao-Zhuang and Buddhist traditions, not one of Zhou's Confucian predecessors had ever regarded desirelessness as an end to be pursued. Truly, neither Confucius nor any of his followers explicitly upholds having no desires; *Wu* language is clearly non-Confucian. Yet, if the pioneering neo-Confucian Zhou Dunyi explicitly advocates having no desire, there must be good reason for this, rather than merely his being influenced; in fact, one can assume that he is, and yet, if he is influenced, one should inquire *why* this idea among many others influenced his thought, and what made him philosophically attracted to it.

Zhu Xi refers to Zhou Dunyi's conception of no desire, in his *Reflections* on neo-Confucian philosophy, explaining that when Zhou relates no desire to tranquility and activity, he implies that desires transform and change, yet never disappear.[92] Having no desire as tranquility is thus a necessary dialectical polarity in the dynamics of transformation, and never a state to rest in. With regard to the expression When tranquil one is empty, Zhu Xi refers to the Confucian sense of emptiness.

Someone said, "Concentration on one thing means complete singleness of mind. Vacuity in tranquility means that the mind is comparable to a clear mirror or still water, without an iota of selfish desire in it. Therefore all its activities ensue from the operation of the principle of nature, and are not disturbed by an iota of selfish desire. Vacuity in tranquility is substance, while straightforwardness in action is function. Is that correct?"

Zhu Xi answered, "Generally correct."[93]

Zhu Xi suggests that Zhou Dunyi's idea of concentrating on one thing is to be taken as single-mindedness. A mind that is fully concentrated on the Way to become a sage must be free from selfish desires, and in this sense only it is empty. This attitude toward emptiness can certainly be accepted in Confucianism as shown by Confucius appreciation the frugality of his disciple Yan Hui, who finds joy "in the eating of coarse rice and the drinking of water," and Mencius advocates reducing the number of desires for "the nurturing of the heart."[94] In this way, it should be understood that the foreign schools contribute the terms and yet, the understanding is already implied in Confucian early texts. While the Daoist idea of *wu* as spontaneous unreflective action is an alternative that works wonders in nature, it remains insufficient for human beings, likewise, Buddhist emptiness, is a pure abstraction that does not land back in reality.[95] If in Buddhism, emptiness is necessary for ridding human suffering as rooted in the self and in Daoism, being empty is necessary in order to wander freely in the world like an empty boat that can never be hurt or a drunken man free from moral responsibility and attachment,[96] the tranquility of TS is a tranquility of the *moral* mind.

For Zhou Dunyi, desirelessness can only make sense as being without external turbulence, or purely moral; as such, it's necessary for impartiality, as a prerequisite for complete morality—that is to say, for being a sage.[97] *Analects* 9:4 describes Confucius as keeping a distance from four things, one of which is being selfish (*wo* 我). Since desires are by nature selfish, they should be eliminated. The nourishing of the mind signifies for Zhu Xi "having fewer and fewer desires until there is none."[98] Only the mind that is not occupied with desires can get closer to a sagely mind. Zhou's saying, therefore, is revealed as having the clear Confucian ethical dimension of eliminating disrupting thoughts (such as of profit) in order to be moral. Having no desire implies two equally significant aspects of sageliness: first, being empty while tranquil, a sage is enlightened and thus penetrates all from within, as if there were no border or limit, similarly to the penetration of the Non-Polar. Second, being upright in action, his knowledge is moral or universal, hence impartial and pervading similarly to Supreme Polarity. The latter is unmistakably Confucian:

straightforwardness in action leading to impartiality or to being unbiased signifies in Confucianism the derivation of actions from morality itself, without regard for selfish concerns. Hence, although Daoist and Buddhist conceptions of self-cultivation undoubtedly influenced Zhou Dunyi, the use of concepts is essentially Confucian.

Zhou's view of tranquility as fundamental is a requirement of self-mastery in studying. If one is reverent, claims Zhu Xi, there will be no idle, impure thoughts and one will naturally be vacuous and tranquil.[99] When discussing learning to be a sage, it is critical that the first concern of the student should be with the mind that faces a process of cultivation and transformation and with the will that must purely and totally wish to learn and to be transformed. Zhu Xi proceeds with a Confucian version to the analogy of the human mind as a mirror, in order to justify Zhou's attitude.[100] Known in China from its Daoist use in the *Zhuangzi*, as well as abundant Buddhist references,[101] Zhu Xi uses the mirror-like mind as the highest state of mind, which signifies no desire, in his own way—to justify a version of a Confucian mirror. Accordingly, this emptiness belongs to the one whose activities ensue directly from the operation of the Order of nature.

Going back to Zhou's conclusion of TS 20, one may still be wondering: can one be a sage or can one only come close to being a sage? Why is Zhou so unclear on a point that is so crucial? And is it possible that he does not want to get rid of the ambiguity? Zhu Xi's commentary on the chapter can be helpful:

> The point of this chapter is of the most vital importance. However, since the meaning of the words is very clear I do not bother explaining it. Those who learn it will be able to delve deeper into study and put it into practice with might. Then they will have some knowledge of the truth of the Nonpolar.[102]

Is the meaning of words indeed so clear, as Zhu Xi writes? If it is, then the riddle is the message—at least it is a significant aspect of it. From the human perspective, we are readdressed to the riddle: How WJTJ?

The suggested ultimate person is dynamic, and this dynamism inherently embodies dialectic between opposing poles that are usually seen as contradictory and cannot be clearly depicted in words. However, as the process is endless, one is a sage by only being near, or being in the process toward sagehood. Being a sage as being in the process is never an absolute infinitude distinguished from the finite myriads. Living the process reveals the new construct WJTJ and its mystery regarding being a sage and not being a sage at once. Being a sage is being (morally) a Supreme Polarity in intentions and deeds, and Nonpolar as not having an ego or desires. Zhou challenges his student and reader to reflect on sagehood *in contradictory terms.*

Neo-Confucianism is an age of sophistication: terminology acquires nuances, and new notions enter the arena. In this spirit, perhaps we should express more trust in Zhou's choice to explicitly reveal through the contradiction in terms, something significant with regard to the Confucian Way. Zhou preserves a valued ambiguity, as if the old notion of sincerity cannot be formed more reasonably, as if this ambiguity is *necessary* for a better understanding of sagehood. In this way, Zhou can restate Confucian ideas from Han and pre-Han periods in the post-Buddhist era, when the conceptual language had changed and interest in metaphysical issues becomes evident.

I want to suggest that understanding the paradox of WJTJ as living riddle does not necessitate hermetically resolving it; rather, it requires a practice as if everyone may attain that which is unattainable, yielding an understanding that in the transforming world, WJTJ is one as manifested in the myriad things. Since the moral way is endless transformation, perpetual realization, and ceaseless striving for perfection, it amounts to the living riddle of WJTJ. The new terminology is used to reaffirm the moral Way, the plurality of its realizations, and the requirement to always be in the process of becoming moral. Accordingly, to be a sage is to always aspire to attain that which cannot be attained or to be and not be at once. The latter obliges practicing, with the textual riddle as a call for its carrying out.

CONCLUDING NOTE: LIVING THE RIDDLE

According to the present analysis, Zhou's suggestion at the end of TJTS to investigate beginnings and endings so as to know death and birth is responded to in TS as the investigation of beginnings and endings in one's practice, in an ongoing process of transcending boundaries between infinitude and finitude, activity and tranquility, doing and undoing, *you* and *wu*. Being one with the universe, a sage is an incomplete set of emergences in the one dynamic process.

According to the present reading, I suggest that for Zhou Dunyi, infinitude in finitude is reflected in the riddle of WJTJ and its response. Bringing to viewing the Confucian foundation of morality as dynamic moral life, living morally is taking part in infinitude as grounded in moral life. The answer for why we should be moral and how we can know right from wrong is that we have inherent human feeling and reason, and that our moral abilities are unbounded. Accordingly, human life and practices deserve serious treatment in philosophical discussion and argumentation as the embodiment of WJTJ. As seen below, Zhou takes up from the very paradox for maintaining morality and reinforcing its intricate nature, rather than giving it up.

TJTS can be taken as the renewed Confucian understanding through riddle, in particular, through the living riddle of WJTJ, or Nonpolar and Supreme Polarity at once. Reminiscent of DM's sincerity being the Way of heaven, as well as that of the person, we meet Zhou's sage as an embodiment of Nonpolar and Supreme Polarity, such that only when tranquility and activity interpenetrate, is intentional action directed toward moral perfection. Under Daoist and Buddhist influence, Zhou emphasizes *wu* aspects as nondesire, tranquility, and no thought; unlike them, he chooses not to give up *you* as thinking and acting morally in the world.

The significance of living the riddle is detected in simple daily practice. Thinking for example of the justification for one's landing a helping hand to another—as concrete, partial, and limited practice—according to the present reading, the deed is implied in the concept of giving, as rooted in WJTJ as something that adds to the giver rather than subtracts from her; as something from which we gain rather than lose. The moral sense of giving reverses the simplistic understanding of the idea from disposing of something to gaining. We can only understand ourselves or express human actions in a language that presupposes moral judgments, and the concept of giving reflects it. When we see a person asking for money, we interpret what we see as—she is in need, it will be helpful to give some extra that I might have. As noted earlier, giving in itself is infinite, and yet it can only be realized in every finite act of giving. In this way, the immediate feeling of distress by any person seeing a child about to fall into a well reflects in this understanding a call to act as emerging from *wu* characteristics of having no (selfish) desire, as morally focused self-reflexivity that culminates in upright activity. A concrete act, in this way, is the positive expression of infinitude. When all physical and emotional resources are directed toward saving the child, thoughts of gaining benefits are considered disruptions of the straightforwardness of action that morality calls for. According to TS, WJTJ in the moral world is known through sincerity, which is the Way of heaven; yet, the Way of human beings is to "sincere" it. The person who sinceres the Way is the human embodiment of WJTJ, or the sage. Through the movement between being and nonbeing, one transforms and gets closer to being a sage, or a human embodiment of WJTJ.

This view is asserted not only in the times of the Song dynasty, but prolongs from then on. Accordingly, not merely the Supreme Polarity is the cause, explanation, and justification of human life; rather, the Supreme Polarity *is* human life and its disposition. One important aspect to the reaffirmation of this line of thought appears later on, in Tang Zhunyi's philosophy, making the point that in Confucianism, human is one of three powers (heaven, earth, and man) that communicate with each other. The individual is encouraged to employ his mind to the utmost and thereby to know his own nature through the knowledge of heaven. In order to attain this, one is expected to "practice the utmost sincerity like spiritual beings."[103] A different example in the same spirit is that of Mou Zongsan's discussing immanent transcendence, suggesting a single process of immanentization, that is, the descending of Heaven's mandate as nature and a transcendentalization in which the human heart-mind forms a triad with heaven and nature.[104] Sincerity, together with humanity and the heart-mind, is a part of what Mou Zongsan refers to as the principle of subjectivity; namely, it departs from the person and develops into a complete approach. Like early Confucians, Mou Zongsan underlines the presence of an objective heaven, due to an emphasis on one's subjectivity. Hence, the only way to know heaven accords with the Mencian line of Confucianism, of a subjective practice of humanity.[105]

When sincerity is presented both as the ideal to aspire to and the daily actions that lead to it, dichotomies, fall apart, including that on infinitude and finitude. Ideals and the actions rooted in them replace ends and means, such that in order to attain sagehood or to get closer to the sincerity of heaven, one acts sincerely and sagely on a daily basis, and when a concrete act is considered, it can be performed only as an expression of the sincerity of heaven, or of WJTJ.

THREE

Emerging through Transcending the In-Out Duality

Shao Yong's Epistemological Shift

....

BLOCK: Who are you?
DEATH: I am Death.
BLOCK: You have come for me?
DEATH: I have been for a long time at your side.
BLOCK: I know.
DEATH: Are you prepared?
BLOCK: My body is afraid, but I am not.
(*Death approaches Block.*)
BLOCK: Wait a moment.
DEATH: You all say that. But I give no respite.
BLOCK: You play chess, do you not?
... If I win, you set me free.

—INGMAR BERGMAN, *The Seventh Seal*

INTRODUCTION: OBSERVER AND PLAYER

The Task: Expanding One's Perspective

Who we are is indeed how we are related with other partakers in the game we take part in. Not game playing as during frivolous leisure as opposed to work, neither as fictitious fantasy as opposed to reality, nor as limited to concrete location and duration as opposed to the boundlessness of space and time of the living world. Rather, games as reflecting views, beliefs, powers, and feelings, such that game and life are in fact rooted in each other. Therefore, there is great significance in familiarity with the rules of the game, mastering its playing techniques, acquiring skills. and applying good strategies, as well as properly pursuing its goals and overcoming the challenges confronting us. Mirroring human intentions and deeds, games serve as microcosms of the world we live in and introduce primary formative elements in our lives. Who one is then the player of games one participates in. Hence, close observation of the game we live may get us closer to the essence of the form of life in which it is played.

Shao Yong 邵雍 (1011–1077), who had noticed the important roles of game and of observation of it, serves the second Song dynasty response to the early Confucian task of broadening the Way, understood also as Zhou Dunyi's riddle of WJTJ. Most interestingly, in his "Great Poem on Observing Weiqi" (*Guanqi dayin* 觀棋大吟), Shao demonstrates clear awareness of the substantial role of games in understanding human life; in particular of Weiqi 圍棋 (better known in the West by its Japanese name, Go).

Similarly to metaphysical discourse, epistemology cannot be considered part of early Confucian discourse. As we have seen, through focusing on the Way and its broadening, Confucian discourse leads to moral-humanistic practice by a person in search of self-realization through morally relating to others. We have seen that Zhou Dunyi broadens the Way by exploring for the fundamental nature of transformations, through an anthropocosmic study of the dynamics of the universe as the interpenetration of motion and tranquility, his investigation transcends the boundary between finitude and infinitude, suggesting an alternative for a metaphysical perspective for understanding the person as ongoing *emergence.*

As suggested here, Shao Yong broadens the Way by looking for the rules of the game he takes part in, from both within the game and outside it. Through a study of games, players, and the dynamics between them, he investigates the extent to which self-knowledge can be acquired, this time by transcending a boundary not addressed so far, that between *in* (*nei* 內) and *out* (*wai* 外). Suggesting an *epistemological* perspective to the person as *observer*, he realizes himself also as player of the game, and expands his cognitive boundaries.

Undeniably, important common features relate games and life. Games are played as sublimation to basic needs and desires; they reflect the nature of the forms of life in which they are played, as well as the culture from which they arise; thus, they can be telling with regard to the life, beliefs, attitudes, and practices of the players. The experience of pleasure and gratification without which life would be unbearable is one of the defining features of game; interaction with others—including support, affection, appreciation, and imitation, as well as competition, struggle, dispute and fight—are equally inherent to game and to life; challenges motivate both game and life; skills are necessary for survival in both; creativity is essential to progress in both; in both game and life, a good strategy leads to better outcomes and prevents failure, and rule-following is necessary for taking part both in a game and in one's life.

Some words on Shao's life can illuminate the significance he allocates to self-knowledge as observing the world he lives in and transcending in-out dichotomy. Shao was born to Lady Li (d. 1032), a devoted Buddhist practitioner, and Shao Gu (986–1064), a teacher and a lover of the Classics. As Shao's philosophy and life attest, both parents greatly influenced their son; the mother primarily inspired his life style, and the father—his love for learning and his scholarly dedication. Although he later on made a conscious choice to avoid involvement in the system of social service, this background was critical to his philosophical development, in particular to the system of values he held onto, and his selfless devotion to elderly family members.[1] From the philosophical perspective, Shao merged ideas from the Chinese Classics with foreign flavors informed by Buddhism and Daoism, while living a life that can be generally considered closer to Buddhism or Daoism than to Confucianism. Soon after the death of his mother, he moved to a new home with his father and started learning. Upon the completion of his studies, he traveled around, and finally settled in Luoyang—in the home of great scholars of the Mencian line in Confucianism. Focusing on the *Book of Change*, Shao did not set up a bed for three years; he was sitting erect day and night, working or thinking. He copied part of the book and pasted it on the walls of his hut, reciting it tens of times per day.[2] Shao developed his own approach to the study: while the majority of scholars of his time adopted the outlook that was accepted as the School of Principle (*li xue* 理學), which was based on moral-metaphysical concepts, Shao alone adopted the Image-Number Study (*xiangshu xue* 象數學), resting on iconographic- and symbolic-based concepts. Perhaps this was the reason why within the accepted Song Confucian tradition as portrayed later by Zhu Xi, Shao Yong was regarded only as a distant member. Unlike Zhou Dunyi, Zhang Zai, and the Cheng brothers, he is not considered part of the main Confucian line of transmission, but rather was perceived more as an observer of this line. However, Shao's philosophy of observation is perhaps, the most important contribution to Confucian epistemology and theoretical systematization up to his time.

During his life, Shao received from his disciples and friends a cottage to live in that he named Nest of Peace and Happiness (*Anle Wo* 安樂窩), in which he hosted visitors and taught his disciples. As an act of gratitude, he then titled himself Mr. Peace and Happiness. He was considered one of the most learned and knowledgeable people of his generation, was offered several official positions, and declined all to continue living in his nest, free from political intrigues or responsibilities, again choosing a position of an observer. Shao married late and became a father at a mature age; he had two sons. The birth of his son Shao Bowen 邵伯溫 (1057–1134) changed his attitude toward his nonconformist choices. Shao Bowen was also the first commentator on his father's philosophy.[3] Shao was befriended by many members of the Luoyang intellectual elite, yet he failed to fully integrate into the social sphere and achieve self-fulfillment within the order of reality dominated by Confucian perceptions. This resulted in inner tensions and frustration, demonstrated with greater might in his poetry, where he expressed a feeling that only he had to endure difficulties.[4] However, later on in his life his poems expressed self-acceptance and serenity.

In this chapter we focus on Shao's understanding of life through observing a game of Weiqi, using the "Great Poem on Observing Weiq," as methodological cue, leading to his broader philosophical ideas.[5] The five-syllabic poem on observing *Weiqi*, was written in the old style (*gushi* 古詩). Its 360 lines—analogous to the 360 days of a year, the 360 degrees of a circle, the 360 revolutions of a cycle, as well as the number of stones in a complete Weiqi set—refer through correlative thinking to life and games at once.[6] The very length of the poem allowed Shao to reflect extensively on phenomenological, historical, and metaphysical reality, addressing his speculative thinking by means of this particular poetic form. The choice of games as a model enables understanding the person both from within as player and from the outside as observer.

Playing in the different parts of the poem with the observer's perspectives of within and without the game brings Shao to transcending the boundary between them, allowing him as observer to enter others' lives through the game and change position from observer to player.

The first part of the present chapter refers to the cultural significance of games and playing in general, then to playing the game of Weiqi. Discussed next is Shao's idea of observation (guan 觀) that opens the poem, assisted by his philosophy of the observation of things (guanwu 觀物), as introduced in the Book of Supreme World Ordering Principles (Huangji jingshi 皇極經世, abbreviated as HJJS), and the central topic of his major philosophical treatise Inner Chapters on Observing of Things (Guanwu Neipian 觀物內篇), usually incorporated in HJJS.[7] Next, we move on to Shao's ideas by reading the poem in three parts, following Chen Zu-yan's division.[8] In the first part, the poet describes observing the game and draws from it analogies to life. Moving from in to out, the observer transcends his own subjective boundaries for understanding the players and the game as a microcosm of one's life. In the second and longer part, the poet describes observing Chinese history from an ethical perspective, moving this time from out to in. Seeing the game in history as revealing the game in one's life brings him to transcending historical boundaries. Last, the ending part of the poem implies a riddle regarding the interpenetration of in and out, for which the response forms a theoretical framework of a perpetual interchange between the perspectives of observing and playing and between game and life, thus transcending the very dichotomy between in and out, leading to seeing the single world order in the basis of life.

Game, Play, Weiqi

Before entering Shao Yong's philosophy, a closer consideration of the game model for knowledge, in particular of Weiqi, is due. The earliest historical evidence of the Weiqi game appears already in the Classics. In the *Analects*, Confucius refers to playing Weiqi, saying only that it is better than doing nothing at all.[9] In *Mencius*, Weiqi is counted, in one instance, among five unfilial behaviors, and then mentioned for the first time in a more positive reference as an art in which one cannot succeed without fully engaging the mind and will.[10] Earlier yet, Weiqi is presented as analogous to life already in the Zuo Zhuan's 左傳 commentary on the *Spring and Autumn Annals* (*Chunqiu* 春秋), stating that if a player of Weiqi moves without a definite object he won't conquer his opponent, just as a ruler cannot escape ruin if he moves with no objective.[11] The prestige associated with Weiqi developed later on, probably during the Song or the Tang dynasties, in which Weiqi was regarded as an appreciated art.[12]

A brief review of how Weiqi is played will contextualize the upcoming discussion of Shao's use of Weiqi in his poem.[13] Similarly to Chess, Weiqi is a competitive territorial board game, noted for its complex strategy, despite its basic simple rules. Weiqi is played by two participants on a nineteen-by-nineteen-line grid board, in which the intersections of called points, and the 360 small and round playing pieces are called stones. The players take turns placing a stone on one of the board's unoccupied intersections. Once a stone is placed on the board, it is not moved until the end of the game. As the stones accumulate, they form groups of one color and connected stones with open territory along the line are alive. The object of the game is to occupy and control a larger area on the board, while a stone or a group that is surrounded by opponent's stones is dead and removed from the board.[14] A player can pass during the game if there is no territory she can occupy, and the game ends when there are two passes in a row, or under agreement of the players to stop. In the end, the stones are totaled and the dead ones are subtracted. The player with the higher total wins.

Two important features of the game have to do with a strong sense of ambiguity during its course. First, at no point during the match can one predict the final result; an apparent superiority of one opponent can change to one's inferiority through a single move. Second, the counting of points is extremely complicated. Hence, at the end of a match no one—not even a skilled Master—knows the accurate final count right away. These two traits are particularly interesting when thinking of the role of the game in the larger cultural context.

Like other games, Weiqi reflects the culture it is played in. In *Homo Ludens* (*Man the Player*, 1938), Johan Huizinga notes that in most languages there is no singular term that groups all of the activities that we refer to as game. No matter what language we think in, we tend to tone down the idea of play to an activity connected with lightness, while concepts such as challenge, danger, risk, chance, or contest must also be considered.[15] The Chinese word for game (*wan*瓩) extends its semantic range from children's games to the verbs: being busy, enjoying something, trifling, romping, jesting, making fun of, making jokes, or not being serious, as well as twiddling ornaments, sniffing at, examining, and feeling. All of the above are broadly referring to as handling in a specific way.[16] However, the Chinese language uses a special expression designated solely for playing Weiqi (*yi* 弈), as if distinguishing the unique features of this specific game from others.

The game of Weiqi corresponds well with Huizinga's reference to game.

> We might call it a free activity standing quite consciously outside "ordinary" life as being "not serious," but at the same time absorbing the player intensely and utterly. It is an activity connected with no material interest, and no profit can be gained by it. It proceeds within its own proper boundaries of time and space according to fixed rules and in orderly manner. It promotes the formation of social groupings which tend to surround themselves with secrecy and to stress their difference from the common world by disguise or other means.[17]

Weiqi, is indeed a free activity, and the playing is never enforced on players; it is outside life and constitutes an alternative board-life, and in this sense only it is not serious. However, not only does it absorb the players, it can, in fact, addict them and twist accepted norms in the ordinary world—as is also expressed in Shao's poem. In itself, the activity is not connected with material interest or profit (although Weiqi is played for money sometimes). Weiqi proceeds within its very limited space, and a game can sometimes last weeks or even months, always according to well-defined and simple fixed rules, in an orderly manner. Last, as Shao shows in his poem, written from an observer's perspective, Weiqi promotes social groupings of players as well as of observers of the game. Not only do the groups surround themselves with a sense of secrecy, but also, since its earliest stages, the game was associated through its legendary inventor Yao with divination and the secrets of foretelling. The game's secretive associations also include the great legendary ancestor Fuxi—the alleged author of the diagrams of the *Book of Change* (interestingly, Weiqi diagrams are depicted similarly).[18]

Huizinga specifies that regarding contest, unlike the general tendency to think that it has an aim, a game in fact is completely self-sufficient; it begins and ends of its own, and in this sense it is largely devoid of purpose or of an object outside itself. Winning a game always presupposes a competitor, such that the very idea is tied to relationships, esteem, or respect and not primarily to material profit. Hence, the point of a game involves the social life that rests on antagonistic structures.[19] In the Chinese context, the play of opposing forces can be depicted through a yin-yang relationship, as the opposing fundamental forces in the cosmic Order.[20] Huizinga associates the two ideas of war and game that were blended in the archaic mind, as specifically significant regarding strategy. Fighting, like game, presupposes limiting rules and requires play quality: opponents in war are regarded as equals, and like in play, war employs determination, strategy, and skill, which are often glorified by poets and chronicles.[21] Huizinga suggests that games create their own detached reality, thus they also contain an element of seriousness as can be seen in the players' attitude.[22]

Roger Caillois takes up from Huizinga, suggesting six criteria for games: games are *free*, namely, playing is not obligatory; they are *separate* in the sense that they are restricted to defined limits of space and time; they involve *uncertainty* of course and result with room for creativity in their moves; games are *unproductive* in that they produce no wealth, material goods, or other new elements external to the game, such that they end in a situation that is identical to that at the beginning of a game; they are *governed by rules* under conventions that establish new legislation; and finally, they include a *make-believe* element, which gives a sense of an alternative reality.[23] All six criteria are true for Weiqi and can be found in Shao Yong's poem. As we will see, Shao considers the freedom of the game to be the participants' creativity. He then presents the separate space and time in the game referring to moral standards in which truth and deceit blend together. Furthermore, the uncertainty of the result is depicted through historical analogies throughout the second part of the poem; the unproductiveness of game is shown through rebuffing the need to mention benefit and detriment. Rule following serves as the framework for "taking or abandoning in the flash of the moment," and make-believe characterizes the scene in which "pearls and jade flow from bosom and sleeves," and "life and death are in the hand."[24] Shao's own skillful creative observation in the game stems from familiarity with rules and strategies, as well as from perceptiveness of temper, disposition, and inclinations of the participants.

As every observation takes place within defined boundaries of space and time, the time and space created by the game of Weiqi have their own status, creating a microcosm—an alternative universe within our own. The game can therefore serve as a model, allowing for an observation that demands an extension of cognitive boundaries, or a play of in and out of the game. By means of entering the game through his observation, Shao transcends the boundaries of his personal cognition.

OBSERVING WEIQI AS TRANSCENDING ONE'S BOUNDARIES

Shao as Observer of Arts

Both the title—"Great Poem on Observing Weiqi"—and its two opening lines introduce its focus on the power of observation, in particular of observing Weiqi games; let us rest on them in the context of Shao's philosophy

> Some are skilled at exploring the arts,
> I have observed Weiqi games. (lines 1–2)

Shao refers to experts in exploring the arts or roaming in arts (*youyi* 游藝), perhaps alluding to Confucius's reference to aspiring to the Way, abiding by virtue, adhering to humanity, and exploring the arts.[25] Shao suggests a clear analogy according to which, similarly to the skills of exploring the arts, observing Weiqi also necessitates skillfulness. One clear shared trait of Weiqi with the Confucian-based Six Arts (*liuyi* 六藝), including rites, music, archery, charioting, calligraphy, and mathematics, is the importance of rule-following for being able to take part in the activity and for attaining a high level of participation. Indeed, rules enable meaningful performance of rites, harmonious playing of music, hitting a target by using a bow and arrow, classily operating a chariot, artfully mastering writing, and solving math riddles with precision and elegance. Art was introduced in China as first and foremost a matter of mastery of technique. Thus, the Chinese six arts can be seen as framework for ongoing disciplined practice. Later on in history, in late imperial time, Weiqi came to be considered one of the Four Arts (*siyi* 四藝) demanded for being a cultivated person, including zither playing, Weiqi playing, calligraphy, and painting.

The poem's two opening lines exemplify Shao's stand regarding the game he describes. The boundaries of the I positioned as observer (*yu chang guan* 予嘗觀) appear clear when opposed by Shao with the some who are skilled or have the proficiency (*you jing* 有精) for exploring the arts. Apparently in sharp contrast, the others are opposed to him: art opposes game; skillful exploration opposes Shao's observation as keen amateur. Positioning himself as an outsider allows Shao to open his observation with an apparently objective perspective toward what he observes, how it is done, and where it leads. Doing so, Shao invites his reader to observe him observe the game, as played in public, surrounded by a gathering of interested spectators, including himself. Throughout the poem, Shao introduces himself step-by-step as an observer of Weiqi, who acquires the required skills of an experienced observer of art. Shao's position is, in this way, somewhat similar to that of a bench player who is familiar with the rules, attentive to every move, and involved and ready to play—even if not actually playing. This attitude allows him to enjoy a dual position of an active observer, who is in the game and outside it at once. The apparent opposition between him and the expert is explored in the poem, showing that the very act of observing Weiqi opens up the observer, endowing him with skill, creativity, and ultimately self-knowledge, which is unbounded by the personal (*si* 私, line 360), as the poem eventually shows.

While the poem refers to the observation of the concrete game, one cannot be oblivious to the much broader context of the term observing in Shao's philosophy. Exploring Shao's perspective regarding observation as an organized skillful deed makes the analogy between game and life more meaningful. Shao's idea of *observation of things* should be considered in the broader context of his writings. In general, the notion *guan* refers to observing as well as beholding, perceiving, contemplating, understanding, and even advising. Using this term rather than its less complex alternatives, such as to see (*jian* 見), watch (*kan* 看), think (*si* 思), or understand (*zhi* 知), emphasizes Shao's intent to probe profoundly with the assistance of the various human faculties, as distinguished from empirical looking.

Shao introduces the important relatedness between what is seen in the senses and what is seen (and understood) by the mind. By means of the act that relies on both the experience of the senses and the analysis of the mind, Shao stresses the significance of the unity of experience and knowledge. Don J. Wyatt asserts that the observation of things became Shao's "practicable methodology, his modus operandi for looking at the world and its components"; therefore, many modern interpreters regard it as Shao's "signature idea."[26] Wyatt notes that the term was originated in the classical schools of Chinese philosophy, in the writings of Xunzi, with reference to the relatedness between one's determination of mind and the certainty of observation. Accordingly, not having a fixed mind increases doubts in one's observation.[27] However, until Shao's application of the term, it appeared only infrequently and nonsystematically.[28] Shao observes everything that is observable including, according to Wyatt: "Chess pieces on a board, fish, Mount Sung's smaller peak, ancient affairs, and the jade spurting geysers south of the Lo River."[29] The evolution of Shao's terminology for the various types of seeing shows, as Wyatt suggests, an "intent on probing as deeply as possible into the constitutions of all conceivable manifestations of existence."[30] This intent designates the uniqueness of human beings. Shao refers to observation as a threefold process.

> By viewing things is not meant viewing them with one's physical eyes, but with one's mind. Nay, not with one's mind but with the principle inherent in things. There is nothing in the universe without principle, nature and destiny. These can be known only when principle has been investigated to the utmost, when nature is completely developed and when destiny is fulfilled. The knowledge of these three is true knowledge. Even the sage cannot go beyond it. Whoever goes beyond it cannot be called a sage. (HJJS 6.26a; Chan 1963, 487)[31]

Siu-chi Huang raises two epistemological questions that follow this statement. First, what, according to Shao Yong, are our sources of knowledge? Second, what can the observer know? Huang responds to the first question saying that according to Shao, although our sense organs are our means to observe the world, the outcome of observation by means of senses alone cannot be considered knowledge.[32] Our sense organs endow us with some channel to sense data as given; knowledge, however, is more than the assemblage of sense information. It necessitates analysis and interpretation by the mind, which brings closer to Order, or to the principles that are inherent in things, which make things what they are and allow us to properly refer to them. Shao's model of knowledge involves senses, mind, and Order.

The Threefold Process of Observation

The three types of observation are, in fact, three perspectives that can be attained in one process. This process involves skills, which are acquired through experience and education—and more importantly, it requires a theoretical and practical infrastructure. What we know according to the first type of observation—through the senses—necessitates the work of the knowing mind and its integration of the information for understanding the inherent Order.

Shao explains in HJJS,

> Man is the most intelligent of all things because his eyes can perceive the colors of all things, his ears can perceive the sounds of all things, his nose can perceive the smell of all things, and his tongue can perceive the tastes

of all things. Color, sound, smell, and taste are the substance of things and the four senses are the functions of all men.... In the interaction of substance and function, the principles of man and things are complete. (HJJS 5:5a; Chan 1963, 485)

For Shao, sense data are the substance of things, and sense perception is its human function; hence, the two cannot be separated. According to his view, the realization of data as its perception, or of substance in its functions, constitutes knowledge; knowledge is then possible due to the operation of Order. Thus, it is important that the observation of things takes place neither solely through our eyes (*mu* 目), which in themselves are a thing, nor solely through the subjective mind (*xin* 心), but rather from the perspective of Order (*li* 理), which is none of the two, and yet embodies the two.

According to Shao, the first type of observation starts with the senses, in particular with the eyes, as mediating. In this sense, what we see is what we know. However, awareness is required in the processing of the mind to yield a reaffirmation. For deciphering sense data, the eyes that make the first acquaintance with the world cannot be separated from the work of the mind. For example, the simple experience of a broken spoon observed in a glass that is only half filled with water has more than one explanation. A naive viewer, perhaps a young child, indeed perceives it as broken; and when taken out of the water, it is whole and unbroken again, like magic. In this case, the eyes take over the mind, such that what the eyes see is what a child or a naive viewer understands, even if this does not correspond with the knowledge of a mature mind. This understanding is not wrong, since it perfectly describes what the eyes see. Moreover, it is necessary in order to later understand the phenomenon of perceptual illusions, to investigate it, and to understand that what the eyes see does not provide us with the full information that enables proper understanding. Observing through the eyes is necessary, but understanding through them alone is according to Shao, only partial. Therefore, what the eye sees comprises only the first and most basic type of observation.

The second, more advanced type of observation involves the mind, and allows one's observation to transcend the boundaries of senses. Referring again to the broken spoon, observing with the mind allows one to understand that the fractured spoon is just an illusion, while in reality it is unbroken. The mind enables the understanding that when a spoon is put in a glass of water, an optical illusion occurs, which makes it seem as something other than what it really is. Then what we see is not a broken spoon anymore, but rather a physical phenomenon called optical refraction, which amounts to the change in direction of a wave due to a change in its speed and creates an apparent illusion. As light bends when it travels from water to air, it looks as if the spoon is broken and when it is taken out of the water, the water does not affect the light anymore, and it appears whole again—as it actually was throughout the experiment. Clearly, no magic is involved. The nuanced understanding applies a mental act of abstraction for seeing in things not just what the eyes observe, but also what the mind extracts. Observing with the mind contributes, in this way, to creating categories such as realism and idealism—or as coined in China around Shao's days, the School of Principle opposed to the School of mind, each suggesting a different framework for better understanding the contents of the world we live in. Notably, however, as we will soon learn, Shao's understanding of Order includes the mind; thus, it is not surprising that he belonged with neither school.

The idea of the observing mind often appears in Shao's writings, in varied contexts. In some cases we read that the mind is Supreme Polarity.[33] Endowing the mind with the highest ontological status, Shao implies that similarly to Supreme Polarity, the mind functions as the ultimate unity, clearly not in a transcendental sense. The mind as Supreme Polarity is everything, existing at every level of reality, with no boundaries of space or of time. While Supreme Polarity cannot be known by the senses, the mind as Supreme Polarity can be known in the sense that myriad things are produced and reflected in it.[34] In this way it involves no dualism in the Cartesian sense.[35] The mind reveals an epistemological element, which is superior to sense organs, since unlike them, it is reflexive.

Shao describes the creative, active role of the human mind in observing things in a poem from 1076.

> To dwell in darkness, but observe the bright;
> To reside in quietude, but observe what moves.
> To dwell in simplicity, yet observe complexity;
> To reside in the trifling, yet observe the weighty.
> Those who take repose (in these things) are few;
> Thus, many (are the things) they observe.
> Since not to dwell (in these things) would be not to observe,
> Of what use would (the concern with) "few" or "many" be?[36]

Senses are principal means in one's acquaintance with the world; however, they never constitute a complete understanding. The human power for understanding demands active mental processing that allows one to be in the dark and yet be able to observe brightness, without being beclouded. Knowledge is both internal and external, and yet mind and senses are not sufficient to truly dwell on knowledge. Knowledge is revealed by a process of transcending boundaries: first, sense data are transcended in being processed by the mind's cognitive faculties, which are then transcended again and by Order—which is the product of neither the mind nor the world exclusively.

Accordingly, the third and most complete type of observation through Order enables true knowledge, which is not subdued by circumstances. Coming back to the glass example, only as understanding through Order, one is able to see neither a broken spoon nor an optical illusion. While one may presume that understanding through Order comprises yet another version in the category of understanding with the mind, Shao clarifies that this is not the case. Order is in everything; namely, in the spoon, in the water, in the glass, and in the perceiving mind. In other words, observing with Order is an observation of the moment as a whole, in which all participating essentials of observation—object, subject, their relation, and the mediation between them—take part in a unified process. In this sense, toward the end of his poem, Order is referred to as fulfilling nature (line 347). This onto-epistemological role of Order has the methodological merit of safeguarding the doctrine against epistemological absurdities. Philosophical schools attempt to assure commonsense beliefs by all possible means, too numerous to recount here: platonic ideas, mental representations, empiricist correspondence theories, rationalistic coherence theories, monisms and dualisms, and so on. By means of Order, Shao can keep faith with common sense and avoids epistemological paradoxes, by the inherent dynamism between things, mind, and Order.

The three types of knowledge articulate a progression from sense experience to consciousness. According to Anne Birdwhistell's view, the final stage is the utmost sagely achievement, enabling one to regard objects without preconditions, and unifies the sage with things. Wyatt sees this understanding as "mystical subjectivism, which calls for total merging of the subject and the perceived object," thus disregarding Shao's unique perspectivism.[37] Wyatt is right to emphasize the importance of the various perspectives in Shao's philosophy, and his various ways of observation do indeed form a unity, with no mystical subjectivism in it. However, it is a unity of multiple perspectives, which jointly form a full understanding of a person who is able to expand his own skills through an epistemological process. Shao seeks to merge the practical-experiential and ethical aspect with the theoretical-systematic sphere, such that he can be viewed neither as an epistemological empiricist nor as an idealist, since the sources of knowledge are drawn from sense data and processed by the active contribution of the perceiving mind, through Order.

Shao's notion of Order is not disconnected from the experiential world, and his epistemology is strongly related to the Confucian moral system, as we will see hereafter. Unlike previous Confucian attitudes, his expansion of the person must be attained through an epistemological shift, using one's creative mental powers as the only way for self-transcending. Moreover, while Order has primal epistemological value, its bond with nature and mandate forces the reader to accept that the only possible manner to follow Order is through the moral Way, the ultimate ideal of perfection, which also comprises the ongoing process of becoming; or in particular, of becoming moral. Shao refers to the Order of the Way in reference to moral cultivation.

> From this we know that the Way is the basis of Heaven and Earth, and that Heaven and Earth are the basis of all things. Viewed from Heaven and Earth, the myriad things are the myriad things (that is, individual entities). When Heaven and Earth are viewed from the Way, then they themselves are also the myriad things. The principle of the Way finds its full development in Heaven; the principle of Heaven, in Earth; the principle of Earth, in the myriad things; and that of the myriad things, in man. (Chan 1963, 485, 5:7a)

> The principles governing Heaven and man are found in all events, great or little. It is the duty of man to cultivate his person. (Chan 1963, 494, 8B:31b)

The acquired skill of weaving all things through one Order, which is ultimately the Way, brings one to observing things as unified and moral. From the perspective of the Way as ultimate, heaven, earth and the myriad things respond to one universal Order. For this very reason they are all things. The Order in heaven, in earth, in the Way, and in things (and in humans as special "things") is fully known when being observed through, which then brings about a knowledge of things from the perspective of things (that is, having the same Order the observer has).

> A mirror reflects because it does not obscure the physical form of things. But water (with its purity) does even better because it reveals the universal character of the physical form of things as they really are. And the sage does still better because he reflects the universal character of the feelings of all things. The sage can do so because he views things as things view themselves; that is not subjectively but from the viewpoint of things. Since

he is able to do this, how can there be anything between him and things? (Chan, 1963 488, 6:26b)

A Reflective Realism

Shao refers to the significance of responsiveness, consciousness, or reflection (*ling* 靈) of things in one's knowledge of them, cognizant of the different levels and different kinds of knowledge. In this way, he refers to knowledge that is expressed in words, reflected in the mind, and performed with the body in a human deed. When knowledge is reflected in the mind, the sage incorporates in it all levels as one. The sagely state of mental perfection is thus a state in which all levels of knowledge, or all means of observation, are unified. According to Shao, knowledge is based on concrete experience and corresponds with the universe, as perception corresponds with reality. This outlook, defined in modern philosophy as direct realism, brings the study of metaphysics to the way people actually experience the world, rejecting the idea of inner mental representations, authoritative sense data, and other intermediaries between the mind and the world.[38] For Shao, an appropriate reflection does not obscure the physical form, and yet, it reveals its universal character.[39] The reflexive capability as a human higher faculty is vital from both moral and epistemological perspectives. Focusing on the epistemological perspective, it is the purest way to know both oneself and other people and things. This point that is so pivotal in Shao's system is expressed again in full volume in a poem from 1074.

> A man mustn't seek his reflection in flowing
> He must seek it in water that is still.
> Flowing water has no fixed form,
> While still water provides a fixed entity.
> (But) neither should a man seek his reflection in water (at all).
> He should seek his reflection in other men.
> Water's mirror may show a man's face,
> But a human mirror exposes a man spirit. (ICCJC 14.53a–b; Wyatt 174)

Reflecting not only the physical but also on mental functions is the sage's unique epistemological faculty. Observing things impartially, or sagely, is observing things *from the perspective of things themselves*, or being fully reflexive. Observing through Order brings the observer back to the world of things through reflexivity, namely, through returning to the perspective of things, rather than one's own perspective. Rather than seeing Order as elevating man from things and bringing him closer to a higher and purer realm (such as Theravada Buddhist nirvana), Order unifies humans with things and brings all back to a single level. Ultimately, there is no supreme knower who knows others better than they know themselves. This perspective is influenced by ideas that were originally foreign to Confucianism, such as the Zhuangzian request to bring his reader down to earth when he discusses the Way from the perspectives of the ant, the grass, the tile, and down to feces;[40] or to the *Awakening of Faith in Mahayana*'s (*Dacheng Qixin Lun* 大乘起信論), introducing reality through four levels, starting with things, elevating to Order, then to a noninterference between things and Order, and last to the noninterference of things with each other, which in fact signifies coming back to earth as the ultimate level of reality.[41] Shao gives this process a Confucian-moral sense.

The sage's special capacity to observe things from the perspective of things also involves viewing things not from a subjective perspective, as a nonego, such that she realizes herself as a thing among things. We thus arrive at knowledge attained through observation, which is by no means a physical faculty; rather, it is acquired through skillful observation of things through inherent Order. The skillful person who observes things in her own terms, or from her own viewpoint, is understood as the full realization of Mencius's "All the myriad things are there in me" (7A:4). No mystical overtones are concealed in Shao's saying; rather, he refers to a sense of directness and an ability to observe the world by its own means, with no need for supernatural beings or transcendental means. According to the Mencian statement, the person who finds the myriad things within himself is sincere. Notably, from the epistemological perspective, this observation is sincere, in the sense that it acquaints us with things as they are in our experience. Yet it is also morally sincere. Through an ongoing practice of observation, a person refines the intuitive skill that incorporates empirical and rational faculties into an impartial vision. Knowledge on this level is absolute and creative at once; it is universal, despite being acquired by inherent and creative means. This reflective ability of the knower allows him to creatively unify his personal viewpoint with the viewpoints of all things, under the guidance of Order that unifies all and brings us knowers to the essence of things. The morality of observation is attained through reflexivity.

Shao offers a methodology of reflective observation (*fanguan* 反觀), the goal of which (according to Birdwhistell's explanation) is to attain a state of consciousness that overcomes the senses and touches reality. As Anne Birdwhistell puts it: "things exist whether observed or not, but they are not completed until seen or otherwise perceived by someone."[42] For a thing to be complete, an awareness of a perceiver is needed, such that while no absolute subjectivity exists, there is constant interaction and codependence among things and persons in the world. However, while every human being has consciousness, the sage alone uses it reflectively. Through reflective observation, or a consciousness that reflects the processes, the sage is able to apply her reflection in thought or deed. Reflective perception is the only means to see the Order, which is one in things and in oneself.

In this way, subject and object become one in the sense that both share the same Order and constitute every component in reality. The sage, or the perfect perceiver, is a unified and unifying self, who, as prerequisite, is impartial and reflective. Observing things in this way necessitates forgetting one's ego and personal interest, or forgetting oneself. By shifting the focus from perception to observation, Shao can discard the ego, in a way that minimizes the contributions of perceivers and of perceptive faculties to that which is perceived. Rather, the perceiver, perceiving, and the perceived are grasped in a single glimpse, as one state of affairs. Just as a mirror shows a single reflected object rather than an object and a reflection, so does the mind of the sage contain the object within it. Yet although clear observation is ego-less observation, it does not demand a total neglect of feelings. Thus, Shao expresses a new sense of being happy or sad.

> When one can be happy or sad with things as though he were the things themselves, one's feelings may be said to have been aroused and to have acted a proper degree. (Chan 1963, 493, 8B:26a)

Shao's idea of feeling as though one is a thing, as expressed in the notion that things themselves are happy or sad with us, differs from the *Zhuangzi*'s view about "[j]oy and anger, sadness and pleasure, anticipation and regret ... like music from an empty tube, or mushrooms from the warm moisture" (2.2). In the *Zhuangzi*, feelings are superfluous, like fungi growing out of moss, when according to Shao they are guided by the mind; one's feelings are introduced—a natural and direct outcome that does not becloud reality. Shao continues,

> We can handle things as they are if we do not impose our ego on them. The sage gives things every benefit and forgets his own ego. To let the ego be unrestrained is to give rein to feelings; to give rein to feelings is to be beclouded; and to be beclouded is to be darkened. To follow the natural principles of things, on the other hand, is to grasp their nature; to grasp

their nature is to be in possession of spiritual power; and to possess spiritual power is to achieve enlightenment. (Chan 1963, 494, 8B:27b)

Shao warns his reader that while feelings do have significance, they should not be given rein. Losing the balance and letting feelings rule blurs our vision, distorts our perception, and muddles the understanding of an event. Unrestrained feelings are the immediate outcome of ego-governing rather than governing by Order. Through Order, one may grasp the true nature of things, which is a high spiritual degree leading to enlightenment. Cultivating this human power is empowering for the human participant in the universe.

> Our nature views things as they are, but our feelings cause us to see things subjectively and egotistically. . . . Man occupies the most honored position in the scheme of things because he combines in him the principles of all species. If he honors his own position and enhances his honor, he can make all species serve him.
>
> The nature of all things is complete in the human species.
>
> The spirit of man is the same as the spirit of Heaven and Earth. (Chan 1963, 492, 8B:16a–17a)

Shao explains the gap between what exists and how it is understood by means of the feelings that process direct experience, and thus must be overcome in order to return to the pure observation that is also our own capability. Forcing feelings on things makes understanding biased and apparent knowledge—a mere superstition. Concrete mental states constitute mistakes and fallacies. The sagely no self is absolute receptivity, in which hearing, seeing, smelling, tasting, and feeling all exist on a nonpersonal level, merely as occurrences in one ongoing process of skillful observation. Shao's poem on observing Weiqi is an observation on observation, which allows him to reflect on life without analyzing it and dismantling its continuity. The game is a model, a microcosm that discloses what life is, rather than failing to describe what it is about.

As we will see next, the observation of the strategic game suggests that we do have a substantial ability to contemplate, deliberate, and calculate our ethical and political moves. The poem introduces a Confucian self who transcends his own boundaries, this time by observation: first, transcending the personal through observing with the eyes, then transcending the eyes with the mind, and finally transcending the mind with Order. In the following we will see how the concrete observing of the Weiqi game exposes Shao's philosophical attitude, as contributing to his idea a methodology of observation through game, which embodies observing through senses, mind, and Order, and suggesting a unified framework for all three. In his translation and short analysis of the poem, Chen Zu-yan suggests that the poem can be read as an archetype for Shao's "three step epistemological methodology."[43] Chen divides the poem into three parts and suggests that it exemplifies the methodology, such that the first fifty-six lines concern observing with the eyes; the second and longer part of the poem refers to observing with the mind; and the third part, the last forty lines, introduces observing with Order (translated by Chen as "principle"). Embracing Chen's suggestion, I seek to make the point that the three types are not distinct from each other, and in this way contribute to an understanding of the unbounded self, who is free from the traditional Chinese in-out dichotomy.

IN TO OUT: THE LIFE OF A GAME

An Observer's Perspective

In the first part of the poem, Shao Yong situates himself as a spectator of Weiqi games that reflect the game of life. Shao, as the subject of the observation, applies his own eyes to observe the game as an object—a thing. Thus, the first part of the poem is a demonstration of observation of things with the senses. This observation introduces a movement from within his own limited self toward an external happening, which necessitates expanding himself through the observation. The special status of an observer of the game allows Shao to slowly progress from a subjective position of an involved observer who gradually enters the game he observes, and expands his own subjectivity. He is thus able not only to know objective data, like the rules of the game and its moves, but also to attain a more intimate acquaintance of subtle motions within it. The game he watches is revealed in this way, as a microcosm of the life he lives.

Shao describes the game through metaphorical expressions, with allusions to life outside the boundaries of game. Through the poem's lines, we learn that the game is not just the board, the stones, or the specific moves; indeed, it also comprises strategies, tactics, manners, and moods. The game is the gathering around the board and the associations it raises. A sense of continuity between corporeal or empirical reality and "game reality" brings the reader to a realization of both as having equal statuses of existence in Shao's philosophy. The idea of an equal status of existence shared by the experienced reality and the game's alternative reality does not imply that one can be mistaken for the other, or that one acts in life according to game rules and vice versa; rather, the notion originates in the contribution of both empirical-reality and game-reality to one's understanding. Life, death, occupation, or victory on the board each has its own significance and implications that do not depend on real life and yet can change one's view and understanding of life. Hence, after the two opening lines in which he states his perspective as a Weiqi observer, Shao shifts the perspective from the observer to the observed, opening with the underlying tension between hidden and seen that incites the game.

> After calculations, creations and evolutions are known,
> Through moves, the trivial and the subtle are seen. (lines 3–4)

Shao endows his reader with the impression that through careful observation of every move, one can not only learn about better or worse Weiqi moves, but also a keen observer sees minute aspects that could have been overlooked otherwise. Moving "outside" the game allows entering the inner, invisible, or hidden. Phenomenological happenings in the game represent an empirical level of the whole. Shao is aware that every move exposes indicative information: with regard to the player, it may expose one's temper, understanding, and disposition; with regard to the world we live in, it may expose its rules of space and time, dynamics, and forces. Every move is a product of an analysis within one's internal sphere, bringing about a creative choice, which evolves into the shift on the board, such that regarding the game, knowledge is transformative in essence (*zhi caihua* 知造化). The inner realm is manifested in this way, in the public realm, in which it is open to other eyes and thoughts through the moves (*zhe* 著) that reveal the aspects of the trivial and external (*wai* 外), as well as the finest subtleties (*jiwei* 幾微).

Observing a game reveals not only the significance of moves but also that of premove dynamics. Like his predecessor Zhou Dunyi, who discusses the importance of subtle activation (*ji* 幾) as the crucial time-instant in which the specific direction of an action is determined, Shao too aspires to penetrate the minute before it fully came into being. He intends to attain this objective through game moves that expose what cannot be expressed in words and intensify what can hardly be seen in everyday practice. The instant beforehand, or the state between nonexistence and existence, is one in which game and life are merged harmoniously, and can be seen as the inspiration for the game. While the calculations, creations, and evolutions cannot be observed, a skillful observer can observe them retrospectively, as part of the precondition of moves. The next lines turn primarily to the internal aspects and the motivations seen in Weiqi moves—or to exposing the tension between the public realm and the interactions through codes of etiquette and politeness, as opposed to genuine personal reality.

> Minds are ceaseless in their desire for victory,
> Intentions of striving for initiative do not subside.
> In front of people, the etiquette of guest and host is thoroughly observed,
> But facing each other, they are like barbarians and savages. (lines 5–8)

Keeping balance and losing it is represented in the poem through the relation between feelings within oneself and behavior in public. The aspiration for victory in the game creates a double standard: just like the calculations that are made before a move is taken (including both conclusions from previous moves and speculations on coming moves), so is the eagerness to win (*haosheng* 好勝) and the intentions (*yixian* 意先) to be first. Shao refers to a Weiqi tactic for winning in the game by its Weiqi-jargon initiative (*xian*先), which makes sense for unfamiliar readers also in its ordinary use.[44] In this way, he brings to the forefront the role of resourcefulness in the game and in life in general, acknowledging the fact that intentions to win are present always, even if unseen. The desire for victory as inherent to the competition is liable to turn shrewdness into deviousness.

As observer, Shao's cognition expands the boundaries of ego and develops an important sense of criticism on social conventions and accepted standards in the society he belongs with. Shao conveys his criticism on the spirit of competition as hidden by etiquette and politeness, which was not foreign to Chinese society of his era. The place of competition in understanding Chinese culture is highlighted by Marcel Granet's claim that, similarly to other societies and cultures, competition animated Chinese society from early times—as detected already in the winter festivities in tournaments of ritualistic dance and song, leading to the actual formation of state institutions, which then shaped the entire hierarchy of the later Chinese state.[45] Even if one does not fully accept Granet's notion, Shao's presenting the desire for victory as having a significant role in a culture that is often praised for its aspiration for harmony clearly demonstrates his acknowledgment of a living tension.[46] Indeed, Shao criticizes the incessant desire for victory that the mind cannot resist when it enters the game, sometimes at the cost of moral standards. In his reference to the board game, Shao naturally implied the political game in which he never agreed to take part.

Huizinga's agonistic principle of game is the connecting of victory with play, as reflected in winning and in what is won—referring first and foremost to showing oneself as superior to others. Accordingly, victory lies in winning something external to the playing itself, such as esteem, prestige, and honor, associated with the various ways in which they can be enjoyed and celebrated with others. In this way, however, victory also comprises an attainment that presupposes a partner or opponent.[47] This point makes sense in the critical Confucian framework of focusing on the other. Since the other is needed for an effective victory, Weiqi can be used as a form for learning about proper and improper human interactions, as Shao shows in the lines regarding the visible aspects of Weiqi interaction.

Shao observes that a person's conduct in public conforms with the general code or the etiquette of guest and host (*dangren jin binzhu* 嘗人儘賓主). What dictates this code in the Confucian context is mainly the rites or the rules of propriety that guide one's behavior and have special significance in the social realm. Through a critical perspective, the poem presents the rites that serve as a moral framework in Confucianism. If not properly internalized, rites pose a risk of creating a double standard with regard to honesty. If the rigidity attached to rules—including rules of propriety—overtakes the morality to which the rules were intended to lead, the outcome is a mechanic and insincere behavior, whereby both the within and the without are detached. Shao describes the hypocritical situation in which in the company of others rules are kept, and yet in a one-on-one interaction with no audience, behavior changes significantly. In fact, according to Shao, it becomes similar to the behavior of barbarians and savages (*manyi* 蠻夷) who follow neither the moral Way nor its rules of propriety.

The public reality outside the game dictates behavior and rules that are agreed under cultural consensus, following norms believed to derive from life, its traditions, and its etiquette. Truly, the game also has its traditions, rules, and outcomes, which express themselves in the game only through gestures and deeds among participants. For example, in the game, players who in other contexts may appear to be friends might behave like enemies, in a situation that is complex as the borders fade out between is and ought, between propriety and hypocrisy. In real-life situations, the participants of the game, just like others, conform to rules of propriety and civility that are intended to reflect inner morality; if the rules do not manifest one's true feelings, they are always intended to develop a true *moral* feeling. The agreement on rules of propriety is itself a game with its own rules, which are by and large ethical ones. However, the simulated conditions of the game free players from accepted norms and codes of behavior, allowing them to switch identities and become occupiers and hunters, releasing a barbarian and savage self, in an alternative reality, while keeping a framework of politeness as external only.

Importantly, the freedom to be savage cannot be true freedom, since it ultimately destroys itself; yet within the framework of game, it can be viewed as part of the essential characteristic of game as free activity.[48] Acknowledging the behavior in the game of Weiqi, as described by Shao, can be taken as an assertion of the Xunzi'an vision of human amoral disposition coming to life when unrestrained by real life's code of propriety.[49] Demonstrating the type of savageness he refers to, Shao keeps on distinguishing between the double standard of the game-reality versus life outside it.

> Money and profit agitate minds,
> Joy and anger show in faces.
> Life and death are in the hand,
> Give or take flame in the cheeks. (lines 9–12)

While clearly morally inappropriate, the world of the game embodies agitations of the mind, such as wealth and profit (*caili* 財利). While the mask of rites guides its followers not to be influenced by profit, when the player's mask takes over, profit is liable to enter the picture, with the justification that it is part of the game. Shao observes this with a critical eye, especially as related to joy and anger in the hedonistic sense, rather than the Confucian moral sense in which joy is a moral feeling that accompanies a good deed, as always opposed to profiting from it.[50] In the picture that Shao draws, the relation changes such that joy and anger (*xinu* 喜怒) reflect the agitations of wealth and profit, losing their moral value. In this way, the joy of the game indistinctly involves both pure joy from the beauty of brilliant moves and beastly or greedy joy based on possible material goods or on rejoicing in another's failure. This extends, according to Shao's observation, to feeling that life and death are *truly* at stake and in one's power: not only do the players' stones live or die, but rather life and death are in their hands (*shengsha zaiyu shou* 生殺在於手).

The Player's Perspective

Since observing a game offers a unique ability to delve, from the observer's perspective into that of a player, the opponents' inner motives are revealed through the moves in the game, such that Shao is able to describe the game—or at least offer some perspectives of it—from *within*. From an insider perspective he sees that it is not as if life and death are in their hands; rather, the game *is* life and death. This key line in the poem reflects Shao's view on Weiqi as a microcosm for human life, which not only models life but also *becomes* life and generates more life.

The lines reveal in this way sensitivity to two important characteristics of a game that lead Shao throughout the poem: first, a game is a form of interaction; second the game creates a world of make-believe. This make-believe characterizes every game as "accompanied by a special awareness of a second reality or of a free unreality, as against life."[51] The idea of living two realities such as war in the game and peace outside it has far-reaching effects. An example can be taken from shamanic-voodoo rituals, in which both the shaman and his audience believe in an invasion of spirits and ghosts who cause frenzies; they also believe that the mask the shaman wears is the character it represents, that supernatural powers do act in the world, and that a voodoo doll pricked with a pin can truly kill.[52] The make belief reality of the ritual may end with a person's death, apparently due to the pricking of a doll. The explanation that "it is only a game" loses its meaning when the game overtakes life. The more absorbing the game is, the less it can offer comfort for a loss. This merging of the in and the out perspectives of Weiqi playing is movingly demonstrated in Yasunari Kawabata's semifictional chronicle of Go master Honinbo Shusai's 1938 retirement game. The story describes the lengthy struggle that took almost six months to complete, after which Honinbo Shusai lost to his younger competitor, and died thereafter. The book, written from different perspectives simultaneously, suggests a detailed description of the game and its moves on the surface, while on deeper levels the very description of the game should be read as the life story of the aging Go master, the clash between tradition and modernity, and perhaps even the story of Japan's defeat in World War II. As the author testifies,

> That play of black upon white, white upon black, has the intent and takes the form of creative art. It has in it a flow of the spirit and a harmony as of music. Everything is lost when suddenly a false note is struck.[53]

Bringing the imagined reality of the game to an extreme, Shao's poem proceeds to discuss human qualities, three of which are moral qualities that change in the game and lose their ordinary references in life.

> Perversity does not differ from ice and charcoal,
> Harmony does not equate to *xun* and *chi*.
> Loyalty does not extend to company and friends,
> Affection does not connect husband and wife. (lines 13–16)

Referring to tyranny or stubbornness (or perversity *li* 戾), harmony (*he* 和), rightness (or loyalty *yi* 義), and affection (*qing* 情), Shao first equates the stubbornness that he sees in the game with the inflexibility and rigidity of ice and charcoal. As ice freezes and charcoal burns, both are unreal in the sense that each presents a natural substance introduced in its extreme state. Ice is water that lost its flow, charcoal is wood that lost its vitality; neither has flexibility, neither can depart from the point of extremity that by nature defines it. The inclination to stick to extremes characterizes the Weiqi world of make-believe, in which killing and dying happen constantly. The fierce fighting driven by the desire to win creates even more serious gaps between desired states and reality, turning people into enemies. While stubbornness is at its extreme, harmony seems to be merely a delusion. Harmony, which is associated with the music played by the wind instruments of *xun* 塤 and *chi* 篪, comprises an appearance, at best. By their hollowness, both wind instruments—made of the natural materials of stone or bone and of bamboo—enable humans to blow air into them, for harmony to be created. Without true harmony, the moral value of rightness, originally indicating one's loyalty to morality, changes in the game to loyalty to one's ego. In the same manner, affection—the basic feeling that is supposedly the foundation of family relatedness—does not connect husband and wife, at least not in the game.

> Shao gives more metaphors taken from external and material world,
>   exemplified by objects such as ornaments, structures, and tools.
>   Pearls and jade flow from bosom and sleeves,
> Dragons and snakes race in liver and spleen.
> Strong fortresses rise from wine cups and meat bowls,
> Swords and spears cross in front of screens and curtains. (lines 17–20)

Pearl and jade stand as metaphors for elegant speech that is exchanged between players; dragons and snakes are analogous to weapons and fighting beneath the external cordiality.[54] While elegance flows from garments and the body, within the body dragons and snakes race. The poem might be hinting at a confusion and mix-up of the five phases that are responsible for harmonious world dynamism, represented in the poem through liver and spleen, which are presented in a disorderly manner. Liver represents wood in body organs, and spleen represents earth; dragon represents water in animals and snake represents metal. The *Yellow Emperor's Inner Canon (Huangdi Neijing* 黃帝內經) sees the liver as the army's general; a properly functioning liver ensures that the tendons are nourished and not too tense or gristly. The normal direction of liver qi is downward; when it rebels, it attacks the spleen, which in turn affects digestion, muscles, and circulation, as perhaps Shao hints. Moreover, the two vital organs host a race or at least a stride (*zou* 走) of dragons and snakes, depicted as attacking each other and seeming not to be in their orderly places.[55]

Thus, Shao's imagery implies that the preoccupation with the drive to win yields deliberate attempts to mislead and deceive others. These implications are suggested in the images of fortresses that appear to rise from too much wine and meat, and swords and spears that rather than being engaged in the battlefield, fight within a domestic set and decoration materials. Shao moves on to a description of underlying powers, connected with time, seasons, and earthly and heavenly space—again described as malfunctioning.

> Ghosts and spirits labor during daytime,
> Flood dragons and hornless dragons coil on the ground.
> Thunder and hail crack in the sky and upon the river,
> Male and female whales are slain on land and sea. (lines 21–24)

The problem reflected in the above lines is the loss of clear functions—not in terms of opening oneself to additional alternatives, but on the contrary as losing ground. If thus far, the deviations were described in the game, they now transgress its borders and penetrate reality. Through the game one learns about life; a player's experience of being lost within it can thus serve as a warning sign for the player. The game enables one to carry out alternatives that are not fancied in reality and should never be fancied. The natural and supernatural forces that Shao describes reflect a crooked cosmic Order in the reality of the game. Ghosts and spirits (*guishen*鬼神) that are forced to serve in an untimely manner during the daytime are not respected and most likely also unhappy; the legendary aquatic dragon (flood dragon *jiao* 蛟), who supposedly controls rain and floods, and the hornless dragon (*chi* 螭) curl on the ground instead of being in the water;[56] thunder and hail, the more aggressive among the natural forces, crack the empty space (*kong* 空); male and female whales, as metaphors for savages acting like big fish who swallow smaller ones, are all slaughtered in the depth of the ocean or displaced on the shore.[57] The lines depict a distorted yin-yang pattern: dark and ghostly versus daily normality, water against ground, audible thunder versus visible-tangible hail, sky above and river below, male and female. While the players as insiders cannot see this, observing the game provides a perspective on Shao's natural elements as confused and twisted.

The four lines (lines 25–28) describing the distraction of Order are followed by a description of the cycle of seasons affecting human temper, referring to a shielded sun and a crescent moon, both sharing light and dark; to rivers and mountains brightening the earth; and to stars naturally gathering in constellations. Through the description, Shao produces a sense of an alternative time and space that are created in the game, which do not correspond with ordinary space-time laws. The designation of space and time of game isolates it from the rest of life and gives it life of its own.[58] In the case of Weiqi, the space on which it happens is the grid board, and nothing that takes place outside this frontier is relevant. As for time, the game starts and ends as agreed; its duration can be fixed in advance or it can continue on. In the example of the six months of game in *The Go Player*, insofar as the game lasts, it takes over the master's life, eventually leading to his death. Accordingly, the game's rules replace the laws of ordinary life, and space and time function according to new rules reflecting new beliefs and values.[59] The exclusive space and time lead to total submerging in the game, causing people to forget their own lives beyond the board. The observing subject, who is absorbed in the game, transcends space-time limits, in a way that reminds what Immanuel Kant taught later on: space and time are revealed as categories of human cognition. In Shao's case, this revelation re-creates the categories that in turn enable a journey of the subject in space and time, as seen later on.

With regard to this context, Caillois asks, with this regard, "what becomes of games when the sharp line dividing their ideal rules from the diffuse and insidious laws of daily life is blurred?" He asserts that the game cannot spread beyond the space of the playing field or the time of its duration. Caillois refers to situations in which the universe of the game is no longer tightly closed within itself, the game as escape turns into obligation accompanied by anxiety, and pleasure turns into obsession. Shao implies that in situations of this kind, the blurring of game space-time with reality space-time corrupts the principle of play. Showing this, he moves on to characteristics of the game as chance, judgment, and unpredictability, as possible unfortunate outcomes of the redefined space and time, which leads to a distortion of accepted *moral* categories.

> Betting on a winning or losing situation,
> One is instead startled on the path of favor or disgrace.
> High and low are easy to judge,
> Back and forth are difficult to catch.
> Once the mind has decided,
> Benefit and detriment need not be mentioned again.
> Rolling up or stretching at the strategic points,
> Taking or abandoning in the flash of a moment. (lines 29–36)

The eight lines criticize the swinging and swaying of mind in the betting situation. Being intellectually, emotionally, and sometimes financially absorbed in the game changes one's judgments and influences the outcomes of judgments. The desire to win is liable to yield deception and cheating. One possible explanation for this phenomenon may involve the difficulty in determining where a game leads to, when any apparent advantage can undo itself in one move. Moreover, the desire to keep the advantage without knowing the result until the end of the game can create an emotional imbalance possibly leading to a loss of the moral standards. This may cause competitive players, as described above, to play *for* something else rather than the game itself. The "something" played for is first and foremost victory, which is enjoyed through prestige and social acknowledgment. The betting adds material value to the victory, which thus turns measurable and appears more real. However, the material prize is never a prize for actual participation, and affects the game itself by shifting its focus, as Shao shows.[60]

In particular, the money at stake startles players to the point of appreciating convoluted techniques and developing ways to deceive that affect the result. While betting is oriented to gaining control over life, it frequently involves superstition rather than examining and verifying data, creating new beliefs according to which players compete. Shao implies that when the competition is *for* something, the very something competed for is at risk of being forgotten or won by trickery. (Examples for corruption in games, forgotten as such and seen at times as part of the game, are abundant in sports; Maradona's famous Hand of God, by which Argentina's soccer team won the 1986 World Cup is such an example. As Maradona testified, the goal was scored "a little with the head of Maradona and a little with the hand of God," revealing his belief that what is considered foul by experts or observers is in fact from the player's perspective divine intervention.)

The fear that one's victory is at risk may cause a player to cheat only within the universe of play, believing that he may keep up with moral standards in life. However, this attempted practice is problematic in both universes: the living universe is under the threat of twisted rules taking over morality, and game universe is at risk of losing its freedom and pleasure.[61] While this is true to some extent, as history tells, pretence—a moral violation in itself—cannot suffice for guarding morality. A violation, for example, taking deceiving as winning, diffuses and can affect reality. Hence, the critical perspective in Shao's model is necessary. Given Shao's position as a Weiqi observer rather than player, he is able to criticize violations, showing how they affect players' mental states, as neither reality nor the game remain intact in a case of deceit.

> The wise are hurt by deceiving others,
> The honest err due to obtuseness.
> Truth and deceit blend together
> Name and reality are both ruined. (lines 37–40)

Shao's Confucian-based moral standards address wisdom in moral personal terms, such that the wise person is hurt by deceiving others and the trustworthy (*xin* 信) err due to their desire to win, and thus lose morality. In more universal terms, the loss of moral standards in the game is a loss of the distinction between truth and deceit (*zhenwei zhixiangza* 真偽之相雜) and a destruction of the appropriate correspondence between name and reality (*mingshi zhidouhui* 名實之都隳). When the correspondence between reality and names collapses, the outcome is a mechanical legalistic system, closer to Han Feizi's (280–233 BC) dangerous understanding, suggesting that names should be determined first and reality is to be shaped accordingly; in fact, he suggests ignoring reality and living the dangerous game that can best serve the empire. According to this view, names follow law and create reality, rather than reality following names. Thus, "there is no literature, but the laws serve as the teaching; there are no sayings of ancient kings but officials act as teachers; and there are no assassins, rather there is courage against the enemy."[62] The crucial correspondence between name and reality, as stressed already in ancient times, comes clearly in Xunzi's view that the reality represented by a name is objective, even if the name is merely conventional.[63] The objectivity of a reference depicted by a proper name keeps the distinction between appropriate (following convention) and inappropriate (violating convention). Hence, there are good names that are simple and direct, which readily bring the referent into one's mind, as opposed to "bad names" or fictitious names that distance from reality. Using names such that the referents are clear is using names correctly. However, when the distinction is ruined, the most basic foundation for human activity is lost. Likewise, Shao states his awareness of the importance of proper denotations, in which names refer to reality, even when playing a game.

Aware of the risk of a mechanistic-legalistic view caused by a total immersion in the game at the expense of abandoning reality, Shao writes,

> Gain is the root of loss,
> Fortune is the ladder to calamity.
> Heaven and Earth branch out into Conflict,
> Fire and Water change into Opposition. (lines 41–44)

Based on yin-yang dynamics, Shao first refers to gain as the root of loss (*de zheshi zhiben* 得者失之本) and to fortune as the ladder to calamity (*fuwei huozhiti* 福爲禍之梯). Shao alludes to the *Book of Change* first by referring to gain and loss, fortune and calamity, and then to specific natural elements that also constitute the hexagrams and trigrams of Heaven (Qian), Earth (Kun), Fire (*Li* 離), and Water (*Kan* 坎). While conflict and opposition comprise part of the game, the hexagrams Conflict (*Song* 訟) and Opposition (*kui* 睽) refer to outcomes of heaven and earth turning against each other in conflict and of fire and water being in opposition (which brings to extinction rather than flourishing). Qian and Kun can be realized in many ways, among which Conflict marks them as opposing powers that are not harmonized.[64]

The dynamic of Qian representing success, creativity, persistence, good fortune, and reward is distorted absent any horizon or support by their oppositions.[65] Similarly, Kun as responsive success, peaceful persistence, and righteousness sinks to regret and inevitable struggle without a dynamism toward yang creativity;[66] likewise with the trigrams Fire and Water. Moving harmoniously in the generative cycle, wood feeds fire; fire creates earth; earth bears metal; metal carries water, and water nourishes wood. Yet when in disagreement, as depicted in the combination of fire on top of water, in hexagram 38 denoting Opposition, then fire moves upward and water move downward like "two women living under one roof whose wishes do not accord."[67] When water and fire are harmonized, they move toward each other in balance and each fulfills its nature; when separate, each takes its own natural course with no balance; then, either water extinguishes fire, or fire evaporates water.

Acknowledging the fine line between reality and game, and the possibility of pretence taking over reality, Shao warns against the dangers of unjustified self-assurance in a somewhat skeptical tone, acknowledging the flux and transformation of reality.

> What was right the previous day
> Could be wrong today.
> What is strong today,
> Could be weak tomorrow. (lines 49–52)

Reaching the end of the first part of the poem, Shao challenges the canonical role of Confucian universal values, by summarizing the harm that can be caused in focusing on victory, rather than on the game as game, as not seeing that this very focus causes one's own fall—in particular, the fall of moral standards. He concludes with his idea of time as related to history, preparing the reader for the transition from the first part of the poem referring to observing the game to its second part on observing history through it.

> Using antiquity to observe later generations,
> The farthest traces are revealed at the end of days.
> Using the present to observe the past,
> How could it stop at Paoxi? (lines 53–56)

The last reference to time as antiquity, later generations, the end of days, present and past, suggests Shao's point that past and present should be used appropriately; yet, the flux of time and its relative nature necessitate eternally ongoing observation. In a poem from 1074, he makes the same poetic argument: "What once upon a time was said to be right, has now, it seems, somehow come to be wrong."[68]

Birdwhistell is right to claim that for Shao Yong, "time was—in a remarkably modern sense—not separable from behavior."[69] Dealing with the boundaries of the in and the out of events, with beginnings and endings, and with designation in time, Shao acknowledges the constant flow of time and one's inability to stop time, for example, through misusing the *Book Change* with superstitious ideas regarding being able to foretell, either within the game and outside it. Using the present to observe the past, one encounters Fuxi 伏羲 (or Paoxi 庖犧)—the legendary ruler who created the hexagrams as the beginning of all observation. However, Shao questions the termination of this inquiry with Fuxi, opening up to his view on the cycle of history as developed in the next part of the poem. The references to Fuxi serves a double purpose: first, it echoes the first part of observing Weiqi with one's eyes, as between legend and reality, Fuxi is, according to the legend, himself a true observer, who through observing nature came up with the trigrams. Second, by transcending inner boundaries and moving outside oneself to a game, reaching Fuxi calls for an exploration of history, to which Shao is now ready to proceed. This time, rather than transcending inner-personal boundaries and expand to the game or looking for life in the game, Shao is looking for the game in human life, or transcends the outer boundaries of the game to reach his own history.

FROM OUT TO IN: HISTORY AND THE GAME OF LIFE

Why, as Shao asks at the end of the first part of the poem, can't the observation of the past from the present stop with Fuxi? Shao's detailed response to the question is found in the second part of the poem, focusing on history and implying his view on time as cyclical. If the first part of the poem observed the game through the eyes, by means of observing movement from the within to the without, and thus transcending subjectivity, the next part of the poem reverses the movement. Moving on to specific historical events, by which the rules of history are exposed as inherently intertwined with moral rules, the second and longer part of the poem introduces the cognitive movement of observing history through the mind. Through the observation of times and events that are not present in one's life and cannot be observed by the senses (and therefore apparently exist outside oneself), this time the observer transcends history in order to return back to his own self as an extended self that embodies history.

The second part of the poem does not use many direct examples from Weiqi, yet some words and lines bear double meanings, which can be read in the framework of the game, as well as in that of life. The lack of references to Weiqi is itself an illustration to Shao's premise regarding the boundlessness of observation and the endless realms toward which a skillful observation of Weiqi can take the observer. If the first part of the poem introduced the life of the game, its second, longer part introduces the game of life, or life as the larger game that, like Weiqi, follows rules and has a framework that has to be acknowledged. The second part of the poem demonstrates the historical cycle through a description of rising, establishing, gaining independence, falling, and then rising again as a new beginning of a new cycle.[70]

Reflecting on history and game, the underlying claim is not only that playing has an important role in the history of civilization; rather, it is more comprehensive. Taking up from Huizinga, it is helpful to see that culture *arises* in the form of play, or that culture "is played" from its very beginning. According to Huizinga, even the most basic activities like fishing and hunting took on the form of play in archaic society. Moreover, through its distinguishing forms of play, a society articulates and conveys its unique understanding of life and the world we live in. In other words, culture has a play character.[71] Similarly, Shao's observation shifts to this play character, and more particularly the Weiqi character of human culture and history, in the Chinese context. Not only we can observe a strategic game and understand history through it (as in the first fifty-six lines in the poem); but also, through observing history, we find out that it embodies its own game, in which we are all players. In other words, if the first part of the poem observes the Weiqi board projecting itself on life, now the game is observed on the board of human history.[72] Shao focuses, accordingly, on a meticulous description of the most influential events in Chinese history. The historical events (depicted mostly from the political sphere from the times of the Three Sovereigns and Five Emperors—*Sanhuang wudi* 三皇五帝—through Shao's era of the Song dynasty) cannot be observed with the eyes, as they are all past and gone. Rather, history is observed and understood temporally with *the mind*; and the observing mind is revealed in the process as necessarily a moral mind.

To appreciate Shao's use of observation of history in the poem, it is crucial to see how understanding the succession of history is one of the important themes that he philosophizes on.

> The law (of history) began with Fuxi, completed in emperor Yao, modified in the period of the Three Kings, reached its limit in the period of the Five Despots, and disappeared in the time of Qin. This is the track of the cycle of peace and chaos throughout the ten thousand generations. (Chan 1963, 491, 8A:32a)

As point of departure for the understanding of past and present, just like in the poem, Fuxi represents the stage of birth. The completion with Yao symbolizes a stage of growth, the modification of Three Kings symbolizes maturity, and the limit with the Five Hegemons (Chen: Despots) symbolizes the beginning of decline culminating in the disappearance of Qin.[73] According to Shao's view, human history follows a repetitive cycle from birth, through growth and maturity, to decline, analogous to the changes of seasons as embodied in the classics. Shao's view of human history presents a correlation with the cyclical course of the four seasons and the stages of life-cycle, which are also tightly connected with moral duty and responsibility.[74] Seeing time as cyclical explains why an observation of the past from the present cannot stop with Fuxi. The period of the formation of Three Sovereigns was the spring of history; the growth of the Five Emperors was the summer; the maturing of the Three Sovereigns was the autumn; and the destruction of the Five Hegemons was the winter.[75] Since human history follows the pattern of the seasons, which is also the human pattern of birth, growth, maturity, and death, the development and decline in human life is as Zhou Dunyi taught, the inevitable way of the universe, which is repeated when the cycle is completed.

Moreover, as Shao said in the ending lines of the first part, "using antiquity for observing subsequent generation" as opposed to using the present for observing the past (lines 53–54) ends up as far as the height of the sky (*zhongtian lo uduanni* 终天露端倪; Chen: the end of days). Shao now observes the past to understand its outcomes and effects; since the pattern is universal and infinite, there is no actual past or present; rather, there is one flow. Human beings, bound to their own limited span of experience in time and space, see it as past, present, and future.

> The past and the present in the universe is comparable to morning and evening. When the present is viewed from the past, it is called the present, but when viewed from posterity, it will become the past. When the past is viewed from the present, it is called the past, but when viewed from the past itself, it would be its present. Thus, neither the present nor the past is necessarily the present or the past as such. The distinction is entirely due to our subjective points of view. People generations ago and people generations to come all have this subjective viewpoint. (Chan 1963, 485–86, 5:14b)

Shao sees how time functions as a category of perception and points to its relativity. Past, present, and future are all names by which we designate experience. Just like color or weight, which characterize things and yet are changing and unfixed, so is the assignment of events in time. In a somewhat Zhuangzian perspective, Shao understands time as a prospect that enables us to see that things we believed to be true, thought to be evident, or said to be right—are frequently proven wrong.[76]

Focusing back on the poem, Shao is ready to move on from Fuxi; the historical part opens, not surprisingly, in reference to Yao and Shun, the legendary rulers who are known in the tradition for upright leadership and pragmatic achievements of political order and morality.

> With hands folded in front, Yao and Shun bowed on yielding the throne,
> And the four evils still hesitated to follow. (lines 57–58)

Shao's first reference to the exemplary rule is in a Confucian spirit, not to Yao and Shun's political achievements, rather to their moral Way of yielding the throne. Yao passed the throne to Shun, who was known for his high morality; in particular, for his filial piety (rather than piety toward his own son, who was not considered virtuous). Shun, in turn, was renounced when Yu, the worthiest official at the time, could take up. Shun banished the four evils (*sixiong* 四兇) who were unwilling to follow the moral Way, and subordinated to Shun only after being punished by him.[77]

The bond between history and human moral duty is created through Shao's idea of the threefold nature of observation, whereby observing history as observing with the mind is located between observing with the eyes and observing with Order, between the personal and the universal, between phenomena and absolute, focusing on the mind—the unique human capability. The human mind being a moral mind requires that from the perspective of *observation with the mind* as a form of human understanding, the game of history must embody an ethical form. Thus, there is a dramatic change of spirit in the second part of the poem: When the mind observes, one sees actions together with their moral value; namely, if it is a human mind that observes, then ethics enters the game more vigorously, with momentous outcomes. Shao moves on from Yao and Shun in a detailed chronology that exemplifies his message on history, related to morality, as observed by the mind.[78] Shao presents a historical moral reflection through the example of the leading figures of Tang of the Shang (1675–1646 BC); his follower Yi Yin (1648–1549 BC); and the Duke of Zhou—none of whom, despite presenting norms to fashion institutions, could avoid a degeneration of morality.[79]

> Benevolence was defeated by fame,
> Righteousness was squeezed by profit.
> Order and chaos don't end by themselves,
> Conventionality or reform occurs only when appropriate.
> Passing the throne to the worthy, but not to the son,
> Flaws and blemishes occur in both the worthy and the foolish.
> Passing it to the son, but not to the worthy,
> Sores and wounds grew in the descendants. (lines 65–72)

Shao rests on the Confucian moral standards, according to which treatment of a malfunction should include internal and not only external parameters. Only at this point does he clearly state his view as derived from his observation in the first part, which was only implied earlier: humanity (Chen: benevolence) and rightness (Chen: righteousness), rather than fame or profit, should guide people. Shao is critical regarding historical situations in which personal moral standards were overcome by egotistic interests or in which humanity was defeated by the wish for fame (*ming* 名). This description of moral personal life is paralleled in the sociopolitical realm with rightness being squeezed by profit (*li* 利).

Thus, he arrives at the Confucian moral position as clearly stated in the opening of *Mencius*, where he encounters King Hui of Liang and rebuffs his presupposition that coming all the way to meet him might have derived from a wish to profit the king or the state. Similarly, in his famous example of the child on the verge of falling into a well, fame and profit are presented as morally unacceptable motivations. Following this view, the historical decline of morality must be understood as a political decline as well, yielding chaos. Given the inability to separate personal ethics from politics (as a case of social ethics), "Order and chaos don't end by themselves, reform occurs only when appropriate," as line 67 reads. Political order (*zhi* 治) should replace chaos (*luan* 亂) through moral effort, rather than by itself (*ziyi* 自已), and reform that is not timely can only take the form of a legalistic—mechanistic-modification, which people never welcome and cannot truly internalize.

Referring to passing the throne, Shao neither merely praises Yao's transferring of the thrown to Shun rather than to his morally unfit son, nor condemns Zhou who passed it to his son rather than to a more remote but moral person. Rather, he is aware of the moral *conflict*, acknowledging the difficulty inherent in passing the throne both to a morally flawed son and to a person who is morally upright, and yet choosing him can hurt one's descendant and harm one's commitment to the family. Shao makes his point regarding the centrality of morality in the observation of human history such that without the human moral perspective, the cycle of history cannot be fully understood and reasoned, and hence one cannot aspire to genuine progress and renewal.

The centrality of morality in Shao's view of history should not be abandoned under the impression that the epistemological perspective he takes is the central message regarding his notion of observation, while in the context of his broader philosophical ideas, his number theory, and to some extent the cyclical view of history should be considered primary. As the poem shows, morality cannot and should not be taken as negligible, or even secondary to Shao's epistemological perspective. In fact, morality can be separated neither from his philosophy of observation nor from his concept of history. In this context, Don Wyatt underscores the centrality of moral thought in Shao's philosophy—not only as restricted to human behavior, but also as applied expansively to the world at large.[80] This rather significant role of morality is read in the second part of the poem, in observing historical political moves, together with their inner moral value. Through this emphasis, Shao clarifies beyond doubt that in his system (in line with traditional Confucianism), ethics, politics, and history are interrelated. Moreover, from an epistemological perspective, observing political history through clear ethical categories introduces morality as inherent in one's categories of observation.

The point is that while ethics is the search for personal good and politics searches for political or common good, they both serve a single game, followed by a single set of rules. A situation in which the personal aspiration is to be moral but the political one is for profit cannot be accepted in this view. If we first observed with Shao that one cannot deceive in a game and be honest in life, now we see that history makes a similar point, yet with more vigor: one cannot take care of the state when personally corrupted. Unlike in modern politics—in which ethics and politics are sometimes perceived an oxymoron, such that ethics is the realm of authenticity and purity and politics is considered somewhat defiled and filled with personal interests—Shao follows the Confucian line, seeing politics as the part of *ethics* that relates to the regulation of clusters such as governments, nations, or states. Morality is considered a necessary prerequisite that cannot be compromised when considering the safety of a state alongside its peace and prosperity throughout generations. As we see in the next lines of the poem, inner strength is one's moral strength, as demanded against foreign control or conquest; thus, giving up morality for the sake of prosperity ends up in destruction. Shao offers a series of historical outcomes of acts that oppose Order by using power to block rather than advance, provoking conflicts, generating suspicion, attacking, defeating, or being cruel, leading to unfortunate outcomes of exile, defeat, and death.[81] Shao, again, pauses for a moral reflection on the first emperor's use of various strategies to maximize power at others' expanse.

> The sky ended where the sun was,
> Earth extended to the endless extremes.
> Far and near were all included
> Vertical and horizontal were all under command. (lines 101–4)

Before moving on to the harmful consequences, the lines first describe a great territorial success, as opposed to a moral decline, ending with the total decline of the Qin dynasty. The examples of Qin Shi Huang 秦始皇 (246–210 BC), who died before the completion of his palace and the fall of his dynasty, serves Shao for an important history-Weiqi analogy, which Chen titled The Strong Die, as one of four main analogies to Weiqi situations in which advantage turns into disadvantage in one move.[82] First, Qin Shi Huang's well-known unification of China, which encompassed a series of major economic and political reforms and involved undertaking gigantic projects (including the construction of the Great Wall, the Terracotta Army, and a massive national road system)—was attained at the expense of human rights and numerous lives. The first emperor's destructive power is not neglected when Shao describes the territorial achievement together with the disastrous outcome in which "swords and arrows were melted" (line 109) to serve the emperor's purposes and disarm the multitudes; "The *Book of History* and *Classic of Poetry* were burned" (line 110) in the emperor's infamous act of book burning in 213 BC; and "the nobility was abolished and prefects established" (line 111) in his massive burning alive of scholars. According to Shao, "The trunk was strengthened and the branches weakened" (line 112); namely, the emperor acted against the natural Order (to which the historical cycle fits) of strengthening the roots, giving life to the trunk, then the branches, the flower, and the fruit, which ends up as seeds for more roots. Believing in the guarding power of the rocks of the Great Wall, the first emperor's thought he cannot be threatened (lines 114–15) and hence "regarded people as ants, treating materials as sand and mud" (lines 119–20).

In the next sixteen lines (lines 125–40), Shao offers another important example, referring to the fight for the throne between Liu Bang (ruling 202–195 BC)—the founder of the Han dynasty and one of the few dynasty founders in Chinese history who emerged from the peasant class—and the military leader Xiang Yu (232–2 BC). The example serves another history-Weiqi analogy that Chen titled The Weak Win, demonstrating a dramatic change in superiority between the two historical figures. This change of superiority can be demonstrated in Weiqi situations, when an apparently weak player ultimately wins the game by good reasoning that leads the opponent into a strategic trap. The Weiqi of history is exemplified in Xiang's loss of superiority in numbers and in political connections to Liu Bang, because of Xiang's arrogance and Liu's good strategies.[83]

Shao moves on to historical examples from the Han dynasty, the period of disunity, and the Jin and the Sui dynasties, before referring to the founding of the Tang dynasty. The latter serves according to Chen, as an analogy of lurking danger strikes, again analogous to Weiqi, as illustrated in Shao's presentation of the power struggle in the Tang court. Shao refers to the official Huan Yanfan (653–706) of the Tang, who was a key figure in the coup that overthrew Empress Wu (625–705) and restored Emperor Zhongzong (656–710). Huan's belief that there is no threat in his deed was apparently revealed in the carelessness of his action: Wu Sansi (d. 707), whom Huan did not consider to be a real threat and thus did not kill, gained power and later exiled Huan under the pretense of false accusations. Ultimately, Huan was killed in exile in a cruel manner. The analogy to death in Weiqi, which can sometimes be an outcome of negligence that can be avoided with more caution and awareness of one's deeds, offers perspective on the full historical game.[84]

Shao then refers to the destruction of both Tang capitals: first the eastern capital Luoyang, and next the western capital Chang'an, as an outcome of the emperor's arrogance (lines 241–48). Titled by Chen The Arrogant Fail, this example serves the last history-Weiqi analogy.[85] As the poem attests, while the emperor was preoccupied with singing and dancing, both capitals fell and were destroyed (line 247). The high cost of this arrogance cannot be overlooked.

> When joy reaches an extreme, then sorrow arrives,
> When favors accumulate, then disasters join hands,
> There was nothing else that could be done;
> Raising the eyes, whom could one be close to? (lines 249–52)

Referring again to the inescapable yin-yang dynamics, the lines describe extreme situations of joy and favor ending up in sorrow and disaster, leading to complete loneliness and helplessness. While definitely true in the game of history, similarly in Weiqi games, a moment of smugness can lead to a defeat that cannot be rendered null and void. Shao refers to the situation toward the end of the Tang, when the government granted increased powers to military governors who, as Shao mentions, had no respect among the subjects (lines 254). The Tang dynasty, which was largely a period of progress, stability, and notable innovations and developments in art and literature, ended up in decline, following the cycle of history, and the yin-yang dynamics of rise and fall. After the destruction of both capitals, the dynasty never recovered from that setback and suffered severe damage, as described in poetic terms.

> A big tail is known as hard to wag,
> And isn't a long whip difficult to wield?
> Fostering evils, worry will definitely come;

Raising a tiger, harm will eventually arrive.
How bumpy and jolty were the paces of the state,
The emperor's mind was ashamed in vain.
When the time comes, flowers blossom;
With momentum gone, leaves wither and are shed. (lines 265–72)

The rule of the last days of the Tang is described as a tail that is too heavy to wag or to protect the body, or a whip that can't wield, fostering evil that results in worry, withering, and falling apart. Thus, the Five Dynasties and Ten Kingdoms (907–960) ensued in quick succession (line 274).

Before moving on to the Song dynasty, Shao pauses once more to philosophize on difficulties, focusing again on one's moral responsibility for them. In this context, he relates torment of body with that of the mind and considers harmfulness of language and the way in which change occurs as often unexpected and not always wished for. "The cunning and the cheat were often gloomy inside; difficulties and sorrows were often self-induced" (lines 289–90). When both the cunning and the fraud find themselves gloomy, this is a sign of the decline of the inner moral self. External pain or harm, depicted in the poem as harming one's skin, can be prevented more easily than solving the pain of one's heart (lines 291–92). A cheat can perhaps act as if he is not in pain, and yet the severely damaged heart is in pain. In life and in game, minute motions have far-reaching outcomes; words may cause disaster if not carefully considered and used (lines 293–94).

The dynamics of life that can never be predetermined or anticipated bring Shao to an awareness of natural desired changes and transformations that occur by themselves and can't be foreseen. At the peak of a yang movement, yin begins to move, and ultimately yin leads to yang. In this way, a dynasty may fall at the highest point of success and flourishing, while another arises at the lowest point of decline. In Shao's words: "About to rise, one still plunges down; On the verge of falling, one is yet held up" (lines 295–96). Then, referring to the significance of the various sources of cure—in health, land cultivation, education, family encounters, and political ventures—Shao writes the following:

Only those who can eradicate serious illness,
May be referred to as excellent doctors.
Lying in waste long, the land is hard and infertile;
Difficult to travel, roads are dangerous and choppy.
Without seeing the emergence of a true master,
What practices can one perform? (lines 299–304)

Approaching the ending of the historical observation, Shao takes up his observation of human pain in returning to Confucian essentials and discussing the significance of practice and ways to correct malpractice, in particular, through assistance of a good teacher, as analogous to a doctor's treating sickness. A doctor that cannot cure from sicknesses is not a good doctor; a land that was not plowed is not good for sowing; a road that was not paved is not good for passage; a Master who does not guide for practice is not a true Master. Moving to on to his own time, demonstrating learning from the past, Shao praises the Song's enabling the development of proper functions and glorifies the peace of his days. In doing so, Shao applies terms of coming back to order and reason, ending the second part with a direct reference to Weiqi players as national hands (*guoshou* 國手) and offering a concluding line that refers back to the analogy between history and the board game, which comprises the basis of the poem. Ready to move on to the last part of the poem, with the finest observation that is attained with Order, the message of the second part is attained through Shao's transcending the outer boundaries of the game so as to return to understanding Chinese history. The history that shaped his personality, or the history that is part of who he is, brings him to the understanding that he should never rely on anything as a granted future promise; rather, through observing the Weiqi of history, he is more capable to play morally.

> Our dynasty of Song thus laid its foundation
> Wise plans were formed everywhere,
> A host of heroes followed with outstretched necks.
> Till now it has been over one hundred years,
> And people have known nothing of weapons and shields.
> Success and failure must follow fate,
> Rise and fall are bound to the times.
> Heaven's designs are not often set up,
> For "national hands" there are no conventional practices.
> Past things are all just vestiges,
> Books from before can only somewhat be relied upon.
> Comparing them to Bo and Weiqi,
> There is not one iota's difference. (lines 305–20)

TRANSCENDING THE IN-OUT DUALITY

Back to Yin-Yang Dynamics

The first part of the poem brings the observer into the game so that subjective or inner boundaries are transcended by one's reflexivity. In the second part, the observer transcends the idea of history through reflecting back on oneself. In its third part, the poem surpasses the very in-out dichotomy. Shao's observation in the first two parts—first on Weiqi as a microcosm for human life (observed with the eyes), then on human history as a game of Weiqi (observed with the mind)—demonstrates the essential role of observation in his philosophy and, moreover, Shao's special attention to structure, rules, and framework. However, the epistemological game reaches its fullest in the last part of the poem, suggesting the most complete level of observation; namely, observation with Order, or the phase at which what the eyes see and how the mind interprets coalesce within the single Order of being and knowing. In this part, Shao's description comes together to form a structured model for a comprehensive view, as derived from his observing Weiqi on the game board and on the board of history.

Anne Birdwhistell writes, "The problem of the structure of events lies at the heart of Shao Yong's questions concerning the phenomena of change."[86] In particular, the notion of structural boundaries is underscored in his discussing beginnings and endings in human thinking and behavior.[87] In this way, Birdwhistell's suggestion that Shao's philosophy presents an attempt at creating a theory (even if he was not aware of creating it) is helpful.[88] This perspective is reaffirmed in the poem, in particular through its last part, which combines the subject's understanding of game as life and of life as game in one unified system.

Shao sums up his understanding of the essential change and transformation in life as rooted in the philosophy of yin and yang. The polarities of rise and fall, win and lose, large and small, internal and external, motion and tranquility, leading and following, forward and backward, future and past, life and death, are all vital, both in the game and in history. Shao opens the final part of the poem in reaffirming the Way—the ultimate standard—as the basis for understanding the world's dynamic structure, in line with both Confucian ideas and some insights from Daoism.

> Waning and waxing as the sky turns,
> Yin and yang are the scope of the Way.
> Weal and woe are the changes for people,
> Motion and quiescence are the keys to events. (lines 321–28)

Shao's observation regarding Order opens in providing the reader with four perspectives on change: first, nature (translated above as sky *tian* 天) is ongoing transformation, or waning and waxing (*xiaozhang* 消长); second, the Way—the utmost perfection and the scope for everything—is presented through the yin-yang dialectic of creation; third, its human expression is in the changes of weal and woe or fortune and misfortune (*jixiong* 吉凶), referring back to the hexagram system of the *Book of Change*; fourth, in daily affairs (*shi* 事), the key for understanding nature, the scope of the Way, and its human manifestation is motion and tranquility (*dongjing* 动静) as the foundation for the philosophy of change.

According to the present understanding, the opening lines of the third part of the poem correspond with lines 39–56 that end its first part. Earlier, Shao described oppositions seen by the eyes and created, or at least contributed, by human beings: "Truth and deceit blend together / Name and reality are both ruined / Gain is the root of loss / Fortune is the ladder of calamity." In other words, in the first part of the poem, by observing with the eyes, Shao sees *outcomes* of the transforming nature of reality when intervened by human beings. Due to the human contribution to experience, the transformation departs from its natural Order. Guided by neither Order, nor even by the mind, the world does not appear to be in proper organization. Yet deceit can be avoided and loss can be overcome if observed by a moral mind, guided by Order, according to which name and reality match. The first part of Shao's poem, in which he introduces oppositions that are humanly created such as deceit as opposed to truth (*zhenwei* 真偽) and name as opposed to reality (*mingshi* 名實), reflects a Laozian understanding of sense-guided dynamics, as in

> The whole world recognizes the beautiful as the beautiful,
>   Yet this is only the ugly;
> the whole world recognizes the good as the good,
>   Yet this is only the bad. (*Laozi*, ch. 2)

The root for Shao's nondualistic attitude can be assisted, again, by *Laozi*'s criticism on the dualistic mode of thinking in which the recognition of beauty or of goodness creates ugliness and evil. One may derive that if human beings had not searched for the beautiful or the good, the distinction would have never been made between the beautiful (or the true, or the good) and its opposite; and hideous (or name, or deceit, or evil) would not have been created. These distinctions distance us from the Way, rather than bringing us closer to it; hence, as the continuing words of the verse in *Laozi* express, ultimately this way of thinking should be discarded. In nature, unlike human artificial creation,

> Something and Nothing produce each other;
> The difficult and the easy complement each other;
> The long and the short off-set each other;
> The high and the low incline towards each other;
> Note and sound harmonize with each other;
> Before and after follow each other.

Similarly for the second part of *Laozi* 2, the third part of Shao's poem offers a nondualistic picture of the natural production. Apparently similar to the changes described in the first part, yet in fact in diametric contrast, the natural process is a process of spontaneous yin-yang transformation, rather than creation of the human dichotomizing mind. The sky turns, or nature moves and changes, and in this movement things decrease and grow. These transformations equally affect the cosmos, the game, and the human deed. In the poem, these changes are understood through one basic rule of yin and yang, for which motion and tranquility serve as key. Shao's view on movement and the Way as a dynamic perfection appears in his broader philosophy.

> The Way creates heaven and earth and all things without showing itself. All these are patterned after the Way. Yang is the function of the Way, while yin is its substance. (Chan 1963, 489, 7A:16a)

The Way as the one creative rule or pattern does not reveal itself and yet is seen in everything one might encounter. Yang, as its active creative aspect, multiplies in various functions, while the tranquility of yin is the substance that allows the functions. Shao presents yin-yang as one force with interdependent directions that can only be known through each other; yet yin is the foundation of yang, and yang the embodiments of yin.[89] The yin-yang movement in the human realm results in appropriate human changes and transformations (*ren bianhua* 人變化) in times of high and low, or fortune and misfortune, whose hinge or key (*shuji* 樞機) lies in activity and tranquility (*dongjing* 動靜), rather than in human attempts to control them. Shao follows Zhou Dunyi's line of thought, stressing the importance of motion in which tranquility comprises an essential part; not as complete stillness or nothingness, but rather as the yin aspect of the cosmic dynamic Order. This sentiment is clearly expressed in his *Supreme Principles*.

> Heaven is born of activity and earth is born of tranquility. The interaction of activity and tranquility gives full development to the Way of heaven and earth. At the first appearance of activity, yang is produced. The interaction of yin and yang gives full development of the functions of heaven. At the first appearance of tranquility, the element of weakness is produced. When weakness reaches its limit, the element of strength is produced. The interaction of these two elements gives full development to the functions of earth. (Chan 1963, 484, 5:1b)

Proceeding through cosmological detailing of the creative process, starting from heaven and earth, to sun, moon, stars, zodiacal spaces, water, fire, earth, soil, stone, day and night, cold and warmth, forms, interactions, plants and animals, Shao arrives at the human being as the most intelligent creature.[90] Notably, Shao's theoretical framework of change sees the world as interaction and transformation, in which both activity and tranquility are essential in one producer. Softness (*rou* 柔) and firmness (*gang* 剛) are related either to yin's tranquility or to yang's activity and thus are inherent to creation. Heaven is the source of yin-yang interaction, and earth responds in strength and weakness.

Shao explains this transformative interdependence in more detail with the use of the idea of the one undifferentiated Supreme Polarity that is known to humans through the movement of the two modes of yin and yang, in a way that reminds of Zhou Dunyi's TJTS, and yet with more emphasis on the symbolism of the *Book of Change*.

> As the Utmost Ultimate becomes differentiated, the Two Modes (yin and yang) appear. Yang descends and interacts with yin, and yin rises to interact with yang, and consequently the four forms (major and minor yin and yang) are constituted. Yin and yang interact and generate the four forms of heaven: the element of weakness and the element of strength interact and generate the four forms of earth; and consequently the eight elements (heaven, water, fire, thunder, wind, water in motion, mountain, and earth) are completed. The eight elements intermingle and generate the myriad things. Therefore the one is differentiated into the two, two into four, four into eight, eight into sixteen, sixteen into thirty-two, and thirty-two into sixty-four. (Chan 1963, 489, 7A:24b)[91]

This differentiation of the one into multiple manifestations is repeated with specific reference to human nature, which is essentially one in type and yet receives its particular embodiments. The poem makes no mention of the Supreme Polarity, and yet in Shao's writing this concept serves as a bridge to human nature, which the first two parts of the poem refer to: the first part personally, and the second part politically.

> Everything follows the evolutionary Order of the Great Ultimate, the Two modes, the Four Forms, and the Eight Elements. Everything also possesses the two forms of time, the past and the present … (A)ll things receive their nature from heaven but the nature of each is peculiar to it. In man it becomes human nature. In animals and plants it becomes the nature of animals and plants. (8B:9b)

Order in the Manifested World

Returning back to the poem, the transformative nature of the universe is shown from an epistemological perspective as the inherent exchange between in and out. Shao's theoretical view of yin and yang reflect knowledge attained from inner sources and knowledge from external sources, which jointly preserve the continuity of being, from Supreme Polarity to human life, this time from an epistemological perspective. Thus, the next lines (325–32) move on from the Order of transformation as "yin and yang is the scope of the Way" and "motion and quiescence is the key of events" to their concrete manifestations and outcomes as known in the human world, then understood with an unexpected twist.

> Fast runners trip first,
> Slow bloomers wither later.
> Rather than being harmed doubly,
> It's better to forget both.
> Pursuing fish, one should use a trammel,
> Catching hares, one should use a snare.
> Once you have it, you should not forget—
> A sheep's constitution yet clad in a tiger's skin.

The idea of motion and tranquility as the creative rule of the Way is pronounced now in concrete terms: fast running leads to tripping, slow blooming allows longer burgeoning. The somewhat surprising apparent anti-epistemological conclusion regarding the process of change and transformation has clear Daoistic overtones: it is better to forget blooming and withering, or in other words, the only way to progress is by letting nature transform in its time and flow. The idea of forgetting both (*liangwang* 兩忘) as known in the *Zhuangzi* tradition receives a moral twist already in Zhou Dunyi's work, as we have seen; forgetting enables one not to get stuck in a fixed perspective and is thus helpful for progress. Shao's reference to the fish and the hares gives the impression that after asserting his Confucian moral stand in the second part, in the third part of the poem, Shao integrates Confucian values with Daoist perspectivisim into one theoretical framework. The "forgetting both" and thus having it, as Shao describes next, necessitates undergoing a significant epistemological shift that can be better understood through Antonio Cua's stressing (in the Zhuangzian context) that we are urged to forget all distinctions to attain the Way and become one with heaven.[92]

The important difference between Shao's view and that of the *Zhuangzi* is the essential significance of framework in Shao's thought, as opposed to the *Zhuangzi*'s ridding of all frameworks. The *Zhuangzi* takes forgetting as a response to the very existence of theories, demonstrated by the example of the fish who forget each other in the river and the lakes (*xiangwang yuwujiang* 相忘於江湖), who moisten each other as if remembering only upon dying.[93] The "both" Shao asks to forget is not each other, in the moral sense; rather, the distinction between fast runners and slow bloomers must be forgotten to avoid labeling and presupposition.

Shao uses the idea of forgetting to reaffirm the necessity of the framework that allows this forgetting. Saying that pursuing fish, one should use a trammel; catching hares, one should use a snare (*qiuyu biyiquan, huotu biyidi* 求魚必以筌, 获兔必以第) he clearly refers to the Zhuangzian analogy, yet with an important critical twist.[94] Like in the *Zhuangzi*, the fish are caught by the trammel, and the hare by the snare. However, rather than stressing the worthlessness of the trammel and snare after catching the fish or hare, Shao stresses their necessity; they *should* be used (*biyi* 必以) for us to be able to hunt and catch.

According to Shao, having the fish or the hare, one cannot forget (*dezhi bunengwang* 得之不能忘) that "a tiger skin can hide a sheep."[95] Analogously, the meaning or the true essence of things is learned through forgetting the presupposed artificial distinctions we make, such as good opposed to bad. Forgetting the presuppositions enables us to see what is, and not what is thought to be seen, or ought to be seen, or selectively wished to be seen. We are called on to develop a disciplined maintenance, watchful of biases and preferences reflected in distinctions, not for the benefit of not-seeing, but rather for the sake of an improved capacity to see. Forgetting both as an outcome of the process of observation leads to depth-vision as a theoretical presupposition. As part of Shao's process of observation, it is bound in a theory. The vision that exposes the true nature of things amounts to using the right theory for observation, as the only tool for getting the true meaning.

Anne Birdwhistell stresses the importance of having a theory of the various forms of change for Shao Yong, as follows:

> He describes the patterns that make up the structure of the universe and the methods by which human beings attain knowledge, as well as the fundamental universal processes, their operations, and their interrelationships. He also discussed the system of symbols—the hexagrams of the *Yijing*....
>
> I do not claim that Shao Yong consciously thought about this theoretical aspect of his philosophy.... By emphasizing the implicit theoretical structure of his thought, I hope to make explicit the theoretical context of his ideas. The theoretical context is important because it provides ideas with their meaning. It is the theory (as form of context) that makes possible the meaning of concepts.[96]

Birdwhistell refers to a passage from HJJSS with the very same allusion to *Zhuangzi*, which is, in fact, a response to his relativistic rejection of any theory.

> The images and the numbers are (like) the net and the trap. Words and ideas are (like) the fish and the hare. When one catches a fish or a hare, and one says that it must have been due to the net and trap, that is permissible. If one discards the net and the trap and seeks for the fish and the hare, then I have not yet seen one be successful. (Birdwhistell 76).

As Birdwhistell claims, in the above passage Shao stresses that structure—in this case represented in his reference to images and numbers—is necessary to perceive the world correctly. While the passage compares images and numbers to trammels and snares, in the poem Shao does not give exact reference to the type of theoretical framework depicted in the poem as a game, having its rules for which it abides and through which it can be understood. In its last part, the poem presents the game and its players as abiding by the same Order. Thus, Shao's attempt to understand something about the world through a Weiqi game as microcosm and then be able to understand the happening in the game through observing history leans on a theoretical presupposition that Order is ultimately one.

The transcending of intertheoretical boundaries is attained when the observing subject moves not *within* theoretical boundaries, but beyond them. Discussing the Weiqi game as a model brings Shao to theoretical conclusions that lead him to a better understanding of practice. By understanding that which should be forgotten and that which shouldn't, Shao develops his idea with reference to both Daoist and Confucian sources.

> "The Way is great," one has heard from Laozi,
> "Talent is difficult to come by," said Confucius.
> Making a shape, one can be easily enlightened,
> Facing the board, why worry about being confused?
> How could black and white be obscured?
> Are death and life enough to rely on?
> Responding to opportunity, act as if to hit the target,
> Meeting a knife blade, tolerate not a hair of error. (lines 333–40)

Through quoting from both Laozi and Confucius, blind veneration of canonical sources is criticized. Referring to the Way by first alluding to *Laozi* 25, has special significance with regard to seeing things as they are versus perceiving them through their given names. The short reference to the Laozian verse is meant to bring to mind the whole verse, in particular, its mentioning the idea of Before Heaven (*xiantian* 先天), which had special significance for Shao. Laozi's verse opens with the chaotic nature of the Way as silent and void—something that cannot be named; that is accomplished in darkness, born before heaven and earth, quiet, unchanging, and chaotic. Since its name is unknown, it is styled by the writer simply as the Way. Henceforth its other titles ensue, the first of which is great. However, no name is right, not even *dao*. Hence, one should ultimately forget names. The verse exemplifies Laozi's view of the inability to define through distinctions, leading to forgetting. Shao wishes to incorporate this forgetting not as a removal of functions, but rather as avoiding the perceptions that are reflected in distinctions, not for the benefit of not-seeing, but so as to gain a capacity to see clearly, or in a Zhuangzian expression, seeing things equally.

Observing without Boundaries

Shao, who could find ample references to the vastness of the Way, refers to it in the specific Laozian context, alluding to the dual citizenship of the Way as that which cannot be said, which is manifested through the myriad things and shapes—as mentioned earlier in the poem, as both substance and function. In other words, that which is unseen in the world allows it to be what it is, or in itself-so (*ziran* 自然). As if to keep the desired balance, following the mentioning of the Laozian connectedness between the greatness of the Way and that of human, Shao immediately provides a Confucian reference to *Analects* 8:20, that talent is hard to find (*cainan* 才難), reminding his reader that very few humans realize their potentiality, and keeping the framework as moral. In this way, a poetic analogy is made between the Way that cannot be grasped, told, or easily attained and is yet so crucial in life, and talent which is hard to find, is not easily defined, and yet is necessary for human life. In particular, the abstract Way can be reflected and observed through concrete human talent. This analogy has special significance in the context of Weiqi, as the next two lines remind us.

"Making a shape" can self-enlighten (*zaoxing neng ziwu* 造形能自悟) refers again to both to making a shape on the Weiqi board and to the form of understanding, through a scheme or a diagram. While in Weiqi, the importance of shape revolves around how well a group creates or removes life and territory, so is the theoretical framework to life. A good shape in Weiqi signifies a position that enables a group to live and is not easy to attack; recognizing the difference between a good shape and a bad shape is essential in becoming a good Weiqi player—and its equivalent in life is just as critical. Finding a "good shape" in life is a necessary condition for everything one does and understands. Through Weiqi, Shao is able to exemplify his view on the necessity of distinctions that are based on corresponding forms, which allow understanding of what is appropriate and what is not (as opposed to distinctions that have no correspondence to form). Moreover, like in life, a shape in Weiqi must take into account its surrounding position, and in the end amounts to transforming a weak position into a strong one.[97] Shao completes the Weiqi analogy by questioning reasons for skilled players' confusion.[98] In other words, Shao sees the board as analogous to a theory of reality, and the reference to "black and white" that cannot be obscured again connects the game stones with the yin-yang symbol and the corresponding active forces of life.

Loyal to the fundamental notions of life and death within the game, Shao reminds his reader that any near-death or ensured life situation can change in an instant. Even the strictest subjective boundaries of birth and death, the clearest boundaries of the person, decompose through the rhetorical question, Are death and life enough to rely on? In the game, the end is unknown, and yet groups of stones are divided into those that are alive, dead, or unsettled. Alive means that the group survives unconditionally if the players make the best moves; namely, any attack can be responded to with a defensive move. "Unsettled" means that an attack can kill the group, and yet if the defensive move is played first, it is saved.[99] Dead stones are removed from the board when the game ends and put back in the bowls. It is considered a mistake to remove the dead stones before such a move is clearly revealed as a tactically helpful move. The loss of a life of a group can signify the loss of the game, but is not necessarily so. Efficiently responding to a challenge may involve making a move that completely transforms the situation. One may know the general status of one's own life or death and of the opponent's life or death and yet, the knowledge never suffices for understanding the full picture. The polar Weiqi conditions—life as opposed to death, winning as opposed to losing, leading as opposed to failing, moving as opposed to resting, black as opposed to white, forward as opposed to backward—follow the polarities of heaven and earth, male and female, motion and quiescence, being and nonbeing, fortune and misfortune, life and death as rooted in the *Book of Change*. All are relative dynamic processes, reflecting the yin-yang constitution of the Way. At this point, Shao is ready to decode his theoretical implications into practical ones and verify them in juxtaposition with the world. Shao moves on to a series of ensuing practical recommendations for action that is harmonious with nature.

> Don't be surprised by a bystander's laughter,
> And don't prevent the glancing of cold eyes.
> As long as you are well-versed in exquisite uses,
> Why worry about many forked roads?
> Conforming with the Way, the Way is also achieved,
> Acting before Heaven, Heaven is not violated.
> Exhaust principles to fulfill human nature,
> Speak freely and deliver the words.
> Looking outward, one then knows simplicity,
> After listening, one discerns silence. (lines 341–50)

Shao offers some general guidelines: The attained skill allows coping with surprises, opening up to the unexpected, and accepting different roads. The idea of attaining the Way, naturally by conforming or being equal to it (*tongdao daoyide* 同道道亦得), seems like a play on *Laozi* 23 saying that in following affairs according to the Way, the follower of the Way is equal to the Way. In *Laozi*, following the Way is being the Way, such that one effaces one's identity and distinctive characteristic and one's self is one's deeds. Shao's wish to *morally* be one with the Way is expressed in his stating that before heaven, heaven is not violated (*xiantian tianfuwei* 先天天弗違), citing the *Book of Change*, connecting heaven and (great) man.[100] Shao's idea about the more speculative type of knowledge—before heaven (*xiantian* 先天)—as opposed to the experiential after heaven (*houtian* 後天) brings him closer to the knowledge of that which has not yet occurred (the before heaven) as more advantageous than of what has already been shown, as the learning of the mind rather than the learning of the traces.[101] Acting in this way, heaven is preserved and Order can be fully realized in human nature.[102]

Shao understands Order as related to nature and mandate: not above things or outside them but rather within them, as the very constitution of things. Order is related to actual practice and revealed in it, similarly to nature that is reflected in one's thought, feelings, and behavior, or to one's mandate known when practiced and experienced. Just like our inability to know a baby's nature until she grows up and it is manifested through her speech and behavior, we cannot know someone's mandate until the person tries it out and we can observe what was done with it. Accordingly, sagehood is the realization of nature, Order, and mandate. Through this perspective, Order is presented as the reality of things. Shao takes up Zhou Dunyi's idea from *Tongshu* chapter 22, titled "Order, Nature, and Mandate," in which Zhou suggests one actuality and ten thousand differentiations (*yishi wenfen* 一實萬分) to express his own understanding of Order.

> It is said in the *Book of Changes*, "investigate Order to the utmost and fully develop nature until destiny is fulfilled."[103] By principle is meant the principle inherent in things. By nature is meant nature endowed by Heaven. And by destiny is meant to abide in principle and one's nature. How else can we abide in principle and our nature except through the Way? (Chan 1963, 485, 5:7a)

Shao stresses that Order is inherent in things (as later on understood also by Zhu Xi and his predecessor Cheng Yi), rather than in the mind. This point is consequential in Shao's view on the three levels of observation. Rather than moving from the most concrete level as things observed with the eyes to the more abstract level in which the mind observes, and finally ending with the universal Order, he returns *back to things*, but with the achievement of seeing through Order (thus avoiding the idealistic-solipsistic trap).

The moral mind is indeed active in knowing the world and understanding its events; yet Order is not a mental configuration. Shao thereby roots his epistemological system back in the world we live in, and brings his philosophy down to earth. The full three-dimensional epistemological process starts in a sensual acquaintance with the myriad things as in-out movement, progresses to the work of mind through reflection, cognition and theorizing, and ends in coming back to the phenomenal world, with refinement and awareness of subtleties as unifying in-out.

Order is revealed an epistemological framework in the sense that it functions as the rules of the game that constitute the Confucian form of life. While a form of life is bound to its own rules, these rules create the outlook; they function as terms of reference and instructions for behavior. On the one hand, these rules, being inherent, create the world; on the other, they constitute the particular way of life of the Confucian follower. Although Order is inherent, these rules are created dynamically according to common doctrines, traditions, and habits. Thus, Order eventually becomes a product of this (moral) world too, and as a product of this world, it can be internalized. Through this internalization, Order constitutes the world and causes one to act in a certain way. In causing one to act in a certain way and know a certain world, Order actuates the Way of life, creates the world, and reshapes it. Hence, it also enables one to make the proper distinctions that are crucial for understanding in general. In this way, Order can represent the true state of affairs, as well as the mental state through which the Confucian acts in the world in harmony. It creates ethical, aesthetic, and, to some extent, logical distinctions: while every person, action, and thing has its own Order, one learns to distinguish between good and evil, right and wrong, the true and false.

The onto-epistemological role of the one Order as the ruling principles keeps faith with commonsense acceptance the inherent dynamism of the universe, while not losing the ground that enables one's to inquire, speculate, and attain knowledge. Expressed as both before heaven and after heaven, the speculative is never disconnected from the experiential. Because of the bond among principles as one Order manifested in one's nature and mandate, the Way comprises the only possible manner to follow Order. Shao sees the highest level of observation as observing the Way, which cannot be done through the senses. Thus, according to the poem, one speaks freely and the message reaches (*qianci* 遣辭); one looks around, and simplicity is known (*zhijian* 知简); one listens while able to recognize silence (*shixi* 識希).[104]

The three lines regarding speaking, looking, and listening (lines 348–50) remind again of *Laozi*'s stating that the Way cannot be made the subject of description; it is ceaselessly in action, and yet cannot be named; and in itself, it is nothing.[105] The *Laozi* describes the Way as the rule of things, which in fact cannot be reached by means of ordinary senses and thus cannot be appropriately described, in a manner that might have inspired Shao's reference to the Way as observed through Order. Shao, however, opposes the Laozian view that even if looked at, the Way cannot be seen; if listened to, it cannot be heard; if reached for, the Way cannot be touched. Shao stresses that even if not heard or seen, through conforming with the Way, what is spoken is delivered, what is looked at is known.

Shao concludes with a series of metaphors describing the naturalness of faultless things that are in themselves-so (*ziran*) and whose knowledge is not mediated.

> Great broth cannot be seasoned,
> "Black wine" cannot be diluted.
> The top army cannot be attacked,
> Clever math cannot be inferred.
> Good words cannot be said,
> Fleeing horse-carriages cannot be chased. (lines 351–56)

Shao anchors his theoretical suggestion by means of using various examples, each taken from a different source: "Great broth cannot be seasoned, Black wine cannot be diluted" is in line with the harmonious simplicity of the non-mediated Way. The lines allude to the *Book of Rites* 禮記 and its practical depiction of harmony, which explains why the broth cannot be seasoned by the need to respect its high quality. One of the three appearances of great soup (or great broth, *dageng* 大羹) is found in the *Record on Music* (*yueji* 樂記), in a discussion on musical instruments and harmonious sounds.[106] Great soup is a broth that does not match any certain flavor among the five flavors, considered the best royal meal as containing all potential possibilities without being identified or limiting itself to one. Shao calls for paying attention to the soup that is properly balanced such that any addition can only harm it.[107] Likewise, black wine (*xuanjiu* 玄揩 or dark/mysterious wine) refers to pure water used instead of wine, considered the best beverage.¹⁰⁸ Shao then offers a military metaphor: The top army cannot be attacked, alluding to *Sunzi*'s idea of the best of best (*shanzhishan* 善之善) in war strategy, as subduing the other army without war.¹⁰⁹ The military example toward the end of the poem on Weiqi, which is essentially a strategic game, has special significance with reference to knowing simplicity as the secret for a perfect move. The next example, "Clever math cannot be inferred" alludes to *Zhuangzi*'s discussion of knowledge in "The Equality of Things" (*Qiwulun* 齊物論), in particular to his reference to the relativity of experience.

Shao reminds his reader of the limitations of knowledge and the significance of the *Zhuangzi*'s "all things and I are one" (*wanwu yuwo weiyi* 萬物與我為一) as the ineffable, or the good words (*shanyan* 善言) that cannot be said, being incomparable to others as reaching the utmost level, and transcending all forms of speech. The allusion to the Laozian perspective regarding the language of the Way can be connected in the ending of the poem to the art of words by which a poem may express the ineffable, at least to some extent.¹¹⁰ Through this brief reference, Shao takes his readers back to the complexity that we create, which distances us from the knowledge acquired in direct observation of things through their own Order—which is also our own. While language assists in understanding specific matters, it can be unhelpful for understanding what life is about. Observing a game can be more helpful in revealing a deeper sense of reality that lies beyond language and concept. Last, Shao refers to fleeing carriages that cannot be chased as a paraphrase of *Chunqiu Zuozhuan* 春秋左傳, "A fleeing horse cannot be stopped."¹¹¹ Being in movement, they not only cannot be stopped, but they cannot even be chased; therefore, one should use extra caution when looking for knowledge. Sophia Katz notes that this level of knowledge, in metaphysical terms, is beyond sight and beyond that which can be heard, and that according to Shao, this level of the ultimate was described by Fuxi in his "Chart on the Order of the Eight Trigrams" and is the main concern of Shao's Before Heaven teaching, seen as the way to attain transformed understanding and sageliness.¹¹²

Shao concludes by returning to the closest and most basic relationships: those of siblings and of parents and children, through which the first step in avoiding of selfishness is taken.

> Brothers devote themselves to love,
> Fathers and sons focus on affection.
> The world also can be passed on
> But this move cannot be selfish. (lines 357–60)

Observing from the perspective of Order comprises the full collapsing of in-out boundaries and the ability to live beyond them. This transcendence not only realizes the epistemological process, it brings Shao's metaphysical Before Heaven teaching down to earth, and applicable in everyday life, as realizing morality. Similarly to Zhou Dunyi's unifying metaphysics beyond the boundaries of One and many, so is Shao Yong's epistemological unified knowledge beyond in and out. Selfishness cannot enter this epistemology. The human ability to go beyond selfish goals of gain and profit links them with ultimate beyond, making the realization of the Before-Heaven teaching possible. The Way of Weiqi thus transforms into a model for understanding the Way of sages.

CONCLUSION: OBSERVING WEIQI AS TRANSCENDING ONE'S BOUNDARIES

Zhou's metaphysical idea involves being as becoming, or the single ongoing transformation as a response to the riddle of WJTJ—infinitude in finitude at once. He transcends the dichotomy between One and many through his understanding the one ongoing creation, of which the human world is one outcome. As we have seen in this chapter, Shao Yong's suggestion turns to an *epistemological* response for the same riddle. As the title suggests, his observation on life takes place within the game of Weiqi, through transcending the in-out boundaries of game. The life of the game and the game of life coalesce in one observation through eyes, mind, and Order.

The poem introduces reflective observation, which may serve as a model for a full theoretical framework. The game, functioning as microcosm for life, is first probed through the eyes, and thus touches on life without analyzing it or dismantling its continuity. The actions of players constitute phenomenological happenings and reveal a dimension that can be seen by everyone as having its own life. This enables a qualified observer to observe human history with the mind, the human moral mind, by means of philosophical speculation in order to uncover the rules of the game inherent within it. The first part of the poem observed human responses through the Weiqi board; in the second part, Weiqi is observed on the board of human history such that not only is game a reflection of life, but life is a game that can be played better or worse, depending on the clarity of one's observation. Shao synthesizes the two perspectives into a full *theoretical* framework, concluding his view on life and game as reflecting a single world Order, that is, the Order of change.[113] The

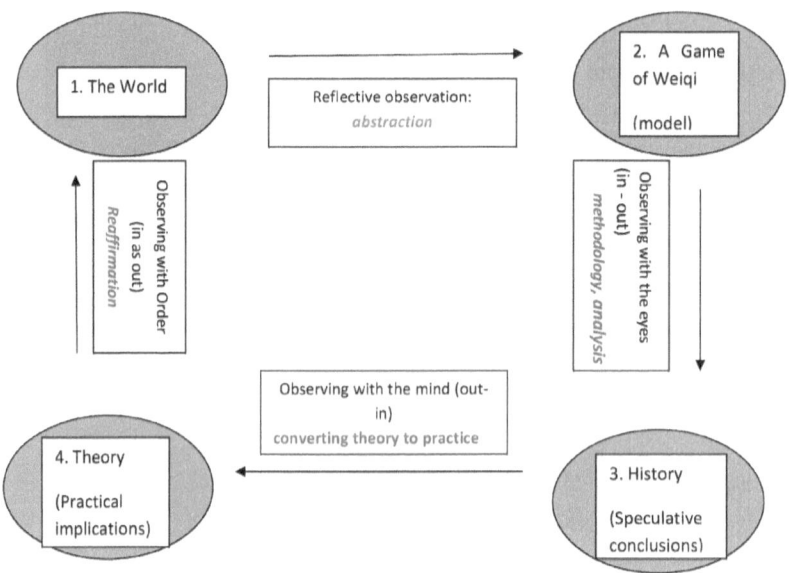

FIGURE 3.1. Shao Yong's observation of Weiqi, as a theoretical framework. *Source*: Fair use.

worldly manifestations of the rules that were first observed in the game *reaffirm* the old Confucian moral framework through a demand to discard the ego in order to attain unbiased observation.

Like Zhou's expansion of the self, Shao's discarding of it is essentially Confucian: when the ego is forgotten, one can relate better with other people or with other aspects of the world. Shao's theoretical suggestion regarding transcending oneself or one's in-out dichotomy through an ongoing process of observation—as his own response to the riddle of the WJTJ—can be graphically illustrated in figure 3.1.

This figure is an attempt to schematize the structure of Shao's observation of Weiqi, as creating a theoretical framework for observing life. Starting from the world we live in (1) Shao applies reflective observation by which he arrives at the game of Weiqi; in theoretical terms Shao starts his search by means of *abstraction* of the world we live in, that leads toward the Weiqi as game *model* (2). Next, according to Shao's methodological framework of observation, the game is observed with the senses, in particular with eyes, leading to a better understanding of history; the theoretical move in this case, is in fact an *analysis* of the game, which takes the direction from in to out, thus allowing to move from model to its first *speculative implications* (3). In order for speculative implications materialize into *practical implications, conversion* is necessary. According to the methodology of observation, human history demands an observation with the mind, this time using out to in direction (4). To complete the theoretical framework, the conclusions are then *reaffirmed* by means of observation that is neither from in to out, nor from out to in, rather it is beyond in-out dichotomy; this is the observation with Order vis-à-vis the world one lives in.

Zhou's riddle How WJTJ? is responded to again through an epistemological perspective, through observation of a Weiqi game, by transcending the boundary between that which lies inside the game and that which lies outside it. A game (or a theory) can be seen as utmost limit in the sense of setting rules and determining boundaries; and yet when played properly, all limits fade—in particular, those of the ego.

FOUR

Emerging Out of Life and Death[1]

Zhang Zai's Pragmatic Point of View

></p>

All go unto one place; all are of the dust, and all turn to dust again.

Who knoweth the spirit of man that goeth upward, and the spirit of the beast that goeth downward to the earth?

Wherefore I perceive that there is nothing better, than that a man should rejoice in his own works; for that is his portion: for who shall bring him to see what shall be after him?

—ECCLESIASTES 3:20–22

INTRODUCTION: THE PERSON AS A UNIVERSAL FAMILY MEMBER

We have already seen how our relations define who we are, and how we know the world we live in. Others influence our thoughts, feelings, and practices; some who had died before we were born, or who will be born after we die, are part in who we are. Zhang Zai 張載 (1020–1077) follows the early Confucian premise that who we are is first and foremost our families, and expands the notion of family to a larger continuity that carries with it commitment and caring. As this chapter shows, according to Zhang Zai, there is a worthy "bonus" in this understanding: within the family one may also live forever. Within the family, fixed individuality dissolves into unlimited responsibility for others. Within the various relationships with living and dead family members, one creates oneself beyond the boundaries of birth and death. This perspective embodies a spiritual salvific flavor, not in a religious sense, but rather one that arises from sheer morality.

In the two previous chapters, we encountered neo-Confucian thinking as a search for broadening the Way by means of transcending accepted self-boundaries, first from a metaphysical perspective and next from an epistemological one. First, Zhou Dunyi transcends the metaphysical boundary between One and many by means of presenting the riddle of WJTJ, and responding to it through an anthropocosmic understanding of infinitude within finitude. Next, Shao Yong transcends the epistemological boundary between in and out through observation, by means of entering a game of *Weiqi* and finding in it the game of life. In the present chapter we focus on Zhang Zai's transcending the most essential boundary—that between birth (*sheng* 生) and death (*si* 死)—through the family. Taking a personal perspective for understanding infinitude and finitude, Zhang Zai's discussing the significance of moral practice of all human beings as sons and daughters, adds a pragmatic weight to the neo-Confucian project, while coming back to its early sources.

In the context of one's most evident boundaries as birth and death, some biographical facts again, can be valuable useful for understanding his philosophical ideas. In particular, Zhang Zai lost his father in early childhood and soon afterward lost his mother, too, having to cope with the heavy loss throughout his life, in poverty and hardship. It is therefore not improbable to read his philosophy as psychologically motivated by a relentless attempt to overcome death, both one's own fear of death and overcoming pain and loss on the death of others; perhaps he even sought to overcome any possibility of loss in the world, as his philosophy of qi may suggest.[2]

Like many in his time, Zhang studied Daoism and Buddhism for a number of years, but realized that the Way can be restored only through Confucian texts. He was fascinated by the *Book of Change* and referred to its philosophy in his writings and lecturing. Indeed, Zhang's point of departure is the natural processes of life—thriving and declining, generating and annihilating, becoming and dying—with important moral implications. While the tendency to see the harmony of the natural world as model for human harmony in the spirit of the *Book of Change* is an almost all-Chinese philosophical trend, the analogy of cosmic harmony to family relations suggests a Confucian flavor.

Zhang's outlook is reminiscent of Shao Yong's and even more so of Zhou Dunyi's. Like Zhou Dunyi, Zhang Zai treats heaven and earth and the human world with the same terminology: a terminology that is essentially based on moral feeling, as a feeling for life in which all things and organisms penetrate each other. In fact, Zhu Xi notes that Cheng Hao observed a similarity not only of ideas but also of personality between Zhou Dunyi and Zhang Zai, with regard to their special treatment of nature: Zhou did not cut the grass and let it grow naturally in its own pace and form, in order not to hurt it; Zhang heard the cry of a donkey and sympathized with the pain, without imposing explanations that may be foreign to his human inclination. Both assumed that all living beings share some manners of behavior, as well as feelings and pains.[3]

Yet, while Zhou transcends the dichotomy between finitude and infinitude in the cosmic universal sense to explain anthropocosmic relatedness, and Shao transcends the epistemological in-out dichotomy to explain the process of observation in the service of expanding knowledge—only Zhang's idea of human transcendence, as oriented to daily practice brings to a holistic view of the universe. Zhang Zai shifts the outlook on knowledge as manifested by both Zhou and Shao from the perspective of knowers to a perspective of an involved seeker of the Way. As a seeker, Zhang's referring to Qian and Kun not simply as metaphorical parents but as *his* parents not only embodies a methodological stand, but actually comprises a new philosophical voice. In this way, heaven and earth are introduced as embodying an ontogenetic nature as the origin and development of the human being, in a way that inherently denotes and delimits one's identity as son or daughter. Yet, the denotation as sons and daughters—necessitating the family as frame of reference—by definition cannot be fixated or limited. Rather, its most distinctive nature is not being bounded by features of space and time, like family members count, age, gender, and so on.[4]

This connectedness attributes the cosmic powers with a human flavor, in terms that are at home with Confucianism. Namely, one's affinity with heaven and earth is depicted as a son's or a daughter's kinship with parents, as family reverence (*xiao* 孝). The use of moral terms in order to explain the universe as a whole, rather than only for understanding humans, increases the weight of the original moral ideas and enables the human understanding of the universe through moral categories. Zhang's call for engagement in the universal Order through moral practice as outgrowing from the near to the distant, completes

Zhou's and Shao's emanation from WJTJ to the myriad things, or from observation to real life. In this way, emerging from earlier buds, Zhang introduces a fullest notion of human's broadening the way.

To follow this understanding, I take up from Zhang Zai's *Western Inscription* (*Ximing* 西銘, hereafter abbreviated WI)—in reference to the broader Works of Zhang Zai (*Zhangzaiji* 張載集, hereafter abbreviated as ZZJ). The first part of this chapter addresses WI as reference to the remarkable view of Qian and Kun as parents; the relatedness within the different branches of the universe as one body; the commitment to the universe as family reverence; and the conclusion that by serving one's parents with reverence during life, one dies in peace. In order to suggest that through true family reverence one transcends the boundary between life and death, we move on to expressing these ideas in terms of Zhang's philosophy of qi as the energy that builds and fills any living creature; its functioning as void; its moral perspective; and its suggesting a continuity that transcends the strict boundary between life and death. In this context I find Zhang Zai's idea of one body (*yiti* 一體) compared with that of the *Zhuangzi*'s as having vital explanatory power. I posit that jointly, the two former perspectives—of living in one family, and as one body or qi—are merged into a unique moral sense of immortality that amounts to *morally living in the present*, or timelessness.

IN THE FAMILY OF *QIAN* AND *KUN*

Zhang Zai's *Western Inscription* begins with an impressive, somewhat grandiose opening referring to Qian and Kun being one's father and mother (taken in this context as Heaven and Earth[5]). Thus, the treatise is understood as an important ecological statement, read also as touching cosmology, as praise for world harmony, as poetic ethics, or as a poignant statement on life and the human experience of it.[6] This richness is perhaps the reason that the text comprises one of the most celebrated neo-Confucian texts and definitely the best known among Zhang Zai's writings. With this perspective, the treatise offers a transcendence of life's boundaries through moral practice. Seen in this light, the closing statement of the treatise "while I am alive, I follow and serve, and when death comes I rest" (*cun wushun shi, mo wuningye* 存,吾順事;沒,吾寧也) is much more than a poetic finale for an ethical text, and not less important than the treatise's opening statement. Indeed, it comprises a significant statement regarding a unique Confucian way to live eternally.

In the all-inclusive, anthropocosmic description in WI, two general points should grab readers' attention. First, unlike other philosophical texts, the text's style is uncommonly written in the first person; the nine appearances of the character *wu* 吾, denoting I or my, cannot be considered coincidental in this short text. While Confucian humanistic tradition refers to human life and experience from an ethical-universal and somewhat remote perspective, Zhang makes a daring articulation of philosophical ideas understood through his own life experience. Addressing the reader in this manner, Zhang manages to stoutly make his point by a universal-cosmological description that is based on one's life experience, rather than through speculative theoretical discourse on creation. The first person address regarding filial life and restful death presents a view whereby despite the universality of ethics, one is forced to acknowledge personal experience in moral life, and moreover, one is allowed (perhaps even encouraged) to consider such experience seriously in the philosophical sphere too. Through this writing style, Zhang clarifies that human life is primarily moral life, and morality cannot be discussed as a remote theory. In addition, regarding its theme, Zhang presents what is commonly considered metaphysical as ethical, by making an unusual link between an opening statement regarding heaven and earth as universal parents, followed by a main body of the text explaining the relatedness within the different branches of the universe as family relations, described through an analogy to filial kinship, and finally concluding with the idea of serving during life and dying in peace.

The unusual link presents the cosmos and the human in it from an intimate perspective as a large yet caring family. These two features of the text appear immediately in the moving opening statement: "Qian is the father, and Kun is the mother; I, the little, dwell within them," connecting the person—essentially through one's own person—with the two fundamental cosmic ancestors, known through the two opening hexagrams of the *Book of Change*.[7] Playing their twofold role as both the cosmic principles of heaven and earth and the earthy manifestations of male and female, Qian and Kun are not introduced as abstract forces that play symbolic roles in human life; rather, they are one's parents. To make his point, Zhang then refers directly to heaven and earth (*tiandi* 天地), using a second image according to which anything between them is one's body (*ti* 體).

> Therefore, what fills heaven and earth is my body, and what rules heaven and earth is my nature. People are my relatives, things are my companions. The great ruler is the eldest son of my parents; his great ministers are stewards. Honor seniors such that an elder is treated as elder; have compassion for the orphan and helpless, such that the young is treated as young.[8]

Emerging Out of Life and Death 167

The five appearances of "I" in the above passage underscore that from Zhang's perspective, the cosmic responsibility is the very responsibility for *one's own body and family*. While all allies in the universe share this body as equal partakers, each is ruled by his or her own moral nature—not in a solipsistic sense but rather in an inclusive humanistic sense, according to which my nature is in fact the one nature that rules the universe, that is shared with every being, and to which each one is committed. The full weight of Zhang's idea can be understood better by comprehending the various sources and senses of *ti* used among various other Chinese terms for "body," in an abstract and philosophical way.[9] Literally signifying "one's body" or "the physical body," the notion is referred to as "the thing itself" (as distinct from its functions), as "original nature" (as opposed to civilized, acquired, and artificial nature), as well as "the substance" or "essence" (as opposed to occurrences and coincidences). Moreover, the term is also used as the verb *to embody*. Nathan Sivin opines that in early Chinese texts, the smallest unit of the *ti* body is the human body, or the four limbs, while the largest unit is the cosmos itself. Thus, the difference between the smallest unit of *ti* and the largest unit of *ti* is not a real or an "essential" difference.[10]

ONE BODY, ONE NATURE, ONE QI

The Body as Metaphor

In general, the term *ti* implies the meaning of a body with neither fixed definition nor defined borders, either physically or conceptually. Zhang's successors considered his seeing the contents of the cosmos as his own body (*wuqiti* 吾其體) as influenced by Buddhist ideas.[11] In particular, the notion was connected with the idealism of Yogacara's mind only, based on a phenomenological analysis of personal experience and turning toward the subjective. However, as in earlier Buddhist versions, Zhang does not focus on oneness to assert the body as ultimately real; rather, it is real in a conventional way, as arising from moment to moment due to fluctuating causes and conditions that are inherent to cosmic creativity. Moreover, the significance of this ongoing fluctuation arises from its effects on human lives—in particular, as Zhang's passage shows, on one's ending up a ruler or minister or instead a helpless orphan. These various human conditions—considered karma in the Buddhist framework and from which one wishes to be liberated—are considered in Confucian terminology essential for one's nature and its active realization.

The idea of one body is found in Chinese philosophy much earlier than the Buddhist arrival to China and its influence on Chinese thought. In both Daoist and Confucian sources, we find references to the concept of a universal *ti*-body, of which we all comprise organs. On the more remote level, the idea was rooted in the *Zhuangzi*'s chapter on "The Equality of Things" (*Qiwulun* 齊物論) to ideas according to which no difference exists between the big and the small—or more precisely, the difference between them is relative rather than real, since big and small are one body. A view that cannot accept distinctions between big and small certainly cannot accept moral distinctions, which are essential in Zhang's philosophy. In the *Zhuangzi* chapter on The Great Honorable Teacher (*Dazong shi* 大宗師), idea is introduced by a riddle that is echoed in Zhang Zai's thought: "Who can think of nothingness as his head, of life as his spine, of death as his buttocks? Who knows that life, death, consciousness and unconsciousness are all one body?"[12] Despite the fact that responding to this riddle was not explicitly one of Zhang Zai's inspirations, the riddle itself is reflected in his attempt to visualize cosmic interconnectedness through the image of the cosmos as one body, related in the end of the treatise to a continuity of life and death. The *Zhuangzi* presents the human form as a mass of flesh, organs, limbs, and bones that implies a larger wholeness; it is encompassed within a larger common body that is a wholeness including both life and death. The *ti*-body does not have discrete boundaries, but rather is a complex organic corpus with infinite boundaries that may be divided into many smaller fragments, each of which is entirely analogous to the whole and is consubstantial with it. As shown in the riddle presented above, the part is then equivalent to the whole, with nothingness as head, death as buttocks, and life as analogous to the spine is linking the nothingness before it and that which is past it. Although a human being appears to have a discrete physical form, the human body is organically consubstantial with the bodies of ancestors and descendants, with the bodies with whom it engages. Participating in the range of universal progressions is being embodied (*ti*) in it. As we will soon see, Zhang Zai describes a similar existential experience of being part of a boundless, unified body.

The moral perspective of the unbounded body is to be found in similar ideas within the framework of early Confucianism, according to which the *ti* body is rarely if ever fragmented, mutilated, or mutated; rather, it is one. Mencius uses the term *ti* as one's body in referring to the body as a larger whole that also includes nonphysical organs. In the analogy between moral virtues and human organs as reflected in the fourfold body (*siti* 四體), the four beginnings (*siduan* 四端) are the moral feelings of commiseration, shame and dislike, modesty, and the complaisance of approving and disapproving, as seeds of the virtues of humanity, rightness, propriety, and knowledge. Lacking a virtue is analogous to lacking a bodily organ, such that morality cannot be disconnected from the unified body (2A:6).[13] In this spirit, Mencius refers to following the great body (*dati* 大體) as including morality, opposed to following the small body (*xiaoti* 小體) or ignoring the innate moral aspect that makes a person great (6A:15).

This idea is reflected in the neo-Confucian context as a case of the understanding that Order is one, manifestations are many (*liyi fenshu* 理一分殊), which developed to its fullest moral sense in the idea of forming one body with heaven and earth and the myriad things (*yitiandi wanwu weiyiti* 以天地萬物爲一體).[14] The complete ethical weight of the idea appears in Wang's explanation that the accomplished person becomes one body with the cosmos, "not because he deliberately wants to do so, but because it is natural to the humane nature of his mind that he do so."[15] According to this view, inherent in the nature of the accomplished person is self-broadening, as one body—created through one's humanity—with everything in this world, including "ruler, minister, husband, wife, and friends, mountains, rivers, spiritual beings, birds, animals and plants."[16] This sense of continuity appears as a true practice of love that realizes humanity, which then enables one's clear character to be completely manifest in one's body as the body of heaven, earth, and the myriad things.

The vision of one body carries the argumentative force of solving open moral questions with regard to otherness (in particular, regarding Levinas's notion of absolute otherness).[17] While there are others and there is otherness for practical understanding, this otherness can never be absolute and distinct from oneself, since each other is ultimately connected with every other as one body, as we see in Zhang's description. An ethical instant is thus the instant in which the boundaries of one body are breached such that a person who faces the pain of another cannot stay indifferent and, in a certain sense, feels the other's pain. Hence, unless one offers help, one's wholeness as a person is damaged. Zhang's view of whatever fills the universe as comprising one's body uses an analogy between body and *family*—not only as one's biological family but as the universal family whose well-being is its members' responsibility.

As one may realize, we *are* our parents whose bodies we comprised an integral part of, before we were born; likewise, our siblings are distinct, yet are one's body, being the outcome of the same genetic process. The important contribution of Zhang's view is in his seeing the family as a body, implying that realizing the Confucian moral virtue of family reverence is in one's natural inclination to preserve the body, which is in fact everything between heaven and earth.

According to Zhang, while in the cosmic sense nature (as *tian*) is that which our bodies fill, *my* nature (as *xing*) directs or governs (*shuai* 帥) it. This idea was echoed later in Mou Zongsan's sense of transcendence, bringing together the apparent contrasts—that which transcends the world, that is seen as independent from the human and beyond human experience, and that which is immanent to the world and depends on it—to cover in one concept both the metaphysical realm and the sensitivities of one's heart and mind.[18] This duality is explained as a simultaneity of opposing movements.

> It can perhaps be best visualized as a mutually intertwined, dynamic two-way traffic: the immanentization process that goes from tian "downward" trough xing to xin and the trasncendentization process that goes from xin through xing to tian. The two processes occur simultaneously and both culminate in the "trinity" of tian, xing, xin.[19]

Notably, both are ways to describe the same process in which a person expands her boundaries and transcends herself in the creation of morality, which is part of the creation of world. According to Mou, through a process of immanentization, the heavenly is internalized in one's nature and heart, such that human beings can absorb cosmic creativity within themselves as part of their true nature and part of their practice and existence. This immanent transcendence in fact is the internalization of the Way in every person. In this sense, selfhood is the form of this transcendent component in human life and realization; it belongs at once to heaven and to the person, such that through constituting human relationships, one relates directly with heaven. [20] As shown earlier, Tu's graphic depiction of concentric circles that begin with the human and expand, first to family, then to community, state, world, and beyond, expresses the expanding self as inherently related to a specific context that enables one's growth, on the one hand, and challenges it, on the other. The family is the closest circle by which we are nourished and through which we may grow and burgeon. The overcoming of challenges and using them as opportunities for moral flourishing, one transcends his boundaries.[21]

When Zhang claims that not only what fills heaven and earth is one's body, but that moreover, that which rules heaven and earth is one's nature—not as universal nature but as one's own nature, a human and moral nature—he makes sure that not only are we are inherently related, but also we are *committed* to our cosmic family. In this way, Zhang offers his own version to the *Analects*' discussion of humans broadening the Way rather than the Way broadening humans; or to *Zhongyong*'s concept of human's "sincering heaven." In this way Zhang imprints his understanding of the body on neo-Confucian generations to follow.

Body as Void Qi-Continuity

To understand Zhang's idea of the body one has to refer to the qi-constitution of the universe as a whole—including both physical and nonphysical events—as presented in his Collection of Work (ZZJ). Qi or vital power is rightly identified as Zhang's most significant original contribution to Chinese philosophy; in the present context, Sui-chi Huang's observation that "his view on *qi* sounds at times like the law of conservation in modern physics" has special appeal.[22] It sometimes seems that Zhang's philosophy comprises in earnest a refusal to accept any type of loss, while his idea of qi is a powerful device for avoiding it. Huang remarks that in the Works of Zhang Zai, terms such as existence (*you* 有) and nonexistence (*wu* 無) are replaced by more dynamic terms explained in terms of qi, such as appearance (*xing* 形) and disappearance (*buxing* 不形), moving (*dong* 動) and resting (*jing* 靜), ascending (*sheng* 升) and descending (*jiang* 降), connoting the idea that despite an apparent disappearance of things, in the constant change of reality, nothing is lost.[23]

As mentioned earlier, the term *qi* denotes the vital power that forms the invisible building blocks of reality, as the intangible and yet essential. Qi is the fabric of life, the filling of the universe and its beings, and the constitution of every experience or event. Trying to capture its essence as a matter that is not solely physical, different interpreters understood it through different ideas and endowed it with creative translations accordingly. Similarly to the idea of power in the Humean sense, qi brings about life, pervades the universe and every being in it, and comprises every phenomenon, being, feeling, thought, or deed—physical as well as mental.[24]

Notably, whatever translation it takes, given the broad and abstract senses of qi, it appears unjustified to label Zhang Zai a materialist (in the traditional Western sense) simply because of the centrality of qi in his philosophy. Seen in its full sense, qi contributes to a high level of abstraction and constitutes phenomena that are not material, such as feelings, thoughts, and personality.

In the present context, it is imperative that qi is also the basic constituent of moral virtues. Based on qi, which expands and has no ends, Zhang's morality can be understood as a morality that is always in a process toward perfection and has no final goal. Rather, one aspires to a moral ideal that cannot be fully attained. Seen in this light, Zhang Zai may be considered a moral idealist.[25] In this context, Jung-Yeup Kim's book on Zhang Zai's philosophy of qi is extremely instructive in its innovative understanding of his notion of qi as enabling dynamic pluralism in the human experience. Challenging the accepted substance-monistic and materialistic understandings, Kim brings into the discourse more proper notions of qi, which include polarity, correlativity, and organic unity as opposed to substance, presenting the term's richness as a creative nonsubstance monism.[26]

In order to justify this view, my discussion on qi first focuses on Zhang's unique understanding of its inherent relation with void (*xu* 虛);[27] next, I return to its implication regarding human nature and the human moral constitution, which will demonstrate how qi as void, on the one hand, and as human nature on the other, enables transcendence of the boundary between life and death.

The innovation in Zhang Zai's understanding of qi reaches its full weight in his bold identification of qi with void, or better put, with his own way of understanding void. For Zhang, qi as the raw material of the universe is in the constitution of life and as such it unifies being and nonbeing. Zhang states,

> The Great Void is without forms—it is the original substance of *qi*. Its condensation and dispersal are but temporary forms of change and transformation. (ZZJ 7.5, Kasoff 1984, 37)[28]

Qi, before taking form, is identified with the great void (*daxu* 太虛), or as Zhang puts it, its original substance (*benti* 本體) is great void.[29] Both his use of great void and his explanation of reality as qi (as being) that is void (nonbeing), echoes Zhou Dunyi's use of Non-Polarity and Supreme Polarity.[30] Zhang relates a new use of void with a prominent neo-Confucian dialectics of description through dynamic polar pairs.

> When you understand that the void is *qi,* then being and non-being, hidden and manifest, *shen* and transformation, nature and destiny are all unitary and not dualistic. If you reflect on condensation and dispersal, leaving and entering, form and no-form, and can trace them to the origin whence they come, then you have a profound grasp of the *Book of Change*. (8.1–2, Kasoff 1984, 40)

Emerging Out of Life and Death   173

Zhang is aware of the distinction in *Xici Zhuan* between the Way prior to taking form (or above form *xinger shang* 形而上) and the concrete things as subsequent to form (or below form *xinger xia* 形而下).[31] Referring to form and no form as dynamic features of reality originating in one process, Zhang shows that no substantial distinction exists between two separate realms as hidden versus manifest, or in modern terminology as metaphysical versus practical. Rather, the nature of qi involves a dual citizenship, which embodies the diversity of experiences. By means of the explanatory vigor of qi as one matter that runs through everything, Zhang invites his readers to understand the world as a unity that must be expressed in oppositions due to its dynamic nature, as opposed to a static dichotomizing nature that can be found in human creations like language.

The explanation in dialectic pairs, together with the reference to the *Book of Change*, implies the understanding of qi as void through the essential yin-yang movement, which endows void with a transformative power. Zhang follows the yin-yang model of continuity, in which being and nonbeing are not two separate ontological states, but rather are ontologically one, and should be seen as dynamic configurations, relative to a process that we are all part of (ZZJ 235.8–10). Void as a nontangible dynamism is necessarily qi and yet, not being specified or realized in any particular form, it is pure transformation. Since everything is in constant flux, no solid and fixed entity exists; in this sense all is empty—namely, it is empty of determinations. Seeing everything (or any embodiment of qi) as empty should not be taken at face value; since everything is in incessant transformation, all is in a process of being emptied from specified essential characteristics and former features, and there is no fixed thing. Qi is void by virtue of its ever-transforming nature; hence, void is an expression of the universe as one. The point in the passage is the *transformations* in which void is manifest through various qi-constitutions, as different objects, events, behaviors, feeling, movements, or anything that characterizes life.

This understanding of void implies a rejection of what Zhang sees as the naturalism of the *Laozi* that gives priority to nonbeing over being in stating that being comes from nonbeing and failing to see the unity of being and nonbeing.[32] As we will see in the following, according to Zhang Zai, void is indeed the source of morality, yet it is not the source of qi, since if it were, void would have been limitless and qi limited in the way that leads directly to the Laozian doctrine of being produced from nonbeing.[33] Void *as* qi is equal to being, invalidating the primacy of nonbeing, and filling it with living dynamism. Qi can still be produced spontaneously, as the Way, the change, or the movement between being and nonbeing. Having the inherent disposition to be realized in specific forms and yet not *substantially* changed, either as void or as a thing, qi is hence one. Using the same dialectic of oppositions, Zhang says,

> The Great Void is pure; being pure, it is without obstruction. Because it is without obstruction, it is marvelous. The opposite of pure is impure. Being impure, it is obstructed. Because it is obstructed it has form. (ZZJ 9.2, Kasoff 1984, 63)

Zhang stresses that although there is great significance to the purity level of qi, the distinction between the marvelous or spirit (*shen* 神) and form (*xing* 形) is not dichotomous. Importantly, this philosophy of qi has no place for the centrality of the well-known mind-body problem, as constituting Western philosophy since the days of René Descartes; void, or pure qi, is spirit, which penetrates and fills all being with life. Zhang explains that when qi is pure it penetrates, and when it is impure, it is blocked and inaccessible. Then, he can go on explaining the dynamics of spirit, such that when purity reaches its limit, spirit subsists, and when spirit condenses, it penetrates. To demonstrate this, Zhang uses an analogy from a dialogue in the opening passage of the second chapter of the *Zhuangzi*, according to which like the breeze moving through the holes of a musical instrument producing tones and carrying them to great distances, so is the purity of void (ZZJ 9.3). The sounds of the earth are the outcome of the void, through which the wind blows, and humans blow intentionally in pipes to make music. Void plays a crucial role in enabling every living sound, vision, touch, and experience; however, as soon as something is experienced, its qi is no longer pure; rather, it becomes visible. Zhang says,

> When *qi* condenses, its visibility comes into effect and there are forms. When *qi* does not condense, its visibility is not in effect and there are no forms. When *qi* condenses, how can we not call it temporary? (ZZJ182.7, Kasoff 1984, 42)[34]

For Zhang, from void to form, at all levels of the process of becoming, everything is qi. While in itself ongoing and never lost, we know it only through temporary forms (such as the human body). Sui-chi Huang's observation mentioned above about Zhang's view on qi as sounding to a modern ear like the laws of conservation in modern physics makes even more sense in this context. She explains,

> The law of conservation of mass or of matter ... states that the mass of substances in a closed system will remain constant, no matter what processes are acting inside the system. It is a different way of stating that though matter may change form, it can be neither created nor destroyed.[35]

Zhang's idea of qi as void is a persuasive device for understanding life and avoiding transience. Yet, how is this applied in human life?

FAMILY, MORALITY, AND VOID

The Family as Model

Zhang's seeing people as siblings whose responsibility for their parents and for each other is their natural predisposition comprises neither a naive mystical belief that heaven and earth are *truly* one's parents nor a mere metaphor used for understanding one thing in terms of another. The world is rather one and continuous *for real*. As a human member in this family, Zhang Zai's only way to understand the universe is a *human* way, that is, as moral. In this way Zhang's view includes a distinctive epistemological stand; cosmic connectedness, from a *human* perspective, is in this way revealed as moral connectedness based on family reverence. Zhang's world is described through an inclusive holistic perspective as a living moral organism that can only be learned and known through human moral categories.

The ability to transcend bodily boundaries, then the boundaries of one's biological family, and ultimately see the cosmos as one's body and its inhabitants as one's family has an important moral implication regarding the status and the role of family reverence. Zhu Xi interestingly points out that family reverence is not the main point in the WI; rather, according to Zhu's understanding, it helps Zhang Zai get across humanity (*ren*). He believes that Zhang uses the idea of family reverence because he is worried that referring to humanity might seem remote and its altruistic connotations could have been at risk of being interpreted in a spirit that is closer to Mozi's utilitarian idea of universal love (*jian ai* 兼愛) than to Confucian moral love with distinctions (*aiyou chadeng* 愛有差等).[36] Earlier yet, Cheng Yi agrees that Zhang might have gone too far; yet, accentuating the importance of Order and manifestations, he clearly rejects the idea of a similarity between Zhang's idea and Mozi's. Accordingly, family reverence must be understood as a concrete manifestation of human morality.[37] Yang Shi (1053–1135), aware of the comparison to Mozi, notes that

Zhang's idea is influenced by Mencius, who in the context of human morality declares that "the accomplished person ... loves all things" (7A:45).[38]

Zhang Zai, who clearly expresses an idea of a Confucian sense of one body understood as a moral body, would have certainly agreed that humanity is the core of his ethics; however, family reverence cannot be taken to be coincidental or to play a minor value in WI. Recalling the classical Confucian framework, one family includes various relationships that unlike in Mozi's conceptualization *do* have distinctions; father relates with son differently than husband with wife, or an older sibling with a younger one. The family ways to relate *as such* serve as basis for broader morality. In other words, seeing all members as belonging to one organic unit, morality is based on a family commitment according to the specific kind of relationship. Examples for this attitude as we have seen earlier are found as early as the *Book of Family Reverence*, in which already in the opening passage, we learn from Confucius's reply to Zengzi that the perfect virtue of the sage kings and the root of excellence is family reverence. Likewise, the *Analects* portray family reverence as the source for humanity (1:2, 1:6).[39] Loyal to this line of thought, Zhang moves on from the closest family circle to broader sociopolitical and cosmic circles, as demonstrated in the next passage of WI.

> The virtue of the sage is harmony, and of the worthy is refinement. All under heaven, weary and infirm, disabled, desolate and lonely, widower, and widowed, all are my elder and younger brothers in distress, without anyone to talk to.[40] Protecting them when the time comes is the care of a son. To be joyful and without anxiety, is to be genuinely filial.

The virtue of the sage is described as harmony, which is by its very nature relational and presupposes a coexistence of a variety of parties and relations.[41] The harmony that is the sage's virtue is based in the human world on family reverence as the family relationships. Unlike in Mozi's conceptualization, love *does* have distinctions when serving as basis for broader morality; therefore, it is specifically family reverence that can play this role in Zhang's understanding of humanity. Implying the immediate connotation to a bloodline that is obvious in a biological family, Zhang is able to lead his reader to a broader notion of inherent moral continuity.

De Bary refers to this continuity in the context of neo-Confucian self-cultivation as a Confucian personalism that stresses and reaffirms the significance of the self as a dynamic center of a bigger whole of biological continuity and of a moral community.[42] Taking this distinctive feature of the Confucian self into account, since humans are by nature connected to the cosmos through moral qualities, going against our cosmic parents is not only violating nature, it is also violating human morality.

> Going against [heaven], is violating virtue; harming humanity is treachery. He who promotes evil is incompetent. He who fulfills his physical appearance resembles [heaven]. When understanding transformations, then their affairs are carried out well, and when penetrating spirit, then their will is followed successfully.

Rather than a view in which heaven is the ultimate source of human activity, we learn that heaven is an ultimate in a different sense, and that it is objective in that it can be known to human beings, insofar as it offers standards that prevent the relativism that could be the outcome of a theory that centers on human beings and their capabilities. By means of knowing heaven, we can improve human practice, such that heaven becomes human, rather than that humans becoming heavenly. Since good family relationships are manifest in one's relationship with heaven and earth, moral practice is spiritual practice, heaven can never be disjointed from human morality, and self-cultivation is essentially caring for the world. The responsibility of a person for the elderly, the weak, and the poor, as well as the connectedness to a broader circle as if it were one's family, is also based on the known Mencian advice to rulers to treat others like family.[43] Relatively to the short treatise, the high number of historical demonstrations to family reverence that Zhang offers in the next passage allows him to make his point that morality stemming from family reverence yields inborn stability. Similarly to Shao Yong, for Zhang Zai too, our history is inseparable from who one is.

> Do nothing shameful in the northwest corner of the house, and bring no dishonor; preserve the mind and cultivate nature without negligence. The son of Chong Bai hated wine, but protected and supported (his parents); Ying Feng-ren advocated benefitting mankind and imparted happiness onto others; Shun with his meritorious deeds (delighted his father); Without trying to escape and awaiting capital punishment, Shen Sheng showed reverence; Shen (Zengzi) received his body (from his parents) and returned it (without blemish), and Bai-qi bravely obeyed the command of his father.[44]

Stressing that honoring parents reflects the traditional idea of preserving proper behavior without transgressing even in private life (*shendu* 慎独), Zhang refers to doing nothing shameful even when not seen by others, or in the northwest corner of the house (*Wulou* 屋漏), which according to tradition is the darkest place in the house, in which one may take a break and seen by nobody.⁴⁵ Morality is not family-dependent; rather, it is realized within the family, and only then beyond it. Then, Zhang offers the six different examples of historical sages from various ages, all demonstrating exemplary family reverence of sons who under challenging conditions never compromised their filiality. In other words, each example demonstrates a case of overcoming one's personal preferences and inclinations for the sake of protecting, supporting, or honoring one's parents.⁴⁶

Void Nature–Void Morality

The one body as moral body can be also expressed in terms of the moral dimension of qi, for which the family serves as model. We have seen above that the nature of qi is the core of all transformations, and for any transformation to appear, void is necessary. An utterly "filled" universe does not allow the necessary space for movement, interactions, and transformation. Thus, there is an essential duality in the nature of qi as connected to change, on the one hand, and to tranquility, on the other. This dual nature is reflected in the human world and serves as a building block for the understanding of the moral sphere. According to Zhang's understanding, qi as void has special significance when we refer to tranquility in human life, such that the qi-nature of the universe as void is manifested in the human sphere in the quality of impartiality, as voidness of inclinations. In this way, qi as void can endow humans with perfect impartiality and a lack of personal bias. The latter is reflected as tranquility in the sphere of human conduct, such that human nature at its source is "completely still and without stimulation" (ZZJ 7.6).

According to Zhang, the human feature of being absolutely tranquil and unaffected by external stimulations is also the foundation of human tranquility as a sign of morality, originating in void (ZZJ 325.14). As already mentioned, Zhang's inspiration for his understanding human nature is Mencius's idea of the relatedness of heaven and humans and the comprehension that human nature is good.⁴⁷ Accordingly, qi pervades and animates the body; it is exceptionally great and exceptionally strong; it is nourished by morality, cannot be harmed, and fills all between heaven and earth. Due to these features, qi is empowering, as referred to by Mencius 2A:2, in being "flood-like *qi*" (*weiqi* 為氣). Being so, qi is a companion of rightness and reason, and a reinforcement to them; it is attained by the accumulation of moral deeds, and without it humans are in moral starvation. As qi fills everything, "knowing one's own nature is knowing heaven" (7A.1).

Zhang follows this understanding in his own terminology.

> (When) a man 'knows his nature he knows heaven'; and then (he understands that) yin and yang, and returning and coming forth, are all merely part of his endowment. (ZZJ 21.14, Kasoff 1984, 70)

However, according to Zhang's version, there are two kinds of nature: the undifferentiated qi as perfectly good is opposed to the individual nature, which is the outcome of the form that qi takes in its condensed mode.[48] Every person can strive to overcome the given limited nature in order to attain nature's perfection through learning. Thus, Zhang Zai arrives at his daring idea in unmistakable clarity.

> Void-ness is the source of humaneness. (ZZJ 325.1, Kasoff 1984, 59)

To ascertain that his idea is not misunderstood, he introduces void as moral virtue, as follows:

> The height of goodness is void-ness. (ZZJ 326.3, Kasoff 1984, 59)

Through learning, our contact with the external world brings about new consciousness and knowledge. Developing nature through moral learning unifies the original formlessness of not being affected by external conditions, with having a concrete form and being affected by others. In this way, even when realized after taking form, a human being is not a thing, since one has the endowed indispensable freedom of creation and is never determined. Thus, Zhang's philosophy of qi as void is not merely a philosophy of void as nothingness; rather, it is a no-thingness in an exclusive Confucian humanistic sense. In other words, regarding human behavior, there are no *determined* states or things; rather, reality is an ongoing process of moral creation by human beings. There are no firm distinctions that create isolation in the human community and therefore human beings cannot behave like things, irresponsibly and careless; as Zhang shows in WI, we are all parts of one family with mutual responsibility for care.

Zhang criticizes the Buddhists, who see void as annihilation and believe that things do lessen and eventually vanish. In this way, according to his understanding, their view ends up identical to the view of religious Daoists who cling to things and believe that one can be immortal and fixed beyond time.[49] While apparently opposing each other, Zhang sees both Buddhists and

Daoists as identical in their tendency to stick to an absolute unchangeable reality, whether as the void in Buddhism or as an eternal deity in later (religious) Daoism. According to his approach, both views, in fact, fail to admit transformation as the true gist of void, and therefore fail to justify the ongoing process of life. Instead of incessant transformation, they refer to replacements of states; hence, rather than presenting a dynamic world, both approaches ultimately present static pictures of it. Accordingly, the Laozian view, fails in not reaffirming the world we live in. As for Buddhism, Zhang criticizes the understanding of the void as nonexistence and thus believing that there is nothing. For Zhang, despite the central role of void in Buddhism, their preoccupation with it as a means to transcendence and escapism brings Buddhists to stress its importance only in part and with negligence of its true essence. Through his critique of the Buddhist lacunae, Zhang Zai affirms his own position of realizing emptiness as positive receptivity.[50]

For Zhang, precisely this world of coming and departing is what reality is about *as void*; it changes, and is yet real; it is a living energy and not an illusion. According to his line of thought, given the nature of the void, there is no annihilation; in particular, in living beings, death is not annihilation.[51]

> The *qi* in man which does not leave him during his life, but which scatters and disperses after his death, is called *hun*. That which condenses to make his physical form, and does not disperse even at death, is called *p'o*. (ZZJ 19.5, Kasoff 1984, 38)

In this context again, Zhang criticizes the Buddhists, for not correctly perceiving *hun* 魂—the yang, spiritual, and ethereal soul—and therefore seeing change as oriented to *samsara* alone. However, *hun* cannot be introduced without *po* 魄—the yin, corporeal, and substantive, which in itself is qi that never disperses and is inherent in every living human. Zhang sees the play of integration and disintegration of qi analogous to freezing and melting of ice to water, in which nothing is lost, and yet everything changes enormously in terms of sight, touch, sound, and more importantly, function. Just as water is the nature of ice even if the ice ceases to exist, so is moral nature for human beings (ZZJ 22.1). Unlike what he sees as a Buddhist and Daoist mistake, Zhang's universe as qi is a moral one, whose yin-yang movement produces, among other things, moral qualities. Morality is an eternal living power, which relates events, and things, such that nothing exists as fixed, defined, separate, and thus inert. Zhang introduces the moral significance of the universal process.

> Its [*qi*'s] two polarities, yin and yang, follow cyclically without cease, and establish the great righteousness of heaven-and-earth. (ZZJ 9.11, Kasoff 1984, 44)[52]

Heaven-and-earth, or the world in its entirety, is moral. Yin and yang are present in human beings in humanity and rightness.[53]

> To preserve void-ness and clarity, to dwell long in the highest virtue, to follow the changes and transformations, to attain 'timeliness and centrality': these are the height of humaneness, the full realization of righteousness. Only after you know 'what is hidden and what is evident,' and unrelentingly continue in goodness, can you complete your Nature. (ZZJ 17.12–13, Kasoff 1984, 105)

The virtues of humanity and rightness (righteousness) are explained in terms of transformation, timeliness, and void. According to Zhang Zai, practicing virtue is realizing nature, while evil violates nature.[54] The spontaneous process of heaven and earth is morally good, since they are productive, nurturing, reliable, and impartial. Similarly, the qi-nature as a yin-yang dynamic, which governs natural processes, is also morally good. Hence, according to Zhang, "The Nature in man is completely good" (ZZJ 22.13, Kasoff 1984, 70).

Despite not being the first to use the notion of void in the neo-Confucian context, Zhang's notion of void was unique and according to Tang Junyi, it was misunderstood. In particular, the metaphysical foundation that this idea of void offers to his view on morality was overlooked. Tang sees the spirit of Zhang's thought as a whole as having special significance in the context of the human moral mind. Identifying qi with void it denotes complete transformation that in the person is to be understood as primarily moral. According to Tang, a thing must have void within itself, in order to absorb another. Since void is always within things and never outside them, it generates qi, which enables the thing to transcend its own corporeal existence.[55] While Tang correctly pinpoints the significance of void as a foundation for Zhang's morality, when this foundation is understood as nonmetaphysical (or at least not solely metaphysical) it seems to gain more explanatory conviction. Understood as existential rather than metaphysical, void qi as all-pervading and all-encompassing is realized in human life as human *interactions*. These interactions comprise the Way for a human being to broaden oneself, as reflecting one's moral choices, or as free moral actions. The moral significance of void enables transformation and relations rather than signifying cessation. In this context, there is special significance to Zhang Zai's understanding of sincerity (誠 *cheng*) as creativity being the capacity to resonate nature. Correlating void with creativity, Zhang is able to see that the potency of nature is void as a "positive receptivity, that is, the capacity to resonate with the multiplicity of things and dimensions of this world." [56] Thus, Zhang's idea of void has to be treated seriously, especially when referring to the human realm.

Zhang Zai sees qi first, as endless continuous transformation, which is identified with void. Second, the qi-constitution of human nature requires that human nature be accordingly continuous and void. Last, since, the heaven-human continuity of qi necessitates that human nature is moral, therefore, morality is continuous, void, and endless or eternal. We will turn back to this discussion after inquiring into the specific sense in which observing rites, in particular death-related rites, enhance qi, and the special sense of void in this context.

Following Confucius with Void Ritual

Early Confucianism suggests that morality is attained through the ongoing practice of rites (*li*), by which humanity is internalized. According to Zhang Zai, this tension is in fact a tension between the virtue of humanity and qi, through the rites. In other words, through practicing rites, one's qi is preserved and its moral potentiality is realized; as cultivating one's qi is attained through various practices, performing the rites is the cultivation of qi as moral. Zhang states that "nothing makes people progress as quickly as ritual" (ZZJ 265.1, Kasoff 1984, 81), reminding his readers the significance of the rites, in the spirit of the *Analects*' teaching that people are quicker to learn from ritual than from punishment, as the latter simply makes them avoid either the deed or the leader, but does not educate (*Analects* 2.3). [57] He then adds,

> When you make your actions all accord with ritual, then your *qi* constitution will spontaneously become good. (265.9)

Zhang complements the *Analects*' understanding of returning to the rites as preserving humanity (12:1) by his own observation as a paraphrase or expansion of the idea. Indeed, he adds the missing link between rites and goodness, as qi; if the *Analects* tells that when actions are in accord with propriety one is human, Zhang elucidates that the practice directly affects one's qi constitution, which then becomes good by itself. He adds,

> Ritual is the means by which you hold on to your Nature. I claim that it originally comes from the Nature. To hold on to your Nature is to return to the origin. All those who have not yet completed their Nature must hold on to it through ritual. If you can adhere to ritual then you will not stray from the Way. (264.2, Kasoff 1984, 82)

In fact, Zhang's approach can locate him as a conciliator between Mencius and Xunzi. While siding with Mencius that our ability to act morally is endowed from heaven, he more explicitly than Mencius endows ritual with a place of honor as the necessary practice that brings one closer to the Way, similarly to Xunzi. Moreover, in the context of family reverence, as mentioned earlier, the rites have special significance not only as putting virtue into practice, but also through their preserving the living line from ancestors to descendents. Yet, despite the acknowledged importance of the ritualistic code, honoring ancestors is first and foremost honoring their Way. Zhang offers an exceptionally daring and moving example, taken again from his own personal experience.

> In my home we have a portrait of Confucius. I have wanted to place it near my side. (But) to sit facing it would not do; to burn incense would not do either; the ritual of bowing and gazing at it would not do either. I was hard pressed to find a solution. I thought about it. The best thing to do is roll it up and put it away, and honor his Way. (289/9–10, 97)

Zhang makes the point that Confucius is the ancestor who deserves to be honored through rites of propriety and yet whose Way is beyond rites. The strict ritualistic code may not suffice; rather, true family reverence is required for living in the moral Way. The above story seems to have somewhat Daoist, even Chan-Buddhist tones, reminiscent of Zhuang Zhou's forgetting rites in the process of becoming one with the Way (*Zhuangzi* 6.9). In a somewhat similar spirit, Zhang's moral perspective of rites cannot compromise the flexibility and freedom that qi demands; in this sense he takes up from more remote philosophies. However, unlike Zhuang Zhou, who forgets propriety and hence forgets humanity, Zhang forgets the rite of propriety in order to preserve humanity and keep his master's Way alive.

As can be expected, Zhu Xi criticized Zhang Zai's radical independence and inventiveness regarding the significance of rule following in the performance of rituals.[58] Unlike the Confucian expectation, Zhang's notion is described in the above example as void of concrete specifications.[59] Despite the clear

Confucian moral understanding, Zhang Zai's moral sense of forgetting rests on a connection between life, death, and ritual in the context of one body as qi and "roaming freely," as seen in three examples from the *Zhuangzi*. First, recall *Zhuangzi*'s story about the three close friends, one of whom died. One of his friends writes a song, the other plays the *qin*, while both sing together, leading to an interesting question regarding their following of the rites. According to the story, Confucius sends Zigong—the Master of rites—to condole.[60] Upon arrival at the funeral, he sees the body laid out for burial, while the deceased's friends surround him singing. Zigong is disconcerted that the two friends are happily singing over their friend's corpse, and wonders how this behavior accords with the rites. The friends reply: "What does this one know about the rites?!"

The Daoist friends do not say that rites are unnecessary, as one might have expected. Rather, they undermine Zigong's expertise, implying that the Confucian expert Zigong is interested only in the external aspect of ritualistic behavior and is concerned with the correct performance of the ceremony according to the rules as defining what exactly should be done—where, when, and how, rather than *why* it is so done. The Daoist response gives an impression that, in fact, the Daoists in the story may acknowledge the significance of the rites in human life, yet not as a fixed ritualistic pattern of behavior, but rather as an expression of authentic feeling. This soft understanding of rites is extremely different from that of those who see propriety as the ceremonial pattern of behavior or the ritual that should be maintained in all circumstances. Rites are, in this case, definitely not what Benjamin Schwartz sees as the guiding rule of a "community that accepts unblinkingly what it regards as the need for hierarchy, status and authority within a universal world Order."[61]

Zhuang Zhou's amoral position allows him to suggest that rites cannot be a mere set of dogmatic or rigid rules of conduct to be obeyed; they are not a list of dos and don'ts. Rather, the suggested view may be understood as seeing in the rites *more* than mere ceremonial manners. Rites reflect a general pattern allowing things to happen naturally, maintaining and expressing feelings and emotions as transient. According to the story, when Zigong returns to Confucius (or the Zhuangzian depiction of him) puzzled about the lack of propriety of these two people, his Master replies: "They travel outside the system, while I travel within." Confucius stresses that he, first and foremost belongs with the sphere of humanity (*ren* 人); thus, his attitude is different from that of Daoists who aspire to the realm of nature or heaven.[62] Rather

Emerging Out of Life and Death   185

than undermining Zhuang Zhou and his followers, he regrets sending Zigong to condole, since his messenger seems to be concerned with ritual formalities rather than humanity itself.

The story appears not to criticize the idea of the rites per se but rather, it criticizes their dogmatic acceptance. Many of their significant ingredients reappear in Zhang Zai's view: first, inhabiting a common body (*tongti* 同體) allows for abiding by qi; second, following qi is cultivated in a proper practice of the rite (as nondogmatic); and last, qi is cultivated through void (reflected in the text through the practice of forgetting). Yet, similarly to Zhou's and Shao's, Zhang's forgetting is leading to morality. The second Zhuangzian story, this time about Yan Hui, the Confucian exemplary humanist, rather than about Zigong, the exemplary ritualist, gives foundation to Zhang's understanding.[63] When Yan Hui asks Confucius about the behavior of Meng-sun Cai upon his mother's death and wonders how Cai did not shed a tear, felt no distress, and exhibited no sorrow, he receives a reply that is somewhat different from the one Zigong received. Unlike Zigong's worry about the rites that function as the behavioral external expression of humanity, Yan Hui cares about the inner experience of the mourner, or the *meaning* of propriety (*liyi* 禮意) that Zigong seemed to overlook. Yan Hui is therefore treated in the *Zhuangzi* with significant respect, gaining a response through a Zhuangzian dream argument, oriented at shaking the dogmatic understanding of reality, then inviting Yan Hui to access the endless transformations.[64] With the Daoist seeing how the eternity of endless transformations unifies with morality, it is easier to understand the Confucian senses of void and forgetting.

Before coming back to Zhang's philosophy, the last example from *Zhuangzi* brings the story of a father coming with his son to condole Laozi's death (*Zhuangzi* 3.5), can serve as reminder that mourning is a family matter and that the son can learn from the occasion. The father cries out three times and goes out. The astonished disciples (and probably the son too) do not primarily question the deed; rather, they refer to the father's *friendship* with their Master. They wonder: Were you not a friend of the Master? . . . Is it proper to mourn in like this? The presupposition again is that if it is an authentic feeling of sadness and true friendship, then it is an appropriate ritualistic manner for mourning. However, the critical reply addresses the way all others were mourning: old men wail as if they lost a son, and young men wail as if they lost their mother. It cannot be taken for granted that everyone among the mourners feels the same or wishes to cry in one way and to say the same words. In fact, to the father, such unison of expression seemed inappropriate, not authentic, and as if "hiding from heaven, turning away from reality, forgetting what we received."[65]

The three friends whose friendship was so close that it sufficed them to look at each other's eyes, smile at each other's face, and simply understand, are characterized as understanding in yet another version of *Zhuangzi*'s one-body riddle: "mounting up into the sky, roaming without limits, forgetting each other and *live forever*" (emphasis my own). The harmony among them, their friendship and its spirit live forever, such that they don't fear death; for them, living in the present in harmony and friendship is immortality.

The uniqueness in Zhang Zai's idea of on body leading to void qi, hence to void morality and rites lies in his not giving up ethics. In other words, the "roaming freely" in harmony as the way to live forever (*sheng wusuo zhongxiong* 生無所終窮) receives the Confucian version of gaining freedom as presented in the *Analects* 2:4, with Confucius telling his life story, when at the age of seventy he internalized morality to the point that he wanted to do what he morally had to do. Zhang Zai seems to accept a view of human roaming in the ongoing transformations, yet according to his understanding, family reverence is just as natural and thus part of this harmony, insofar as human beings are discussed.

Rethinking rites, one should recall that the real Confucius as well is known to care about inner expression, rather than sticking with formal codes. For example, in *Analects* 3:26, he criticizes the act of keeping mourning rites with no sadness. In *Analects* 17:21, in the example of the Master's accepting Zai Wo's giving up on the ritualistic demand of a three-year mourning period, the Master refers to Zai Wo's lack of inner expression of virtue. In 3:4, when a disciple asks to know the first thing to be attended to in the rites, the Master replies that in mourning rites, deep sorrow is more important than minute attention to observances; in 11:11, the Master rejects his disciples' wish to perform a large ceremony on Yan Hui's death, since he wanted to bury him like his own son; in 17:11, Confucius criticizes those who claim "it is according to rites, it is according to rites" (*liyun liyun* 禮云禮云), asking: "are gems and silk all that is meant by propriety?" to stresses the precedence of inner feelings over external meticulousness.

An even more interesting example appears in the *Book of Rites*' chapter "Confucius at Home at Leisure" (*Kongzi Xian Ju* 孔子閑居), which offers a perspective advocating propriety that does not require specific or necessary externalization. In the text, Zi Xia wonders about the proper ruler, who can be called the people's father and mother (*fuminzhi fumuyi* 夫民之父母乎).

Emerging Out of Life and Death 187

Confucius replies that he must have penetrated the principles of the rites and music to the five extremes (*wuzhi* 五至) and three nones (*sanwu* 三無), explaining then, that the three nones are music with no sound; rites with no body, and mourning with no mourning clothes (*wusheng zhiyue, wuti zhili, wufu zhisang* 無聲之樂, 無體之禮 , 無服之喪).[66] Even at the core of the Confucian canon of rites, we find appreciation for an understanding of the rites through a nonbounding definition, in a via negativa, understanding what propriety is really about: no specified body of behaviors, no limited sound (such as a crying sound), no dress code. In other words, the rites cannot be understood exclusively as the ceremonial practice itself.

Returning to Zhang Zai's story about the inability to mourn for Confucius according to any dictated rite, it appears again that Zhang Zai adopts some Daoistic lessons, without contradicting Confucian views. In his personal treatment of human life and morality, he justifies that first no single fixed way exists for mourning. Also, acting dogmatically over one's death exposes a severe lack of understanding of qi transformations and roaming in them. Similarly to Zhuang Zhou, Zhang Zai seems to imply that the people who pay attention to formal, external aspects alone do not understand the true significance of the rites. By implying that under certain circumstances, revering Confucius's memory and heritage can be accomplished without formalistically sticking to accepted rituals and that this is properly honoring the Way, Zhang Zai appears closer to Zhuang Zhou than to his Confucian Master.

Later, Confucian interpreters stressed the inner aspect of rites, such that while rites refer to norms of behavior in which active participation is of high value, humanity gives them their meaning. In this spirit, Tu Weiming says, "Man cannot live without *li*, but when *li* becomes wholly determinative, he is no longer really man."[67] From a different perspective, Herbert Fingarette, who sees the centrality of the rites, claims that the effortlessness in performing rites cannot be mechanical or automatic: a certain spirit in the ceremony gives it life. As Fingarette notes, holiness exists in human existence that is central in Confucianism and is expressed in the attitude toward the simplest daily affairs.[68] The true essence of ritual does not lie in its outer shell.

When, in the above example of Confucius portrait, Zhang Zai asks to honor Confucius by *not* performing the ritual of honoring his master, he follows the Confucian Way as his Way, without rejecting ritual. In his reference to honoring Confucius, he finds room for greater flexibility regarding the rites as a realization of moral qi. In doing so, he implies the basic idea that death—in particular a death of a person who lived a full life—is not a tragedy.

The foundation for this approach is that acting according to fixed paradigms cannot be in harmony with qi. The rites have special significance in intimate family practices; revering family is a compelling commitment and responsibility in Confucianism, yet it cannot be accomplished by sticking to external codes alone. This is perhaps also the point that Zhu Xi wishes to make in saying that Zhang Zai's WI is in fact on humanity rather than solely on family reverence, as mentioned earlier.

Connecting the significance of family reverence as a model for the continuity of morality with void rites as means for realizing qi as moral, one should pay special attention to ancestral worshiping, as worshiping of moral life. Through the rites, the deceased comes back to life, or in other words, the moral Way never dies. This leads to Zhang's transcending boundaries in his view on moral life and moral death.

A CONFUCIAN SENSE OF IMMORTALITY

Transcending Life and Death through Joyful Family Relations

From the centrality of family reverence as a model for human morality, Zhang's WI reaches its concluding idea of restful death, understood as primarily moral. Since it is morality by which one relates to the universe, one gains a sense of transcendence through morality, which annuls the fear of death. The idea is preceded in a less explicit manner through the association between heaven and human continuity, in Mencius's approach that by retaining the heart and nurturing one's nature, one is serving heaven. Then, whether one is going to die young or live to an old age makes no difference to one's moral dedication (7A.1). The point that if one is moral, dying young or living to an old age becomes pointless is connected, again, to the early Confucian understanding that morality is about having joy in one's deeds, in the present.

As noted earlier, this approach is already apparent in Mencius's personal statement that "There is no greater joy for me than to find, on self-examination, that I am true to myself" (7A.4), as well as the idea of joy in morality (as learning and hospitalizing friends) as appears already in the very opening of the *Analects*.[69] Joy and pleasure as human feelings that accompany a moral deed have moral significance that reveals a moral idealism of a special practical kind, within which the ideal is practiced daily. Moral duty as joy, peace of mind, or what Albert Camus refers to as the will to happiness is possible when an individual becomes conscious of the necessary and inseparable relationship of life and moral duty. It is a conscious choice to act morally, which is responded to in one's happiness as the moral requirement according to which "Your one duty is to live and be happy."[70]

The consciousness of happiness as a choice is attained through authentically loving others. The philosophical attitude that gives moral significance to joy not only allows life to be lived joyfully, but also requires the moral person to seeing the existential imperative as an imperative to joyful life, which enables resting in peace at the end of life. The Mencian point that self-reflection brings to knowledge of others and care for them is restated by Zhang, who elsewhere paraphrases *Analects* 12:1 "overcoming oneself and returning to propriety."

> To overcome oneself and behave by the rules is to be a virtuous man; to rejoice in oneself and be able to serve as the pattern [for others] is to be a sage.[71]

In this sense, Zhang Zai's saying "protecting them [my parents] when the time comes is the care of a son; to be joyful and without anxiety, is to be genuinely filial" (*leqie buyou chunhu, xiaozheye*樂且不憂，純乎孝者也), shows that family reverence is caring as being happy, having no anxiety and no fear. In particular, as Zhang implies in his conclusion, there is no fear of death.

In his treatise, Zhang introduces his own version of Confucian idealistic morality by first presenting all humans as one family; second, explaining that as such we are all morally committed to our cosmic parents through family reverence; third, concluding with the idea that this filial morality brings joy in life and peace in death.

> Wealth, nobility, and good fortune will enrich my life; Poverty, lowliness and sorrow, accomplish my deed.
> In life I follow and serve. When death arrives I rest.

The uniqueness of Zhang Zai's inclusive humanistic suggestion receives an intensifying tone by referring to its Zhuangzian amoral counterpart. Chapter 6 of the *Zhuangzi* refers twice to the great Mass of nature in which one finds "support of body," namely, in death. Zhuang Zhou sees life as toiling on it (*laowo yisheng*勞我以生); old age as seeking ease on it; and death as find rest in it (*xiwo yisi*息我以死). Therefore, what makes one's life good makes one's death good as well (*Zhuangzi* 6.2, 6.5). One can wonder whether this may be an earlier version of the concluding sentences in WI, "In life I follow and serve. When death arrives I rest"; the Zhuangzian labor leading to rest seems rather close in spirit to the labor Zhang Zai refers to. Without explicitly mentioning family reverence, both occurrences of the phrase in the *Zhuangzi* are preceded by reference to parents and the obligation to love and serve one's father and mother—be they cosmic or personal. In *Zhuangzi* 6.2, we read that "Death and life are ordained. There are those who specially regard Heaven as their father, and they still love it...." However, not only for him death and life are ordained and cannot be chosen, moreover, as soon as Zhuang Zhou acknowledges the power of family reverence and attributes this relationship to men and nature, he immediately makes the following reservation: "how much more should they love that which stands out!" Unlike Zhuang Zhou's heaven and earth that are beyond humans, Zhang Zai sees heaven and earth as one's father and mother. In a similar spirit, after the story about the four who become friends through understanding the riddle of life and death, we read in *Zhuangzi* 6.5.

> Wherever a parent tells a son to go, east, west, south, or north, he simply follows the command. The Yin and Yang are more to a man than his parents are. If they are hastening my death, and I do not quietly submit to them, I shall be obstinate and rebellious.

Zhuang Zhou moves on to presenting the cosmic poles of yin and yang as parents, offering an interesting Daoist twist regarding what family reverence is about. In the *Zhuangzi*, the implication is first and foremost that if heaven or nature wishes so, it would be stupid to wrestle against it, and trusting our parents is being able to die peacefully. For Zhuang Zhou, yin-yang's status as father and mother is a metaphor, while in fact they are more than that. He, therefore, sees this relatedness as second best, holding that preferably, people should not limit themselves to father and mother.

When Zhang Zai uses the analogies to parents and to ruler for describing the relatedness between earth and humans, he unifies a sentiment that is similar to the one in Zhuang Zhou's philosophy, with a Confucian moral attitude. Heaven and earth as parents demand that we accept transformations that enable peaceful death. For him, the one ongoing process of transformation of life and death necessarily includes the moral perspective of seeing the cosmic one body as one family. As such, we are all *morally* committed to our cosmic parents through family reverence bringing joy in life and peace in death.

In the present picture, morality begins with family reverence in the closer circles and expands to all parts of the universe as an ability to embody the universe.[72] The person is depicted as an expanding entity in a moral sense, as one who cultivates morality. The body does not start with one's toes and end at the tips of the hair; rather, one's body is that which fills heaven and earth; it is more than physical form. For this reason, whatever happens to others affects oneself, or happens to one's (expanded) body. In this way nothing, in fact, happens to others, since there is no absolute other. Living well is living harmoniously, and living harmoniously is essentially living an interconnected moral life, leading to peaceful death. Just as dynamic living characterizes nature, so does morality characterize human beings.

One crucial implication of this understanding is seeing death as a phenomenon that is to be treated in the intimate familial context through family reverence and ancestral worship, which thus preserves continuity between life and death. This continuity is attained through following the Confucian humanistic system, which from the practical perspective is reflected in the rites of propriety. As Confucius instructed, "When your parents are alive, observe the rites in serving them; when they die, observe the rites in burying them" (2:5).[73] An interesting feature of this life-death moral continuity is that through preserving one's parents' rites, the parents are in some sense always present. Thereby, through filial care not only is the tradition preserved, but also every human being, by virtue of being somebody's son or daughter, can last after death.

This moral attitude of suspending one's existential boundaries is extremely intriguing with regard to a possible moral sense of immortality. Can it be taken as neither mystical nor metaphysical? What sense can moral eternity or morally transcending the boundaries between life and death make in Zhang's broader philosophy? Zhang's notion of qi corresponds with these open questions.

Moral Qi as Timelessness (Explained with a Wittgensteinean Tip)

As indicated above, morality as realizing qi transcends all boundaries, even the boundary between life and death. Questions to address in this context include whether Zhang Zai, in fact, suggests an idea of eternal life, and if so, what sense of eternity he refers to, and how can it be sought. The idea of the void as endless and eternal and, therefore, seeking eternity is seeking voidness, can serve as a starting point for this inquiry. Since the human eye cannot ordinarily notice void, Zhang suggests seeking it by other means.

> The blueness of *qi* (in the sky) is where the eye stops. The sun and moon, stars and planets, are visible images. (From the visible,) you should seek the void-ness of heaven with your mind. (ZZJ 326.1, Kasoff 1984, 59)

Zhang Zai uses the visual field as an image to express his attitude toward what is seen and what is invisible, what dies and what forever lives. While the visual field is endless, the eye rests on visible images; the eye stops where it is blue, yet void fills everything. Thus, since according to Zhang Zai, one should seek the invisible and endless, or the void, one should seek it with the mind, and not with the eye. The human mind is moral and morality, as we have seen, is ultimately void (ZZJ 325.1, 59; 326.3, 59). This feature of morality embodies an important seed for hope. Zhang says,

> The Way and virtue, Nature and destiny: these are all things which exist forever, never dying. The individual dies, but these always exist. (ZZJ 273.7, 68)

Within the continuity of qi from heaven to the human sphere, the human aspect of nature is the moral nature (*daode* 道德). Since the Way lives forever, with no spatial boundaries or obstacles that defeat it, morality as void and continuous is hence endless or eternal; it is always existent. Kim refers to the same idea from the perspective of learning. Accordingly, for Zhang Zai stopping learning is dying, signifying real death as the death of the heart-mind; a body without learning is a body with no heart-mind that is inert.[74] Zhang thereby creates an idea of moral eternity or an alternative sense of immortality.

The philosophical weight of this moral eternity can be better appreciated in light of the philosophy of Ludwig Wittgenstein (1889–1951). According to Wittgenstein's *Notebooks*: "For life in the present there is no death" (75e). By living in the present, such that there is no death, Wittgenstein seeks to stress that life neither consequentially refers to a future end, nor does it refer to history as a possible deterministic mechanism. Later on, in *Tractatus Logico-Philosophicus* (hereafter abbreviated as *Tractatus*), Wittgenstein elaborates.

> Death is not an event in life: we do not live to experience death. If we take eternity to mean not infinite temporal duration but timelessness, then eternal life belongs to those who live in the present. Our life has no end in just the way in which our visual field has no limits. (6.4311)[75]

Wittgenstein uses an analogy to the limitless visual field that reaches everywhere and has no concrete spatial limits, which can be interestingly compared to Zhang Zai's referring to the limited eye (see above ZZJ 326.1), as opposed to the boundless voidness of nature. The visual field, unlike the auditory range, is timeless; in it, things appear as analogous, on one plain and always in an eternal present. A visual field always intersects with other fields ad infinitum, and no one can point to where it begins or ends. Likewise, life is much more than merely physical existence. Like in Zhang's philosophy, life is duration as movement, change, and continuity; therefore, as per Wittgenstein's understanding, death as cessation is not within life: when death occurs, life ends. Hence, from the perspective of the person—the *living*—the present is eternal, and those who live in the present live eternal life. Wittgenstein redefines the notion of eternity as one that is not subject to time, but rather exists outside the realm of time, or as timelessness, like the visual field. Therefore, Wittgenstein's saying that "Death is not an event of life. One does not live to experience death," should not be interpreted to mean that death *cannot* be said to be experienced, because from the individual perspective it occurs after life. Wittgenstein is clearly not concerned with immortality of the soul in the Platonic or neo-Platonic sense; he does not refer to death as an endless cycle, as read in the dialogue *Phaedo*; the point is not whether the body rots or is rejuvenated. Yet, if so, why mention eternity as something that exists in some sense, if Wittgenstein actually only intended to say that death is outside life in the above sense?

Wittgenstein's "Lectures on Religious Belief" (abbreviated as LRB) opens with a clue.

> An Austrian general said to someone: "I shall think of you after my death, if that should be possible." We can imagine one group who would find this ludicrous, another who wouldn't.[76]

By focusing not on death, but rather on *attitudes* toward death, Wittgenstein explores the distinction between different *forms of life* (*lebensform*). In brief, a form of life—as a nontechnical term that connotes the sociological, historical, linguistic, physiological, and behavioral determinants comprising the matrix within which a given language has meaning—is distinguished by its own language game (*sprachspiel*) defining its framework and its rules. According to Wittgenstein, it is a form of life within which death plays a major role.[77] Moreover, the role of death is suggested in LRB as defining a form of life (in particular, death comprises the difference between religious versus nonreligious forms of life). For example, LRB stresses the important point that belief in the Last Judgment comprises a basis for or foundation of a form of life that Wittgenstein does not share, and this belief marks the line between him and his interlocutor.[78]

Wittgenstein is not concerned with what *in fact* happens after death; rather, he is interested in the form of life that is lived as embodying a certain faith regarding death. For Wittgenstein, as the nonreligious party in the conversations, the point in death cannot be metaphysical; death refers neither to divine providence nor to immortality and afterlife, and yet its significance is great.

Accordingly, one's view of eternal life, not in the sense of temporal immortality, provides a basis for one's understanding of life and death. Within the life we lead, death has no perspective of its own; rather, the living attitude to death provides *guidance* for one's *entire life*, such that every deed within the form of life is oriented toward it.[79] For example, within an orthodox monotheistic form of life, the attitude of heaven and hell guides every action from blessing God when one wakes up, through expressing gratefulness before taking all food and drink, to blaming oneself for one's own sickness taken as a divine response for a sinful deed, or hoping to meet a friend again after she passed away.

The guidance Wittgenstein refers to is oriented toward deeds, and human deeds are moral deeds. Understanding this connects to Wittgenstein's living in the present as living *morally*; in a way in which eternal life begins in the present (that is, during life). Since life as moral is continuous and endless, death comprises ethical death or the death of the *moral* agent.[80] Immortality receives a moral dimension: the moral approach, not the concrete person, is timeless and becomes immortal in this sense. Realizing that this is the point with regard to death, Wittgenstein says, "There I begin to attach ideas, perhaps ethical ideas of responsibility."[81] Responsibility as part of moral beliefs is allowing life as an eternal present, and unlike the body it cannot rot or disintegrate. He writes,

> A great writer said that when he was a boy, his father set him a task, and suddenly felt that nothing, not even death, could take away his responsibility [in doing the task]; this was his duty to do so, and that even death couldn't stop it being his duty. He said that this was, in a way a proof of immortality of the soul—because if this lives on [the responsibility won't die].[82]

When Wittgenstein refers to duty as timeless, he means that duty and its relation to moral beliefs are values in themselves, and not subject to time—duty is not associated to a belief in immortality in the traditional sense. Wittgenstein refers to the moral attitude as becoming immortal in allowing one to attach ideas, such as responsibility and duty. Like in the Confucian context, Wittgenstein represents an ideal-oriented view of ethics, as opposed to traditional religious views of immortality typifying the means-end moral theory, since the latter represent a "live now and pay later" policy (reflecting the consequentialist view of ethics). For Wittgenstein, reward or punishment in the afterlife are irrelevant; the moral ideal has intrinsic value in itself, and thus as a duty has timeless moral value. Similarly, in "Lectures on Ethics" (LE), the absolute good is referred to as something that a practitioner feels compelled to enact in life.

> And similarly the absolute good, if it is a describable state of affairs, would be one which everybody, independent of his tastes and inclinations, would necessarily bring about or feel guilty for not bringing about. (LE 7)

In a somewhat Mencian spirit, realizing morality, independently of tastes or of inclinations, is presented as a natural and necessary human tendency. Wittgenstein's proponent, D. Z. Phillips, expanded this notion by developing the alternative understanding of death and immortality, through his idea of living life virtuously in order to overcome death. Unlike Plato's proposing that the philosopher prepares for death as external to life, during life through virtue, Phillips "overcomes death" through living life morally or with what he calls a sense of decency.

> Immortality might mean ... moral attitudes ... Eternal life would mean living and dying in a way which could not be rendered pointless by death.[83]

In the Wittgensteinean line, Phillips rejects all types of traditional arguments regarding immortality. According to the traditional Western view, immortality serves as a basis for ethical behavior in this life in the shade of future salvation.[84] Phillips revises the traditional view, such that the immortal is not something after life, but rather it exists alongside life. In this way, immortality refers to present life, rather than to an extension of life or something beyond it. Phillips conceives of immortality as in the present, as something inseparable from the ethical behavior of the individual during his lifetime. While the immortal is concurrent with the present, Phillips's view of immortality also necessitates an important shift from the temporal to the eternal.[85]

Phillips states that according to his view, the discussion on death is rendered pointless by a moral sense of decency and in that sense, death is overcome. Death is no longer to be feared, since death in itself is temporal; and yet, importantly, it is the *moral attitude* of an individual that become eternal. Death is rendered pointless because it is the ethical content of existence that matters.

> Immortality of soul, and its eternal predicate, lies in the moral beliefs of the believer and his relationship to God as eternal. Therefore, the temporal quality of death is overcome by the eternal when the believer lives according to God's moral precepts or God's life.[86]

Wittgenstein says, "Ethics, if it is anything, is supernatural," in the sense that "[a] teacup will only hold a teacup full of water if I were to pour out a gallon over it" (LE, 7). In other words, according to Wittgenstein, ethics as supernatural involves absolute values in one's life.[87] The important relationship between form of life, death, and ethics in Wittgenstein's paradigm, ends up such that metaphysics loses its meaning, and the primary significance of death is ethical. Similarly to the Confucian perspective, ethical choices are those that enable the individual to lead a happy, nonfearful life: Wittgenstein says, "A man who is happy must have no fear. Not even in the face of death" (*Notebooks* 74e). For death to be feared, death must be a future event, reflecting the traditional view of death. However, the eternal present or timelessness cannot refer to death in a linear sense, as an end. When Wittgenstein writes: "For life in the present, there is no death," he means that death is overcome, as Phillips suggests, when an individual lives morally or joyfully in the present.

Merging the ideas discussed so far with the Wittgensteinean tip from the West, we realize that Zhang Zai's idea of serving heaven and earth like parents leads to a restful death, if we understand that being filial reflects a moral attitude to life that defines one's form of life as moral and is reflected in the attitude toward death. The moral attitude overcomes death through endless duty, which is also joy. The Confucian form of life is defined by the system of rites as reflecting morality, for which family reverence is the source. Death rituals, especially ancestral worshiping, *guide* one with rites as filial, not only through life but also through death. Thereby, family reverence—as both morally steady and perpetual—endows the notion of eternity with the sense of living timelessly, or morally living in the present. According to Zhang Zai, eternity is embodied in qi, and is morally realized through the rites. The system of rites can be treated as the language game or the rules that enable the knowledge of the world and proper conduct, namely, the Confucian form of life. Thus, the Confucian form of life is also a form of death. There is neither a dichotomy between the dead and the living nor a beyondism of another world, which is beyond the human and superior to it in justifying human action.

Wittgenstein's limitless visual field as analogous to life sheds light on the Confucian view of the infinite and eternal ever-expanding net of morally related selves. Through moral feelings, knowledge, and deeds, one transcends one's own life and reaches unto others' lives, thus losing any concrete end. In this way, each individual lives in other places and in other persons, as all things in the universe intertwine eternally. Moral Life endows a human being with a sense of immortality. The continuity that early Confucianism stresses can also be expressed as filling heaven and earth with one's body, which grows into a larger whole beyond the biological being. This continuity keeps our parents in us, even when physically they are gone, and obliges us, as *self-cultivators*, to be family reverent. This continuity embodies a sense of immortality, while in fact it is a sense of morality. It is about our own living morally in the present, which enables us to carry on our ancestors' lives and respect their traditions. Family reverence is continuous, timeless, and beyond concrete existence in time.

In the Confucian context, we may use the terminology of overcoming death in this sense as an acceptance that brings to no fear and to moral eternity.[88] Confucianism is a philosophy and a practice that honors the traditions of the past such that history is a living agent in the tradition, and one's genealogy and family history is essential for who one is. In particular, Zhang Zai's idea of family reverence as the root for humanity from which the Way grows enables one to overcome death in Phillips's terminology, or "to hear the Way in the morning, and to possibly die in the evening," as suggested in the *Analects* 4:8 (*zhao wendao xisi keyi* 朝聞道, 夕死可矣). When one understands the timelessness in the Way as its eternity, then one gains eternity by tying oneself to a being of eternity (as the Way) and thus overcoming death by accepting it without fighting it or wishing to eliminate or defy it (as in religious Daoism).

Sageliness as Transcending Life and Death

If Zhou Dunyi's sage is the cultivated person who transcended finitude-infinitude boundary and lives in reality as one, and Shao Yong's sage transcends in-out dichotomy, knowing the world as one—Zhang Zai's sage transcends life-death boundary and lives forever. Zhang's idea that unlike the individual or the individual's body (*shen* 身), morality lasts forever (273.7) is a statement of complete faith in human moral power. Interestingly, it also enfolds in it a moral hope as alternative to the religious promise for afterlife. Since in Confucianism there is no idea of retribution or outcome of moral deeds that is different from the deed itself, this sense of immortality as coined by D. Z. Phillips, is gained in one's life, as morally lived in the present. As neither a promise for afterlife nor a guarantee that one will never die, this immortality is a power to overcome death—not in the sense of fighting a gigantic enemy and defying it, but in the sense of making it pointless for discussion. In this sense Confucius's avoidance of discussing death becomes more meaningful than ever.

In the context of Zhang's philosophy, this overcoming death is inherent in human existence as qi—the vital power that ignites and comprises life, which enables the moral continuum, in particular as manifested in family reverence—and by nature is eternal, or making death pointless. While the individual dies, heavenly moral nature never dies; morality overcomes death.

In this way, morality is immortal, such that this immortality is the ultimate moral attainment one can aspire to. One can attain sagehood by learning and transforming the qi-constitution for a morally better constitution, and sagely understanding is the understanding of the transformation.

According to Zhang Zai, the sagely mind, the moral transforming mind, is naturally void (324.13); it is void of fixities and devoid of sensual turbidity. As such, the moral mind (just like a void) lasts forever. Yet, it lasts not as an entity, but rather as the unique dynamism of unceasing, ever-lasting moral development. Thus, Zhang refers to the sage, the ultimate moral exemplar, as the one who attained ultimate voidness (325.10). In this moral Way a sage lives eternally, and his morality is always present. For Zhang, being content with knowledge gained from sensory perception only is being stupid (307.8), as moral knowledge does not stem from sensory perception (24.11–13). A sage recognizes the unity of all things and understands that all phenomena—human as nonhuman—are governed by the same course of interaction and succession of polar forces.[89] This understanding enables a sage to transcend self-interest and regard his or her own physical being as a thing—but also to transcend this thingness.

> When the principles of heaven are always present, yourself and things are all seen; then you are not selfish, [because you realize] you are also a thing. (In this manner,) people often transcend their own bodies, and thus achieve clarity. (ZZJ 285.4–6, 107)

The voidness of sagely qi is manifested through being without a self, or in the Confucian sense, as not being selfish. The idea combines the understanding of the *Analects* regarding the sage caring for others and having the same predisposition as others, with a flavor of the Buddhist Mahayana notion of no self (*anatman*), which centers on the absence of a metaphysical self and stresses moral responsibility toward others (rather than an annihilation of the self).[90] Being a sagely self, which is not ontologically founded as a self, or which is a no self, enables living after death as pure morality and an ongoing responsibility toward others. Thus, one only becomes a "self-like" that is not oneself in the sense that he or she is inherently connected to and nourished by other members of the human community and other parts of the universe.

Being able to partake of everything in the world is the sage's way of expanding family reverence; according to WI: "that which fills the universe is my body and that which directs it is my nature." The sage's body fills the universe through moral relatedness as a moral and eternal family member. Being at ease with the endless transformations of body, the sage is at ease with the void (as the ongoing transformations) and is not disturbed in facing death. Being empty, Zhang Zai's sage is ultimately also without knowledge.

> Being 'without knowledge' lies in there being nothing you do not know. If you say you have knowledge, then there are things you do not know. Only because (Confucius) was 'without knowledge' was he able to fully present both sides. This is what the *Change* calls 'quiescent and unmoving; when stimulated then it penetrates.' (ZZJ 200.7–8, Kasoff 1984, 108)

Zhang Zai takes being without knowledge to mean lacking a knowledge of knowledge, or simply living life as is; this is the ability to be impartial and to see the whole picture. Zhang Zai refers to no knowledge as responsiveness. The sage manifests his comprehensiveness when he is called to.

> The great bell never makes a sound (itself); it makes a sound only when it is struck. The sage never has knowledge; he has knowledge only when he is questioned. (ZZJ 31.14, Kasoff 1984, 109)

Unlike Western carillon bells, the Chinese bell has no clapper and it is struck from outside. This structure serves as a symbol for the important functional aspect of emptiness.[91] The bell, empty in itself and thus soundless, produces a wonderful sound when struck. Notably, the sound does *not* originate in the bell (as the metal cast); rather, sound emerges from the meeting of the metal shell, the external struck, and the emptiness within. The instant of this meeting—the sound—endows emptiness with this unique operative value, making the bell into a bell. If that emptiness could have been removed from the bell, it would not have produced the chiming sound; it would not have been a bell. This emptiness cannot be destroyed, and while its intrinsic nature is eternal and unchanging, in relation to things it is specifiable and limited. Zhang Zai demonstrates the importance of the functionality of emptiness with the assistance of the *Zhuangzi*.

> The clarity of the sage is just like Cook Ding's butchering an Ox. He knows all the cervices; the blade passes through the empty spaces. "The whole ox" is not (what he sees). (JJZ 335.10, Kasoff 1984, 111)

To make his point regarding the usefulness of emptiness, Zhang Zai refers to *Zhuangzi*'s cook Ding, whose wisdom is shown through his professional attitude, exhibiting perfect harmony.[92] His movement, the sound of his knife, and the sight of his action all merge to produce a work of art; they become the dance of *dao*. Indeed, at first he saw an ox, then he ceased seeing the whole ox, and only then, similarly to Zhang Zai's later suggestion, he was able to meet it with the spirit, not with the eyes. Thus, the use of the senses was discarded, and the spirit could act. The cook explains that he can now observe the natural lines, allowing the knife to match harmoniously and with no effort, such that it "slips through the great crevices and slides through the great cavities, taking advantage of the facilities thus presented."[93] The sagely art is not an art of force or strength; rather it is an art of finding the empty spaces that are easy to penetrate, such that obstacles disappear. The art of connecting with emptiness is the art of no knowledge. Critically, this notion definitely also implies not fearing death.

When Zhuang Zhou refers to the sage who "considers early death or old age, his beginning and his ending, all to be good" (6.2), this is possible because the sage forgot morality. Zhang Zai's view of no knowledge is likewise connected with the art of life, death, and the sage, yet, seeing the sage as moral opposes Zhuang Zhou's view. For Zhang Zai, morality is a necessity without which the human world cannot be understood. In Zhang Zai's philosophy, being without the knowledge of knowledge should be positively stated as having knowledge internalized, similarly to what Confucius sees in Emperor Shun who rules with no action because he completely internalized the rites. Rather than behaving like a Zhuangzian spontaneous fish, he acts like a cultivated practitioner of the rites, sitting facing north.[94] In the passage quoted above, Zhang Zai makes this point clear when he refers to Confucius as the one who was without knowledge and thus was able to fully present both sides; namely, knowledge was part of who he was. Morality can be spontaneous when wholly internalized.

The important difference between the two attitudes in the context of transcending the boundary between life and death becomes obvious on recalling the three Zhuangzian friends whose friendship was so close that the rites were not needed for them to mourn, who *knew* the true meaning of his one body riddle as "mounting up into the sky, roaming without limits, forgetting each other and *live forever*" (6.6, emphasis mine). The harmony among them, their friendship and its spirit live forever, such that they don't fear death; for them, immortality is living in the present in harmony and friendship. The roaming freely in harmony as the way to live forever (*sheng wusuo zhongxiong* 生無所終窮) receives a humanistic Confucian version of internalized morality in Zhang Zai's philosophy. Zhang Zai seems to accept a view of human roaming in the ongoing transformation, yet according to his understanding, for humans morality beginning with family reverence is just as natural and thus part of this harmony. For Zhang Zai, "what the *Change* calls 'quiescent and unmoving'; when stimulated then it penetrates" (ZZJ 200.7–8, 108) is necessarily moral too. Following the Mencian Confucian line, sagehood for Zhang is the given human natural endowment, as moral knowing not to know; yet there is always mutual play between the natural (moral) endowment and the moral act, which must be balanced.

> The great sea does not moisten; it moistens (only) because there is thirst. The greatest humaneness is without kindness; there is kindness (only) because there is insufficiency. (ZZJ 34.14, Kasoff 1984, 109)

The sagely virtue is voidness as true openness to others, as *qi* meeting *qi* and void meeting void, which keeps the moral balance. In fact, this voidness is the ability to penetrate and transform. No-knowledge in this case amounts to not limiting oneself, giving up prefixed ideas for the sake of simply responding to the matter at stake. The sage's openness is given form and function in moral responses; his practice influences the world's moral growth and reflects back as moral immortality.

CONCLUSION: MORALITY AS (A SENSE OF) IMMORTALITY

When Zhang Zai refers to heaven and earth as father and mother, he broadens the circle of the family and grants family reverence rootedness in the Confucian form of life, as well as in one's predisposition. A close reading of WI reveals that family reverence allows one to transcend not only family moral boundaries, but also the boundary between life and death. However, while the moral perspective is quite clear, the existential leap to life and death might still be puzzling. While the Daoist attitude connects the idea of one body (as qi) directly with immortality, it is not coincidental that Zhang Zai uses the family as a link between the idea of one body and that of his moral sense of immortality.

The choice of family as a model gives a rather solid ground for transcending one's boundaries through universality, naturalness, transformation, connectedness, and continuity. As for universality and naturalness, we all are family members; each and every person is someone's son or daughter, each and every person carries her parents' DNA; we are all born into families. With regard to transformation, the family is a microcosm for differences, which presupposes diversity and dynamism. A family relates members who are old with others who can be so young that their views cannot even be expressed in words; members of different genders with different attitudes and practical preferences; members who have different backgrounds, who are related by marriage or adoption, but are equally obliged to the family. As for connectedness, the family calls for a practice of caring. In the family, the responsibility for others is an outcome of the incessant search for one's realizing oneself. Family necessitates dialogue as a ceaseless ongoing practice that cannot be considered attained following a lonely, one-time occurrence. It embodies a channel to moral life through the virtue of family reverence. The life commitment of family reverence that Confucianism accentuates leans on the understanding that the family serves as a practical guide for life, tightly connected to a ritualistic code of behavior. In theory, we may talk about building our relationship with people and with the world explained through grand principles; yet in practice, any relationship begins from the relationship with one's parents.

Last, family is by definition an ongoing, everlasting continuity. Family requires us to see the need to transcend ourselves and reach others, and as self-transcending we reveal that the family gives us power to keep living beyond the limits of our actual lives, as part of the family. In this way, it overcomes dichotomies of immanence and transcendence, life and death.

With this in mind can the Confucian explanation of one body be given in terms of qi. Zhang's discussion on qi expands the understanding of the latter, such that the moral body of family in fact is revealed as a realization of the qi that fills the space between heaven and earth, as a matter that is never lost and transcends existential boundaries, including the boundary between life and death. While death is cessation in the physical sense, the moral qi of a person—cultivated in the family through the rites—is not annihilated in death. The practice of the rites and ancestral worship in particular is worshiping life, namely, the life of our ancestors, which thus is maintained consistently during life and death. One should serve the dead as if they were alive, such that family reverence clearly keeps a living thread of morality.[95] Thereby, moral qi overcomes the fear of death, and turns death pointless for discussion. Being filial, thus, reflects an individual's attitude toward morality that overcomes death.

This attitude is rooted in the opening of the *Book of Family Reverence*, with reference to human disposition, such that every physical or mental character that one has is parental endowment.[96] This continuity is Zhang's one body, which also involves keeping our parents in us, even when they are physically gone, and obliges us, as self-cultivators, to be filial. The outcome of this practice is gaining a sense of immortality, which in fact comprises morality. In this way, family reverence is timeless; it is beyond concrete existence in time.

Zhang's philosophical renewal is the nurturing qi through family practice, which unifies the old distinct ideas of moral continuity with qi-continuity.

Zhang's idea of expanding family reverence accentuates the pragmatic foundation of the moral view, such that the justification is organic and inherent. His philosophy of qi expands the practical foundation of the moral view such that the matter of which all life is comprised of necessarily contains morality, which guides us on how to live and die, in the sense that physical death becomes pointless in the face of morality.[97] For Zhang, living well is necessarily living morally, which also prepares one for death. Zhang Zai's philosophy, in this way, keeps faith with Confucianism and focuses on life; and indeed, human life is to be lived morally in the present, and thus there is no fearing death (as Wittgenstein suggests).

Confucius, who passes over in silence after the painful death of his beloved disciple Yan Yuan in *Analects* 11:12, does not tell us whether he implies that death cannot be known, should not be known, or simply is not known; however, in his discussions with disciples, he clearly gives priority to knowing life—in particular, knowing *how* to live. Indeed, it is life as *moral* through which one can overcome death and gain moral eternity, which also makes death pointless for discussion. This is perhaps the meaning of both Wittgenstein's saying, "What we cannot speak about we must pass over in silence" (*Tractatus* 7), and Confucius's choice to pass over in silence regarding his beloved disciple's death.[98]

It is said that prior to his death, Zhang Zai had been preparing a piece of land for instituting the well-field system, in which he believed throughout his life.[99] Propagating the system, which serves a continuity of generations, perhaps expresses the belief that he held until his last day—showing that Zhang Zai did indeed overcome death. Using his personal writing style in this spirit, on approaching his death Zhang Zai wrote a moving statement that expresses the simple wish to live and an appreciation for life, including old age, sleep difficulties, and the ability to reflect. Yet calmness of mind characterizes Zhang, rather than fear; according to his own approach, this is a true sign of morality. As a paraphrase on Confucius's wish to study the *Change* had he been given more time to live, his only request is a continuity of the Way within his family, or a wish to live morally in the present, forever.

> Idle by day, I go to sleep when it is not yet late. In the middle of the night I am already awake, my mind calm and vast, and I think and consider (things) until dawn. If I were given a few more years, and at sixty (could see) the Way practiced in my family, that would be sufficient. (291.14, 124)

APPENDIX

A Brief Methodological Remark

Chan Buddhism and Living Riddles

....

> The next Question that was started, was, What is the Thing we receive, without being ever thankful for it; which we enjoy, without knowing how we came by it; which we give away to others, without knowing where 'tis to be found; and which we lose, without being any ways conscious of our Misfortune? ...
>
> *Zadig* was the only Person that concluded it was LIFE.
>
> —VOLTAIRE, *Zadig*

A PHILOSOPHY OF NONDUALITY

The nontheoretical nature of early Confucianism results in a philosophy of Way without concrete conceptual boundaries. The indefinite framework for discussing the Way and the person who broadens it implies a view of the person as an ever-changing, ever-expanding web of relations. The realized self attains continuity beyond place, time and symbolic limits. The understanding that life is an ongoing endless transformation is rooted in the *Book of Change* (*Yijing* 易經) and the Chinese yin-yang system, depicted by lines, arranged in hexagrams that are deciphered as clues for understanding one's person and one's life. According to the present suggestion this understanding embodies a riddle that has to be responded in one's life. In this context, Chan riddling system and practice was not foreign to the Chinese ancient system of thought. In fact, in a certain sense it corresponds with the older Chinese system that had major influence on Song dynasty philosophers.[1] The understandings vary among the different philosophies, all three Song philosophers as discussed here, propose to transcend subjective boundaries before landing back in life.

The contribution of the later philosophical development—that of Chan Buddhism—cannot be overrated in considering the Chinese understanding of transcending boundaries. In particular, the Chinese tradition of Chan developed a methodology for understanding that the emptiness of reality, or the lack of boundaries thereof, can only be expressed in riddles; as such, it turned communicating in riddles into a practice and a performative methodology.[2] Chan's use of riddles, in particular in the practice of *gong-an* (Jap. koan), introduced a methodology that explicitly confronts accepted distinctions and boundaries, thus allowing more systematic discussions and more elaborated insights regarding the person as self-transcending. The idea that inherently cannot be put into clearly defined theories or into distinct systematic boundaries has significant implications in the present scope. In the following, I only briefly refer to some of its major implications from the methodological perspective, focusing on its nondual language as introduced by the Indian monk Bodhidharma (Damo 達摩, ca. 440–ca. 528), then to some following examples.[3]

The legend says that after a long journey from India, Bodhidharma visited Emperor Wu of Liang, known for his good deeds as a keen benefactor of Buddhism. The Emperor addressed the Indian monk with a question: "How much karmic merit have I earned for ordaining Buddhist monks, building monasteries, having sutras copied, and commissioning Buddha images?" Bodhidharma's apparently discourteous reply was: None. This None is succinctly responding to the wondering about karmic merit as something that accumulates through moral deeds, directed toward gaining a better life when this one ends. The response with a riddle shakes the solid ground that underlies the emperor's question and his general attitude toward Buddhism. Through the terse response, Bodhidharma teaches that favorable deeds and fondness for Buddhism grant nothing; in particular, they grant nothing regarding the afterlife, thus turning of karma—the causal wheel of rebirths, leading from one life to a new life—into a riddle.[4] Indeed, according to the teachings of the Buddha, all of us will eventually pass away in our present form as part in the natural process of birth, old age, and death. Death is the end of the concrete form this limited body inhabited in the present life, and how one will be reborn results from past deeds, the accumulation of positive and negative action, and the resultant cause and effect. Therefore, from the perspective of the Indian Buddhist world, Bodhidharma's claim can be considered heresy. Undeniably, Bodhidharma points to a critical problem with the received notion of karma: a person can neither perform moral acts, nor can one accumulate deeds in this life for better incarnating in a subsequent life. Accordingly, deeds are done for their own sake, with no external aim in mind. As in the Chinese view, consequentialism cannot be admitted within the framework of human life.[5]

Returning to the legend, the astonished emperor asked a second question: "What is the highest meaning of holy teaching?" To this question, the monk replied: "There is no holy teaching, there is only emptiness" (*kuoran* 廓然). Bodhidharma's second response targets the very dichotomy between holy and profane, teaching that nothing is sacred in the all-pervading living realm; accordingly, the holy teaching is indeed empty. In other words, within the unified single existence, there is no holy teaching. Emptiness is the lack of distinct boundaries and essential attributes of the ongoing transformation; it pervades all existence as the being of all in all, such that everything—the monk, the Emperor, as well as a dog on the road, or a worm in a hole—are all pure and impure at once. The fixed boundaries that we attach to words are created only in artificial linguistic spaces. The teaching, aiming at a unified vision, is expressed in terms such as emptiness; not as distinguished from fullness, but rather as the wholeness of nondistinctions. The Emperor's mistake lies in the very question that holds onto the distinction between holy and profane, presupposing two dichotomous states of existence. Dropping the boundary between cause and effect, and then that between holy and profane, turns the ideas into what I call here *living riddles*.

At this point, Bodhidharma is ready to wipe out the last and ultimate boundary: that is, the boundary between self and other. When the emperor asks who stands in front of him, he is exposed as repeating the same mistake. The very question *who* stands before me? exposes a search for a distinguished definition of oneself: Is the one standing in front a Buddhist? What faith does he hold onto? How can he be characterized? What motivates him? Bodhidharma is kind enough to repeat his reply again in a slightly different version—this time perhaps a more personal version, or at least more oriented to the human perspective: "I do not know (*buzhi* 不識)." Bodhidharma's last reply transcends personal boundaries, noting the absence of self-identity. The question of who it is presupposes a distinct consistent self with limits and definition, cognition, feelings, and desires. Yet in his short reply, Bodhidharma implies that a person who looks for the self distinguishes it from others, and thus is expressing a lack of trust in human nature. Bodhidharma, on the other hand, shows that he has no identity, definitely not one of a "great teacher," and he certainly does not aspire to an identity of this kind.

A MIRROR OF SUCHNESS

In later years, when the neo-Confucian philosophies that were discussed in *100 Verses on Old Cases* (*songgu baize* 頌古百則), compiled by Xuedou Zhongxian (980–1052), we read a version of this legend.[6] Xuedou appears to be looking at the present moment with a mind that transcends dualities and attains tranquility.[7]

> The holy teaching? "Emptiness!"
> What is the secret here?
> Again, "Who stands before me?"
> "No knowing!"
> Inevitable, the thorns and briars springing up;
> Secretly, by night he crossed the river.
> All the people could not bring him back.
> Now, so many gone by,
> Still Bodhidharma fills your mind—in vain.
> Stop thinking of him!
> A gentle breeze pervades the universe.
> The Master looks around:
> "Is the patriarch there?
> —Yes! "Bring him to me,
> And he can wash my feet."[8]

The recorded dialogue between Bodhidharma and the emperor reflects mature Chan ideology regarding nonduality in the universe. The verse continues on to describe how Bodhidharma left Liang and went to Wei, then referring to the emperor's preoccupation with bringing back the great patriarch.[9]

According to the teaching, the mistake can only be fixed when the unity is seen, whereby Bodhidharma is as important as a gentle breeze. If the teaching of Bodhidharma is understood, then there is no holiness of doctrine, of place, or of person. Therefore, Bodhidharma is as good as the last servant who washes the emperor's feet. The idea of transcending the basic distinctions of the human mind is thus put in riddle, and its understanding may be attained in riddle only.

Since Emptiness as ongoing transformation is always present in human life, in a mirror-like mind, it is giving the mind a power to reflect. It is the lack of inherent nature, a nothing, in the sense of emptiness from existence of distinctions. Emptiness is thus presented as the constant transformation of things as one energy rather than as separate entities in particular shapes at specific points of time. Seeing in this way is attained by letting the mind go beyond borders and limits, to places where eyes and ears never reach, unless they suspend the sensual capacities of seeing and hearing. Since emptiness refers to the transforming world, the intellectual power of the Buddhist sage seems to be redirected to involvement in the myriad things. A perfect person is distinguished by a comprehension beyond borders that transcends obstacles and keeps close contact with the transforming world. Worldly transformations nullify the singularity of phenomena in the evaluative sense. No dichotomous distinction exists between the transforming world and the sagely mind. The clear and pure mirror-like mind, traditionally signifying no sensation, no thought and above all, no intention (to become enlightened), is ready to accept "all the objects in the world."[10] This methodology of mind-work that reaffirms the world is the ability to transcend conventional categories, thereby enabling acceptance of transformations, as put by Cheng Chung-ying.

> The key to enlightened understanding apparently is to transcend both affirmation and negation in order to embrace both affirmation and negation. This is to realize or enact a positive realization of emptiness in a particular instance of A, where A is also seen as an occasion for making this realization possible.[11]

Cheng's idea of a positive realization stresses that emptiness does not mean nonexistence. A perfect person sees properly by letting the mind go beyond borders and limits.[12] This idea had special significance in Tang dynasty, traditionally regarded as the golden age of Chan Buddhism. The Chan idea of enlightenment sprouts from the vision of an inherent Buddha-nature that is to be found in this very world. The daring unification between the phenomenal world of becoming and ceasing as samsara and the absolute as nirvana rang familiar within Chinese ideas such as Order and things (*li-shi*理事), which influenced the Chan and reflected back on neo-Confucianism, as we will later see.[13]

Indeed, within Chan Buddhism, the understanding of suchness and its lack of essential boundaries is observed again in the mirror simile by Hui Neng, the sixth and last patriarch.[14] According to the Platform Sutra (Liuzu Tanjing 六祖壇經), when the fifth patriarch made reference to his origin, Hui Neng replied: "Although people exist as northerners and southerners, in the Buddha nature there is neither north nor south"; thus, he was admitted to the monastery. The reply by means of ridding boundaries became the heart of the doctrine, reaching a new peak in Hui Neng's famous poem, which endowed him with the patriarchy. As the Sutra tells, the fifth patriarch called his disciples to a contest in the monastery, in which they were asked to show understanding of the essence of the mind.[15] Shenxiu, responded with the following poem:

> The body is the Bodhi tree,
> The mind is a standing mirror bright.
> At all times polish it diligently,
> And let no dust alight.[16]

Hui Neng responded to this reasoning, which presented a substantiality of knowledge through a clear duality of body and mind and a constant demand for diligent practice.

> Bodhi is fundamentally without any tree.
> The bright mirror is also not a stand.
> Fundamentally there is not a single thing.
> Where could any dust be attracted?[17]

Apparently not so far from Shen Xiu's poem thematically, Hui Neng's poem addresses its reader in a riddle-like manner rather than a statement on dharma. Shen Xiu used familiar similes to express ideas: the body as a bodhi tree (namely, the place where enlightenment was attained by the historic Buddha, Shakyamuni); the mind as a bright stable mirror, ready to reflect; and practice as ceaseless industrious dusting. Hui Neng broke all familiar conventions: in his poem, bodhi is knowledge or perfect wisdom that is *fundamentally* not a tree—not even metaphorically; the mind cannot be compared to a standing mirror, as the mirror has no fixed stand, position, or framework; and finally, since nothing exists, dust finds no place, or enlightenment is not the outcome of hard work. Beckoning its readers to decipher meaning in the form of a riddle, the poem also suggests that wiping the dust is not the desired attitude for attaining knowledge.

RIDDLING AS A WAY OF LIFE

The new perspectives is reflected in a methodological contribution that cannot be overlooked, which started with Mazu Daoyi (709–788), who is usually regarded a successor in the lineage of Hui Neng.[18] In particular, the Hongzhou school of Mazu Daoyi developed shock techniques, including shouting, beating, and bodily gestures, in order to astonish students and bring them to realization.[19] The new techniques, alongside an assimilation of Daoist views and ways of argumentation, were integrated into a new style of teacher-disciple encounters that were later collected, and reached a climax paradigm in the Song dynasty.[20]

The perception of the person and one's life is characterized by endless paradoxes that bring about a new understanding that the living self is to be read always as a *riddle* of a special kind; namely, a riddle that has no theoretical solution but rather is responded to in practice. The Chan practice of *gong-an* falls like an overripe fruit within the Chinese philosophic scene. A koan is a riddle or a paradox to be meditated on, used to train monks for abandoning dependence on reason and compelling them into gaining sudden intuitive enlightenment. Therefore, an answer to a koan cannot be attained through an analytical process of reasoning; rather, it is a response, which may be expressed by new uses of language or by nonliteral utterances. A cry, a laugh, a body gesture, or a sound can all comprise appropriate responses to a koan. While the koan functions as a riddle, a response to a koan may seem like a riddle in its own virtue and demand yet another process of responding, which again cannot be attained intellectually. As such, koan is an ongoing practice that is usually repeated more than once; hence, the mere repetition of a suitable response can never be considered appropriate. What matters is the process that yields the response, and some element in each response must be shown to be original.

Koans appear to be nonsensical; yet when a response is attained, the riddle makes sense, and more importantly offers a new insight. Cheng Chung-ying stresses the logical and semantic significances of the dialogic exchange of koan: its ontological basis as an ontic noncommitment and its methodological basis as contextual demonstration. Given their ontic noncommitment, the koans are revealed as extraordinarily meaningful tools for reaching or revealing enlightenment. In this sense, the paradoxicality results from the disconnect between their semantic and ontological structures. This gap creates a need for an understanding that does not depend on world-language correspondence, but rather signifies inner reflection and observation, which is independent of the phenomenal world. On the basis of contextual demonstration, the use of koan language embodies freedom and creativity, which demands a shift of perspective, or a leap that brings to new understanding.[21] Once a person is enlightened, the exchange that seems paradoxical at first is no longer paradox for her; rather, it comprises a practice. Thus, it can serve to verify enlightenment and appears to be self-resolving, intending to force a transformation of the person who attempts to respond to the riddle.

The discarding of dichotomous thinking by creating a language that functions differently is demonstrated in many cases Xuedou Zhongxian encounters, as recorded in the *Blue Cliff Record* (*Biyan Lu* 碧巖錄, Jap. *Hekiganroku*).[22] Case 19, for example, tells the story of Master Jinhua Juzhi who, whenever asked a question, responded by raising a finger.[23] The raising of finger responds to Chan requirements: The nonverbal response avoids dichotomous verbalization and denotes oneness, as opposed to using words for explaining that the very positing of a question is wrong, since any question presupposes something that cannot be real and distinguishes it from others. It may be the presupposition of a subject in a "who" question, of a designed technique in a "how" question, or of a cause in a "why" question—the very reliance on words, grammar, or linguistic patterns that by nature are discriminating. The physical gesture says without words, and shakes the common consensus of what a good question amounts to. This can be shown through lecturing on the sutra by means of mounting the platform, striking the desk with a button and descending; or through replying to what is the teaching that transcends the Buddha and patriarchs by sesame bun; or when asked What is Buddha? and replying "three pounds of flax."[24] In all these examples, the response exposes an appreciation for the riddle and thus exhibits understanding. The greatness of the Buddha, of perfection, or of the doctrine that teaches it is beyond verbalization, or accepted boundaries. It cannot be described ordinarily; it calls for using language differently and creatively.

A KOAN OF DEATH AND LIFE

The koan system of practice uses expressions that are not self-explanatory, which one has to meditate on, in order to understand their meaning. In many cases, no one correct meaning exists; rather, the riddling expression forces the disciple to ponder the idea he is inquiring about. In one important example of this kind, Master Zhao Zhou refers to death as continuing the ongoing transformation of life (case 41).[25] "Great death" functions in this case as metaphor for the condition that appears in absolute Samadhi—the ultimate stage of meditation, when the person is out of physical consciousness. In Samadhi, the mind and soul are in equal balance, hence attaining a nondualistic state of consciousness in which the consciousness of the experiencing subject transcends its own limitations and becomes one with the experienced object, thus bringing the mind to stillness. Asking "what if a man of Great Death comes back to life again?" challenges the idea that life ends with death and implies that just as Samadhi is not disconnected from everyday practice, neither is death from life. The koan requires an epistemological shift that affects one's boundaries, bringing about a new way of living and of dying.[26] Seeing that Samadhi is the state in which the present is ever renewed and thus beyond time is understanding that one can attain in life a state that is beyond dichotomies, even beyond that between life and death.[27] Xuedou clarifies this by means of yet another riddle.

> Open-eyed, he was all the more as if dead;
> What use [is it] to test the Master with something taboo?
> Even the Buddha said he had not reached there;
> Who knows when to throw ashes in another's eyes?

The verse refers to Zhao Zhou's knowledge as if dead, namely, like one who had undergone Great Death, yet behaved ignorantly while asking the question regarding the return of one who had never left. Xuedou implies that asking the question that shouldn't be asked, Zhao Zhou tried his interlocutor, or used his generosity to bring the other to understanding. Next, the verse emphasizes the extreme difficulty and importance of doing so, through provocatively saying that "even the Buddha did not reach there." The verse ends with reference to throwing ashes in others' eyes, indicating the blinding that is sometimes needed in order for others to see clearly. The koan ties together a new use of linguistic expressions that causes the listener to rethink accepted references. Through an expression of Samadhi as death, or cessation, Zhao Zhou implies a positive and fearless perspective to death and a non-dual vision regarding life and death.

A Similar reference to the end of life can be found in the story of the chief priest visiting Master Mazu Daoyi when he was sick, asking him for his feeling. The Master replied: "Sun-faced Buddha, Moon-faced Buddha," implying, in the ambiguous saying, that everything is condensed in the present moment, in which all is eternal. The Sun-faced Buddha allegedly lived for 1,800 years, and the Moon-faced Buddha—one day and one night.[28] Words cannot describe human life, which is as short as the life of the Moon-faced Buddha when compared to eternity, and as long as the Sun-faced Buddha when compared to an instant, yet both are equally good for representing Mazu's feeling at that moment. Xuedou's verse brings the ordinary tools of measuring greatness to an extreme by exposing the absurdity in the question, how do you feel? Compared to a dying person, a sick person can be considered to not be doing too bad.

Likewise, when the emperor asks Master Zhong Guoshi what can be done for him after his death, the Master replies: "Make a seamless pagoda." When the Emperor inquires about the style of the pagoda, the Master remains silent, then adds that his disciple will explain it.[29] The seamless pagoda represents to the formlessness of the Dharmakaya Buddha, or the Absolute essence of the universe as the unmanifested unity of all things and beings, beyond existence or nonexistence, and definitely beyond concepts. After the death of the Master, his disciple makes the point by telling a short story of a boat reaching an empty palace, remarking that "no holy one exists in the emerald palace you see."[30] Xuedou responds with "All is finished." By transferring the reply to his disciple, the Master brings up an understanding regarding the formlessness of the universe and the lack (or seamlessness) of dichotomies. Then, Xuedou brings his own disciples to understanding by adding the famous remark about the "soundless sound of one hand." As for what will be done after the Master's death, the building of the seamless pagoda is already accomplished; building the formless and empty pagoda is attained with the Master's death, dissolving into unity and in need of nothing.

The attitude toward one's bodily boundaries is expressed in a monk's question: "Man's body will ultimately decompose; what is the indestructible Dharma body?" The Master then replied: "Flowers cover the hillside like brocade. The vale lies deep in shade." Xuedou added his verse.

> The question came from ignorance;
> The answer was not understood.
> The moon is clear, the wind is cool,
> The wintry pine stands on the peak.
> I laugh heartily to hear the saying,
> "When you encounter a man of the way,
> Meet him with neither words nor non-words." (case 82)

The thought that ultimately we will all perish terrifies human beings and leads people to seek eternity, something indestructible. The question "what is the indestructible Dharma body?" exposes a common hope to overcome death and a wish that the practice of Chan might bring one to eternity. This state of mind, however, will not lead one to find the truth: that flowers cover the hill, or that the valley is in the shade. Everything is indeed destructible: flowers wither, shade moves. Hence, the response takes the inquirer who is looking for a definitive truth as noumena away from a conceptual understanding of phenomenal reality. Xuedou stresses in his verse the ignorance in the very presupposition of the question, and kindly repeats the answer, reminding that the moon is clear and the wind is cool, yet not forever. The moon will be eclipsed again, and the wind will pass. Nature transforms, and life is eternally transient. An awakened mind can see this. Hinting at the non-dual view, the monk receives a laugh, and a suggestion to meet a man of the Way with neither words, nor nonwords.[31] How can this be done? Perhaps similarly to Zhuangzi's wish to exchange some words with someone who forgot words.[32] Perhaps when we meet with meanings, words become what they are—nonwords, or words that lost their surplus weight; just words.

A different case refers to Master Daowu's visiting a funeral with a disciple to express empathy with the mourners.[33] The disciple touched the coffin and asked: "Tell me please, is this life or is this death?" The Master refused to reply and the disciple asked again, this time threatening to hit the Master if he refuses to provide an answer. Daowu asked his disciple to strike him. When Daowu passed away, the disciple told the story to yet another Master, who again refused to respond. The disciple attained realization. The content disciple went searching for the spiritual remains of Daowu, and was told that the Master's spiritual remains are there.[34] While the disciple was deeply bothered with the problem of death, Master Daowu showed understanding in refraining from response. The disciple used the question to escape the presence of death, while the Master answered directly and sincerely. A conceptual manipulation of death is useless; it is more helpful to hint at the understanding that death cannot be escaped. Daowu's silence was the first clue, implying that while the meaning of death cannot be expressed in words, one cannot escape it. Since the clue was not sufficient, the Master gave a second clue, letting the disciple strike him. As for pain, the Master is no different from his disciple; moreover, striking one's teacher is a great transgression, after which the disciple realized that there are no shortcuts and was left to commence his own search. Xuedou's verse adds,

> Hares and horses have horns,
> Cows and goats have none.
> It is quite infinitesimal,
> It piles up mountain-high.
> The golden relic exists,
> It still exists now.
> Foaming waves wash the sky.
> Where can you put it?—No, nowhere!
> The single sandal returned to India
> And is lost forever.[35]

Words hide more than they reveal: How do hares, horses, cows, or goats have anything to do with the story about visiting the mourning family? What is the "it" that is quite infinitesimal and piling up mountain-high? What does the single sandal that returned to India and became lost forever signify? To understand the poem's meaning, one must ponder through words, metaphors, and symbols that function like riddles. Regarding the hares and horses having horns, and cows and goats having none, the text functions like a spur to show that the distinction between life and death is erroneous. Understanding this is infinitesimal, and yet it piles mountain-high. The Master disappeared and his wisdom exists, like Bodhidharma's, who according to the legend returned to India after his death carrying a sandal, breaking yet another dichotomy. Since understanding cannot be attained by means of an ordinary use of language, the Chan practice of riddles offers both a methodology and a way of living. In this way, it shows the inability to express the mystery of a life that is constantly ceasing and becoming and the ambiguity of a person as a known, defined being.

In this book, I posit that the neo-Confucian thinkers discussed here suggest more systematic and elaborate discussions on Ways of self-transcendence: Zhou Dunyi transcends the boundaries of person through *metaphysical* embodiment; Shao Yong transcends one's boundaries through an *epistemological* perspective; Zhang Zai transcends boundaries through a *pragmatic humanistic* act. All embody a riddle to demonstrate that there is no strict beginning or definitive end. The possibility that they were helped by though not committed to the Chan understanding of living riddle calls for a further research.

NOTES

NOTES TO INTRODUCTION

1. See, Peter Winch, "Understanding a Primitive Society," in *Ethics and Action* (London: Routledge & Kegan Paul, 1972), 33.
2. Discussions on the issue are abundant from classical philosophy to modern social sciences. For just a few examples see *Immanuel Kant, Critique of Pure Reason*, trans. Norman Kemp Smith (London: Macmillan, 1929), 22; Jeff E. Malpas, *Donald Davidson and the Mirror of Meaning: Holism, Truth, Interpretation* (Cambridge, UK: Cambridge University Press, 1992), 192; David Swartz, *Culture and Power: The Sociology of Pierre Bourdieu* (Chicago: University of Chicago Press, 1998), 55; Max Velmans, *Understanding Consciousness*. 2nd ed. (New York: Routledge, 2009), 3.
3. On Confucian Virtue Ethics see, David B. Wong, *Natural Moralities: A Defense of Pluralistic Relativism* (New York: Oxford University Press, 2006); Bryan Van Norden, *Virtue Ethics and Consequentialism in Early Chinese Philosophy* (New York: Cambridge University Press, 2007); Stephen C. Angle and Michael Slote (eds.) *Virtue Ethics and Confucianism* (NY: Routledge, 2013). On Confucian Role Ethics, see Roger T. Ames, *Confucian Role Ethics: A Vocabulary* (Hawaii, University of Hawai'i Press, 2011); Henry Rosemont Jr. and Roger T. Ames, *Confucian Role Ethics: A Moral Vision for the 21st Century?* (Göttingen Germany, V&R Academic, 2016).
4. Compare with *Analects* 6:30. Citations from *The Doctrine of the Mean* use Charles A. Muller translation, http://www.acmuller.net/con-dao/docofmean.html. For a comprehensive discussion on *The Doctrine of the Mean* as focusing on the problem of transcendence and immanence as the problem of heaven and humans, see Also see Liu Shu-Hsien, "The Confucian Approach to the Problem of Transcendence and Immanence," *Philosophy East and West* 22, no. 1 (1972): 45–52.

5   Zongsan Mou (牟宗三), *Xinti yu Xingti* (心體與性體) (Taipei, Taiwan: Zhengzhong Books正中书局, 1968-1969).
6   On Confucian religiosity see, Tu Weiming, *Centrality and Commonality: An Essay on Confucian Religiousness* (Albany: State University of New York Press, 1989); Rodney Taylor, *The Religious Dimensions of Confucianism* (Albany: State University of New York Press, 1990).
7   See the appendix on Chan Buddhism.
8   The riddle methodology takes up Cora Diamond's post-Wittgensteinean suggestion as applied in my earlier work. See Galia Patt-Shamir, "To Live a Riddle—The Case of the Binding of Isaac," *Philosophy and Literature* 27, no. 2 (October 2003): 269–83; "The Effectiveness of Contradiction in Understanding Human Practice: The Rhetoric of Goal-ideal in Confucianism," *Journal of Chinese Philosophy* 32, no. 3 (August 2005): 455–76.
9   See Carl G. Jung, Foreword to *The I Ching, or, Book of Changes*, trans., Richard Wilhelm and Cary F. Baynes, with Preface by Hellmut Wilhelm (Princeton, NJ: Princeton University Press, 1967).
10 See, Galia Patt-Shamir, "To Live a Riddle: The Transformative Aspect of the Laozi," *Journal of Chinese Philosophy* 36, no. 3 (June 2009): 408–23; "The 'Dual Citizenship'" of Emptiness: A Reading of Bu Zhenkong Lun," *Journal of Chinese Philosophy* 38, no. 3 (September 2011): 474–90. Some Lao-Zhuang perspectives will be integrated hereafter, according to their relevance; for the practice of *gong-an* as the most straightforward practice of riddle to be meditated on, see the appendix.
11 Ludwig Wittgenstein, *Tractatus Logico-Philosophicus*, trans. David. F. Pears and Brian McGuinness (London: Routlege and Kegan Paul, 1961), 6.4312; see Cora Diamond, "Riddles and Anselm's Riddle," in *The Realistic Spirit: Wittgenstein, Philosophy, and the Mind* (Cambridge, MA: MIT Press, 1991), 26, 267–89.
12 The different periods in Wittgenstein's philosophizing are presented here without distinction. See Gustav Bergmann, "The Glory and the Misery of Ludwig Wittgenstein," in *Logic and Reality* (Madison: University of Wisconsin Press, 1964), 245–71, as opposed to Mark Lazenby, *The Early Wittgenstein on Religion* (London UK: Continuum, 2006).
13 Ludwig Wittgenstein, *Philosophical Investigations*, trans. G. E. M. Anscombe (Oxford, UK: Basil Blackwell, 1988), 143–44, §531.
14 This methodology also connects to the earlier Wittgensteinean observation that "living in the present" (*Tractatus* 6.4311) or timelessness, is "the solution to the riddle of life in space and time" (6.4312). Since "for life in the present there is no death" (*Notebooks* 75e), and morality is living in the present while changing "the limits of the world" (*Tractatus* 6.43) it is connected to eternity.
15 The assumption that a year is comprised of 360 days was based on accepted knowledge in Shao's time. See Anne D. Birdwhistell, *Transition to Neo-Confucianism: Shao Yung on Knowledge and Symbols of Reality* (Stanford, CA: Stanford University Press, 1989), 141.

16 Separate studies in Western languages on each of the discussed philosophers give accounts of the mentioned issues, as referred to hereafter.

NOTES TO CHAPTER ONE

1 Note that in the *Analects* there is good and "non-good," or the lack of good, in a way that leaves no ontological status to badness.
2 Zigong 自貢 is Duanmu Ci's 端木賜 courtesy name. He is known for his sharpness and straightforward strictness and is one of the Confucius's students most commonly referred to in the *Analects* (see 9:6, 9:13, 11:13, 13:20, 14:17, 17:19). Confucius criticizes him for being too strict with others (*Analects* 5:12; 14:29).
3 I translate *da* 達 as "realizing," which seems most appropriate in the Confucian context. It is also translated as arriving or accomplishing.
4 Ziyou 子有 is Ran Qiu's (冉求) courtesy name (522–489 BCE). He was noted for his versatile abilities and talents. Confucius praised his administrative ability (*Analects* 5:8); yet, once he disappointed Confucius, saying he lacked the strength to pursue the Way (*Analects* 6:12). Zilu 季路 is Zhong You's 仲由 courtesy name (542–480 BCE). He was known for his love of the sword. After he studied with Confucius, the Master praised Zilu for having an exceptional ability to manage an army of a state (*Analects* 5:8).
5 Most importantly, while 4:4 refers to setting the will, 4:3 refers to already being human hearted.
6 Fan Xu's 樊須 courtesy name was Zichi (子遲). He distinguished himself as a military commander.
7 All references to the text follow Andrew Plaks, *Da Xue* 大學 *Torat Hagadol* (Jerusalem: Bialik Institute and Harry S. Truman Research Institute, 1997).
8 See also *Analects* 13:18; *Mencius* 4A:19; 7A:15; 7A:35. See discussion in Galia Patt-Shamir, "Way as Dao; Way as Halakha: Confucianism, Judaism and Way Metaphors," *Dao: A Journal of Comparative Philosophy* 5, no. 2 (January 2005): 137–58.
9 Zeng Shen 曾參 (505–436), courtesy name Zeng Ziyu 曾子輿, known as Zengzi 曾子. Zengzi is known for paying great attention to the cultivation of the self. He is credited with the authorship of the *Rites of the elder Dai* (*dadaili* 大戴禮) and possibly of *The Great Learning* (*daxue* 大學) and *Classic of Family Reverence* (*Xiaojing* 孝經). Zengzi was noted for his family reverence, and according to one story, after the death of his parents, he could not read the rites of mourning without being led to think of them and moved to tears. Regarding the authorship of the text, see Henry Rosemont Jr. and Roger T. Ames, *The Chinese Classic of Family Reverence: A Philosophical Translation of the Xiaojing* (Honolulu: University of Hawai'i Press, 2009), 19–20.
10 References to *Classic of Family Reverence* use Rosemont and Ames's translation.
11 The story raised doubts regarding Confucian morality as it was suggested that

Confucianism encourages family favoritism and corruption. See Qingping Liu, "Confucianism and Corruption: An Analysis of Shun's Two Actions Described by Mencius," *Dao: A Journal of Comparative Studies* 6, no. 1 (March 2007): 1–20. Also, see responses in *Dao: A Journal of Comparative Philosophy* 7, no. 2 (June 2008).

12 For the discussion on the structure of first and last and the possibility of simultaneity, see Plaks, *Torat Hagadol*, 31–47.
13 Tu Weiming, "Selfhood and Otherness: The Father-Son Relationship in Confucian Thought," in *Confucian Thought: Selfhood as Creative Transformation* (Albany: State University of New York Press, 1985), 113–30.
14 Tu, 1994, 183.
15 See Wei-ming Tu, *Centrality and Commonality: An Essay on Confucian Religiousness* (New York: State University of New York Press, 1989), 23–38.
16 Tu Weiming, "Embodying the Universe: A Note on Confucian Self-Realization," in *Self as Person in Asian Theory and Practice*, eds. Roger T. Ames, Wimal Dissanayake, and Thomas P. Kasulis (Albany: State University of New York Press, 1994), 177–87.
17 Tu Weiming, "Selfhood and Otherness: The Father-Son Relationship in Confucian Thought," in *Confucian Thought: Selfhood as Creative Transformation* (Albany: State University of New York Press, 1985), 113–30, 113.
18 David L. Hall and Roger T. Ames, *Thinking Trough Confucius* (Albany: State University of New York Press, 1998), 26.
19 Ibid., 26.
20 Ibid., 40.
21 Ibid., 27.
22 David B. Wong, "Relational and autonomous selves," *Journal of Chinese Philosophy* 31 (2004): 419–32, 420.
23 Ibid., 421, See *Analects* 11:22.
24 Ibid., 422.
25 Li Chen-yang, "The Confucian Concept of Jen and the Feminist Ethics of Care: A Comparative Study," *Hypatia* 9 (Winter 1994): 70–89; 72–73.
26 Ibid., 75.
27 Li Chen-yang, ed., *The Sage and The Second Sex: Confucianism, Ethics and Gender.* (Chicago and La Salle, IL: Open Court, 2000), 11–12.
28 Michael Puett, "Ritual and the Subjunctive," in *Ritual and Its Consequences*, eds. Adam B. Seligman, Robert P. Weller, Michael J. Puett, and Simon, Bennet (Oxford, UK: Oxford University Press, 2008), 17–27; *"Ritualization as Domestication: Ritual Theory from Classical China,"* in *A Ritual Dynamics and the Science of Ritual*: vol. 1: *Grammars and Morphologies of Ritual Practices in Asia*, ed. Axel Michaels (Wiesbaden, Germany: Harrassowitz Verlag, 2010), 365–76.
29 Henry Rosemont Jr., and Roger T. Ames, *Confucian Role Ethics*.
30 Robin Wang, *Yinyang: The Way of Heaven and Earth in Chinese Thought and Culture*, (New York: Cambridge University Press, 2012).

31 Cheng Chung-ying, "Confucian Onto-Hermeneutics: Morality and Ontology," *Journal of Chinese Philosophy* 27, no. 1 (March 2000): 33–68, 33.

32 Tu, *Centrality and Commonality*, 77. The character *cheng* is written with the word radical (*yan* 言) and "to accomplish" (*cheng* 成). It is, therefore, natural to refer to its original meaning as "realizing words" or "accomplishing words." In this spirit, it is translated as sincerity or integrity. However, in its all-pervading aspect as expressed in the *Zhongyong*, it has unequivocal spiritual sense since classical times. In the quest to capture the broader sense of *cheng*, it was translated more recently as authenticity. See Kidder Smith Jr., Peter K. Bol, Joseph A. Adler, and Don J. Wyatt, *Sung Dynasty Uses of the I Ching* (Princeton, NJ: Princeton University Press, 1990), 195. My choice of "sincerity" intends to preserve the strict moral weight of the term, while maintaining a reference to the moral dimension of the entire universe.

33 For elaboration on this perspective of the text, See, Tu, *Centrality and Commonality*, 67–91; Roger Ames, "Reading the *Zhongyong* Metaphysically," in *Chinese Metaphysics and Its Problems*, eds. Chenyang Li and Franklin Perkins (Cambridge, UK: Cambridge University Press, 2015), 85–104.

34 The passage uses the question form, "*buyi* . . . *hu*" (不亦 。。。 乎), which does not allow a negative response, thus expressing the unequivocal nature of the issue at hand: it is impossible that learning and then practicing is not a pleasure, that having friends is not a joy, and that not taking offense when not sufficiently appreciated is not being morally accomplished.

35 Emphasis my own. Yan Hui's 顏回 courtesy name is Yan Yuan顏淵or Ziyuan 子淵 (521–481 BCE). He became Confucius's disciple when he was very young, and as we see here, he was the disciple the Master most appreciated.

36 Compare the idea with Immanuel Kant, *Critique of Practical Reason*, trans. L. W. Beck (New York: Macmillan,1956), 136.

37 See Galia Patt-Shamir, "The Effectiveness of Contradiction in Understanding Human Practice: The Rhetoric of 'Goal-ideal' in Confucianism," *Journal of Chinese Philosophy* 32, no. 3 (August 2005): 455–76.

38 See Tu Weiming, "Neo-Confucian Ontology: A Preliminary Questioning," *Journal of Chinese Philosophy* 7 (June 1980): 94.

39 Stephen Darwell makes the distinction between empathy as taking over the other's distress as one's own and Sympathy, as the feeling that calls for action. See Stephen Darwell, "Empathy, Sympathy, Care," *Philosophical Studies* 89 (March 1998): 261–82.

40 For more elaborate discussions on this point, see, Tu Weiming, "Happiness in the Confucian Way," in *In Pursuit of Happiness*, ed. Leroy S. Rouner (Notre Dame, IN: Notre Dame University Press, 1995), 104–21; Galia Patt-Shamir, "Seeds for Dialogue: On Learning in Confucianism and Judaism," *Journal of Ecumenical Studies* 40, no. 1–2 (2004): 201–15; Yong Huang, "Why Be Moral? The Cheng Brothers' Neo-Confucian Answer," *Journal of Religious Ethics* 36, no. 2 (June 2008): 321–53; Yong Huang, "Confucius and Mencius on the Motivation

to Be Moral," *Philosophy East and West* 60, no. 1 (January 2010): 65–87; Henry Rosemont Jr. and Roger T. Ames, *The Chinese Classic of Family Reverence*, 75–76.

41 The term *li*禮 is translated throughout this book in three different ways, representing various aspects of the same idea. "Propriety" is used to express the idea of *li* as acting properly; "ritual" refers to a concrete practice; and "rites" to the full system of rules of practice.

42 For more on this view see Michael Puett, "Ritual and the Subjunctive," 17–27.

43 See Rosemont and Ames, *The Chinese Classic of Family Reverence*, 61.

44 Ziwo子我 is Zai Yu's宰予courtesy name. Although he had a sense for argumentation and rhetoric, as we see in the passage, the Master did not hold his moral depth in high regard.

45 Mencius expresses a similar sentiment in the story about the death of Duke Ding. The prince inquired about the duty to his father, and Mencius advised him to keep the ritual of three years' mourning period. The passage cites from the *Analects* to make the point that it is not about the external grandeur, but rather that the inner feeling matters and makes others identify (3A:2).

46 See discussion in Herbert Fingarette, *Confucius: The Secular as Sacred* (New York: Harper and Row, 1972), 1–17.

47 See Amy Olberding and P. J. Ivanhoe, eds., *Mortality in Traditional Chinese Thought* (Albany: State University of New York Press, 2011).

48 Huang Kan 皇侃 (488–545) specialized in early ritual texts, the *Book of Family Reverence* and *Analects* and in "matching ideas" from Confucianism, Buddhism and Daoism. Chen Tianxiang 蕆天祥 (1230–1316) was a scholar, an official, and a general. Zhu Xi朱熹 (1130–1200 AD) the Song dynasty leading Confucian scholar, is known as the leader of the rationalistic School of Principle *lixue* 理學. His contributions to Confucian thought include assembling the four books (*sishu* 四書) together; establishing a Confucian academy; synthesizing all fundamental Confucian concepts; and forming a "Confucian line" of scholars. See Edward Slingerland, *Analects: With Selections from Traditional Commentaries* (Indianapolis, IN: Hackett, 2003), 115, 256, 259.

49 Ibid.

50 P. J. Ivanhoe notes that one must understand life to understand death. See "Death and Dying in the *Analects*," in *Confucian Spirituality*, vol. 1, eds. Weiming Tu and Mary Evelyn Tucker (New York: Crossroad, 2002), 220–32. On the same line are Amy Olberding, "The Consummation of Sorrow: An Analysis of Confucius' Grief for Yan Hui," *Philosophy East and West* 53, no. 3 (July 2004): 279–301 and "Slowing Death Down: Mourning in the *Analects*," in *Confucius Now*, ed. David Jones (LaSalle, IL: Open Court, 2008), 137–49; Mathew A. Foust, "Grief and Mourning in Confucius's *Analects*," *Journal of Chinese Philosophy* 36, no. 2 (June 2009): 348–58. All take up this perspective with respect to grieving and mourning and their role in providing humans with a "map" to life. While I agree with this point, I depart hereafter from their points regarding "the finality of death."

NOTES TO CHAPTER TWO

1 In fact, modern physics' quest for a theory of everything (ToE), suggesting that matter interacts with all other matter in the universe, wishing to fully explain and link together all physical aspects of the universe (while nonphysical is either reduced to physical or nonexistent), can be taken as a new hope for finding the missing link between finitude and infinitude. Nonetheless, from a philosophical perspective it appears almost obvious that human life and practice not only remains outside a unified theory of this kind, it is also necessary and desired for the pluralism and openness of understanding it. See, Steven Weinberg, *Dreams of a Final Theory: The Scientist's Search for the Ultimate Laws of Nature* (New York: Knopf Doubleday, 2011).

2 See Roger T. Ames, 2015. "Reading *Zhongyong* "metaphysically," in *Chinese Metaphysics and Its Problems*, eds. Li Chenyang and Franklin Perkins (Cambridge, UK: Cambridge University Press, 2015); Galia Patt-Shamir, "Li and Qi as Supra Metaphysics," *Dao Companion to Zhu Xi's Philosophy*, eds. Kai-chiu Ng and Yong Huang (Switzerland: Springer, 2020), 243–63.

3 Julia Ching, *The Religious Thought of Chu Hsi* (New York: Oxford University Press, 2000), 19.

4 *Song Yuan xuean* 宋元學案, ch. 11. See Herbert Franke (ed.), *Song Yuan Biographies* (Wiesbaden, Germany: Franz Steiner Verlag GMBH, 1976), 278.

5 The "two Cheng masters" (*ercheng* 二程), namely, Cheng Hao 程顥 (Cheng Mingdao 程明道, 1032–1085) and Cheng Yi 程頤 (Cheng Yichuan 程伊川, 1033–1107), were sent by their father to study under Zhou in 1046–1047, at the ages of fifteen and fourteen. The two became outstanding philosophers in their own right. Their temperaments were utterly different, and though they agreed on many issues, Cheng Yi is considered the founder of the rationalistic school of Neo-Confucianism, together with Zhu Xi, and Cheng Hao is considered to have a more idealistic tendency.

6 Franke, *Song Yuan Biographies*, 277. Bounghown Kim questioned the traditional assumption of Zhou's intellectual background. He offers a broader perspective on the second chapter of his dissertation. Bounghown Kim, *A Study of Chou Tun-i's Thought* (Arizona: University of Arizona Press, 1996).

7 See Ching, *The Religious Thought of Chu Hsi*, 19.

8 I follow Adler's translation of *taiji* as Supreme Polarity and *wuji* as Nonpolar. See Joseph A. Adler, *Reconstructing the Confucian Dao: Zhu Xi's Appropriation of Zhou Dunyi* (Albany: State University of New York Press, 2014), 113. Adler affirms that there is no denying the idea of *taiji* as farthest, highest, extreme, or ultimate. Still, he opines that Song dynasty Confucians did not think in linear terms, but rather in terms of yin-yang dynamics, where the farthest point is never the "last stop on a one-way line." See 122–25.

9 See ibid., 49–75.

10   Ibid., 100–6.
11   See Smith et al., *Sung Dynasty Uses of the I Ching*.
12   According to the Lu version of the *Analects*, yi 易 ("*Change*" taken as the book's title) should be replaced by yi 亦 in the passage, thus meaning "If I were granted many more years, and could devote 50 of them for learning, surely I would be able to be free of major faults." See Edward Slingerland, *Analects: With Selections from Traditional Commentaries* (Indiana: Hackett, 2003), 69–70.
13   Carl. G. Jung, *Collected Works*, vol. 8, *The Structure and Dynamics of the Psyche* (New York: Bollingen Foundation, 1960), editorial preface, vii.
14   Joseph Needham, *Science and Civilisation in China*, vol. 2 (Cambridge, UK: Cambridge University Press, 1956), 280–81.
15   Frederick W. Mote, *Intellectual Foundations of China* (New York: McGraw-Hill, 1971), 19.
16   The term *qi* encapsulates the evasive nature of the intangible matter of life. Trying to capture its essence as a substance that is not solely physical, qi was rendered ether, matter energy, passion-nature, material force, vital force, pneuma, essential matter, ether of materialization, and psychophysical force. See "Discussion" in Patt-Shamir, "Li and Qi as Supra-Metaphysics," 244.
17   In general, I translate *li* 理 as Order, implying an arrangement in accordance with universal rule. It is sometimes equated with reason and the Aristotelian notion of form. In its original meaning, the word *li* referred to the patterns in things, the markings in jade or the veins. Later on, it acquired the meaning of principle. It is translated also as pattern, principle, law, and inherent normative patterns. When citing a translated source, I follow the original choice of the translator, while generally it is referred to hereafter as Order, and in specific contexts, where it seems more appropriate, I refer to the term as principle (see discussion on the various translations of *li* in Patt-Shamir, "Li and Qi as Supra Metaphysics," 244–45). For *li xue* 理學, I use the accepted translation—School of Principle.
18   Cheng Chung-ying, "Li and Qi in the *Yijing*: A Reconsideration of Being and Nonbeing in Chinese Philosophy," *Journal of Chinese Philosophy*, 36, supplement 1 (December 2009), 11–36, 24.
19   Despite being mentioned only in the in the appendices of the *Book of Change*, the book reflects the image *Xiang* 象 (thinking) basically as analogical reasoning in which one image schema is used to conceptualize another domain. See Wang, 2012, *Yinyang: The Way of Heaven and Earth in Chinese Thought and Culture* (New York: Cambridge University Press), 22. Accordingly, each hexagram includes an illustration (*guaxiang* 卦象), a title (*guaming* 卦名), a corresponding condition explaining its meaning (*guaci* 卦辭), and a verbal account for each line (*yaoci* 爻辭). The symbols together with the literal expressions serve as tool for understanding the meaning of sixty-four different archetypal conditions, which may vary according to diverse circumstances.
20   This view also matches the understanding according to which for every "pure" yin or yang line, one should also look up the opposing hexagram. For example,

according to the three coins system, a yang line can be the outcome of either three threes (three coins which fell on heads) considered pure, or one three and two twos (one head and two tails), which is "mixed"; accordingly, a yin line is the outcome of three twos (three tails) as pure yin or one two and two threes (one tail and two heads) as mixed. For every pure line, one should look at its opposite. For example, if one got the *Qian* hexagram as the top and bottom pure lines and the rest are mixed, one should also look up hexagram 28 of four yang lines with yin lines on bottom and on top. Hence, the varieties for each hexagram amount to sixty-four readings.

21 See C. G. Jung, Foreword to Richard Wilhelm's translation of the *I Ching*, 1950.
22 http://www.iging.com/intro/foreword.htm.
23 For views that emphasize the metaphysical aspect in neo-Confucianism, see Wing-tsit Chan, *Chu Hsi, Life and Thought* (Hong Kong: Chinese University Press, 1987), 108–12; Carsun Chang, *The Development of Neo-Confucian Thought* (New Haven, CT: College and University Press, 1963), 140, 153–58; Angus C. Graham, *Two Chinese Philosophers: Cheng Ming Tao and Cheng Yi Chuan* (London: Lund Humphries, 1967), 153–58; William T. de Bary, "Some Common Tendencies in Neo-Confucianism," in *Confucianism in Action*, eds. David Nivson and Arthur Wright (Stanford, CA: Stanford University Press, 1959), 33; Sui-chi Huang, "The Concept of *T'ai-Chi* in Sung Neo-Confucian Philosophy," *Journal of Chinese Philosophy* 1, no. 3–4 (August 1974): 275–94, 289; Sui-chi Huang, "Chu-Hsi's Ethical Rationalism," *Journal of Chinese Philosophy* 5 (June 1978): 175–93; Robin R. Wang, "Zhou Dunyi's Diagram of the Supreme Ultimate Explained (Taijitu shuo): A Construction of the Confucian Metaphysics," *Journal of the History of Ideas* 66, no. 3 (2005): 307–23; Mingdong Gu, "The Taiji Diagram: A Meta-Sign in Chinese Thought," *Journal of Chinese Philosophy* 30, no. 2 (May 2003): 195–218.
24 The terminology is borrowed from Kierkegaard's *Sickness Unto Death*. Despite the different context, the balanced self for Kierkegaard is a composite of elements of finitude and infinitude. See Søren Kierkegaard, *The Sickness unto Death: A Christian Psychological Exposition of Edification and Awakening by Anti-Climacus*, trans. Alastair Hannay (London: Penguin Classics, 1989), 65.
25 Regarding the status of *you* and *wu*, see Chungying Cheng, "Dimensions of the Dao and Onto-Ethics in Light of the *DDJ*," *Journal of Chinese Philosophy* 31, no. 2 (2004): 177; Tongdong Bai, "An Ontological Interpretation of *You* and *Wu* in the *Laozi*." *Journal of Chinese Philosophy* 35, no. 2 (2008): 339–51.
26 Benjamin Schwartz, "Knowing Words: Wisdom and Cunning in the Classical Traditions of China and Greece by Lisa Ralphs," A Review, *Harvard Journal of Asiatic Studies* 56, no. 1 (1996): 230–31. Schwartz makes this statement in the context of a comparison with Greek thought being "fundamentally obsessed with knowing that.
27 Chen Tuan 陳摶 (d. 989) was said to be a student and practitioner of the yin-yang system of the *Yijing*, as well as of Confucian classics. He had special

fondness for Daoist philosophy, medical principles, astronomy, and geography; energy cultivation; sleeping meditation; Qigong; and Gongfu. According to the legend, he had planned a career at the Imperial court but failed the state examination and became a hermit sage. See Wang *Yinyang*, 310–11.

28. Ibid., 41–82. See also Donggu Ming, "The Taiji Diagram: A Meta-Sign in Chinese Thought," *Journal of Chinese Philosophy* 30, no. 2 (May 2003): 198–99.
29. See Diamond Cora, "Riddles and Anselm's Riddle," in *The Realistic Spirit: Wittgenstein, Philosophy, and the Mind*, 267–90 (Cambridge MA: MIT Press, 1991), 267–89.
30. For extensive discussion on the translation, see Adler *Reconstructing*, 118, 123–25.
31. See Patt-Shamir, "To Live a Riddle."
32. See Cheng, "Dimensions of the *Dao*," 146–47.
33. Master Zhu's commentary on TJTS, *Yulei*, 94: 3,122; Adler *Reconstructing*, 123
34. Ibid. 94: 3,127, Adler *Reconstructing*, 125.
35. Compare also with the Kabbalah notion of *Einsof* (infinity) or *Keter* (Crown) and the Diagram of Sefirot. See *Zohar* attributed to Rabbi Shimon Bar Yochai, part ii, section "Bo," 42b. http://www.ashlagbaroch.org/Zohar/.
36. The text can also be read, "the limit of tranquility is movement," referring to the simple fact that when activity is exhausted it reaches stillness, or the limit and end of movement is tranquility. While this is an appropriate translation as well, I wish to stress the simultaneity and mutual containment of movement and tranquility.
37. See *Zhou Lianxi xiansheng quanji* 周濂溪先生全集, section 1. Unless stated otherwise, the translations here of TJTS and TS passages are my own. TS is referred to according to part and chapter; Zhu's commentary is referred to similarly, with the addition of the letter *c*.
38. Wang, *Yinyang*, 8–12.
39. Ibid., 19–20.
40. Ibid., 158.
41. *Yangbian yinhe* 陽變陰合 can also be read: "the alternation and combination of *yang* and *yin*." See Adler, *Appropriating*, 179.
42. Henri Bergson, *L'evolution Creatrice* (Paris: Libraries Felix Alcan et Guillaumin Reunies, 1911), *Creative Evolution*, trans. by Arthur Mitchell (Lanham, MD: University Press of America, 1983), 13, 98. This statement comprises a part of a criticism on mechanism and teleology that overlook the idea of movement.
43. *L'evolution Creatrice*, 13.
44. *Book of Change*, "Appended Remarks," A.1.4. *Chinese Text Project*. http://ctext.org/book-of-changes/qian.
45. The commenting or appendix part, the *Yizhuan* 易傳, also called the "Great commentary" *Yi dazhuan* 易大傳, consisting of "Ten Wings" (*shiyi* 十翼). The Ten Wings include two Canons of *Tuan* 彖 on the judgment; two Canons of *Xiang* 象 on the "appearance"; *Wenyan* 文言 on the characters; two Commentaries of *Xici* 繫辭 on the relationship of the hexagrams; *Shuogua* 說卦 explaining the hexagrams;

Xugua 序卦 on the order of the hexagrams; and *Zagua* 雜卦 referring to miscellaneous hexagrams. The word *wings* is used to express alleviated understanding of the Classics, as wings serve to make a bird fly higher for a more all-encompassing perspective.

46. John R. Lynn (trans.), *The Classic of Changes: A New Translation of the I Ching as Interpreted by Wang Bi* (New York: Columbia University Press, 1994), 129. In the context of Zhou Dunyi's work, *Book of Change* passages use Lynn's translation of Wang Bi's 王弼 *Zhouyi zhu*, 周易注, as Wang Bi's commentary was already the dominant in Song dynasty times, and undoubtedly impacted Zhou's understanding.
47. Ibid., 143.
48. Ibid., 158.
49. The term *correlative thinking* was coined by Granet. See *Marcel Granet, La Pensee Chinoise* (Paris: Albin Michel, 1950). See also Angus C. Graham, *Yin-Yang and the Nature of Correlative Thinking*, Occasional Paper and Monograph Series, no. 6 (Kent Ridge, Singapore: The Institute of East Asian Philosophy, 1986), 1; Needham, *Science and Civilization*, 280–81.
50. For the traditional Jewish version of the serpent as evil inclination (*yetzer hara*), see Babylonian Talmud, *Baba-batra*, 15:1; See discussion in, Nechama Leibowitz, *Iyunim Chadashim B'sefer B'reshit* (Jerusalem, Israel: Maor, 1994), 22–33. In this context I do not deal with the interpretation that the serpent is Satan. For a comprehensive discussion see James L. Kugel, *The Bible as It Was* (Cambridge MA: Harvard University Press, 1997), 72–75.
51. Both parenthetical additions are Zhou's explanatory remark from chapters 6 and 20 in TS. See Adler *Appropriating*, 188.
52. *Changes*, Qian, hexagram 1.
53. *Changes* Remarks on Trigrams (*Shuogua*) 2; *Zhouzi chuanshu*, 1–2, 4–32.
54. *Appended Remarks*, 1.4.2.
55. Zhu Xi's comment on TJTS, Adler, *Appropriating*, 193.
56. Zhu does not provide his reader with an explanation regarding why humanity is yang and rightness is yin; however, this view of his is repeated in his *Treatise on Ren* (*renshuo* 仁說), where he presents the relatedness of humanity and "the mind of heaven and earth," which is "to produce things." This mind is characterized by four qualities, of which origination and prosperity are analogous to humanity and rightness, such that in human beings, humanity is origination, and origination in humans is first and foremost origination of morality. Rightness—a more "mature" virtue—can be understood in the tradition of the *Book of Change* as completion (which is the beginning of decline). *Renshuo* 720–21. See Chan *Source Book*, 593.
57. See ibid., 460.
58. See Adler *Appropriating*, 299. Adler suggests an explanation to Zhu's choice of TJTS as the pioneering Confucian text in the Song dynasty, as the outcome of a spiritual crisis he underwent, 67–75.

59 Adler *Appropriating*, 129.
60 Referring respectively to chapters 1–3 on sincerity, chapter 20 on motion and tranquility, and chapter 22 on order, nature, and destiny.
61 Adler *Appropriating*, 129.
62 See Franke *Song Yuan*, 280.
63 See Tu Weiming, Milan Hejmánek and Alan Wachman (eds.), *The Confucian World Observed* (Honolulu, Hawaii: East Asian Center, 1992), 118–19. According to Schwartz, in the original context, this attitude is also "profoundly religious" in the sense that the universe is routinized in a meaningful way. See Schwartz, "Knowing Words," 231.
64 From *Yijing*, commentary on the first hexagram—*Qian*, see Lynn, *The Classic of Change*, 129.
65 From the Commentary on the first hexagram, see ibid. Lynn's translation of *ming* as "destiny" is replaced here with "mandate," suggesting an emphasis not on predestination and predetermination, rather it is on future possibilities.
66 Ibid., Commentary on the Appended Phrases, pt. 1, section 5, 53.
67 Unless stated otherwise, TS is brought here with chapter number in my translation.
68 DM 20.342.
69 Zhu Xi implies here that sincerity is "to be complete," following DM 25.1. See Legge, *The Four Books*, 402.
70 See *Mencius* 2A:2.
71 *Yulei*, 9.96, Chan, *Source Book*, 633. The Chinese term *ti* 體 is typically translated as "substance" (see Russel Hatton, "A Comparison of 'Li' and Substantial Form," *Journal of Chinese Philosophy* 9 (March 1982): 49–76; Chan, *Source Book*, 485–89, 517, 535, 541, 570, 596–97, 696–97). However, as coupled with uses, roles, or functions (*yong* 用), one should note that the term is closer to one's idea of a structure that is embodied in the various instances. While I follow the accepted translation, it is important to differentiate *ti* from Western substance-theory and its connotations of substance, as an essence that serves as a key concept in ontology and metaphysics, and suggesting an ontological sense of objecthood, which posits that a substance is distinct from its properties. According to the present attitude *ti* is supra-metaphysically oriented: Being responsible for the unity, it is also responsible for primary differences in practice, and never distinguished from properties. Rather, it is unified with the various functions.
72 *Yulei* 11.118, see ibid., 640.
73 Quotation from the *Yijing*, commentary on the *Qian* hexagram. See, *The Classic of Changes*, 133.
74 Quotations taken respectively from the Commentary on the Images of the *Sun* hexagram (see ibid., 388), and of the *Yi* hexagram (see ibid., 397).
75 The text refers to women (*furen* 婦人) as the source of separation, bringing the example of hexagram 38 describing two women under one roof. I believe that a

proper progressive understanding demands that the source of separation is plurality of women under one roof, rather than simply women.

76 The importance of the possibility of turning back is also discussed in chapters 3 and 27. It is interesting to reflect back on chapter 3 and compare the idea that returning is "turning back and bring it about" (*fanerzhi* 反二致) with the Hebrew expression *tshuva*. In the Hebrew language, returning (*lashuv*) and bringing about or repenting (*tshuva*) originate in the same root. Returning implies the possibility of rectification.

77 Graham, *Two Chinese Philosophers*, 68.

78 Adler, *Reconstructing*, 74–77.

79 From the Commentary on the Appended Phrases, part one, section 8. See Lynn, *The Classic of Changes*, 57.

80 DM 20.343.

81 See examples in Hatton, "A Comparison of 'Li' and Substantial Form," 55–59.

82 Zhu Xi's predecessor Cheng Yi developed this perspective in treating order as the quest for moral knowledge. For a comprehensive discussion of Cheng's views, see Peter K. Bol, *This Culture of Ours* (Stanford, CA: Stanford University, 1992), 316–27.

83 Thome H. Fang, *Chinese Philosophy: Its Spirit and Its Development* (Taipei: Linking Publishing, 1981), 352–53.

84 *Ji* 幾 is rendered here subtle activation. This translation of *ji* emphasizes the power that is inherent in the origin of things (as distinguished from power inherent in position; see TS ch. 27). This translation is a combination of the two meanings of the word suggested in the *Yijing*: subtlety, or infinitesimally small beginning (see Lynn, *The Classic of Changes*, 84, 267–68), and first sprouts or origin (see ibid., 498). Chan suggests "subtle incipient activating force" (see Chan *Source Book*, 466); Smith, Bol, Adler, and Wyatt use "incipience" to translate *ji* (see Kidder Jr. et al., *Sung Dynasty Uses of the I Ching*, 189–90.

85 See *Zhuangzi* 2.7.

86 In a comparison with Greek thought being "fundamentally obsessed with 'knowing that,'" Schwartz observes that this type of knowledge is the outcome of a lack of a practice/knowledge antithesis. See Schwartz, "Knowing Words," 231.

87 This section is based on previous work, see Galia Patt-Shamir, "Way as Dao; Way as Halakha: Confucianism, Judaism and Way Metaphors," *Dao: A Journal of Comparative Philosophy* 5, no. 2 (December 2005): 137–58.

88 See Tu Weiming, "Neo-Confucian Ontology: A Preliminary Questioning," *Journal of Chinese Philosophy* 7 (June 1980): 94.

89 For Zhu Xi's comment, see the *Wanyou wenku* edition of *Zhouzi quanshu*, 165; see also Chan, *Source Book*, 473.

90 See Chan, ibid., 473–74; on Buddhist influence on the neo-Confucian concept of sage, see Pratoon Angurarohita, "Buddhist Influence on the Neo-Confucian Concept of the Sage," *Sino-Platonic Papers* 10 (June 1989): 6–16.

91 Wing-tsit Chan, *China* (Berkeley and Los Angeles: University of California Press, 1946), 268.
92 Zhu Xi, *Jinsi lun* 近思論—Zhu Xi's reflections on neo-Confucian philosophy. The first appearance of the idea is to be found in the *Yiishu* 遺書. See Wing-tsit Chan (trans.), *Reflections on Things at Hand: The Neo-Confucian Anthology* compiled by Chu Hsi and Lu Tsu-Chien (New York: Columbia University Press, 1967), 163. Here, Zhu Xi uses the example of fondness for hunt, given by Zhou Dunyi himself.
93 Ibid., 4.1. See Chan, *Reflections*, 1967, 123.
94 Respectively, *Analects* 7:15; *Mencius* 7b:35. Other examples of this kind may be found in *Analects* 6:9 and 1:15.
95 See Edward T. Chien, "The Neo-Confucian Confrontation with Buddhism: A Structural and Historical Analysis," *Journal of Chinese Philosophy* 15 (December 1998): 347–70, 347–488.
96 Respectively, *Zhuangzi*, chapter 20.2; 19.2.
97 See Chan *Source Book*, 479.
98 Zhu Xi, *Jinsi lun*, 4.70, 5.1–2. See Chan, *Reflections*, 154–55.
99 See ibid.
100 Ibid., 4.48, see Chan, *Reflections*, 143.
101 See, for example, *Zhuangzi* 7.6, saying that the perfect person uses his heart like a mirror, responding without storing or retaining (*yinger buzhang* 應而不藏).
102 Zhu Xi refers here to the "images" and "appearances" of the *Book of Change*.
103 Tang Junyi in Douglas Lancashire ed. *Chinese Essays on Religion and Faith*. San Francisco, CA: Chinese Materials Center, 1981, 49.
104 Mou borrows the notions "immanence" and "transcendence" from Kant. See, Mou, *Xinti yu Xingti*, 20. 49. For a full discussion on the dual process, see Lin Tongqi and Qin Zhou, "The Dynamism and Tension in the Anthropocosmic vision of Mou Zongsan: A Reflection on Confucian Concept of *Tianren Heyi*," *Journal of Chinese Philosophy* 22, no. 4 (December 1995): 405–16.
105 See ibid., 419.

NOTES TO CHAPTER THREE

1 See discussion in Sophia Katz, "From Observing to Listening. The Intellectual/Spiritual Path of Shao Yong as Reflected in the *Yichuan Jiranji*," *Monumenta Serica* 61(2013): 141–82, 157–58. Ping-tzu Chu suggests that Shao tried unsuccessfully to obtain an official position. See Ping-tzu Chu, "Transmission of Shao Yong's Yi Learning," *Monumenta Serica* 61 (2013): 227–68, 227–31.
2 Katz, "From Observing to Listening," 157–58.
3 See Sui-chi Huang, *Essentials of Neo-Confucianism: Eight Major Philosophies of the Song and Ming Periods* (London: Greenwood Press, 1999), 37–38; Anne D. Birdwhistell, *Transition to Neo-Confucianism: Shao Yung on Knowledge and*

Symbols of Reality (Stanford, CA: Stanford University Press, 1989), 20–41; Don J. Wyatt, *The Recluse of Loyang: Shao Yung and the Moral Evolution of Early Sung Thought* (Honolulu: University of Hawai'i Press, 1996), 1–10.

4 Katz, "From Observing to Listening," 158.

5 The date of the poem is unknown; evidence taken from the poem's text supports that it was written between 1060 and 1077, when Shao Yong was between fifty-one and sixty-seven years old. See Zu-yan Chen, "Shao Yong's *Great Chant on Observing Weiqi*: An Archetype of Neo-Confucian Poetry," *Journal of the American Oriental Society* 126, no. 2 (April–June 2006): 200n7. Note that there is also a shorter poem titled, "Long Ode to Watching Wéiqí" (Guanqi changyin 觀棋長吟).

6 The assumption regarding the 360 days of the year was based on accepted knowledge in Shao's time. See Birdwhistell, *Transition to Neo-Confucianism*, 141.

7 Less frequent but necessary reference is also made to the *Yi River Striking the Earth Collection* (*Yichuan Jiran ji* 伊川擊壤集). The very title of this work is partially derived from a game that was allegedly played in the court in old times, tossing sticks at a larger stick on the ground while singing.

8 Chen Zu-yan's suggestion in his article about the poem from 2006 is of great significance to the present understanding. All references to the poem use his translation.

9 *Analects* 17:22. The term *boyi*博弈 raised some vagueness regarding the precise translation of the expression in the *Analects* passage. It is now quite accepted that *bo* refers to the ancient popular gambling game *liubo* 六博, whereas *yi*弈 is the playing of Weiqi. For details see Lien-sheng Yang, "A Note on the So-called TLV-Mirrors and the Game Liu-Po," *Harvard Journal of Asiatic Studies* 9 (February 1947): 202–20, 202.

10 Respectively, *Mencius* 4B:58; 6A:9.

11 *Zuo Zhuan*, 9.25.2 (Duke Xiang, 25th year, pt. 2 襄公二十五年).

12 Donald Potter, "Go in the Classics," *Go World* 37 (1985): 16–18, 18.

13 The frequent mentioning of Weiqi in vol. 5 of the *Yichuan Jirangji* was rather unusual. Apart of being mentioned in one poem in vol. 1 (YCJRJ 1:1:4), it appears one time in vol. 2 (YCJRJ 2:10:10); two times in vol. 4 (YCJRJ 4:10:25, 4:34:29); one time in vols. 7–8 (YCJRJ 7:12:45, 8:7:51); two times in vol. 11 (YCJRJ 11:33:82, 11:46:84); one time in vol. 12 (YCJRJ 12:40:90); two times in vol. 17 (YCJRJ 17:52: 128, 17:62: 129); and in vol. 20, the term is mentioned seven times, appearing first in 1072. See YCJRJ 20:1: 148–58 (poems 15, 29, 79, 99, 114, 119, 120).

14 For more, see Peter Shotwell, *Go! More than a Game* (Rutland, VT: Tuttle Publishing, 2003).

15 Johan Huizinga, *Homo Ludens: A Study of the Play Element in Culture* (Boston, MA: Beacon Press, 1950), 33–40. An interesting relation between game and laugh appears also in the Semitic languages. For example, in Hebrew, the root ש.ח.ק) *s.h.k*(denotes game and laugh.

16 In Chinese (as well as in Greek and Sanskrit), *wan* is not used for games of skill, contests, gambling, or theatrical performance, thus the words for contest are distinct from those of play. Huizanga also refers to the modern word that denotes an organized contest, *sai*賽 (Huizinga, *Homo Ludens*, 32–33).

17 Huizinga, *Homo Ludens*, 13.

18 John Fairbaim, "Go in Ancient China," http://www.pandanet.co.jp/English/essay/goancientchina.html (1995), 3.

19 See Huizinga *Homo Ludens*, 28, 49–53. Caillois criticizes this point believing that Huizinga's definition excludes games of chance played for money. See Roger Caillois, *Man, Play and Games* (Chicago, IL: University of Illinois Press, 2001), 9, 145–60. Notably, Weiqi competitions are sometimes played for money, too.

20 Marcel Granet derives the whole hierarchy of the Chinese state from primitive customs including contests. See *Marcel Granet, La Pensee Chinoise* (Paris: Albin Michel, 1950), 204.

21 Huizanga, *Homo Ludens*, 89–97, 119.

22 Huizanga, *Homo Ludens*, 198. Weiqi, which the study does not refer to directly, easily fits in this category too.

23 Caillois, *Man, Play and Games*, 9–10.

24 Respectively, lines 1–4, 39, 33, 6, 17, 11.

25 *Analects* 7.6. See more in Chen's "Shao Yong's *Great Chant*," 200n10. In the poem, Shao refers to the game of Weiqi by its traditional reference, qi 棋. For more detail, see Potter, "Go in the Classics"; Fairbaim, "Go in Ancient China." Some believe that in classical Chinese *qi* could also refer to other games, such as chess or the more popular game of *xiangqi* (象棋); doubtlessly, Shao Yong's poem refers to Weiqi.

26 Wyatt, *The Recluse*, 177.

27 See John Knoblock, *Xunzi: A translation and Study of the Complete Works* (Stanford, CA: Stanford University Press, 1998), vol. 3, 108. See Wyatt, *The Recluse*, 275n34.

28 See John Knoblock, *Xunzi*.

29 See John Knoblock, *Xunzi*, 180. In the above quotation, Wyatt uses "Chess" to include Weiqi.

30 John Knoblock, Xunzi, 181.

31 Compare with Wyatt, *The Recluse*, 186; Birdwhistell, *Transition to Neo-Confucianism*, 181.

32 Huang, *Essentials*, 47.

33 HJJS 8B:25a; Chan 1963, 493.

34 HJJS 8B:29a.

35 See Birdwhistell, *Transition to Neo-Confucianism*, 56.

36 Wyatt, *The Recluse*, 192.

37 See Birdwhistell *Transition to Neo-Confucianism*, 164–66; Wyatt, *The Recluse* 1996,186–87.

38 This type of direct realism can be compared to Hilary Putnam's direct realism, aiming to bring the study of metaphysics back to the way people experience the world, rejecting intermediaries between the mind and the world. See Hilary Putnam, *Renewing Philosophy*, Cambridge MA: Harvard University Press, 1999.

39 Shao considers water to reflect better than a mirror, probably because mirrors in his times were silver-mercury amalgams and not as bright as water. Alternately, since water is a natural resource, he may have considered it better at revealing the universal form.

40 In 22.6.

41 The four levels are referred to respectively as *shi* 事; *li* 理; *lishi wuwai* 理事無礙; and *shishi wuwai* 事事無礙. See Yoshito S. Hakeda trans, *The Awakening of Faith, Attributed to Asvagosha* (New York: Columbia University Press, 1967).

42 Birdwhistell, *Transition to Neo-Confucianism*, 180.

43 Chen, "Shao Yong's Great Chant," 218.

44 In this situation, a player takes the lead in a certain part of the board and forces the opponent to respond to his moves rather than initiate his own move. Otherwise, the opponent risks greater damage. See Chen, "Shao Yong's Great Chant," 201n11.

45 See Granet *La Pense*, 272–73.

46 For example, see Chenyang Li, "The Confucian Ideal of Harmony," *Philosophy East & West* 56, no. 4 (October 2006): 583–603.

47 Huizinga, *Homo Ludens*, 50.

48 Huizinga first notes the need for freedom (Huizinga, *Homo Ludens*, 7–8). Caillois relates it with joy (Caillois, *Man, Play and Games*, 8).

49 See Xunzi, chapter 23.

50 See the discussion in chapter 1.

51 Caillois, *Man, Play and Games*, 10

52 See Caillois, *Man, Play and Games*, 87–97.

53 Yasunari Kawabata, *The Master of Go*, Edward G. Seidensticker trans. (New York: Vintage International 1996), 165.

54 See Chen, "Shao Yong's 'Great Chant," 201f13, 14.

55 Chen suggests that "dragons and snakes" refers to weapons, based on *Lu Wen* 呂溫 (772–811). See "Shao Yong's Great Chant," 201n14. This analysis does not explain how the weapons are related to the liver and spleen. According to the *Hanyu da cidian* 漢語大詞典, *longshe* 龙蛇 can also refer to "an eminent or distinguished person." The sentence could be read along the lines, of "The eminent person arises from the liver and the spleen." (Interestingly, the combination is also reference to the soon to be mentioned Han founding emperor Liu Bang and his adversary Xiang Yu as a pair.)

56 For more elaboration on the dragon, see Edward H. Schafer, *The Vermillion Bird: T'ang Images of the South* (Berkeley: University of California Press, 1967).

57 See Chen, "Shao Yong's Great Chant," 201n15.

58 Caillois, *Man, Play and Games*, 9.
59 See Caillois, *Man, Play and Games*, 6–7.
60 Huizinga even mentions the curiosity in the relatedness of "prize," "price," and "praise," all derived from one Latin source. See Huizinga, *Homo Ludens*, 50–51.
61 Caillois notes that, interestingly, in most cases even a player who violates the rules of the game pretends to respect them and behaves as if following accepted ethical norms, therefore guarding the rules he violates or wishes to rid himself of, since otherwise he would be caught and would be disqualified to play. Caillois, *Man, Play and Games*, 43–45.
62 See *Hanfeizi*, 49, SBCK 5a; Wing-tsit Chan, *Source Book*, 260.
63 See *Xunzi*, chapter 22. See also the *Analects* 13:3, stressing the relatedness of names and actions in the political sphere.
64 Respectively, hexagrams 1, 2, and 6.
65 See remarks on the lines of the first hexagram, John Blofeld, trans., *I Ching: The Book of Change* (New York: Penguin Books, 1968), 87.
66 See John Blofeld, trans., *I Ching*, 93.
67 See John Blofeld, trans., *I Ching*, 161.
68 Wyatt, *The Recluse*, 182.
69 Birdwhistell, *Transition to Neo-Confucianism*, 17.
70 Wing-tsit Chan notes that Shao's concept of cycles of history is closely related to his theory of number as the essence of the universe. In the historical context, the theory opens with the unit of thirty years for a generation, making a complete revolution in twelve generations and defined by an epoch of thirty revolutions, all analogous to the months of the year and the periods of the day. Note that not all scholars agree with the understanding of Shao's view of history as cyclical (see Birdwhistell, *Transition to Neo-Confucianism*, 149). The scheme and the theory of numbers will not be discussed in the present context. For more, see Chan *Source Book*, 485–87; Huang, *Essentials*, 38–45; Birdwhistell, *Transition to Neo-Confucianism*, 145–61.
71 Huizinga, *Homo Ludens*, 46.
72 Chen adds that Weiqi is a "play-substitute" for the actual art of war and, hence, popular among generals and statesmen, who conducted their wars on the larger board (Chen 2006, 218–19).
73 The Three Kings were King Wen, King Wu, and the Duke of Zhou. The Five Despots were Duke Huan of Qi, Duke Mu of Qin, Duke Xiang of Song, Duke wen of Qin, and King Zhuang of Chu. For Shao's account on the Three Kings and Five Hegemons, see Birdwhistell, *Transition to Neo-Confucianism*, 147.
74 See Birdwhistell, *Transition to Neo-Confucianism*, 144–61.
75 See 6:15a Chan, *Source Book*, 487.
76 That is, "There is no one more long-lived than a child which dies prematurely, and Peng Zu did not live out his time" (*Zhuangzi* 2.9). In this spirit, Qu Bo-yu changed so often in the course of his life. (Chan, *Source Book*, 25.8).

77 The "Four evils" include the Sanmiao tribe 三庙 that Shun deported and three morally corrupt influential leaders. See Chen, "Shao Yong's Great Chant," 202n20.
78 This chronology will not be followed in details here; rather, we will use a few examples that serve the present purpose.
79 Yi Yin 伊尹 was a minister of the early Shang. He helped Tang of Shang 商湯, the founder of the Shang dynasty, to defeat King Jie of Xia. The Duke of Zhou 周公 played a major role in the Zhou dynasty. He is credited with writing the *Book of Change* and the *Book of Poetry* and with establishing the rites for fashioning institutions.
80 Wyatt, *The Recluse*, 114–18.
81 Lines 73–99 are dense with historical examples. For detailed reference to each instance, see Chen, "Shao Yong's Great Chant," 203–4nn25–50.
82 Chen, "Shao Yong's Great Chant," 219.
83 For details, see Chen, "Shao Yong's Great Chant," 205–6nn63–73, 219.
84 See Chen, "Shao Yong's Great Chant," 219.
85 Chen, "Shao Yong's Great Chant," 219.
86 Birdwhistell, *Transition to Neo-Confucianism*, 16.
87 The concept of "the ends of beginnings of heaven and earth" (*tiandi zhi zhongshi* 天地之終始) refers to cyclical patterns of time, as also illustrated in the Chart of the Four Images of Heaven and Earth (*Jingshi tiandi xiangtu* 經世天地四象圖). See more in Birdwhistell, *Transition to Neo-Confucianism*, 133–44.
88 See Birdwhistell, *Transition to Neo-Confucianism*, 49–65.
89 7A:17a Chan, *Source Book*, 489.
90 Chan, *Source Book*, 5:5a.
91 The passage also demonstrates Shao's philosophy of numbers, on which the discussion lies beyond the present scope.
92 Antonio S. Cua, "Forgetting Morality: Reflections on a Theme in *Chuang Tzu*," *Journal of Chinese Philosophy* 4, no. 4 (December 1997): 305–328, 306.
93 See *Zhuangzi* 6.2; 14.6.
94 Compare *Zhuangzi*, chapter 26.
95 Chen notes the reference to Yang Xiong's fable: "a sheep's constitution, yet clad in a tiger's skin; happy to see grass, it still trembles to see a jackal, forgetting that its skin was that of a tiger." See Chen, "Shao Yong's Great Chant," 215n158.
96 Birdwhistell, *Transition to Neo-Confucianism*, 42–43. Notably, Birdwhistell's analysis grants substantial importance to Shao's numerological system, which I deal with here only in passing. For her thorough analysis, see Birdwhistell, *Transition to Neo-Confucianism*, 42–94.
97 See James Davies, *Tesuji* vol. 3 (Tokyo, Japan: Ishi Press, 1975), 164. Davies also notes that in many cases, making a shape demands "sacrifice tactics."
98 Chen refers to the saying of Liu Xu 刘昫 (887–946) that one is confused when facing the game board, but when watching from the side one examines carefully. See Chen, "Shao Yong's Great Chant," 215n161.

99 A group can be considered "alive," "dead," or "unsettled," based on its having "eyes," regardless of the players' moves. See Davies, *Tesuji*, vol. 4.
100 *Zhouyi* 1.5b (in appended phrases to Qian hexagram). See Chen, "Shao Yong's Great Chant," 216n163.
101 Chen, "Shao Yong's Great Chant," 216; Wyatt, *The Recluse*, 198. I do not delve into the Before Heaven diagram and the After Heaven diagram, and their concrete significance in Shao's philosophy here. See discussion in Wyatt, *The Recluse*, 195–207. See also Birdwhistell, *Transition to Neo-Confucianism*, 88.
102 See Chen, "Shao Yong's Great Chant," 216n163–64.
103 *Changes*, "Remarks on Certain Trigrams," chapter 1. Legge, *The Chinese Classics*, 422.
104 Line 348 on speaking actually closes the above lines, rather than opening the following ones. I use it together with the next two lines because the idea in this transition is strongly related.
105 See *Laozi*, 14.
106 See *Liji*, 10.12; 11.30; 19.6.
107 Interestingly, Li Chenyang refers to the soup metaphor for harmony in a passage on preparing a balanced soup in *Zuozhuan* 左傳, stressing the importance of avoiding excessive flavors. Chenyang Li, "The Confucian Ideal of Harmony," 585.
108 Both of the images of great soup and black wine are also used to describe tasteful and elegant writing. See Katz, "From Observing to Listening," 126n129.
109 *Sunzi* 4a. See Chen, "Shao Yong's Great Chant," 220n182.
110 The use of the term *shanyan* can be found in *Laozi* 27. Interestingly, the simplicity of "good words" is to be found also in *Mencius* 7B:32. As Chen notes, there he refers to "good words" as ones that are near at hand, but far reaching. See Chen, "Shao Yong's Great Chant," 216n170.
111 CQZZ 25.192c.
112 Katz notes that Fuxi's Chart on the Order of Eight Trigrams is usually described as "The Four Charts of Fuxi" (*Fuxi situ* 伏羲四圖) or "The Four Charts of the Before-Heaven" (*Xiantian situ* 先天四圖). See Katz, "From Observing to Listening," 127n132. The charts related to the "before-Heaven" and "after-Heaven" order of trigrams and hexagrams became common in scholarly use only during the Song dynasty, in a very significant degree due to Shao Yong's scholarly contribution. According to tradition, these charts were allegedly drawn by Fuxi and Wen Wang, respectively. The teaching was transmitted to Chen Tuan (871–989), and then to Shao Yong. However, since very little evidence for the circulation of these concepts before Shao can be found in literature, it is sometimes suggested that Shao Yong was in fact the one who "invented" these schemes. See discussion in Wyatt, *The Recluse*, 195–207.
113 Shao's occupation with Weiqi as a microcosm for history and life demonstrates the significance he attributes to structure, rules, and frameworks. In this regard, I refer to Anne Birdwhistell's perspective on "the problem of the structure of events" (Birdwhistell, *Transition to Neo-Confucianism*, 16). The theoretical

framework suggested here is based on Boaz Patt-Shamir's idea (personal communication).

NOTES TO CHAPTER FOUR

1. Many thanks to the participants in the neo-Confucian Studies Seminar at Columbia University (2010) for their kind, insightful comments on an earlier version of this chapter. An earlier shorter version of this chapter titled "Filial Piety, Vital Power, and a Moral Sense of Immortality in Zhang Zai's Philosophy" was published in *Dao: A Journal of Comparative Philosophy* 11, no. 2 (June 2012): 223–39.
2. Following Ben-Ami Scharfstein's point that one's philosophy reflects the philosopher's life story. See Ben-Ami Scharfstein, *The Philosophers: Their Life and the Nature of Their Thought* (New York: Oxford University Press, 1980.(
3. Chan, *Reflections*, 302–3.
4. See Galia Patt-Shamir, Ping Zhang, "Expanding Family Reverence: A Confucian-Jewish Dialogue," in *The Blackwell Companion on Interreligious Dialogue*, ed. Catherine Cornille (Oxford, UK: Wiley-Blackwell, 2013), 450–67.
5. For example, Chan translated Qian and Kun as Heaven and Earth. Chan, *Source Book*, 497.
6. See Wei-ming Tu, "The Ecological Turn in New Confucian Humanism: Implication for China and the World," *Daedalus* 130, no. 4 (Fall 2001): 243–64.
7. A possible reading may be that the *hun* 混 (in *hunran zhongzhu* 混然中處) must be translated as "chaos" rather than as a verb (to be mixed within), hence the phrase should read: "I dwell within chaos." While the suggestion remains loyal to the idea of cosmic connectedness, it is extremely intriguing with regard to Daoist influences on the text. In particular, in this case, the next line hints at the cosmic process as one in which the human consciousness identifies itself with the Way. While Daoist texts move directly to immortality, Zhang turns to a moral discussion, bringing him to a notion of morality as immortality, as we will see. Special thanks to Gil Raz for bringing up this possibility.
8. See *Mencius*, "*Mengzi* 孟子" 1A:7.
9. According to Deborah Sommer, there are four main terms that form together the full idea of body throughout the text. In addition to *ti*, the most recurring terms are 形 (*xing*), literally meaning shape, form, pattern, design, and manifest appearance (appearing ninety-eight times in the whole text); and 身 (*shen*), meaning the body, the trunk, the self, in person, or I myself. The term 躬 (*gong*) means body, person, oneself, in person, personally, or to bend (the body) and is used quite frequently in the *Analects*, where it receives a meaning of the ritualized body. See Deborah Sommer, "Concepts of the Body in the *Zhuangzi*," in *Experimental Essays on Zhuangzi*, ed. Victor H. Mair. 2nd ed. (Dunedin, FL: Three Pines, 2010), 212–14.

10. See ibid.; Nathan Sivin, "State, Cosmos, and Body in the Last Three Centuries B.C.," *Harvard Journal of Asiatic Studies* 55, no. 1 (June 1995): 14.
11. The Cheng brothers believed that Zhang's ideas were too close to Buddhist notions, yet that the idea of Zhang's WI "is perfect." For more, see Chan, *Reflections*, 79; Ira E. Kasoff, *The Thought of Chang Tsai* (London: Cambridge University Press, 1984), 140–43. Notably, Zhang's criticism of Buddhism is quite severe. In particular, he criticized Buddhist subjective idealism. See Huang, *Essentials of Neo-Confucianism*, 59–60, 63–68).
12. *Zhuangzi* 6.5. I thank my former student Sharon Small for this reference. See Sharon Y. Small, *Zhuangzi: The Film: Visualizing Zhuangzi's Riddle of One Body*. MA thesis, Tel Aviv University, 2014, 34–47.
13. See also *Mencius* 7A:21.
14. Discussion in Chan, *Source Book*, 497–99.
15. See Wang Yangming's, "Inquiry on the Great Learning" (*Daxue wen* 大學問), Chan, *Source Book*, 272. Wang Yangming, 王陽明 (Wang Shouren 王守仁, 1472–1529) is commonly regarded the most important neo-Confucian thinker of the School of the Mind (*xinxue* 心學), with antirationalistic, antidualistic views, opposing the orthodox philosophy of Zhu Xi.
16. Chan, *Source Book*, 273.
17. Indeed, in *The Infinite Other*, pure alterity is first encountered and the "Other" is superior or prior to the self. Since the other is transcendent rather than oneself, the ability to reach each other is limited. Levinas sees "Metaphysics, transcendence, the welcoming of the other by the same, of the Other by me" as "concretely produced as ... ethics." See Emmanuel Levinas, *Totality and Infinity*, trans. Lingis Alphonso (Pittsburgh, PA: Duquense University Press, 1969), 43. I am grateful to my former student Niva Sharon for bringing this to my attention.
18. See Lin Tongqi and Qin Zhou, "The Dynamism and Tension in the Anthropocosmic vision of Mou Zongsan: A Reflection on Confucian Concept of *Tianren Heyi*," *Journal of Chinese Philosophy* 22, no. 4 (December 1995): 401–40, 404.
19. Ibid., 413.
20. See, Tu Weiming, "Selfhood and Otherness: The Father-Son Relationship in Confucian Thought," in *Confucian Thought: Selfhood as Creative Transformation* (Albany: State University of New York Press, 1985), 113–30.
21. That is, see Tu Weiming, "Beyond the Enlightenment Mentality," in *Worldviews & Ecology*, ed. Mary Evelyn Tucker (NY: Orbis Books, 1994), 182.
22. Huang Siu-chi, "Chang Tsai's Concept of *Ch'i*," *Philosophy East and West* 18 (October 1968): 247–60, 247.
23. Huang, ibid., 58–61. In the present context, I do not deal with each idea separately. However, the central role of Zhang's dynamic view—in particular, his presenting opposing pairs as continuous and nondichotomous—is demonstrated throughout the chapter. See the discussion in Part B below.

24. Compare with the Humean idea of power as expressed in his *Treatise of Human Nature* in the observation that "the terms of *efficacy, agency, power, force, energy, necessity, connexion,* and *productive quality,* are all nearly synonymous." David Hume, *A Treatise of Human Nature,* ed. L. A. Selby-Bigge (Oxford, UK: Oxford University Press, 1978), 157.

25. On morality as ideal-oriented versus goal-oriented, see Galia Patt-Shamir, "The Effectiveness of Contradiction in Understanding Human Practice: The Rhetoric of 'Goal-Ideal' in Confucianism," *Journal of Chinese Philosophy* 32, no. 3 (September 2005): 455–76. See also Huang, "Chang Tsai's Concept of Ch'i," 258; Wang, Robin R. and Ding Weixiang, "Zhang Zai Theory of Vital Energy," in *Dao Companion to Neo-Confucian Philosophy,* ed. John Makeham. NY: Springer Books, 2010, 39–58.

26. Kim describes the grounds for mistaking Zhang Zai's vertical qi as substance monism: under the understanding that there is ultimately only one being, the many entities are understood to be manifestations only, and thus distinct from the ultimate. This understanding of materialistic qi has resulted in its rendering as substance, ether, or matter. See Jung-Yeup Kim, *Zhang Zai's Philosophy of Qi: A Practical Understanding* (NY: Lexington Books, 2015), esp. 2–10; 37–42.

27. *Xu* 虛 is translated here as void. However, one should note that, as explained hereafter, it definitely does not carry a sense of "vacuum" nor the sense of being "in vein," "useless," or containing nothing. It is rather being without something specified (as in de*void* of excess).

28. Kasoff transliterates qi in three different ways to distinguish its different roles. See Kasoff, *The Thought of Chang Tsai,* 37.

29. For extensive discussions of original substance, see, Cheng Yi 程頤, *Yizhuan* 易傳, Taipei: Shijie, 1972, 145–61.

30. Wang and Ding also mention that this view echoes Guo Xiang's ontology; however, according to Zhang, the great void does not produce vital power. Wang and Ding, "Zhang Zai's Theory," 46.

31. See *Xici Zhuan,* A12.

32. See *Laozi,* 33.

33. Kasoff, *The Thought of Chang Tsai,* 39, 41.

34. Kasoff makes reference to an earlier text in which the last line is different, asking: "How can we not call it being 有?" Kasoff, ibid., 42. For the present purpose, the difference should not be crucial. Certainly, the world of "being" is a world of temporariness, and the latter text seems to nuance the earlier.

35. Similarly, energy can neither be created nor destroyed: it can only be transformed and change form (for instance, chemical energy can become kinetic energy). *ISCID Encyclopedia of Science and Philosophy,* 2011. International Society for Complexity, Information, and Design. http://www.iscid.org/encyclopedia/Law_of_Conservation_of_Mass.

36. Huang, *Essentials of Neo-Confucianism,* 71.

37 Chan, *Source Book,* 550; *Reflections,* 80.
38 Chan *Source Book,* 497–99.
39 See also the *Analects* 13:18; *Mencius* 4A:19; 7A:15; 7A:35. Discussion in Patt-Shamir, "Way as Dao; Way as Halakha."
40 *Mencius* 1B:5.
41 Li, "The Confucian Ideal of Harmony," 589.
42 William T. de Bary, "Neo-Confucian Individualism and holism," in *Individualism and Holism: Studies in Confucian and Taoist values,* ed. Donald J. Munro (Ann Arbor: University of Michigan Press, 1985), 331–35.
43 For example, see, 1A.7.
44 See Huang, *Essentials of Neo-Confucianism,* 82–83, notes 41–46, for basic reference regarding each of the mentioned historical figures.
45 The term is taken from the *Book of Poetry,* Ode 256.
46 For elaborations on the historical examples of the son of Chong Bai, Ying Feng-ren, Shun Shen Sheng, and Bai-qi, see Chan, *Source Book,* 498nn6–11.
47 Wang Fuzhi 王夫之 (1619–1692) observed that whereas Mencius stresses both innate ability and innate knowledge, Zhang stressed only innate ability. See Chan, *Source Book,* 509.
48 See discussion in Wang and Ding, "Zhang Zai's Theory of Vital Energy," 50–53.
49 See Chan, *Source Book,* 501. Also Huang, "Chang Tsai's Concept of *Ch'i*," 254–59; T'ang Chün-yi, "Chang Tsai's Theory of mind and its Metaphysical Basis," *Philosophy East and West* 6, no. 2 (July 1956): 113–36, 115–19.
50 For a thorough comprehensive discussion on Zhang Zai's criticism on the Buddhist notion of void, see Kim, *Zhang Zai's Philosophy of Qi,* 17–44.
51 See Chan, *Source Book,* 502. Zhang's understanding of Buddhism, in particular the richness of schools and the various understandings of emptiness, is beyond the scope of this chapter. Interestingly, Zhang Boxing remarks that Zhang's claim that death is not annihilation is indeed "dangerously close" to Buddhism, hence one must be aware of the indestructibility of vital power. Ibid., 501–2.
52 Kasoff refers to an isolated passage in which yin is identified with the presence of material desires and yang with virtuosity. Kasoff, *The Thought of Chang Tsai,* 44. (See discussion on yin-yang on 43–53.)
53 Like his neo-Confucian predecessors, Zhang as well does not provide his readers with an explanation as to why humanity is yang and rightness is yin.
54 See Angus C. Graham, *Two Chinese Philosophers: Cheng Ming Tao and Cheng Yi Chuan* (London: Lund Humphries, 1967), 46.
55 T'ang, "Chang Tsai's Theory of Mind," 114–15.
56 Kim, *Zhang Zai's Philosophy of Qi,* 20. Importantly, Kim thoroughly appropriates Tang Junyi's "vertical" and "horizontal" dimensions of qi in Zhang Zai's philosophy for arriving at his understanding.
57 The words *minmian erwuchi* 民免而無恥 do not clearly specify whether the people avoid the punishment or the ruler.

58 Zhu Xi, *Zhuziyulei*, 84:2183.
59 The *Zhuangzi* expresses more than one attitude toward propriety. Zhuang Zhou of chapters 1–7 explicitly refrains from applying stern distinctions between behaviors that are "natural" or "unnatural" even though he acknowledges that such distinctions do exist, while in the latter chapters, different phenomena and deeds are divided into these categories. In the "Outer Chapters," we read a "wilder" and more antiformalistic and antiethical view, which explicitly devaluates family reverence and the rites. For example, in 14.2, "wolves and tigers are *ren* . . . wolves and tigers are *xiao*." Also see 18.2, 18.4, 32.16.
60 An important story in the present context is that following Confucius's death, many of the disciples built huts near the master's grave and spent three years mourning for him. Zigong alone pedantically kept mourning rituals not only for three years like one mourns over a father's death, but rather for six full years. Through the double amount of strictness and pedantry, he expressed his admiration for his Master.
61 Benjamin Schwartz, *The World of Thought in Ancient China* (Cambridge, MA: Harvard University Press, 1985), 68.
62 See the *Analects* 5:12; 7:20; 11:11.
63 See *Analects*, 6:5.
64 Porat, Roy. *REN and TIAN: Analysis of the "Confucian Episodes" in chapter 6 of the Zhuangzi*. The seventeenth Conference of the ISCP, EHESS, Paris.
65 Qin Shi, through his comment, also bears criticism on Laozi, the great Master himself, who despite criticizing the rites severely as the lowest point in the degeneration of the Way was not successful enough to educate his students to avoid this practice. Cf. *Laozi* 38.
66 *Book of Rites* 29.3.
67 Tu Weiming, *Humanity and Self-Cultivation, Essays in Confucian Thought* (Berkeley, CA: Asian Humanities Press, 1979, 13).
68 Herbert Fingarette, *Confucius: The Secular as Sacred* (New York: Harper and Row, 1972), 8.
69 On morality as joy, see note 56 of chapter 1.
70 Albert Camus, *A Happy Death* (London: Penguin Books, 1971), 31.
71 ZZJ 46.9, Kasoff, *The Thought of Chang Tsai*, 117. Unless stated otherwise, all Zhang Zai's quotations stem from Kasoff's (1984) translation, referring to the original passage number followed by the page number from Kasoff's book.
72 For the full elaboration of this embodiment, see Tu Weiming, "Embodying the Universe: A Note on Confucian Self-Realization," in *Confucian Thought: Selfhood as Creative Transformation* (Albany: State University of New York Press), 171–81. My student Keinan Mariasin takes up from Tu's idea and brilliantly elucidates how the body thus becomes the ground for morality.
73 See also the *Analects* 1:11; 4:20.
74 Kim, *Zhang Zai's Philosophy of Qi*, 46.

75 For additional understandings of "we do not live to experience death," see Brian R. Clack, *An Introduction to Wittgenstein's Philosophy of Religion* (Edinburgh, UK: Edinburgh University Press, 1999), 95.
76 LRB, 52
77 Ludwig Wittgenstein, *Philosophical Investigations*, trans. G. E. M. Anscombe (Oxford: Basil Blackwell, 1988), 23.
78 LRB, 52. Interpreters of Wittgenstein find themselves puzzled regarding this issue: Alan Keightley highlights the fact that Wittgenstein's attitude is not "a theory about," but something else (Clack, *An Introduction to Wittgenstein's*, 55). Iris Murdoch has called Wittgenstein's expression on religious belief "exasperating hints (ibid., 75). Anthony Flew finds them "scrappy and inconclusive" (ibid.), while Cora Diamond might see in this a "great riddle" (Diamond, "Riddles and Anselm's Riddle," 267–90).
79 LRB, 52. Also see Cyril Barrett, *Wittgenstein on Ethics and Religious Belief* (Oxford, UK: Blackwell, 1991), 132.
80 See reference to LRB as a "moral interpretation of religion" in Clack, *An Introduction to Wittgenstein's*, 71.
81 LRB, 70.
82 Ibid.
83 When Wittgenstein writes: "this was his duty to do so, and that even death couldn't stop it being his duty," he reflects the Kantian notion of "duty." Interestingly, Kant also connects duty with his notion of immortality. See Barrett, *Wittgenstein on Ethics*, 33.
84 D. Z. Phillips, *Death and Immortality* (London: Macmillan, 1970), 50.
85 Ibid., xi.
86 Ibid., 55.
87 Ibid.
88 The term *supernatural* is taken sometimes as that which is beyond human reason. See Barrett, *Wittgenstein on Ethics*, 231.
89 One should note that the Wittgensteinian terminology is taken from a linguistic space in which death is perceived as an apparent enemy. The latter is not necessarily true in Confucianism.
90 Kasoff, *The Thought of Chang Tsai*, 107.
91 Peter Harvey, *The Selfless Mind* (London: Curzon Press, 1995), 33.
92 See Thomas P. Kasulis, "The Absolute and the Relative in Taoist Philosophy," *Journal of Chinese Philosophy* 4, no. 4 (December 1977): 388–90.
93 *Zhuangzi* 3.2.
94 Ibid.
95 *Analects*, 15:4.
96 *Doctrine of the Mean*, 19; *Book of Family Reverence*, 18; 24; *Book of Rites*, 9.7.
97 See also the *Analects* 8:32; *Book of Rites*, 4:20.
98 Blakeley suggests possible explanations for why Confucius did not discuss death and critically responds to all. I do believe that his first suggestion that living well should in itself prepare one for death and the process of dying without anxiety

about death or regrets about life, can be applicable to Confucianism, especially for Zhang Zai. See Donald Blakeley, "The *Analects* on Death," *Journal of Chinese Philosophy* 37, no. 3 (September 2010): 397–78.

99   Peter K. Bol, *Neo-Confucianism in History* (Cambridge, MA: Harvard University Press, 2008), 142–43.

NOTES TO THE APPENDIX

1. See Smith et al., *Sung Dynasty Uses of the I Ching*.
2. By performative I refer to Austin's idea of sentences that are not only describing a given reality, but also changing the social reality they are describing. See J. L. Austin, *How to Do Things with Words* (Oxford, UK: Clarendon, 1962).
3. On Buddhism's arrival to China, see Heinrich Dumoulin, *Zen Buddhism: A History. Volume 1: India and China* (New York: Random House, 2005).
4. Lin Yutang, "Crossing the Gate of Death in Chinese Buddhist Culture," Hawaii, 1995, 1-11. http://www.yogichen.org/gurulin/efiles/mb/mbk16.html.
5. Moreover, the response to the emperor also conceals within it an ideology that there are no "better" or "worse" reincarnations, and measuring deeds against each other amounts to using ridiculous, clear-cut categorizations that are doomed to fail. Jeffrey L. Broughton, *The Bodhidharma Anthology: The Earliest Records of Zen* (Berkeley: University of California Press, 1999), 2–3.
6. Xuedou Zhongxian 雪竇重顯 (Jap. Setcho Juken). Xuedou's collection is the basis for the famous Koan collection titled, *Blue Cliff Record* (*Biyan Lu* 碧巖錄, Jap. *Hekiganroku*), which also includes Yuanwu Keqin's 圓悟克勤 (1063–1135) annotations and commentary on Xuedou Zhongxian's cases.
7. See Ding-hwa Hsie, "Poetry and Chan Gong-an: From Xue dou Congxian to Wumen Huikai," *Journal of Song-Yuan Studies* 40 (2010): 52.
8. See Sekida Katsuki, trans., *Two Zen Classics: Mumonkan & Hekianroku* (New York: Waterhill, 1977), 147.
9. According to the legend, after the meeting with Emperor Wu of Liang and then failing in Southern China, Bodhidharma left to the northern kingdom of Wei to the Shaolin Monastery. He lived in a nearby cave, where he sat in silence for nine years. According to one of the legends, he refused to resume teaching, until Hui ke (慧可487–593) eventually cut off his own arm and handed it to the Master in ultimate demonstration of earnestness, and thus become the first disciple and the second Chan patriarch. The patriarchs who followed were Sengcan (僧璨) ?–606; Daoxin (道信) 580–651; Hongren (弘忍) 601–674; and Hui Neng (慧能) 638–713. See also John McRae, *Seeing Through Zen. Encounter, Transformation, and Genealogy in Chinese Chan Buddhism* (Berkeley: University of California Press, 2003), 60–65.
10. See, Yoshito S. Hakeda trans., *The Awakening of Faith, Attributed to Asvagosha* (New York: Columbia University Press, 1967), 42.

11. Chung-ying Cheng, "'Unity of Three Truths' and Three forms of Creativity: Lotus Sutra and Process Philosophy," *Journal of Chinese Philosophy* 28 (December 2001): 451.
12. See Walter Liebenthal, trans. *Chao Lun* (Hong Kong: Hong Kong University Press, 1968), 54.
13. See Dumoulin, *Zen Buddhism*, 45–49. See also Kang-nam Oh, "The Taoist Influence on Hua-yen Buddhism: A Case of the Scinicization of Buddhism in China," *Chung-Hwa Buddhist Journal* 13, no. 2 (May 2000): 277–97.
14. Dajian Huineng 大鑒惠能 (638–710) is the author of *The Platform Sutra of the Sixth Patriarch* (Liuzu Tanjing 六祖壇經).
15. See John McRae, *The Platform Sutra of the Sixth Patriarch* (Berkeley, CA: Numata Center for Buddhist Translation and Research, 2000), 31.
16. Ibid. Yuquan Shenxiu 玉泉神秀 (606?–706) (Jap. Jinshu) was one of the most influential Chan Buddhist Masters of his day and the expected heir of the fifth patriarch, who according to the legend, lost his patriarchy in a verse contest to Hui Neng.
17. Ibid., 33.
18. While thematically close, Hui Neng's historical connection with Mazu is questioned by McRae. See McRae, *Seeing through Zen*, 82. See also John Jorgensen, *Inventing Hui-neng, the Sixth Patriarch Hagiography and Biography in Early Ch'an* (Leiden, the Netherlands: Brill, 2005).
19. Mazu Daoyi 馬祖道一 (Jap. Baso 709–788 AD) lead the *Hongzhou Zong* 洪州宗. The school survived the great persecution of the Buddhist schools in China during 845–846. This surviving rural Chan developed into the Five Houses (*wu-jia* 五家) of Chan, from which most Chan lineages throughout Asia and the rest of the world originally grew. After the fall of the Tang dynasty and the resultant turmoil in China, during the Song dynasty, Chan was used by the government and grew to become the largest sect in Chinese Buddhism. For details see Philip Yampolski, "Chan: A Historical Sketch," in *Buddhist Spirituality: Later China, Korea, Japan and the Modern World*, ed. Takeuchi Yoshinori (Delhi, India: Motilal Banarsidass, 2003), 15; Thomas P. Kasulis, *Ch'an Spirituality*, in *Buddhist Spirituality. Later China, Korea, Japan and the Modern World*, ed. Takeuchi Yoshinori (Delhi, India: Motilal Banarsidass, 2003), 28–29. Also see Chungyuan Chang, "Ch'an Buddhism: Logical and Illogical," *Philosophy East and West* 17, no. 1 (January–October 1967): 37–49.
20. See McRae, *Seeing Through Zen*, 119–20.
21. Cheng Chung-ying, "On Zen (Chan) Language and Zen Paradoxes," *Journal of Chinese Philosophy* 1(December 1973): 77–102.
22. Xuedou Zhongxian 雪竇重顯 (980–1052), the original compiler of the hundred cases that later served as the basis for the *Blue Cliff Record*, used the term *gong-an* just once in that collection.
23. Jinhua Juzhi 金華俱胝 810–880. Jap. Kinka Gutei. Sekida, *Two Zen Classics*, 197.

24　References, respectively, to case 67, ibid., 326; case 77, ibid., 349; and case 12, ibid., 179.
25　Zhao Zhou 趙州 (778–897, Jap. Joshu) was a successor of Mazu Daoyi who eventually received the Dharma from him. He is frequently touted as the greatest Chan Master of Tang dynasty China. Many koans in the *Blue Cliff Record* concern him.
26　See Sekida, *Two Zen Classics*, 258–61. Also see Young Ahn Jun, *Malady of Meditation, Prolegomenon on the Study of Illness and Zen*, PhD dissertation. University of California Berkeley, 2007, 102.
27　Case 50 on "particle after particle samadhi" replied, "rice in a bowl, water in the pail" by (Yunmen Wenyan 雲門文偃 [Jap. Ummon, 862 or 864–949]). See Sekida, *Two Zen Classics*, 284–87.
28　Case 3. See ibid., 152–53.
29　Chan Master Zhong Guoshi 忠國師 (675–775, Jap. Chu Kokushi), case 18. See ibid., 198.
30　Case 18. See ibid., 194.
31　Ibid., 358–60. See also David Loy, *Nonduality: A Study in Comparative Philosophy* (New York: Humanity Books, 1998).
32　See 26.13.
33　Daowu 道悟 769–835, Jap. Dogo.
34　Case 55. Sekida, *Two Zen Classics*, 298–301.
35　Ibid., 298–89.

BIBLIOGRAPHY

Adler, Joseph A. "Response and Responsibility: Chou Tun-i and Confucian Resources for Environmental Ethics." In *Confucianism and Ecology: The Interrelation of Heaven, Earth, and Human*, edited by Mary Evelyn Tucker and John H. Berthrong, 123–49. Cambridge, MA: Harvard University Press, 1998.

———, trans. "Explanation of the Supreme Polarity Diagram" (*Taijitu shuo*) by Zhou Dunyi, Commentary by Zhu Xi (*Zhuzi Taijitu shuo jie*), 2010. http://www2.kenyon.edu/Depts/Religion/Fac/Adler/Writings/TJTS-Zhu.pdf.

———. *Reconstructing the Confucian Dao: Zhu Xi's Appropriation of Zhou Dunyi*. Albany: State University of New York Press, 2014.

Allinson, Robert E. "The Beautiful as Metaphor: The Symbol of Metamorphosis." In *Chuang-Tzu for Spiritual Transformation: An Analysis of the Inner Chapters*, 71–110. Albany: State University of New York Press, 1989.

Ames, Roger T. "The Meaning of Body in Classical Chinese Thought." *International Philosophical Quarterly* 24, no. 1 (March 1984): 39–54.

———. *Confucian Role Ethics: A Vocabulary*. Honolulu: University of Hawai'i Press, 2011.

———. "Reading the Zhongyong Metaphysically." In *Chinese Metaphysics and Its Problems*, edited by Chenyang Li and Franklin Perkins, 85–104. Cambridge, UK: Cambridge University Press, 2015.

Angle, Stephen C., and Michael Slot, eds. *Virtue Ethics and Confucianism*. London: Routledge, 2013.

Angurarohita, Pratoon. "Buddhist Influence on the Neo-Confucian Concept of the Sage." *Sino-Platonic Papers* 10 (June 1989): 1–23.

Ariel, Yoav. *K'ung-ts'ung-tzu: A Study & Translation of Chapters 15–23 with a Reconstruction of the Hsiao Erh-ya Dictionary*. Leiden, the Netherlands: E. J. Brill, 1996.

Austin, J. L. *How to Do Things with Words*. Oxford, UK: Clarendon Press, 1962.

Bai, Tongdong. "An Ontological Interpretation of *You* and *Wu* in the *Laozi*." *Journal of Chinese Philosophy* 35, no. 2 (June 2008): 339–51.
Barrett, Cyril. *Wittgenstein on Ethics and Religious Belief.* Oxford, UK: Blackwell, 1991.
Becker, Ernest. *The Denial of Death.* New York: Free Press, 1973.
Bergmann, Gustav. "The Glory and the Misery of Ludwig Wittgenstein." In *Logic and Reality*, 245–71. Madison: University of Wisconsin Press, 1964.
Bergson, Henri. *L'evolution Creatrice.* Paris: Libraries Felix Alcan et Guillaumin Reunies, 1911. *Creative Evolution,* translated by Arthur Mitchell. Lanham, MD: University Press of America, 1983.
Berthrong, John. "Chu Hsi's Ethics: Jen and Ch'eng." *Journal of Chinese Philosophy* 14, no. 2 (June 1987): 161–78.
———. "Master Chu's Self-Realization: The Role of Ch'eng." *Philosophy East and West* 43, no. 1 (January 1993): 39–64.
Bhikkhu, Bodhi, trans. *The Connected Discourses of the Buddha: A Translation of the Saṃyutta Nikāya.* Somerville, MA: Wisdom Publications, 2000.
Bialik, Hayyim Nahman, and Yehoshua H. Ravnitsky. *Sefer Haagadah: Mivhar Haagadot sheba Talmud uvamidrashim.* Tel Aviv, Israel: Devir, 1966.
Birdwhistell, Anne D. *Transition to Neo-Confucianism: Shao Yung on Knowledge and Symbols of Reality.* Stanford, CA: Stanford University Press, 1989.
Blakeley, Donald. "The *Analects* on Death." *Journal of Chinese Philosophy* 37, no. 3 (September 2010): 397–416.
Blofeld, John, trans. *I Ching: The Book of Change.* New York: Penguin Books, 1968.
Bol, Peter K. *This Culture of Ours.* Stanford, CA: Stanford University, 1992.
———. *Neo-Confucianism in History.* Cambridge, MA: Harvard University Press, 2008.
Broughton, Jeffrey L. *The Bodhidharma Anthology: The Earliest Records of Zen.* Berkeley: University of California Press, 1999.
Bruce, J. Percy. *Chu Hsi and His Masters.* London: Probsthain, 1923.
Caillois, Roger. *Man, Play and Games.* Chicago, IL: University of Illinois Press, 2001.
Camus, Albert. *A Happy Death.* London: Penguin Books, 1971.
Chan, Alan, K. L. "The *Daodejing* and Its Tradition." In *Daoism Handbook,* edited by Livia Kohn, 1–29. Leiden, the Netherlands: E. J. Brill, 1999.
Chan, Wing-tsit. *China.* Berkeley: University of California Press, 1946.
———. *A Source Book in Chinese Philosophy.* Princeton, NJ: Princeton University Press, 1963.
———, trans. *Reflections on Things at Hand: The Neo-Confucian Anthology compiled by Chu Hsi.* New York: Columbia University Press, 1967.
———. *Chu Hsi, Life and Thought.* Hong Kong: Chinese University Press, 1987.
Chang, Carsun. *The Development of Neo-Confucian Thought.* New Haven, CT: College and University Press, 1963.
Chang, Chung-yuan. "Ch'an Buddhism: Logical and Illogical." *Philosophy East and West* 17, no. 1 (January–October 1967): 37–49.

Chen, Kenneth Kuan Sheng. *Buddhism in China: A Historical Survey.* Princeton, NJ: Princeton University Press, 1964.
Chen, Zu-yan. "Shao Yong's 'Great Chant on Observing Weiqi': An Archetype of Neo-Confucian Poetry." *Journal of the American Oriental Society* 126, no. 2 (April–June 2006), 199–221. Cheng, Chung-ying. "On Zen (Chan) Language and Zen Paradoxes." *Journal of Chinese Philosophy* 1, no. 1 (December 1973): 77–102.
———. *New Dimension of Confucian and Neo-Confucian Philosophy.* Albany: State University of New York Press, 1991.
———. "Confucian Onto-Hermeneutics: Morality and Ontology." *Journal of Chinese Philosophy* 27, no. 1 (March 2000): 33–68.
———. "Unity of Three Truths and Three forms of Creativity: Lotus sutra and Process Philosophy." *Journal of Chinese Philosophy* 28, no. 4 (December 2001): 449–56.
———. "On the Metaphysical Significance of *Ti* (Body-Embodyment) in Chinese Philosophy: *Benti* (Origin-Substance) and *Ti-Yong* (Substance and Function)." *Journal of Chinese Philosophy* 29, no. 2 (December 2002): 145–61.
———. "Dimensions of the *Dao* and Onto-Ethics in Light of the *DDJ.*" *Journal of Chinese Philosophy* 31, no. 2 (June 2004): 143–82.
———. "*Li* and *Qi* in the *Yijing*: A Reconsideration of Being and Nonbeing in Chinese Philosophy." *Journal of Chinese Philosophy* 36, Supplement (December 2009), 73–100.
Cheng Hao 程灝, and Cheng Yi 程頤. *Ercheng ji* 二程集 (Collection of the Two Chengs). 4 vols. Peking, China: Zhonghua shuju, 1981.
Cheng Yi 程頤. *Yizhuan* 易傳. Taipei, Taiwan: Shijie, 1972.
Chien, Edward T. "The Neo-Confucian Confrontation with Buddhism: A Structural and Historical Analysis." *Journal of Chinese Philosophy* 15, no. 4 (December 1998): 347–70.
Ching, Julia. *The Religious Thought of Chu Hsi.* New York: Oxford University Press, 2000.
Chu, Ping-tzu. Transmission of Shao Yong's Yi Learning. *Monumenta Serica* 61 (2013): 227–68.
Clack, Brian R. *An Introduction to Wittgenstein's Philosophy of Religion.* Edinburgh, UK: Edinburgh University Press, 1999.
Conze, Edward. *Buddhism: A Short History.* Oxford, UK: One World, 2000.
Cook, Francis. *Hua-yen Buddhism: The Jewel Net of Indra.* University Park: Pennsylvania State University Press, 1977.
Creel, Herlee G. *Chinese Thought, From Confucius to Mao Tse-tung.* Chicago, IL: University of Chicago Press, 1953.
Cua, Antonio S. "Forgetting Morality: Reflections on a Theme in *Chuang Tzu.*" *Journal of Chinese Philosophy* 4, no. 4 (December 1977): 305–28.
———, ed. *Enyclopedia of Chinese Philosophy.* New York: Routledge, 2003.
Daor, Dan, and Yoav Ariel. *The Book of Dao.* Tel Aviv, Israel: Xargol, 2007.
Darwell, Stephen. "Empathy, Sympathy, Care." *Philosophical Studies* 89, no. 2/3 (March 1998): 261–82.

Davies, James. *Tesuji*. Tokyo, Japan: Ishi Press, 1975.

———. *Life and Death Elementary Go Series*. Tokyo: Ishi Press, 1975.

Daxue 大學. In *Xueyongzhangju yinde* 學庸章句引得. Taipei, Taiwan: Zhonghuaminguo Kongmengxuehui, 1970.

de Bary, William T. "Some Common Tendencies in Neo-Confucianism." In *Confucianism in Action*, edited by David Nivson and Arthur Wright. Stanford, CA: Stanford University Press, 1959.

———. *Sources of Chinese Tradition*. vol. 1. New York: Columbia University Press, 1960.

———. "Neo-Confucian Individualism and Holism." In *Individualism and Holism: Studies in Confucian and Taoist Values*, edited by Donald J. Munro, 331–58. Ann Arbor, University of Michigan Press, 1985.

Diamond, Cora. "Riddles and Anselm's Riddle." In *The Realistic Spirit: Wittgenstein, Philosophy, and the Mind*, 267–90. Cambridge, MA: MIT Press, 1991.

Dumoulin, Heinrich. *Zen Buddhism: A History*. vol. 1: *India and China*. New York: Random House, 2005.

Ebrey, Patricia. *Confucianism and Family Rituals in Imperial China: A Social History of Writing about Rites*. Princeton, NJ: Princeton University Press, 1991.

Fairbaim, John. "Go in Ancient China," 1995. http://www.pandanet.co.jp/English/essay/goancientchina.html.

Fang, Thome H. *Chinese Philosophy: Its Spirit and Its Development*. Taipei, Taiwan: Linking, 1981.

Fingarette, Herbert. *Confucius: The Secular as Sacred*. New York: Harper and Row, 1972.

Foust, Mathew A. "Grief and Mourning in Confucius's *Analects*." *Journal of Chinese Philosophy*, 36, no. 2 (May 2009): 348–58.

Franke, Herbert ed. *Song Biographies*. Wiesbaden, Germany: Franz Steiner Verlag, 1976.

Fung, Yu-lan. *A History of Chinese Philosophy*. Princeton, NJ: Princeton University Press, 1952.

Goldin, Paul Ratika. "The View of Women in Early Confucianism." In *The Sage and the Second Sex*, ed. Li Chengyang, 133–62. Chicago, IL: Open Court, 2000

Goldman, Rene. "Moral Leadership in Society: Some Parallels between the Confucian Nobleman and the Jewish Zaddik." *Philosophy East and West* 45, no. 3 (July 1995(: 399–465.

Graham, Angus C. *Two Chinese Philosophers: Cheng Ming Tao and Cheng Yi Chuan*. London: Lund Humphries, 1967.

———, trans. *Chuang Tzu: The Inner Chapters*. London: Mandala Books, 1981.

———. *Yin-Yang and the Nature of Correlative Thinking*. Occasional Paper and Monograph Series, no. 6. Kent Ridge, Singapore: Institute of East Asian Philosophy, 1986.

———. *Studies in Chinese Philosophy and Philosophical Literature*. Albany: State University of New York Press, 1990.

Granet, Marcel. *La Pensee Chinoise*. Paris: Albin Michel, 1950.

———. *Chinese Civilization*. Translated by Kathleen Innes and Mabel Brailsford. London: Routledge, 1996.

Gu, Ming-dong. "The Taiji Diagram: A Meta-Sign in Chinese Thought." *Journal of Chinese Philosophy* 30, no. 2 (June 2003): 195–218.
Hakeda, Yoshito S., trans. *The Awakening of Faith, Attributed to Asvagosha*. New York: Columbia University Press, 1967.
Hall, David L., and Roger T. Ames. "Getting It Right: On Saving Confucius from the Confucians." *Philosophy East and West* 34, no. 1 (January 1984): 3–23.
———. *Thinking through Confucius*. Albany: State University of New York Press, 1987.
Hansen, Chad. *Language and Logic in Ancient China*. Ann Arbor: University of Michigan Press, 1983.
———. "Should the Ancient Masters Value Reason?" In *Chinese Texts and Philosophical Contexts*, ed. Henry Jr. Rosemont, 209–26. La Salle, IL: Open Court, 1991.
Harvey, Peter. *The Selfless Mind*. London: Curzon Press, 1995.
Hatton, Russell. "A Comparison of Li and Substantial Form." *Journal of Chinese Philosophy* 9, no. 1 (March 1982): 49–76.
Henderson, John B. *The Development and Decline of Chinese Cosmology*. New York: Columbia University Press, 1984.
Hoffert, Brian. "Distinguishing the 'Rational' from the 'Irrational' in the Early Zhuangzi Lineage." *Journal of Chinese Philosophy* 33, no. 1 (February 2006): 159–73.
Holzman, Donald. "The Place of Filial Piety in Ancient China." *Journal of the American Oriental Society* 118, no. 2 (April–June 1998): 185–99.
Hsiao, Kung-chuan. *A History of Chinese Political Thought*. vol. 1. Translated by Frederik W. Mote. Princeton, NJ: Princeton University Press, 1979.
Hsieh, Ding-hwa. "Poetry and Chan Gong-an: From Xue dou Congxian to Wumen Huikai." *Journal of Song-Yuan Studies* 40 (2010): 39–70.
Hsu, Sung-Peng. "Two Kinds of Changes in Lao Tzu's Thought." *Journal of Chinese Philosophy* 4, no. 4 (December 1997): 329–55.
Huang, Siu-chi. "Chang Tsai's Concept of Ch'i." *Philosophy East and West* 18, no. 4 (October 1968): 247–60.
———. "The Moral Point of View of Chang Tsai." *Philosophy East and West* 21, no. 2 (April 1971): 141–56.
———. "The Concept of T'ai-Chi in Sung Neo-Confucian Philosophy." *Journal of Chinese Philosophy* 1, no. 3–4 (1974): 275–94.
———. "Chu-Hsi's Ethical Rationalism." *Journal of Chinese Philosophy* 5, no. 2 (June 1978): 175–93.
———. *Essentials of Neo-Confucianism: Eight Major Philosophies of the Song and Ming Periods*. London: Greenwood, 1999.
Huang, Yong. "Why Be Moral? The Cheng Brothers' Neo-Confucian Answer." *Journal of Religious Ethics* 36, no. 2 (June 2008): 321–53.
———. "Confucius and Mencius on the Motivation to Be Moral." *Philosophy East and West* 60, no. 1 (January 2010): 65–87.
Hudson, Donald. *Wittgenstein and Religious Belief*. London: Macmillan, 1975.

Huizinga, Johan. *Homo Ludens: A Study of the Play Element in Culture*. Boston, MA: Beacon Press, 1950.

Hume, David. *A Treatise of Human Nature*, edited by L. A. Selby-Bigge. Oxford, UK: Oxford University Press, 1978.

Ivanhoe, Phillip J. "Death and Dying in the *Analects*." In *Confucian Spirituality*, vol. 1, edited by Wei-ming Tu and Mary Evelyn Tucker, 220–32. New York: Crossroad, 2002.

Jorgensen, John. *Inventing Hui-neng, the Sixth Patriarch Hagiography and Biography in Early Ch'an*. Leiden, the Netherlands: Brill, 2005.

Jun, Young Ahn. "Malady of Meditation, Prolegomenon on the Study of Illness and Zen." PhD dissertation. University of California Berkeley, 2007.

Jung, C. G. Foreword to Richard Wilhelm's translation of the *I Ching*, 1950. http://www.iging.com/intro/foreword.htm.

———. *Collected Works*, vol. 8, *The Structure and Dynamics of the Psyche*. New York: Bollingen Foundation, 1960.

Kant, Immanuel. *Critique of Pure Reason*. Translated by Norman Kemp Smith. London: Macmillan, 1929.

———. *Critique of Practical Reason*. Translated by L. W. Beck. London: Macmillan, 1956.

Kasoff, Ira E. *The Thought of Chang Tsai*. London: Cambridge University Press, 1984.

Kasulis, Thomas P. "The Absolute and the Relative in Taoist Philosophy." *Journal of Chinese Philosophy* 4, no. 4 (December 1977): 383–94.

———. "Ch'an Spirituality." In *Buddhist Spirituality. Later China, Korea, Japan and the Modern World*, edited by Takeuchi Yoshinori. Delhi, India: Motilal Banarsidass, 2003.

Katz, Sophia. "From Observing to Listening: The Intellectual/Spiritual Path of Shao Yong as Reflected in the *Yichuan Jiranji*." *Monumenta Serica* 61, no. 1 (January 2013): 141–82.

Katsuki Sekida trans. *Two Zen Classics: Mumonkan & Hekianroku*. New York: Waterhill, 1977.

Kawabata, Yasunari. *The Master of Go*. Translated by Edward G. Seidensticker. UK: Vintage International, 1972.

Kierkegaard, Søren. *The Sickness unto Death: A Christian Psychological Exposition of Edification & Awakening by Anti-Climacus*. Translated by Alastair Hannay. London: Penguin Classics, 1989.

Kim, Bounghown. "A Study of Chou Tun-i's Thought." PhD dissertation, University of Arizona, 1996.

Kim, Jung-Yeup. *Zhang Zai's Philosophy of Qi: A Practical Understanding*. New York: Lexington Books, 2015.

Knoblock, John. *Xunzi: A Translation and Study of the Complete Works*, vol. 1. Stanford, CA: Stanford University Press, 1988.

Kohn, Livia. "The Lao-tzu Myth." In *Lao-tzu and the Tao-te-ching*, edited by Livia

Kohn and Michael La Fargue, 41–62. Albany: State University of New York Press, 1998.

Kohn, Livia, and Michael La Fargue, eds. *Lao-tzu and the Tao-te-ching.* Albany: State University of New York Press, 1998.

Kugel, James L. *The Bible as It Was.* Cambridge, MA: Harvard University Press, 1997.

Lancashire, Douglas, ed. and trans. *Chinese Essays on Religion and Faith.* San Francisco, CA: Chinese Materials Center, 1981.

Laozi Daodejing 老子道德經 (*er juan yinyi yi juan* 二卷音义一卷) (春秋)李耳撰、 (晋)王弼注 FB.59:9.273(1), vol. 3 (*Laozi Daodejing* Commentary by Wang Bi). *Sibu beiyao* 四部備要 "Hand Library of Important Writings of the Four Categories." Beijing, China: Zhonghua Publishing House 中華書局, 1936.

Lau, D. C., trans. *Tao Te Ching.* London: Penguin Books, 1963.

———, trans. *Confucius, The Analects (Lun yü).* Hong Kong: Chinese University Press, 1983.

———, trans. *Mencius.* 2 vols. Hong Kong: Chinese University Press, 1984.

Lazenby, Mark J. *The Early Wittgenstein on Religion.* London: Continuum, 2006.

Legge, James trans. *The Texts of Taoism.* With an introduction by T. D. Suzuki. New York: Julian, 1959.

———, trans. *The Chinese Classics.* 5 vols., reprint. Hong Kong: Hong Kong University Press, 1961.

———, trans. *The Four Books.* New York: Paragon Book, 1966.

———, trans. *Lichi, Book of Rites.* 2 vols., reprint. New York: University Books, 1967.

———, trans. *The Works of Mencius.* New York: Dover, 1970.

———, trans. *The Book of Change. Chinese Text Project.* http://ctext.org/book-of-changes/qian. Accessed February 4, 2021.

———, trans. *Zhuangzi. Chinese Text Project.* http://ctext.org/zhuangzi/great-and-most-honoured-Master. Accessed February 4, 2021.

Leibowitz, Nechama. *Iyunim Chadashim B'sefer B'reshit.* Jerusalem, Israel: Maor, 1994.

Lévinas, Emmanuel. *Totality and Infinity.* Translated by Alphonso Lingis. Pittsburg: Duquense University Press, 1969.

Li Chen-yang. "The Confucian Concept of Jen and the Feminist Ethics of Care: A Comparative Study," *Hypatia* 9, no. 1 (Winter 1994): 70–89.

———, ed. *The Sage and the Second Sex: Confucianism, Ethics and Gender.* La Salle, IL: Open Court, 2000.

———. "The Confucian Ideal of Harmony." *Philosophy East & West* 56, no. 4 (October 2006): 583–603.

Liebenthal, Walter trans. *Chao Lun.* Hong Kong: Hong Kong University Press, 1968.

Lin, Yutang. "Crossing the Gate of Death in Chinese Buddhist Culture." University of Hawai'i, 1995. http://www.yogichen.org/gurulin/efiles/mb/mbk16.html.

Lin, Tongqi, and Zhou Qin. "The Dynamism and Tension in the Anthropocosmic Vision of Mou Zongsan: A Reflection on Confucian Concept of *Tianren Heyi.*" *Journal of Chinese Philosophy* 22, no. 4 (December 1995): 401–40.

Liu, Qingping. "Confucianism and Corruption: An Analysis of Shun's Two Actions Described by Mencius." *Dao: A Journal of Comparative Philosophy* 6, no. 1 (March 2007): 1–20.

Liu Shu-Hsien. "The Confucian Approach to the Problem of Transcendence and Immanence." *Philosophy East and West* 22, no. 1 (January 1972): 45–52.

Loy, David. *Nonduality: A Study in Comparative Philosophy.* New York: Humanity Books, 1998.

Lu Xiangshan xianshen quanji 陆象山先生全集 (三十六卷) (宋)陆九渊撰、(清)李绂评点FB.59:9.290 (vol. 3). "Collection of Complete Writings of Lu Xiangshan." (Commentary by Li Fu.) *Sibu beiyao* 四部備要 "Hand Library of Important Writings of the Four Categories." Zhonghua Publishing House 中華書局, Beijing, China, 1936.

Lun yu 論語 (*ershi juan* 二十卷) (魏) *Heyan jijie* 何晏集解. (vol. 1.) (Analects of Confucius, Annotated by He Yan.) *Sibu beiyao* 四部備要 "Hand Library of Important Writings of the Four Categories." Beijing, China: Zhonghua shuju, 1936.

Lunyu yinde 論語引得. Peiping: Harvard-Yenching Institute Sinological Index Series, 1941.

Lundberg, Brian. "A Meditation on Friendship." In *Wandering at Ease in the Zhuangzi*, edited by Roger Ames, 211–18. Albany: State University of New York Press, 1998.

Lynn, John R., trans. *The Classic of Changes: A New Translation of the I Ching as Interpreted by Wang Bi.* New York: Columbia University Press, 1994.

Maguire, Jack. *Essential Buddhism.* New York: Pocket Books, 2001.

McRae, John. *The Platform Sutra of the Sixth Patriarch.* Berkeley, CA: Numata Center for Buddhist Translation and Research, 2000.

———. *Seeing through Zen. Encounter, Transformation, and Genealogy in Chinese Chan Buddhism.* Berkeley: University of California Press, 2004.

Malcolm, Norman. *Wittgenstein: A Religious Point of View.* London: Routledge, 1993.

Malpas, Jeff E. *Donald Davidson and the Mirror of Meaning: Holism, Truth, Interpretation.* Cambridge, UK: Cambridge University, 1992.

Mengzi 孟子. *Sibucongkan* 四部叢刊 (SBCK). Sibu congkan 四部叢刊 "Collection of the Four Categories," compiled by Zhang Yuanji 張元濟.

Mengzi yinde 孟子引得. Peiping: Harvard-Yenching Institute Sinological Index Series, 1941.

Ming, Dong-gu. "The Taiji Diagram: A Meta-Sign in Chinese Thought." *Journal of Chinese Philosophy* 30, no. 2 (June 2003): 195–218.

Moeller, Hans-Georg. *Daoism Explained: From the Dream of the Butterfly to the Fishnet Allegory.* Chicago, IL: Open Court, 2004.

Mote, Frederick W. *Intellectual Foundations of China.* New York: McGraw-Hill, 1971.

Mou Zongsan 牟宗三. *Xinti yu xingti* 心體與性體. Taipei, Taiwan: Zhengzhung, 1968–1969.

Muller, Charles A., trans. *Doctrine of the Mean.* http://www.acmuller.net/con-dao/docofmean.html. Accessed February 4, 2021.

Needham, Joseph. *Science and Civilisation in China*, vol. 2: *History of Scientific Thought*. Cambridge, UK: Cambridge University Press, 1956.
Nivison, David S., and Arthur F. Wright, eds. *Confucianism in Action*. Stanford, CA: Stanford University Press, 1959.
Oh, Kang-nam. "The Taoist Influence on Hua-yen Buddhism: A Case of the Sinicization of Buddhism in China." *Chung-Hwa Buddhist Journal* 13, no. 2 (May 2000): 277–97.
Olberding, Amy. "The Consummation of Sorrow: An Analysis of Confucius's Grief for Yan Hui." *Philosophy East and West* 53, no. 3 (July 2004): 279–301.
———. "Slowing Death Down: Mourning in the *Analects*." In *Confucius Now*, edited by David Jones, 137–49. LaSalle, IL: Open Court, 2008.
Olberding, Amy, and P. J. Ivanhoe, eds. *Mortality in Traditional Chinese Thought*. Albany: State University of New York Press, 2011.
Patt-Shamir, Galia. "To Live a Riddle: The Case of the Binding of Isaac." *Philosophy and Literature* 27, no. 2 (October 2003): 269–83.
———. "Seeds for Dialogue—On Learning in Confucianism and Judaism." *Journal of Ecumenical Studies* 40, no. 1–2 (Spring 2004): 201–15.
———. "The Effectiveness of Contradiction in Understanding Human Practice: The Rhetoric of Goal-Ideal in Confucianism." *Journal of Chinese Philosophy* 32, no. 3 (September 2005): 455–76.
———. "Way as Dao; Way as Halakha: Confucianism, Judaism and Way Metaphors." *Dao: A Journal of Comparative Philosophy* 5, no. 2 (December 2005): 137–58.
———. *To Broaden the Way: A Confucian-Jewish Dialogue*. New York: Lexington Books, 2006.
———. "Living *Li* as Knowing through *Li*." In *The Imperative of Reading: Chinese Philosophy, Comparative Philosophy, and Onto-Hermeneutics* edited by Ng On-cho, 156–73. New York: Global Scholarly, 2007–2008.
———. "To Live a Riddle: The Transformative Aspect of the Laozi." *Journal of Chinese Philosophy* 36, no. 3 (August 2009): 408–23.
———. "The 'Dual Citizenship' of Emptiness: A Reading of *Bu Zhenkong Lun*." *Journal of Chinese Philosophy* 38, no. 3 (August 2011): 474–90.
———. "Filial Piety, Vital Power, and a Moral Sense of Immortality in Zhang Zai's Philosophy." *Dao: A Journal of Comparative Philosophy* 11, no. 2 (April 2012): 223–39.
———. "Li and Qi as Supra Metaphysics." in *Dao Companion to Zhu Xi's Philosophy*, edited by Kai-chiu Ng and Yong Huang, 243–63. Cham, Switzerland: Springer, 2020.
Patt-Shamir, Galia, and Ping Zhang. "Expanding Family Reverence: A Confucian–Jewish Dialogue." In *The Blackwell Companion on Interreligious Dialogue*, edited by Catherine Cornille, *450–67*. Oxford, UK: Wiley-Blackwell, 2013.
Phillips, Dewi Z. *Death and Immortality*. London: Macmillan, 1970.
Plaks, Andrew. *Torat Hagadol: Da Xue*. Jerusalem, Israel: Magnes, 1997

Porat, Roy. "Ren and Tian: Analysis of the 'Confucian Episodes' in chapter 6 of the *Zhuangzi*." 17th Conference of the ISCP, EHESS, Paris, 2011.

Potter, Donald. "Go in the Classics." *Go World* 37 (1985): 16–21.

Puett, Michael. "Ritual and the Subjunctive." In *Ritual and Its Consequences*. Adam B. Seligman, Robert P. Weller, Michael J. Puett, and Bennet Simon. Oxford, UK. Oxford University Press, 2008, 17–27.

———. "Ritualization as Domestication: Ritual Theory from Classical China." In *A Ritual Dynamics and the Science of Ritual: I: Grammars and Morphologies of Ritual Practices in Asia*, edited by Axel Michaels, 365–76. Wiesbaden, Germany: Harrassowitz Verlag, 2010.

Putnam, Hilary. *Renewing Philosophy*. Cambridge, MA: Harvard University Press, 1992.

Robinet, Isabelle. *Taoism: Growth of a Religion*. Stanford, CA: Stanford University Press, 1999.

Robinson, Richard H. *Early Madhyamika in India and China*. Madison: University of Wisconsin Press, 1967.

Rosemont, Henry Jr., and Roger T. Ames. *The Chinese Classic of Family Reverence: A Philosophical Translation of the Xiaojing*. Honolulu: University of Hawai'i Press, 2009.

———. *Confucian Role Ethics: A Moral Vision for the 21st Century?* Taipei, Taiwan: V&R Academic, 2016.

Roth, Harold. *Original Tao: Inward Training and the Foundations of Taoist Mysticism*. New York: Columbia University Press, 1999.

Ryle, Gilbert. "On Forgetting the Difference between Right and Wrong." In *Essays in Moral Philosophy*, edited by A. I. Melden, 147–59. Seattle: University of Washington Press, 1958.

Ruan Yuan 阮元, ed. *Shisanjing zhushu* 十三經注疏. Taipei, Taiwan: Jianxin, 1979.

Saunders, Kenneth J. "Buddhism in China: A Historical Sketch." *Journal of Religion* 3, no. 3 (May 1923): 256–75.

Schafer, Edward H. *The Vermillion Bird: T'ang Images of the South*. Berkeley: University of California Press, 1967.

Scharfstein, Ben-Ami. *The Philosophers: Their Life and the Nature of Their Thought*. New York: Oxford University Press, 1980.

Schultz, William Todd. "The Riddle That Doesn't Exist: Ludwig Wittgenstein's Transmogrification of Death." *Psychoanalytic Review* 86, no. 2 (April 1998): 1–23.

Schwartz, Benjamin. *The World of Thought in Ancient China*. Cambridge, MA: Harvard University Press, 1985.

———. "A Review of *Knowing Words: Wisdom and Cunning in the Classical Traditions of China and Greece* by Lisa Ralphs." *Harvard Journal of Asiatic Studies* 56, no. 1 (June 1996): 227–44.

Sekida, Katsuki. *Two Zen Classics: Mumonkan and Hekiganroku*. New York: John Weatherhill, 1977.

Shao Yong 邵雍. *Huangji jingshi* 皇極經世. *Sibu congkan* 四部叢刊 "Collection of the

Four Categories." Editor: Zhang Yuanji 張元濟. Shanghai, China: Shanghai shangwu yinshu guan, 1922.

———. *Jirang Ji* 擊壤集, *Sikuquanshu* 四庫全書 "Complete Library in Four Sections." Ji Yun 紀昀. Shanghai, China: Shanghai guji chu banshe, 2003.

Shotwell, Peter. *Go! More Than a Game*. Vermont: Tuttle Publishing, 2003.

Sivin, Nathan. "Drawing Insights from Chinese Medicine." *Journal of Chinese Philosophy* 34, no. 1 (December 2007): 43–55.

———. "State, Cosmos, and Body in the Last Three Centuries B.C." *Harvard Journal of Asiatic Studies* 55, no. 1 (June 1995): 5–37.

Slingerland, Edward. *Analects: With Selections from Traditional Commentaries*. Indianapolis, IN: Hackett, 2003.

Small, Sharon Y. *Zhuangzi: The Film—Visualizing Zhuangzi's Riddle of One Body*. MA thesis, Tel Aviv University, 2014.

Smith, Kidder, Jr., Peter K. Bol, Joseph A. Adler, and Don J. Wyatt. *Sung Dynasty Uses of the I Ching*. Princeton, NJ: Princeton University Press, 1990.

Sommer, Deborah. "Concepts of the Body in the *Zhuangzi*." In *Experimental Essays on Zhuangzi*, edited by Victor H. Mair, 212–28. Dunedin, FL: Three Pines, 2010.

Song Yuan xuean 宋元學案. "Scholarly Annals of Song and Yuan Periods," compiled by Huang Zongxi 黃宗羲 and Quan Zuwang 全祖望. Taipei, Taiwan: Shi jie Publishing House, 1961.

Song Yuan xuean buyi (10 vols.) "Addendum to the Scholarly Annals of Song and Yuan Periods"宋元学案补遗（全十册, compiled by Wang Zicai 王梓材and Feng Yunhao 馮雲濠. Beijing, China: Zhonghua shuju, 2011.

Songren zhuanji ziliao suo yin 宋人傳紀資料索引 "Biographical Resources of Song Writers," compiled by Chang Bide 昌彼得 and Wang Deyi 王德毅. Taipei, Taiwan: Dingwen shuju, 1976.

Suzuki Daisetsu T. "Introduction." In *Texts of Taoism*, translated by James Legge. New York: Julian, 1959.

Swartz, David. *Culture and Power: The Sociology of Pierre Bourdieu*, 2nd ed. Chicago, IL: University of Chicago Press, 1998.

Taylor, Rodney. *The Religious Dimensions of Confucianism*. New York: State University of New York Press, 1990.

T'ang, Chüni. "Chang Tsai's Theory of Mind and Its Metaphysical Basis." *Philosophy East and West* 6, no. 2 (July 1956): 113–36.

———. "The T'ienming (Heavenly Ordinance) in PreCh'in China." *Philosophy East & West* 11, no. 4 (January 1962): 195–218.

Trilling, Lionel. *Sincerity and Authenticity*. Cambridge, MA: Harvard University Press, 1971.

Tu, Wei-ming. "The Creative Tension between Jen and Li." *Philosophy East and West* 18, no. 1–2 (January–April 1968): 29–39.

———. "Li as Process of Humanization." *Philosophy East and West* 22, no. 2 (April 1972): 187–201.

———. *Humanity and Self-Cultivation: Essays in Confucian Thought.* Berkeley, CA: Asian Humanities, 1979.
———. "Neo-Confucian Ontology: A Preliminary Questioning." *Journal of Chinese Philosophy* 7, no. 2 (June 1980): 93–117.
———. *Confucian Thought: Selfhood as Creative Transformation.* Albany: State University of New York Press, 1985.
———. "Embodying the Universe: A Note on Confucian Self-Realization." In *Confucian Thought: Selfhood as Creative Transformation*, 171–81. Albany: State University of New York Press, 1985.
———. "Selfhood and Otherness: The Father-Son Relationship in Confucian Thought." In *Confucian Thought: Selfhood as Creative Transformation*, 113–30. Albany: State University of New York Press, 1985.
———. *Centrality and Commonality: An Essay on Confucian Religiousness.* Albany: State University of New York Press, 1989.
———. "Embodying the Universe: A Note on Confucian Self-Realization." In *Self as Person in Asian Theory and Practice*, edited by Roger T. Ames, Wimal Dissanayake, and Thomas P. Kasulis, 177–87. Albany: State University of New York Press, 1994.
———. "Happiness in the Confucian Way." In *In Pursuit of Happiness*. Edited by Leroy S. Rouner, 104–21. Notre Dame, IN: Notre Dame University Press, 1995.
———. "The Ecological Turn in New Confucian Humanism: Implication for China and the World." *Daedalus* 130, no. 4 (Fall 2001): 243–64.
Tu, Wei-ming, Milan Hejmánek, and Alan Wachman, eds. *The Confucian World Observed.* Honolulu, Hawaii: East Asian Center, 1992.
Van Norden, Bryan. *Virtue Ethics and Consequentialism in Early Chinese Philosophy.* New York: Cambridge University Press, 2007.
Velmans, Max. *Understanding Consciousness*, 2nd ed. New York: Routledge, 2009.
Wang, Robin R. "Zhou Dunyi's Diagram of the Supreme Ultimate Explained (Taijitu shuo): A Construction of the Confucian Metaphysics." *Journal of the History of Ideas* 66, no. 3 (July 2005): 307–23.
———. *Yinyang: The Way of Heaven and Earth in Chinese Thought and Culture.* New York: Cambridge University Press, 2012.
Wang, Robin, and Ding Weixiang. "Zhang Zai's Theory of Vital Energy." In *Dao Companion to Neo-Confucian Philosophy*, edited by John Makeham, 39–58. New York: Springer, 2010.
Wang, Yangming. "Instructions for Practical Living, Part I." In *Instructions for Practical Living and Other Neo-Confucian Writings.* Translated by Wing-tsit Chan, 3–87. New York: Columbia University Press, 1963.
———. "Inquiry on the Great Learning." In *Instructions for Practical Living and Other Neo-Confucian Writings.* Translated by Wing-tsit Chan, 271–80. New York: Columbia University Press, 1963.
Watson, Burton trans. *Chuang Tzu: Basic Writings.* New York: Columbia University Press, 1964.

———, trans. *The Complete Works of Chuang-Tzu.* New York: Columbia University Press, 1968.

———. *The Zen Teachings of Master Lin-Chi: A Translation of the Lin-chi lu.* New York: Columbia University Press, 1999.

Weinberg, Steven. *Dreams of a Final Theory: The Scientist's Search for the Ultimate Laws of Nature.* New York: Knopf Doubleday, 2011.

Welch, Holmes. *The Buddhist Revival in China.* Cambridge, MA: Harvard University Press, 1968.

Wilhelm, Richard. *Lectures on the I Ching: Constancy and Change.* Translated by Irene Eber. Princeton, NJ: Princeton University Press, 1979.

Winch, Peter. "Understanding a Primitive Society." In *Ethics and Action.* London: Routledge & Kegan Paul, 1972.

Wittgenstein, Ludwig. "Lectures on Religious Belief." In *Lectures and Conversations*, 53–72. Berkeley: University of California Press, 1955.

———. *Tractatus Logico-Philosophicus.* Translated by D. F. Pears and B. McGuinness. London: Routledge and Kegan Paul, 1961.

———. "A Lecture on Ethics." *Philosophical Review* 74, no. 1 (January 1965): 3–12.

———. *Notebooks 1914–1916.* Translated by G. E. M. Anscombe, edited by G. H. von Wright. Oxford: Basil Blackwell, 1979.

———. *Philosophical Investigations.* Translated by G. E. M. Anscombe. Oxford: Basil Blackwell, 1988.

Wong, David B. *Natural Moralities: A Defense of Pluralistic Relativism.* New York: Oxford University Press, 2006.

———. "Relational and Autonomous Selves," *Journal of Chinese Philosophy.* 31, no. 4 (November 2004): 419–32.

Wyatt, Don J. *The Recluse of Loyang: Shao Yung and the Moral Evolution of Early Sung Thought.* Honolulu: University of Hawai'i, 1996.

Yampolski, Philip. "Chan, A Historical Sketch." In *Buddhist Spirituality: Later China, Korea, Japan and the Modern World*, edited by Takeuchi Yoshinori, 3–23. Delhi, India: Motilal Banarsidass, 2003.

Yang Lien-sheng. "A Note on the So-Called TLV-Mirrors and the Game Liu-Po." *Harvard Journal of Asiatic Studies* 9, no. 3/4 (February 1947): 202–6.

Zhang Delin 張德麟. *Zhou Lianxi yanjiu* 周濂溪研究. Taipei, Taiwan: Jiaxin, 1979. Zhangzi quanshu張子全書 (十五卷) (宋)張載撰、(宋)朱熹注釋 FB.59:9.28(2) (vol. 3). (Complete Writings of Zhang Zai, annotated by Zhu Xi). Sibu beiyao 四部備要 "Hand Library of Important Writings of the Four Categories." Beijing, China: Zhonghua Publishing House 中華書局, 1936.

Zhongyong 中庸. In *Xueyongzhangju yinde* 學庸章句引得. Taipei, Taiwan: Zhonghua minguo Kongmeng xuehui, 1970.

Zhou Dunyi 周敦頤. *Tongshu* 通書. In *Zhou Lianxi xiansheng quanji* 周濂溪先生全集. Section 5, *Guoxuse jiben congshu*, edited by Zhang Boxing. Shanghai, China: Shangwuyin shuguan, 1937.

———. *Taijitu shuo* 太極圖說. In *Zhou Lianxi xiansheng quanji* 周濂溪先生全集. Section

1. *Guoxuse jiben congshu*, edited by Zhang Boxing. Shanghai, China: Shangwuyin shuguan, 1937.

*Zhouyi*周易. Sibu congkan 四部叢刊 "Collection of the Four Categories," edited by Zhang Yuanji 張元濟. Shanghai, China: Shanghai shangwu yinshu guan, 1922. Zhuangzi 莊子(十卷) (戰國)庄周撰、(晋)郭象注 FB.59:9.27(4) (vol.3) (Zhuangzi, commentary by Guo Xiang). Sibu beiyao 四部備要. "Hand Library of Important Writings of the Four Categories." Beijing, Zhonghua shuju, 1936.

Zohar, attributed to Rabbi Shimon Bar Yochai, http://www.ashlagbaroch.org/Zohar/. Accessed February 4, 2021.

INDEX

Aactivity and tranquility (*dong jing* 動靜), 12, 51–55, 61, 68–80, 84–86, 96–100, 104, 145–149, 179, 226n36, 228n60

Adler, Joseph A., 51, 83–84, 223n8, 227n58

Ames, Roger T., 50. *See also* Hall and Ames; Rosemont, Henry, Jr., and Roger T. Ames

Analects (*Lunyu* 論語), 3, 10, 18–21, 24–25, 33, 35, 37, 46, 87, 107, 183, 189–190

anthropocosmic, 12–13, 53–54, 56

Awakening of Faith in Mahayana (*Dasheng qixin lun* 大乘起信論), 119

Bergman, Ingmar, *The Seventh Seal*, 103

Bergson, Henri, 63

Birdwhistell, Anne D., 116, 119, 134, 145, 151, 235n96

Blakeley, Donald, 242–243n98

Blue Cliff Record (*Biyan lu* 碧巖錄, Jap. *Hekiganroku*), 212–215, 245n27, 245n29

body and embodiment, 7, 12–13, 15, 23, 39, 46, 49, 66–72, 74, 167–172, 175–179, 187, 201, 210, 214, 216, 237n9, 245n29

Book of Change (*Yijing* 易經), 9–10, 49, 52–55, 64–65, 70–71, 76–77, 224n12, 226–227n45
    and Shao Yong, 109, 134–135, 146
    and Zhang Zai, 167–168, 174, 204, 206
    and Zhou Dunyi, 12–13, 53–54, 56, 60, 64, 69–72, 100–102

Book of Documents (*Shang Shu* 尚书), 30, 61, 141

Book of Family Reverence (*Xiaojing* 孝經), 23, 30, 38, 177, 203, 219n9

Book of Rites (*Liji* 禮記), 38–40, 157, 187–188

Book of Supreme World Ordering Principles (*Huangji jingshi* 皇極經世) (HJJS), 14, 107, 148. *See also* Shao Yong

Boundaries, 5, 6–9, 18–19, 29, 36–37, 45–46, 70, 145, 156, 159–161

Buber, Martin, 46

Buddhism, 10, 98, 105, 119, 199

Caillois, Roger, 110, 232n19, 233n48, 234n61

Camus, Albert, 189–190

care-ethics, 28–29

Carrol, Lewis, *Alice's Adventures in Wonderland*, 1–2

Chan Buddhism, 10, 205–216

Chan, Wing-tsit, 96, 234n70

Chen Tianxiang 陳天祥, 43, 222n48

Chen, Zu-yan, 233n55, 235n95, 235n98, 107, 122

Cheng brothers (Cheng Hao 程顥 and Cheng Yi 程頤), 50, 165, 176, 223n5, 229n82, 238n11

261

Cheng Chung-ying, 53, 209, 211–212
Chunqiu Zuozhuan, 春秋左傳, 107, 158, 236n107
  Confucius (Kongzi 孔子), 39–46, 107, 204, 241n60, 242–243n98. *See also Analects*
  commonality (*yong* 庸), 3. *See also Doctrine of the Mean*; Tu Weiming
Cua, Antonio S., 150

Daoism, 58, 85, 93, 105
Daowu 道悟 (Jap. Dogo), 215, 245n33
Darwell, Stephen, 221
Davies, James, 235n97
death and immortality, 39–46, 71, 164, 166–172, 176–179 189–192, 194–195, 197–199, 201–204, 242n83, 242–243n98
Descartes, René, 49, 175
Diagram of Supreme Polarity Explained. *See Taijitu shuo* (TJTS)
dialogue, 5–8, 19–23, 45–46, 211–212
Diamond, Cora, 218n8, 242n78
dichotomies and dichotomous thinking, 14, 26–31, 49–50, 55–56, 58, 68–69, 94–95, 99–101, 104–107, 165, 198
  Doctrine of the Mean (*Zhongyong* 中庸) (DM), 7, 18, 32, 38, 87, 172, 221n32
Donne, John, "No Man Is an Island," 17
Duke of Zhou (*Zhougong* 周公), 38, 136, 138, 234n73, 235n79

Ecclesiastes (Ecc.), 3:20–22, 163
eightfold Confucian path (*batiamu* 八條目), 21–23, 73. *See also Great Learning*
einsof (infinity in Kabalah), 60, 226n35
emptiness, 84–85, 95–99, 174–175, 209
"The Equality of Things" (*Qiwulun* 齊物論), 158, 169
expanding self-boundaries, 18–19, 25–31

  family, 5–6, 13–14, 20, 23–25, 30, 37–39, 164, 166, 176–177, 189, 191, 197–199, 199–204, 219n9, 222n45
Fan Xu 樊ス (courtesy name Zichi 子遲), 21, 219n6

Fang, Thome H., 93
Fingarette, Herbert, 188
finitude and infinitude. *See* infinity and the limitless
Flew, Anthony, 242n78
Four Arts (*siyi* 四藝), 106–107, 111
Four Books (*sishu* 四書), 222n48. *See Analects*; *Doctrine of the Mean*; *Great Learning*; *Mencius*
Foust, Mathew A., 222n50
Fuxi 伏羲, 109, 134–135
Fuxi situ 伏羲四圖 ("The Four Charts of Fuxi" or "Chart on the Order of the Eight Trigrams"), 158, 236n112

games and gaming, 108–110, 122–128, 152–161, 232n16–20, 231n15, 233n48, 234n60. *See also* Shao Yong; "Great Poem on Observing Weiqi"; Weiqi
Genesis, 3, 28, 33, 68, 227n50
gong-an 公安 (Jap. koan), 10, 205–216
good words (*shanyan* 善言), 157, 158, 236n110
Granet, Marcel, 124, 232n20
"The Great Honorable Teacher" (*Dazong shi* 齊物論), 169, 187, 201
Great Appendix (*Xici Zhuan* 繫辭傳 or 大傳 *Dazhuan*). *See Book of Change*
Great Learning (*Daxue* 大學) (GL), 18, 21–23, 72–73
great harmony (*dahe* 大和)
"Great Poem on Observing Weiqi" (*Guanqi dayin* 觀棋大吟), 13–14, 104–108, 122–127, 130–134, 152–161

Hall and Ames, 27-31
happiness and joy, 33, 35, 50, 189–190, 193–197
harmony (*he* 和), 14, 31, 63– 68, 99, 124, 127–128, 156–157, 164–166, 177, 189–189, 200–202, 236n107
Huang Kan 皇侃, 43, 222n48
Huang, Siu-chi, 113, 172, 175
Huineng 慧能, 210
Huizinga, Johann, 108–110, 136, 232n16, 232n19, 233n48, 234n60
humanity (*ren* 仁), 5–6, 10, 20–21, 23–24,

28–29, 37, 87, 176–177, 183, 189–190. See also personhood

Image-Number Study (*xiangshu xue* 象數學), 106
immanent transcendance (*neizai chaoyue* 內在超越), 7, 102, 171, 230n104
ineffability, 3, 59, 157, 158, 236n110
infinity and the limitless, 3–5, 12–13, 46, 49–50, 55–56, 59–60, 68–69, 71–74, 94–95, 99–101, 130, 159–161, 225n24, 226n35. See also Non-polar and Supreme Polarity
Inner Chapters on Observing of things (*Guanwu Neipian* 觀物內篇), 14, 107. See also *Book of Supreme World Ordering Principles*; Shao Yong
Ivanhoe, Phillip J., 43, 222n50

Jung, C. G., explanation of the sixty-four hexagrams, 9, 52, 54
junzi 君子 (accomplished person), 33–36. See also personhood

Kaku, Michio, 47
Kant, Immanuel, 4, 48, 50, 242n83
Katz, Sophia, 158, 236n112
Keightley, Alan, 242n78
Kierkegaard, Søren, 225n24
Kim, Bounghown, 223n6
Kim, Jung-Yeup, on Zhang Zai's philosophy of qi, 173, 239n26
King Wu, 38, 136, 234n73
Kun 坤 (hexagram), 9, 65–66, 70–71

Laozi 老子, 59, 146–147, 152, 236n110
laughing and laughter, 211, 214, 215, 241n15
Levinas, Emmanuel, 170, 238n17
Li 理 (Order, principle, pattern), 59–63, 70–73, 77–78, 90–9, 144–149, 151, 224n17
Li Chen-yang, 28–29, 236n107
Liji 禮記. See *Book of Rites*
Liu Bang 劉邦, 151, 233n55
living morally in the present, 36, 71, 189–192, 197–198
living riddles. See riddling and living riddles

Mazu Daoyi 馬祖道 (Jap. Baso), 211, 213–214, 223–224, 245n19
Mencius (Mengzi 孟子), 5–6, 20, 24–25, 31–33, 36, 44–45, 76, 89, 91, 101,107, 119, 139, 170, 179–180, 189, 222n45, 236n110
mirror and mirroring, 13, 20, 99, 104–106, 118–119, 152–161, 230n10, 233n391
Mote, Frederick W., 53
Mou Zongsan 牟宗三, 7, 102, 171, 230n104
Murdoch, Iris, 242n78

Needham, Joseph, 53
Neo-Confucianism See Shao Yong, Zhang Zai, Zhou Dunyi
Non-polar and Supreme Polarity (*Wuji er Taiji* 無極而太極) [WJTJ]):
and the *Book of Change*, 12–13, 53–56, 60, 64
human embodiment of, 56, 58–60, 94–95, 99–101
living morally identified with, 100–102
as a living riddle, 12–13, 53–63, 66–72, 74, 100–102
Shao Yong's presentation of yin-yang compared with, 147–148

observation (*guan* 觀), 13–14
as an organized skillful deed, 113–114
observing history, 134–145, 158, 235n87
observation with Order, 144–149, 151
observation of Weiqi, 122–126, 132–134, 160f3.1
Olberding, Amy, 222n50

Penetrating Book, The. See *Tongshu* (TS)
personhood, 3,18–19, 46, 72–73
as a Confucian task, 2–9, 18–19, 22–23, 46, 73
epistemological perspective in Shao Yong's work, 12, 46, 104–105, 216
as metaphysical embodiment in Zhou Dunyi's work, 12–13, 46, 56, 71, 74–75, 95–96, 99, 101, 164, 216
as pragmatic humanistic act in Zhang Zai's work, 14, 164, 216

Phillips, Dewi Z., 196, 198
   prior to form (*xingershang* 形而上) and subsequent to form (*xinger shang* 形而下), 77, 174

play (*wan* 玩), 108, 231n9
Puett, Michael, 29, 37
Putnam, Hilary, 233n38

qi 氣 (energy, vital power), 15, 172–175, 188–199, 203–204, 224n16, 239n26
Qian 乾 (hexagram), 9, 64–65, 70–71, 76, 80–81, 167–168

relational self, 28–29
riddling and living riddles, 3–5, 11–12, 46
   and the Wittgensteinean philosophical spirit, 10–11, 72, 218n14
   and the *Book of Change*, 9–10, 12–13, 53–64, 69–72, 100–102, 109, 134, 206
   as a methodology, 1–11, 58
   and *gong-an*, 10, 205–216
   and *Zhuangzi*, 169, 187, 201
rites and rituals, 38–39, 45–46, 183, 188. See also *Book of Family Reverence*; *Book of Rites*
reflective observation (*fanguan* 反觀), 119, 233n42
Rosemont, Henry, Jr., and Roger T. Ames, 29–30

sagehood:
   in the *Book of Change*, 65, 76
   in early Confucianism, 29, 36–40
   according to Mou Zongsan, 7, 102
   Zhou Dunyi's view of, 12–13, 56, 58, 68–69, 75–80, 87, 91–95, 99–102
   Shao Yong's view of, 113, 118–122, 155–156, 159–161
   Zhang Zai's view of, 177, 190, 198–202
Scharfstein, Ben-Ami, 237n2
Schwartz, Benjamin, 74, 185, 225n26, 228n63, 229n86
Shao Yong 邵雍:
   biographical details, 105–106
   epistemological perspective, 11–13, 46, 104–106, 148, 152–161

life and game, 13–14, 104–108, 122–127, 152–16
   and time 135–137, 234n70
   on observation, 13–14, 113–114, 134–149, 151, 158, 235n87
   on Weiqi as a theoretical framework, 122–126, 132–134, 160–161, 231n13
   and Zhuangzi, 150–151
   See also *Book of Supreme World Ordering Principles*; "Great Poem on Observing Weiqi"; observation

School of Principle (*li xue* 理學), 105–106, 115, 222n48
sincerity (*cheng* 誠), 6–7, 13, 31–32, 65, 75–76, 80–81, 83, 87, 91, 94, 100–102, 171–172
Sivin, Nathan, 168, 168
Slingerland, Edward, 43
Sommer, Deborah, 237n9
spontaneity (*ziran* 自然), 89, 93, 98, 153, 157–158
St. Anselm's riddle, 3, 58
Sunzi, idea of the best of the best (*shanzhishan* 善之善), 158

Taijitu shuo 太極圖說 (*Diagram of Supreme Polarity Explained*) (TJTS), 12–13, 51, 57f2.1
Taiji diagram 太極圖, 56, 61, 62, 66, 58, 66–68
Tongshu 通書 (*The Penetrating Book*) (TS):
   and personhood, 2–4, 8–9, 18, 22–23, 73
   on sagehood, 72, 74–80, 87, 91–92, 95–97, 97f2.2, 99, 102, 185
   on sincerity, 75, 80–81, 83, 87, 91, 94
   embodying WJTJ, 13, 95–96, 99, 101
transcendence of infinitude-finitude boundary, 49–50, 55–56, 104, 165, 198
transcendence of in-out boundary, 105, 107, 117–122, 145, 156, 159–161, 198
transcendence of the life-death boundary, 164, 166, 197–199, 201–204
true Order (*shili* 實理), 89, 93
Tu Weiming, 3, 26–27, 171, 188

understanding as living riddle. See riddling and living riddles

Voltaire *Zadig*, 205

Wang Bi 王弼, 227n46
Wang Fuzhi 王夫之, 240n47
Wang Yangming 王陽明, 238n15
Wang, Robin R., 30–31, 58, 61, 66
Way (*dao* 道), 2, 6–8, 18–19, 46. *See also* Shao Yong; Zhang Zai; Zhou Dunyi
Weiqi 圍棋 (Jap. Go), 106–111, 136, 231n13, 234n72. *See also* "Great Poem on Observing Weiqi"
Wittgenstein, Ludwig, 10–11, 72, 194–197, 218n14, 204
Western Inscription (*Ximing* 西銘) (WI), 15, 166–171, 177–179, 188–190
Wong, David B., 28
Wuji er taiji. *See* Non-polar and Supreme Polarity
wuwei 無為 (non action), 58, 93
Wyatt, Don J., 112–113, 116, 140

Xiang Yu 項羽, 151, 233n55
Xici Zhuan 繫辭傳 (the *Great Appendix* 大傳 *Dazhuan*), 9, 70, 77, 174. *See Book of Change*
Ximing 西銘 (*Western Inscription*) (WI). *See* Zhang Zai 張載
Xuedou Zhongxian 雪竇重顯 (Jap. Setcho Juken), 208, 213, 243n6, 244n22

Yan Hui 顏回 (Yanzi) (courtesy name Yan Yuan 顏淵), 3, 33–34, 42–44, 50, 92, 204, 221n35
yi 弈 (playing Weiqi), 108, 231n9
Yijing 易經. *See Book of Change*
Yin-yang 陰陽, 12–13, 30, 51–55, 58, 61–71, 74, 76–79, 85, 88–91, 109, 130, 133, 142–143, 145–149, 153–154, 174, 180–182, 191, 206, 220n30
youwei 有為 (having action), 58
Yuquan Shenxiu 玉泉神秀 (Jap. Jinshu), 244n16

Zaiwo 子我 (courtesy name of Zai Yu 宰予), 39, 187, 222n44
Zengzi 曾子, 23, 39, 178, 219n9
Zhang Zai 張載:
    biographical details, 164
    on cosmic interconnectedness, 15, 167–172, 176–179
    on living morally, 11–14, 176–177, 189–192, 216
    pragmatic sense, 12, 46
    the transcendence of the life-death boundary, 166–167, 189–190, 199–200, 202
    See also Western Inscription; *Zhangzaiji*
Zhangzaiji 張載集 (ZZJ), 15, 172–174, 202
Zhao Zhou 趙州 (Jap. Joshu)), 213, 245n25
Zhong Guoshi 忠國師 (Jap. Chu Kokushi), 214, 245n29
Zhongyong 中庸. *See Doctrine of the Mean*
Zhou Dunyi 周敦頤:
    biographical details, 50–51
    living riddle in his philosophy, 12–13, 55–56, 60, 66–72, 74, 94–95, 99–102
    metaphysical perspective, 12, 46, 50, 216
    on morality, 11–12, 72–74
    transcendence of infinitude-finitude, 12–13, 46, 49–50, 53–63, 70–72, 99–104, 165, 198
    See also Non-polar and Supreme Polarity; *Taijitu shuo*; *Tongshu*
Zhu Xi 朱熹, 20, 43, 51, 70–73, 78–79, 81, 83–85, 90–91, 99, 176, 189, 222n48
Zhuangzi 莊子, 94, 99, 119, 137, 150, 158, 169, 187, 191, 200–201, 230n101, 234n76, 237n9
Zigong 子貢, (courtesy name of Duanmu Ci 端木賜), 20, 241n60
Zilu 季路 (courtesy name of Zhong You 仲由), 20–21, 41, 42, 219n6
Ziwo 子我 (courtesy name of Zai Yu 宰予), 21, 219n6
Ziyou 子有 (courtesy name of Ran Qiu 冉求), 21, 219n6

www.ingramcontent.com/pod-product-compliance
Lightning Source LLC
Chambersburg PA
CBHW030532230426
43665CB00010B/860